THE World IN 1977

The management and staff of The Associated Press take pride in dedicating this volume to Paul Miller who served as President and Chairman of the Board of The Associated Press for 14 years.

Mr. Miller had a unique understanding of the principles and operation of this news cooperative, having served as an employee rising to the rank of Assistant General Manager before he left in 1947 to join Gannett Newspapers.

His unfailing dedication to the AP was an inspiration to us all.

Mr. Miller stepped down from his chairmanship of the AP in 1977 but continues to serve as a member of the Board.

THE World IN 1977

HISTORY AS WE LIVED IT

By the Writers, Photographers, Artists and Editors of THE ASSOCIATED PRESS

CONTENTS

FOREWORD

THE YEAR 1977 saw a change in the national administration, with Jimmy Carter assuming office as the first Democrat president since the late President Lyndon Johnson.

Weighty problems, some old and some new, greeted the new president and his cabinet, presenting perhaps as great a challenge as any non-war year in modern history.

The United States had suddenly run low on fossil fuel, creating an energy crisis that could only be temporarily solved by great foreign importation. These imports in their turn created a gigantic unfavorable balance of trade for this nation. The results were a tumbling dollar value abroad, a shaky stock market and an anemic economy struggling to emerge from the stagnation of the mid-1970's.

It was a year also that displayed a rash of terrorism around the world. Terrorist kidnappings for ransom and for murder burgeoned as a threat to the peace of the world.

Fighting continued in Northern Ireland, the Middle East and Africa, flaring and waning fitfully through the year.

At year's end a ray of hope was introduced with the dramatic peace overture shared by President Anwar Sadat of Egypt and Prime Minister Menahem Begin of Israel.

Against this generally dismal backdrop of world events, Americans found little at home to cheer about. Unemployment remained static; a record heat wave gripped the nation following a record cold wave early in the year; New York City experienced its second major blackout; and the western United States was plagued with forest fires and drought through the summer.

The men and women of The Associated Press who had to handle these depressing stories day in and day out during 1977 took no pleasure in the content of the news only in the knowledge that they presented the facts straightforwardly and without bias or prejudice.

Keith Fuller
President and General Manager

JANUARY

The Carters Gave a Homespun Touch to Inaugural Ceremony

The new President and his wife delighted the crowd by marching at the head of the parade

There had been signs Jimmy Carter's inauguration would be different. All those Georgians coming for the Jan. 20 celebration on their own train. Nobody would be allowed into the parties without paying the $25 entry fee, VIPs included. Carter's square dance teacher would lead an evening of folk dancing. And Rosalynn would wear an old dress.

But no one expected the new president and his wife to walk hand-in-hand for the full mile-and-a-half length of the inaugural parade. Walk they did, to the unease of the Secret Service and the delight of an estimated 350,000 persons who lined the parade route on a sunny, icy-cold January day.

Waving and smiling as they strolled down Pennsylvania Avenue, the Carters were joined by sons Jack, Chip and Jeff, and Chip's wife Caron.

Then four blocks from the White House, Amy Carter, 9, slid between her parents, holding each by the hand, and hopped and skipped in high-top boots to parade's end, there to take a front row seat in the solar-heated reviewing stand. The walk was a common touch addition to a euphoric day of good grace and the simple pleasure of political triumph.

For Carter, the day began with a special service at the First Baptist Church where his family later joined the congregation. Across town, there was another equally notable prayer service, led by Carter's evangelist sister, Ruth Stapleton, the Rev. Martin Luther King Sr., father of the slain civil rights leader, and Carter's pastor from Plains, Ga., the Rev. Bruce Edwards. Fourteen years before, the younger King had given his "I have a dream" speech on the same ground in front of the Lincoln Memorial. "I stand here with a bit of reluctancy and timidity upon these hallowed grounds," said King Sr. on the day the first Deep South president since Reconstruction took office.

It was to be a day uncommonly full of symbols and gestures of change. There had been bitter words exchanged between the 38th president and the man who so intensely sought to be the 39th. But campaign rhetoric was forgotten this day. Gerald R. Ford fought back the tears, as he bade farewell to 75 White House staff members earlier in the day. But by the time the Carters crossed Pennsylvania Avenue from Blair House to the White House for the traditional meeting with the departing First Family, Ford was grinning. In the White House Blue Room, Jimmy and Rosalynn Carter and Jerry and Betty Ford chatted over coffee, while the new and old vice presidents Walter F. Mondale and Nelson A. Rockefeller and their wives Joan and Happy, had their own meeting.

As the ceremony time arrived, Carter took his place on the inaugural stand to the strains of the Navy Hymn, so familiar to an Annapolis graduate. Open broadcast microphones caught Ford's appraisal of those who had come to watch. "Great crowd," he said. "Really is," agreed Carter. Most of the throng of 150,000 who stretched across the Capitol grounds were bundled up against the windy weather with temperatures in the 20s. Not Carter. Despite the chill, he was protected by neither hat nor overcoat. He wore instead a vested, navy blue suit, disdaining the formal dress of some former presidents. Mrs. Carter wore a navy blue dress, with a striking blue-green coat.

First to take the simple oath of office was Vice President Mondale. Then it was Carter's turn. With Mrs. Carter holding a family Bible, Chief Justice Warren Burger asked, "Are you prepared to take the oath of office?" Replied Carter; "I am."

He repeated the oath set out in the constitution: "I do solemnly swear that I will faithfully execute the oath of President of the United States, and will to the best of my ability, preserve, protect and defend the Constitution of the United States." As others had he added, "So help me God."

Moments after taking office the new president turned to his predecessor and paid a personal tribute. Carter opened his inaugural address by saying directly to Ford, "For myself and our nation, I want to thank my predecessor for all he has done to heal our land."

The magnanimity of the gesture caught Ford slightly off guard. He nodded, then stood, and the two men shook hands. They stood together for several seconds, drawing applause and cheers from the crowd. Then with echoes of a 21-gun salute still ringing across the Capitol grounds, Carter resumed an inaugural address notable for its brevity (12 minutes) and its religious theme. "Let us create together a new national spirit of unity and trust . . . let us learn together and laugh together and work together

President Carter gave his inaugural address from a stand outside the Capitol

and pray together, confident that in the end we will triumph together in the right,'' Carter said in a speech interrupted seven times by applause.

The new president declared that the country should improve upon an ideal already in place. ''Two centuries ago, our nation's birth was a milestone in the long quest for freedom, but the

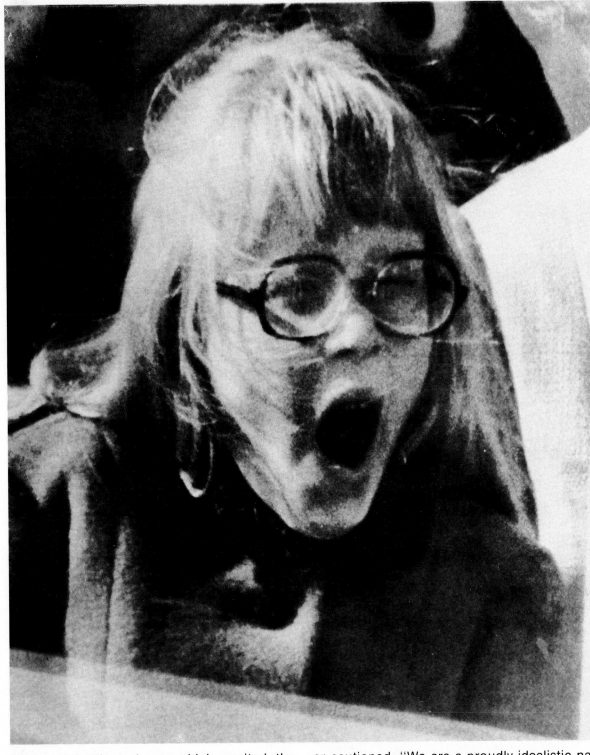

Amy Carter displayed her feelings during the ceremony making her father president

bold and brilliant dream which excited the founders of our nation still awaits its consummation," Carter said. "I have no new dream to set forth today, but rather urge a fresh faith in the old spirit." Then in a theme sounded repeatedly during the election campaign, the president said, "Our government must at the same time be both competent and compassionate."

There was one oblique reference to the Watergate scandals which drove Richard M. Nixon from the White House and made Ford the first appointed president. "Let our recent mistakes bring a resurgent commitment to the basic principles of our nation, for we know that if we despise our own government, we have no future," he said.

To real or potential adversaries abroad, Cart-

er cautioned, "We are a proudly idealistic nation, but let no one confuse our idealism with weakness." Amy Carter rushed to her father's side and hugged the new president as his speech ended. Then, after a lengthy benediction, the ceremony was over.

Ford walked briskly across the snow-covered Capitol grounds he knew so well as a Michigan congressman of 25 years and he and Mrs. Ford boarded a helicopter. The craft circled the city for a last look, and then carried the former President to Andrews Air Force base and a 21-gun salute. There, the Fords boarded a presidential jetliner to take up residence in Palm Desert, Calif.

The Carters began the march near the head of their own parade. The Secret Service, notified three weeks ahead, had advised that walk-

9

Breaking precedent, the new president and his wife, Rosalynn, walked along Washington's Pennsylvania Avenue after the swearing in

Former president Gerald Ford, former vice president Nelson Rockefeller and their wives stood at attention during the playing of the National Anthem

In his first official act, President Carter signed papers submitting the names of his cabinet nominees to Congress.

vas all right "as long as we kept it quiet," ⌐r said.

the end, the Carters and the principals of new administration viewed the parade's ▪antry from a solar-heated stand protected ullet-proof glass. The two-hour procession ands and floats was closed with 40-foot ▪ut-shaped balloon. The parade over, ⌐r walked to the executive mansion, de-ng, "I thought I'd look around."

ere wasn't much time for inspection, how-. After changing to formal dress, the new ■dent and his wife hop-scotched across ▪, for 3½ hours, hosting seven different ⌐es. They were parties, not inaugural balls, ▪use Carter said so.

⌐s. Carter wore the same blue dress she had ▪ when Carter became governor of Georgia ▪71. "Hail to the Chief" was not heard at any

of the affairs. It was replaced by Carter's lively campaign song, "Why Not the Best."

At each party, Carter asked the crowd, "Do you think you live in the greatest country on earth?"

"Do you think you can help make the country work even better."

"Don't you like my wife's old dress?"

The answer from each of the crowded ball-room floors was always a shouted "Yes" or "Whoopee."

Appropriately, the Carters ended their day at the D.C. Armory where friends from Georgia were gathered. "Today is the greatest day in the life of the Carter family," he said. "I see here so many of you who helped me when I didn't have any friends . . . I want this evening of joy and friendship and caring for each other to last for the next four years."

11

Ford Farewell

As Gerald Ford prepared to leave the White House where he had spent 29 months, AP Special Correspondent Eddie Adams took these pictures of the last days of the president and his wife, Betty

Below, the president's desk was almost bare as he spent his final hours in the Oval Office. Right, Ford strode across his office as he prepared to vacate the White House. Opposite page, top, the president took a walk across the White House grounds on the eve of his departure. Opposite page bottom, First Lady Betty Ford paused in her packing to look over some mementos in her White House bedroom.

Oakland linebacker Willie Hall held the ball high in the air after recovering a fumble by the Vikings

Oakland's Triumph Marked Fourth Super Bowl Defeat For the Minnesota Vikings

Rarely in the decade since the National Football League created the Super Bowl had this American sports extravaganza presented two more contrasting teams than it did in January when the Minnesota Vikings and Oakland Raiders played for pro football's world championship. The differences were obvious everywhere from top to bottom. Max Winter, a small, pleasant, white-haired man, was president of the Vikings but much less visible than some other NFL executives. Oakland's chief owner was Al Davis, the survivor in a long court action fought for control of the team. Considered by some of his peers to be one of pro football's most mysterious executives, he was sometimes called secretive, sometimes called sinister, but always respected for his knowledge of the game. On the field, the Vikings were run by slender Bud Grant, a crew-cut coaching throwback with a dry sense of humor whose expression rarely changed win or lose. His face seemed to have been frozen by the frigid Minnesota tundra. Oakland's bench, on the other hand, was ruled by rotund John Madden, a mountain of a man whose modish hair flopped over his forehead as he dashed up and down the sidelines.

The quarterbacks offered the same kind of contrast. Minnesota's offense was operated by Fran Tarkenton, who held most of the important NFL career passing records. Clean-shaven and with boyish good looks, he could be a poster boy instead of a quarterback.

The Raider quarterback was Ken Stabler, an unconventional, left-hander, who once jumped the team because he wasn't being played and left another time to sign with the now-defunct World Football League.

In the back-field with Tarkenton, the Vikings had Chuck Foreman, a multi-talented player who could catch a pass or take a handoff and produce big yardage both ways, and Brent McClanahan, a solid if unspectacular runner. Oakland's ground game belonged to Mark van Eeghen, an unlikely 1,000-yard man from Colgate, and Clarence Davis, best known as the running back caretaker at the University of Southern California between the eras of O.J. Simpson and Anthony Davis.

The Vikings were mostly home-grown, assembled primarily through the draft. But many of the important Raiders were pro football refugees, imported through trades or signed as free agents to fill gaps. The contrast was complete as the two teams took the field at the sun-splashed Rose Bowl in Pasadena, Calif., to settle the NFL championship. As Vicki Carr recited the words to "America the Beautiful," the stadium filled with more than 100,000 fans, fell silent.

On one sideline stood the Vikings, side-by-side and rigid, helmets under their arms. Across the field, facing every which way, some wearing their helmets, some sitting on them, were the Raiders, looking like no army you ever saw. Two very different football teams were ready to play for the championship.

Oakland won the coin toss and Minnesota kicked off. Stabler's first two plays were hand-offs to Davis and van Eeghen, both aimed at the left side. It was the start of a trend that would continue all day long.

On third-and-five, Stabler hit Dave Casper for 25 yards and a first down at the Viking 36. Then Davis ripped off 24 more yards on the next two carries and Oakland was on the Vikings' 12. Suddenly, the Minnesota defenders stiffened. Three plays netted just one yard and on fourth down, Errol Mann tried a 29-yard field goal. The ball glanced off the left upright and the impressive Oakland march had come up empty.

On the sidelines, Madden sizzled until Stabler sidled up to him. "Don't worry," the quarterback said. "There's plenty more where that came from." And he was right.

Minnesota's first two offensive series produced nothing, but the Raiders were still doing a good job of moving the right side of the Viking defense manned by Jim Marshall and Alan Page. Repeatedly, Stabler would send Davis in that direction for good yardage.

After the game, Davis asked what he saw on that left side that kept him going there. "Well," he said, "let's see. I saw (Oakland left tackle) Art Shell, (guard) Gene Upshaw and (tight end) Dave Casper."

With just over five minutes left in the first period, Oakland's Ray Guy set up for a punt. Never in four NFL seasons had one of Guy's kicks been blocked but the Viking special teams had become experts at torpedoing punts and placements and they got to Guy.

Linebacker Fred McNeill burst in from the left side as Guy took the snap. "There was an alley way for me," said McNeill. "I took four or five steps and dived to a point about six yards in front of where Guy originally lined up. Fortunately, the timing was good. It's very easy to miss the ball. In this case, it just barely nicked my arm."

Above, behind perfect protection, Oakland quarterback Ken Stabler completed a pass. Left, with the Raiders' 273-pound Otis Sistrunk climbing his back, Vikings' quarterback Fran Tarkenton debated his next move

The blocked punt bounced crazily towards the Raider end zone with the Vikings, and Guy, in frantic pursuit. McNeill recovered the ball at the three and Minnesota was on the Oakland doorstep.

Two plays later, however, the door was slammed in the faces of the Vikes. "We kept yelling, 'Give 'em three. Give 'em three,' " recalled linebacker Phil Villipiano. The Raiders were willing to concede a field goal but not a touchdown. Minnesota got neither.

Foreman tried the right side for one yard on first down. On Minnesota's second play, Mc-Clanahan went at the middle of the Raider defense. Villipiano and Dave Rowe jarred the ball loose and Willie Hall fell on it for Oakland.

Stabler needed some working room but he didn't get much on the first two plays with Pete Banaszak netting just three yards. On third-and-seven from the six-yard line, Davis tried the left side again. Shell, Upshaw and Casper cleared the way and the sweep gained 35 yards. Now, Stabler took to the air, hitting Carl Garrett for 11 yards and Casper for 25. At the 25, the Raiders went back to the ground with van Eeghen, Davis and Banaszak chewing up chunks of yardage. When the period ended, Oakland was on the eight-yard line.

There, the drive stalled and Mann came on for a 24-yard field goal that gave the Raiders the game's first points.

It didn't take long for Oakland to get more of them. On the Raiders' next possession, Stabler picked the Vikings apart. Garrett ground out 20 yards on three straight carries and Stabler completed five straight passes, the last one an easy toss that Casper grabbed in the end zone at least five yards away from the nearest Minnesota defender.

After one more fruitless Viking series, Neil Clabo punted and Neal Colzie's 25-yard return put the Raiders on the Viking 35. Five plays later, Oakland was on the scoreboard again with Banaszak busting over right tackle from the one-yard line. Like Casper's TD before it, the score was set up by Fred Biletnikoff's diving catch of a Stabler pass at the one.

Mann's extra point try missed but now it was 16-0 and the Raiders were in clear command. Stabler was doing exactly what he wanted and the Viking defense seemed unable to do anything about it. "We came out to open up the game," said the quarterback. "We did not want to play conservatively. We wanted to let it all hang out." By halftime, the Vikings were hanging.

An intermission spectacular orchestrated by Walt Disney Productions bathed the Rose Bowl in a sea of colors. In the dressing room, Viking coach Grant tried to recoup. "I said, 'We can't fold our tent now. We've been down by 16 points before and have come back to score 17 and win,' " the Minnesota coach recalled.

Madden reminded the Raiders that the Vikings weren't dead yet. "There wasn't any danger of us relaxing with a 16-0 lead," he said. "I told the team that no matter what happens—Good or bad—in the early part of the game, we have to keep moving." And that's just what Oakland did.

Minnesota managed one first down at the start of the third quarter before surrendering the ball on downs. On their second possession of the period, Stabler moved the Raiders to the Viking 23 and Mann, who had missed a short field goal and an even shorter extra point earlier, kicked a 40-yarder to increase the Oakland lead to 19-0.

Now the Vikings were in deep trouble. They needed some points and they needed them in a hurry. The fastest way was through the air and that's where Tarkenton went. A roughing-the-kicker penalty enabled the Vikes to maintain possession and Tarkenton took them to the touchdown, hitting rookie wide receiver Sammy White with a 10-yard pass for the score just before the end of the quarter.

Twelve points behind with 15 minutes to play,

Vikings wide receiver Sammy White lost his helmet as two Raider defenders hit him

the Vikings still had a chance. If their offense could generate momentum, two touchdowns weren't out of the question. Tarkenton went to work.

Completions of 14 and 18 yards to White produced two first downs and moved the ball from the Viking 22 to the Raider 37. On third-and-three, Tarkenton was forced out of the pocket and started a mad scramble with linebacker Ted Hendricks in pursuit. Just as the quarterback ran out of room, he threw an ill-advised pass that linebacker Willie Hall intercepted at the 30 and returned to the Oakland 46.

Three plays later, Stabler found Biletnikoff wide open over the middle and the 48-yard pass play put the Raiders on the two. Banaszak went in on the next play, making it 26-7. It was the third time in the game that a Biletnikoff catch

Tight end Dave Casper took a Ken Stabler pass in the end zone for the Raiders' first touchdown

had set up an Oakland touchdown. In all, he caught four for 79 yards.

"I really appreciate Kenny," said Biletnikoff. "He throws the ball where I can catch it, low and away from people. To me, Kenny Stabler is the best quarterback to play football. He doesn't pop off. We know what Kenny can do, and he knows what we can do."

The Vikings, too, were learning what the Raiders could do. So far, the offense had taught an impressive lesson. Now it was the defense's turn to put some points on the board.

Tarkenton, forced to keep pitching in a desperate attempt at playing catch-up football, had the Vikes at the Oakland 28 on the next series when he tossed a swing pass that Willie Brown picked off at the 25. Down the sideline sped the veteran cornerback, 75 yards to another Oakland touchdown.

"You play 14 years, you can anticipate a lot of things," said Brown. "I anticipated a quick-out and I was there to get it." With the game wrapped up, both teams went to their reserves for the final minutes. Minnesota scored a meaningless last-minute TD on a 13-yard pass from backup quarterback Bob Lee to tight end Stu Voight, making the final score 32-14.

When it was over, Davis had shredded the Viking defense for a career-high 137 yards. Stabler had connected on 12 of 19 passes for 180 yards and the Raiders had scored a decisive, one-sided victory, sending Minnesota to its fourth Super Bowl loss in as many appearances.

Among the Oakland heroes were Biletnikoff, who set up three TDs, Banaszak, who scored two, Brown, who returned the interception for another, and Upshaw, who was a devastating blocker all day long. Those four were the only Raiders left from Oakland's only other Super Bowl appearance, a 33-14 humiliation by the Green Bay Packers in 1968.

After that loss, Oakland assembled pro football's finest regular season record and won eight division championships in nine years. But the Raiders always seemed to stumble in the playoffs and never made it back to the Super Bowl. Until this point, they were post-season flubs. The victory over the Vikes, however, erased that aura of failure.

"They said for years we couldn't win the big one," said Stabler. Now I guess we'll hear, 'Will the Raiders be able to win it twice.'"

Minnesota, meanwhile, knew what it would hear. The Vikings had made more Super Bowl appearances than any team in pro football. They had not won one yet, though, and they were embarrassed with their latest performance. "If you find an easier way to lose, let me know," said Grant.

"Let's see," said Tarkenton, trying to inject some levity in the morbid Minnesota dressing room. "We've lost to Kansas City, Miami, Pittsburgh and Oakland. I guess we're going to have to keep looking for an AFC team we can beat."

Execution of Gary Gilmore Climaxed A Bizarre Drama

The convicted murderer won nationwide attention by demanding that death penalty be carried out

Gary Gilmore, the murderer, demanded death. He got his wish on Jan. 17, but only after taking center stage in one of the most bizarre dramas in American criminal history.

It started routinely, this tale that led to the nation's first execution in nearly 10 years. Gilmore, who had spent half his life in prison, was sentenced to death for the July 1976 shooting of a motel clerk. But instead of entering the perfunctory notice of appeal, the type that today keeps scores of killers alive on Death Row, the dark-haired drifter dropped a bombshell on a quiet Provo, Utah, courtroom on Nov. 1, 1976. He said he wanted his execution carried out.

"You sentenced me to die," he told the judge. "Unless it's a joke or something, I want to go ahead and do it." Gilmore later was to confess the motel killing and the shooting of a gas station attendant, saying his random victims were slain in cold blood on successive nights after he had quarreled with his divorcee girlfriend. Showing no remorse, Gilmore said he killed them execution-style, putting a .22 caliber pistol to their heads after ordering them to lie down. Both were young men working their way through school. Both left widows and small children.

"It was something that couldn't be stopped," he told the jury. In an earlier letter to his girlfriend, he said: "Murder is just a thing of itself, a rage, and rage is not reason, so why does it matter who? It vents a rage."

Jurors prayed and wept before ordering the death penalty. But Gilmore said he'd rather die than spend another day in prison. And he proved he meant it. Waiving all appeals, he described as "moral cowards" the public officials who delayed his execution. He told capital-punishment opponents to "butt out." He even rejected an appeal from his mother, saying he loved her but would rather die. Despite Gilmore's demand, his wait was prolonged by stays granted against his will and the intervention of those who claimed the state had no right to take a life. Four times his execution was stayed—by the Utah governor, by the Utah Supreme Court, by the U.S. Supreme Court, and by a Salt Lake City federal judge who personally saw that a stay order was delivered to the prison only hours before the execution.

All were lifted, but in the long weeks of waiting Gilmore twice attempted suicide through drug overdoses. He became an international sensation when the world learned of his girlfriend and his artistic talents. His picture adorned magazine covers, his story reached newspapers around the world, and his imminent execution became a worldwide rallying point for capital-punishment protestors.

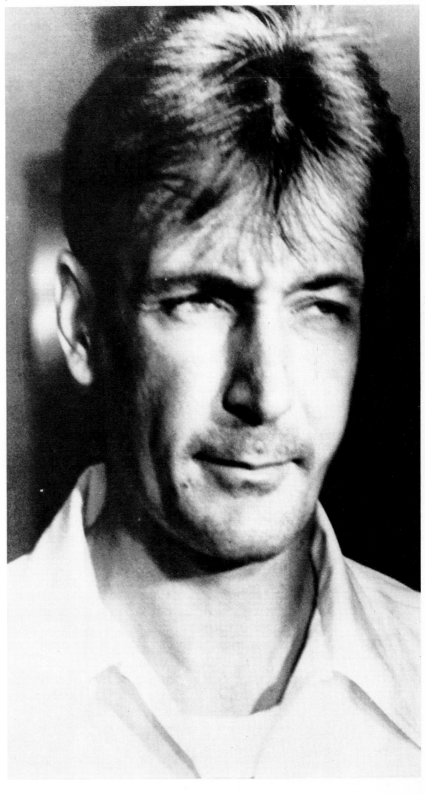

Convicted killer Gary Gilmore won nationwide attention when he declared that he wanted to be executed

Finally, on an icy Monday morning, the enigmatic 36-year-old killer got his way. Minutes after the nation's highest courts had cleared away a thicket of last-gasp obstacles, a firing squad pumped four bullets through his heart as he sat strapped in a chair, a hood covering his head. Gilmore was calm at the end, in contrast to an obscenity-filled outburst of hours earlier when he learned the federal judge had ordered a stay, a stay that was to be lifted after a frantic 500-mile flight by Utah's attorney general, a staff of assistants, and a federal appeals judge.

"Let's do it," Gilmore told Warden Sam Smith and then spoke his last words: the Latin phrase "Dominus vobiscum," which means "The Lord be with you." He said them after the warden stepped aside and as the prison chaplain administered last rites of the Roman Catholic church, into which Gilmore was baptized but to which he had professed no allegiance. It surprised the clergyman, but he quickly gave the liturgical response. And then the firing squad performed its grim chore, rifles protruding through a sailcloth screen. So ended the life of Gary Gilmore, and a stranger-than-fiction case created by a dramatic legal battle and a perplexing personality. Gary Gilmore, born as his parents passed through McCamey, Tex., got into trouble early for breaking windows and was in trouble ever after. Confinement apparently embittered him. His mother, a widow for 14 years who lived bedridden in Milwaukie, Ore., said he seemed to change for the worse after getting out of reform school. His girlfriend, Nicole Barrett, 20, said he was a "beautiful person" made "bitter and ugly inside," by prison life resulting from assault, robbery and car theft terms. Some authorities said he was a disruptive loner, a man who rejected moral values and was beyond rehabilitation.

Relatives tried to help him, but he couldn't hold a job. He was violent and drinking made him worse. He was on parole from Illinois when he came to Utah and began his fatal spree. It was after drinking and a falling-out with Mrs. Barrett that he turned to murder. The victims had never met the man who walked in and coldly executed them. One shooting one night, another the next. Gilmore said later he would have killed again if he had not been caught.

He vented his violence in custody, writing obscenity-laden notes, uttering racial slurs and fiercely rejecting the aid of persons who tried to save his life. In a hospital after the first of his two suicide attempts, he jerked intravenous tubes from his arms. He hit, bit and spit on nurses. Back in prison, he threw food on the floor and smashed a light.

Still, the killer showed another side. Receiving thousands of letters during his confinement, he responded thoughtfully to children. His poetry and letters showed a flair for artistic expression, as did his drawings. He declared himself "rational, and more intelligent than an average person." Authorities agreed.

He appeared personally before the Utah Supreme Court and the State Board of Pardons, in both cases arguing clearly and forcefully for death. "I believe I was given a fair trial, and I think the sentence was proper," he asserted. Turning the tables on death-penalty opponents, he claimed that prolonging his life would be "cruel, unusual and inhuman punishment."

Gilmore fired four attorneys before embracing two who agreed to support his campaign for death. "I desire death for two reasons" he wrote to Mrs. Barrett. "To atone—whatever that means—to become less evil, more worthy. And to escape the unpleasantness of a lifetime in prison. I am the landlord of my house. I built this house and I must live in it. I've got to clean it up. It becomes unbearable. My soul is on fire, and is screaming to vacate this ugly house."

He invited Mrs. Barrett to join him in death, and she tried. On Nov. 16, the two were found unconscious from drug overdoses, Gilmore in his prison cell, Mrs. Barrett in her apartment. She was clutching a photo of Gilmore. Both recovered, and at her family's request, Mrs. Barrett was committed to a mental hospital.

Gilmore, angry because he no longer could communicate with her, went on a 25-day hunger strike, drinking only coffee. He began eating again only after the U.S. Supreme Court lifted a stay it had granted at his mother's request. The high court ruled 5-4 that Gilmore had voluntarily waived his appeal rights. That was to be a vital ruling, echoed by the appeals panel that overturned the final stay.

The Gilmore-Barrett relationship as much as anything projected the killer into celebrity status. The divorcee had visited him daily until the suicide attempt. At one point, during a court appearance for resentencing of his death date, he shouted to a newsman: "Tell her I love her more than life itself." He was also quoted as saying he wanted to encourage her to be happy and to live a good life. But on another occasion, he told a lawyer he'd rather die even than spend the rest of his life free with Nicole. "I want to leave this planet," he said. Another lawyer said Gilmore told him: "If they don't do it, I'm going to do it myself. "I'm not going to spend the rest of my life in prison."

Gilmore tried to take his own life again on Dec. 16, a day after the setting of his final execution date. In accordance with state law, the judge pronounced a date more than 30 days in advance. Outraged at the delay, Gilmore assaulted the judge verbally in court. The next morning, jailers found him unconscious from an overdose. Again, he recovered.

Prison Warden Samuel Smith said he felt no guilt over Gilmore's ability to obtain drugs in prison. "If a man of intelligence wants to commit suicide," the warden said, "he's going to find a way."

Gilmore was at once gentle and explosive. Lisa La Rochelle, a girl from Holyoke, Mass., wrote to Gilmore and several other prominent

carnation, saying he felt he would be rewarded on a "higher level" because he had not tried to escape punishment for his acts. Gilmore once said he thought he had been an Indian in a previous life because he got along well with Indians in this one. After his death, it was revealed that he also had carried on a long correspondence with an 11-year-old Salt Lake City girl known locally for her boxing exploits. He saw that she got a bicycle, a movie projector and some cash. He praised youth involvement in sports and admonished his young correspondent to "knock them all out for me."

This same Gilmore who wrote tenderly to children also issued open statements filled with

Left, prison chaplain, Rev. Thomas Mearsman, bag in hand, walked across the prison yard to visit Gilmore on the eve of his execution. Right, Utah Atty. Gen. Robert Hansen talked with reporters after a court of appeals overturned a stay of execution. Ten minutes after the stay was lifted, Gilmore was killed

persons as part of a religion class, asking "What will be the first question you will ask God when you see him?" Politely, Gilmore wrote: "First, I'm not a prominent person. I've just gained some unwanted notoriety . . . I sort of believe that we are all God . . . I don't feel any questions will be necessary."

To others, Gilmore expressed a belief in rein-

21

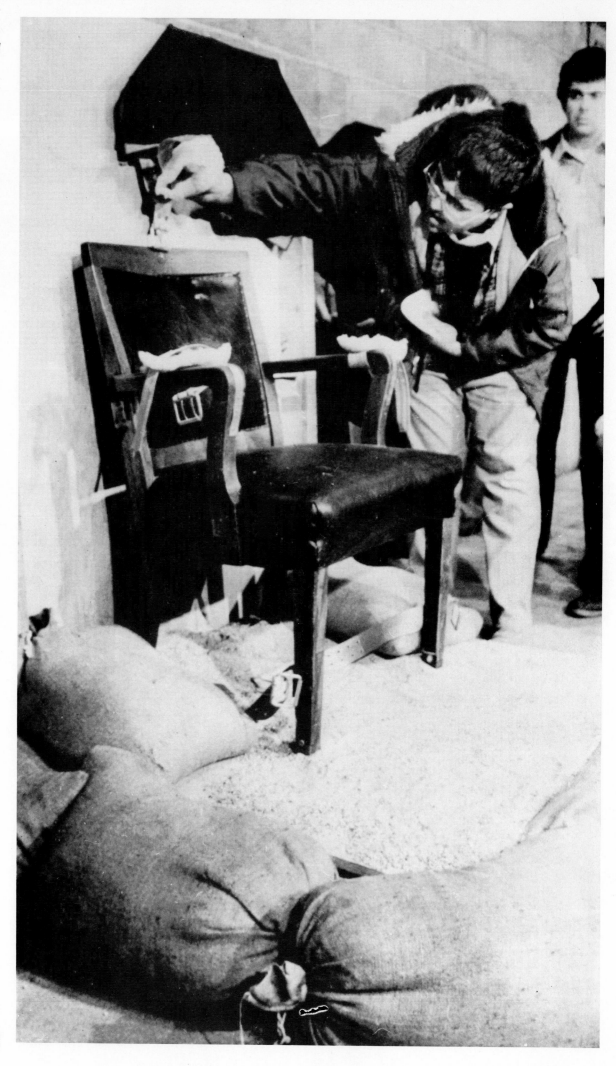

venom. After the U.S. Supreme Court announced a stay, he exclaimed: "I wish my mother, the niggers and sons of bitches would butt out of my life . . . If I have a right to a speedy trial, why don't I have a right to a speedy execution?"

As his final week began, he again lashed out at death-penalty opponents, telling the American Civil Liberties Union "You take one stand on abortion which is actually execution: you're all for that. And then you take another stand against capital punishment. You're against that. Where are your true convictions?"

There was more than life and death at stake in Gilmore's case. There was money. Lawrence Schiller, a promoter, convinced Gilmore to sign a contract for commercial rights. That, coupled with the warden's blockade against media access to the killer, closed off direct contact with the press except for two newspaper interviews granted under a brief and later-overturned court order. So while attorneys talked freely about Gilmore's reactions to developments, and while Gilmore's own open letters were relayed throughout the world, he remained something of a mystery.

Utah law, making no mention of news coverage, permitted the condemned to designate five witnesses to his execution. Schiller, the two attorneys, Gilmore's uncle, and Mrs. Barrett were named. The naming of his girlfriend was symbolic, since she was confined to the mental hospital. It was Schiller who described the execution to newsmen in a briefing room.

There was talk of a movie and songs. There was one report that Gilmore wanted to auction off seats to his exectuion. Estimates of the value of his story soared into the hundreds of thousands of dollars. After his death, an easterner began selling "Let's do it" T-shirts.

But his victims were not forgotten. Well before the execution, and insurance company sought $45,000 to reclaim benefits it said were paid to the family of Max David Jensen, 24, the gas-station attendant. The family of Bennie Bushnell, 25, the motel clerk for whose death Gilmore paid the ultimate penalty, sought $1 million. Schiller said some of his profits would go to the victims' families.

During the penalty-setting phase of his trial, Gilmore was asked if he had killed Bushnell. Gilmore said: "Yes, I guess I did. I don't know why. I felt like there was no way what happened could have been avoided. There was no other choice or chance for Mr. Bushnell. It was something that couldn't be stopped."

There were legal warnings on both sides. Some supporters of capital punishment argued that Gilmore might have to be set free if not executed within 60 days of his original sentencing, and that appeals would delay the case a year or two. Some opponents claimed Gilmore's execution would open the way to mass slaughter of others on Death Row.

Opponents of capital punishment, gambled on winning a last-minute reprieve too late to permit successful appeal by state authorities committed to carry out the sentence.

They waited until Friday, Jan. 15, the final working day before the Monday sunrise execution, to make their strongest move. Then, in rapid succession, they went before a federal judge, a state court, a Utah Supreme Court justice, and the governor. They failed at every turn.

There seemed nothing left for foes of capital punishment, but they pressed on. On Sunday, they failed to get relief from U.S. Supreme Court justices Bryon White and Harry Blackmun.

Sunday night, the prison began giving hourly reports on Gilmore's activities: how he requested country music songs played over a local radio station; how he took only coffee and milk when the evening meal was offered; and how he seemed to be in good spirits as he placed phone calls to relatives. Gilmore's attorneys added further details: how he tried to cheer them up, teach them to dance and box a bit; how he turned handstands.

Then, came a dramatic last-minute development. Shirley Pedler, Utah ACLU director, said U.S. District Judge Willis Ritter had called to say he understood the ACLU was trying to reach him. So it had been, she said, and a hearing was scheduled for late sunday night.

After midnight, seven hours before the execution, Ritter ordered a stay, citing "obvious, serious doubts" in the Utah law. He rode with a U.S. Marshal to the prison for delivery of the order. But Utah Atty. Gen. Robert Hansen was ready. Calling aides to duty, he ordered papers prepared and arranged for an emergency flight to Denver in the company of David T. Lewis, chief judge of the 10th U.S. Circuit Court of Appeals, and a Salt Lake City resident; four assistants; and an ACLU attorney. Hansen had said earlier that if the execution did not occur by sunrise, a delay of more than 30 days would be necessary under state law.

Gilmore, infuriated by Ritter's decision, eventually caught some sleep as his now-uncertain execution time neared. Then he awoke for a breakfast of eggs, hamburger, potatoes and coffee.

The final events unfolded rapidly. In Denver, headquarters of the appeals court, a special three-judge panel convened less than an hour before sunrise and quickly vacated Ritter's order. The state judge who had originally set the sunrise time changed his order to permit the execution at any time during the day. And, as Gilmore was led from his cell and loaded into a van for transporting to the execution site, opponents made their final appeals to the U.S. Supreme Court. Justices White and Thurgood Marshall declined, and finally the full court agreed the execution should proceed.

Then prison spokesman answered a telephone in the briefing room and announced: "The order of the 4th District Court has been carried out. Gary Mark Gilmore is dead."

Anthony Eden, as prime minister in 1956, shook hands with Sir Winston Churchill, following a luncheon at No. 10 Downing Street

EDEN'S DEATH RECALLED A CAREER MARKED BY TRIUMPH AND TRAGEDY

Anthony Eden was best remembered for the courageous stand against Nazi Germany that raised him to stardom and the disastrous 1956 Suez invasion that left his career in ruins.

When the former British prime minister died Jan. 14 at the age of 79, the government hailed his role as the architect of Britain's foreign policy four centuries earlier. "To those who grew up in the '30s," the official statement said, "Anthony Eden will always be remembered as a staunch opponent of fascism and the fascist dictators."

The British Press Association looked regretfully at the other side of the coin. It commented that the tragedy of Eden's political career had been his identification with the Suez invasion in which British and French forces tried to take control of the canal after it had been nationalized by Egypt.

Handsome, suave and aristocratic, usually clad in impeccably tailored pinstripe suits and a black Homburg, Eden in his day was a model for diplomats. His popularity which survived, despite the Suez fiasco was traceable in part to his glamor. A World War I hero, he became foreign secretary in 1935 at the age of 38. He soon won a reputation as a polished statesman, but one who was tough enough to stand up to the totalitarian dictators of Europe. He was a staunch advocate of rearmament and called for a firm stand against Hitler and Mussolini. When Prime Minister Neville Chamberlain refused to adopt such a hard position, Eden resigned in 1938 as a stand against appeasement. But he

was back as foreign secretary when Winston Churchill became prime minister following the outbreak of World War II.

After the war, Eden left his post when Churchill's government was voted out, but he returned in 1951 when Churchill and the Conservatives were brought back. Eden succeeded the aged Churchill in 1955 as prime minister, and a year later he was confronted with the Suez crisis.

The trouble began when Egyptian President Gamal Abdel Nasser nationalized the vital canal. Eden insisted that the West should join forces against Nasser, who he said could not be trusted to keep the waterway open. The United States refused to go along with Eden but he proceeded to make secret plans with Premier Guy Mollet of France.

After Israel invaded the Sinai Desert in October of 1956 and advanced on the Suez Canal, British and French forces were dispatched to join the invasion and secure the waterway. The United States refused to join them, and Soviet threats forced Britain and France to withdraw, leaving Nasser in firm control.

Eden insisted the invasion had prevented a larger war in the Middle East and thus stabilized the situation there, but his policy was now a shambles and his health poor. The unhappy statesman resigned Jan. 9, 1957.

In 1961, Eden was elevated to the peerage as the Earl of Avon. Between bouts of illness, he spent his time vacationing abroad and working on his political memoirs. In the three-volume work, Eden was surprisingly kind to men who had been bitter opponents, most of whom he had outlived.

"So many of them are dead now," he once explained. "You cannot very well be unkind to the dead. In fairness you would have to be unkind to those who are alive too, and that would create complications."

OOD RIOTS ERUPTED IN AIRO AND ALEXANDRIA

hen Egypt's army rolled across the Suez Canal in the 973 war with Israel, many Egyptians began to hope that e would get better. But it did not work out that way.

Instead daily existence for most of the 40 million Egyp-ans grew more and more intolerable as progress towards eace remained stalled and heavy military spending contin-ed. Many had to work overtime and then borrow from rela-ves to make ends meet even though they lived in an Arab orld peopled by oil-rich sheiks. But little of this petroleum ealth found its way to Egypt.

Plagued by spiraling inflation, the future looked bleak for e average Egyptian. The issue suddenly came to a head an. 18, when the government reduced subsidies for ciga-ettes, food and many other items, sending prices skyrock-ting.

By nightfall, thousands of infuriated Egyptians had ex-oded into action in Cairo and the Mediterranean port city f Alexandria, stoning cars, and buses and attacking po-ce. Mobs set fire to a police station and massed outside e official Cairo residence of President Anwar Sadat who eemed to be the main target of their fury.

Informed that the president was 600 miles south in the inter resort town of Aswan awaiting an official visit by ugoslavia's President Tito, the rioters got still madder.

"You are living it up in Aswan while we eat stones," they cried.

As the worst rioting to hit Egypt in 25 years threatened to spread, Sadat revoked the price increases on food and other products that his government had triggered. At the same time, authorities ordered a 14-hour curfew in several cities and gave riot police orders to shoot anyone found straying outside without a pass. But battles between police and demonstrators were reported still raging in several areas.

After two days of violence, the dust began to settle and authorities tried to figure out the damage. At least 40 per-sons were dead, some 700 injured and about 1,200 had been arrested.

Newspapers said the arrests had netted many leftists and Communists, accused by the Ministry of Interior of plotting to "burn Cairo." The semiofficial newspaper Al Ahram said investigation of 200 suspected Communists picked up in the rioting showed they had formed four secret organiza-tions to overthrow the government by force.

The charges brought denials from leftist leaders, one of whom retorted that the food riots had been a "natural pop-ular outbreak" and did not involve any Communist moti-vation.

Most observers agreed on one point. Unless Sadat came up with some tangible help for his people, trouble could erupt again.

Demonstrators, pro-testing increased food prices, massed on a rubble-strewn street in Cairo

Vice President Walter Mondale, left, and Joseph Luns, secretary-general of the North Atlantic Treaty Organization, pictured after a session of the North Atlantic Treaty Council at NATO headquarters in Brussels

FRANCE CAUSED UPROAR WITH CAPTURE AND RELEASE OF TERRORIST SUSPECT

Terrorism is always an explosive issue but this time it touched off an international uproar involving half a dozen nations.

The uproar started when French counterintelligence agents arrested an official of the Palestine Liberation Organization accused by Israel of planning the murder of 11 Israeli athletes in the 1972 Munich massacre.

The suspect, Abu Daoud, had slipped into Paris under an assumed name to attend the funeral of a PLO activist who had been gunned down in the French capital.

Daoud's arrest triggered demands from both Israel and West Germany for his extradition so that he could be tried for the Munich murders. It also prompted Arab ambassadors to march on the French Foreign Ministry and protest the "unfriendly action" by France in arresting a member of an official PLO delegation.

West Germany and France both began claiming that the other had initiated the arrest of Daoud whose capture appeared increasingly embarrassing to the French. Then suddenly a hastily-convened French court rejected both the Israeli and West German extradition demands and Daoud was placed on a plane bound for freedom in Algeria.

French newspapers and political figures joined in the criticism of the circumstances of Daoud's release which came after 20 minutes of deliberations by a court that under normal circumstances would not have convened until six days later. But the hottest reaction was from abroad.

An infuriated Israeli government recalled its ambassador to France, and in Tel Aviv Foreign Minister Yigal Allon denounced the court decision as "nothing but a disgraceful capitulation to the pressure of Arab states and the threat of terrorist organizations."

The West German Foreign Ministry chimed in, declaring that "the fight against international terrorism has not become easier" with Daoud's release.

Response from Washington was also swift. State Department spokesman John Trattner said "our dismay reflects our abhorrence over the brutal and mindless murders at Munich and our strong conviction that terrorists should be dealt with sternly and firmly by legal authorities of all countries."

Stung by the U.S. reaction, the French government declared that it "constituted inadmissable comment on the acts of the French courts."

As the denunciations grew, French President Valery Giscard d'Estaing stepped into the picture and defended France's role in releasing Daoud. He wound up with an attack on what he called a "campaign of insults which tried to strike at France's dignity and honor."

The French response did nothing to appease Israel whose anger over the freeing of Daoud reached a new pitch with reports from Paris that France had sold 200 Mirage F-1 fighter-bombers to Egypt. This news touched off wide speculation that the impending sale had been one reason for French haste in freeing Daoud.

Meanwhile, Daoud, safe and sound in Algiers, told a news conference his arrest had been due to "purely political considerations." He charged that elements of the French police were "working in the interests of Zionsm." In a telephone interview with The Associated Press, Daoud declared that he was a revolutionary not a terrorist. He declared that he would be willing to testify before a West German court that he was innocent in the Munich massacre.

German police told a different story. They said they had proof that Daoud had been at the hotel used by the Palestinan raiders just before they launched the 1972 attack which cost the lives of the Israeli athletes.

BARCELONA COLLISION KILLED 48 U.S. SEAMEN

When the American helicopter carrier Guam and the USS Trenton, an amphibious transport ship, anchored at Barcelona, Spain, on a goodwill visit to the Mediterranean port, many of the seamen aboard were given permission to go ashore.

Among those who did were the 126 sailors and marines who decided to return to their ships early Jan. 17 aboard a 56-foot landing craft that was serving as a harbor launch. At about 2:20 a.m. the launch was just pulling out and rounding a pier to ferry the men back to the U.S. 6th Fleet ships when, according to Marine Cpl. Herb Braxton, "We saw a ship coming at us suddenly and it kept coming. People started to yell, 'Dammit, watch out,' but the ship kept coming. The bump didn't do much damage but the ship just kept coming on into us and that's what turned us over."

Braxton, a nonswimmer, was one of the men trapped under the launch when it rolled over after colliding with the 380-ton Spanish freighter, Urela. He and others who clung in a small airspace below the inverted deck were saved when Spanish tugboats sped to the scene and righted the overturned launch. Scores of others who were dumped into the dark, 50-degree waters swam to safety. Others were not so fortunate. When rescue operations were completed, the number of dead was reported at 48.

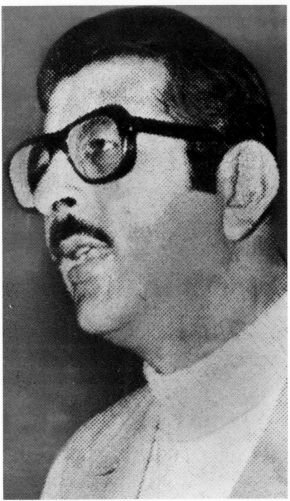

The Israeli government released this photograph which it identified as terrorist suspect Abu Daoud

Spanish frogmen loaded the body of a U.S. seaman onto a launch after it was pulled out of Barcelona harbor

The collapsed Granville Bridge lay atop a commuter train on the outskirts of Sydney, Australia

AUSTRALIAN TRAIN WRECK CLAIMED 81 LIVES

It was still quite early in the morning as the commuter train sped along on its 50-mile trip from Australia's Blue Mountains to Sydney. As the train rounded a curve about 20 miles out of Sydney at 8:12 a.m. Jan. 18 it jumped the tracks and plowed into a bridge support pylon. As the train lay stricken, the 200-ton concrete bridge tumbled down upon it. Three autos which had been on the bridge plunged down onto the train.

The scene, a survivor recalled in horror, resembled "a bloody battlefield." The screams of trapped passengers merged with the cries of hystrical persons who had come to the site looking for relatives.

Rescuers rushed to the area. One was a Roman Catholic priest. He crawled into one of the carriages pinned under the bridge girders. When he came out again he said he had given last rites to about 20 persons—many of them already dead.

A man who staggered out of one of the front cars said, "I was in the war and I never thought I'd see anything like that again. We were upside down, inside out, and then the carriage burst like a sardine tin."

Neville McDonald, a journalist, said he was thrown to the floor after the train braked suddenly. "I had time to pick myself up and stick my head out of the window before the bridge came down," he said. "A great cloud of dust went up and I thought the train was exploding. Everyone was stunned and silent. Then the overhead power lines came down, spitting sparks."

All available policemen and ambulances were rushed to the scene from Sydney. Sgt. Joe Becroft, a member of the police rescue squad, recalled, "It was terrible. We just could not get them out. We could see dozens of bodies all over the place. There was one amputation performed—a young girl's arm was taken off. The dead in there are of all ages and, quite frankly, some of them are so badly mutilated we just can't tell who they are."

Rescue teams worked through the night in an effort to reach the injured and the dead. When they had finished, the death toll stood at 81.

FOR THE RECORD

PARDONED. Iva Toguri D'Aquino, the women known to millions of World War II servicemen as "Tokyo Rose." Mrs. D'Aquino, who was one of several women who made regular propaganda radio broadcasts designed to demoralize American servicemen in the Pacific, was pardoned Jan. 19 by President Ford. She was convicted of treason in 1949 in San Francisco and served 6½ years in prison. Mrs. D'Aquino, 60, was graduated from college in 1941 and traveled to Japan to care for a sick relative before the attack on Pearl Harbor. Stuck in Japan with the outbreak of war, she said she was ordered to make the propaganda broadcasts by Japanese officials. She said later an American officer who was a prisoner of war told her the broadcasts would do no harm.

The crisp winter air made these horses dance and frolic in an isolated mountain pasture near Banner Elk, N.C.

Hindu pilgrims converged by the millions on the dust-choked banks of the Ganges River at Allahabad, India, during a 43-day ritual bathing festival celebrated every 12 years

FEBRUARY

American Criticism Of Uganda Killings Angered Idi Amin

The message that crackled over the air in a routine Radio Uganda newscast Friday, Feb. 25, held menacing overtones for the United States and its new president, Jimmy Carter: Field Marshal Idi Amin Dada, the flamboyant unpredictable president-for-life of the landlocked East African nation, had barred all American residents from leaving the country until meeting with him in the capital three days hence.

Carter, whose election Amin had initially welcomed, had apparently angered the African president with his stinging criticisms on human rights in Uganda. Recent events in Uganda, Carter said — referring to reports of a new wave of killings in the country and the mysterious deaths of an Anglican archbishop and two cabinet ministers — "have disgusted the entire civilized world."

The American president added that he supported a British demand that the United Nations send a fact-finding mission to Uganda to assess the horrible murders that are apparently taking place in that country, the persecution of those who have aroused the ire of Mr. Amin."

The radio announcement said Amin had ordered provincial officials to make a complete list of the 200-odd Americans in Uganda as well as their possessions, including "chickens goats, pigs and other animals." The Americans were ordered to prepare a memorandum explaining their activities, saying if they had been mistreated and if they wished to remain in the country.

Meanwhile Uganda's security forces were ordered not to allow any of the Americans, the majority of them missionaries living in remote rural areas, to travel abroad.

Amin was already in the middle of an internal crisis, claiming to have uncovered an abortive plot to topple him from power. He charged it was masterminded by the man he himself ousted from power six years earlier, former President Milton Obote, now living in exile in neighboring Tanzania. Details of the alleged plot

Uganda President Idi Amin wore a uniform ablaze with medals when he attended the Arab-African summit in Cairo in March

were revealed at an open-air confession ceremony attended by 3,000 of Amin's loyal soldiers, specially trucked into the capital of Kampala, cabinet ministers, diplomats and other "invited guests."

Three participants in the alleged plot recited documents incriminating themselves. One hundred Chinese automatic weapons, thousands of rounds of ammunition and hundreds of hand grenades were laid out alongside 22 steel trunks in which they were allegedly found. One of the men read a long memorandum allegedly drawn up by Obote in which he suggested ways of mobilizing opposition to Amin and said arms could be shipped into the country to be passed on to Uganda's Anglican archbishop, Janani Luwum.

Luwum, who was present at the ceremony with other Anglican bishops in purple robes, shook his head in denial. Nevertheless he was arrested less than 24 hours later, along with two other government ministers, Lt. Col. Erinayo Oryema, responsible for land and water resources, and Charles Oboth-Ofumbi, in charge of internal affairs. They were charged with complicity in the anti-Amin plot. Their arrest was rapidly followed by an official Radio Uganda announcement which informed a dubious world that the three men died in a car crash as they tried to escape while being driven to interrogation. The deaths, especially that of Luwum, sparked a worldwide wave of protest and charges that the three were murdered b' Amin's security police.

Only two days before barring the American: from leaving the country Amin, a burly, 6-foot-« former army private who often packs a pisto strapped to his right hip, accused the Unitec States, Britain and Israel of involvement in the plot to end his rule. Amin, who had a reputatior for offering gratuitous advice to world leaders did not substantiate his claim. And the three nations denied involvement.

Amin's orders rang alarm bells in the White House and Presidential Press Secretary Jod' Powell told reporters: "The president will take whatever steps he thinks are necessary anc proper to protect American lives." As he spoke a four-vessel U.S. Navy task force, headed b' the nuclear-powered aircraft carrier Enterprise cruised off the East African coast as Americar military officials kept watch on the situation in case the Americans needed rescuing. But bar ring an unexpected break in the bizarre pat terns of Amin's behavior it appeared unlikel' their lives were directly threatened. Amin': vengeance was normally directed at his own people.

Only three whites were believed to have beer killed during his rule: Mrs. Dora Bloch, the Is raeli air hijack hostage whose death has neve been satisfactorily explained, and two Ameri can freelance journalists, Nicholas Stroh anc Robert Siedle, who died when they went to in vestigate a reported military rebellion shortl' after Amin took power.

First confirmation that the Americans appar ently had nothing to fear came from a Minis try of Information official in Kampala, who sai' they would be free to leave after meeting Amir "There's no cause for alarm," he said. "There' no cause for fear at all." Indications that Ugan da was backing off from the possibility of a di rect confrontation also came from Paul Chep kwurui Amin's charge d'affaires in Washingtor Summoned by the State Department he sai' the Ugandan president "merely wants to reas sure them that nothing will happen to them."

Radio Uganda helped ease the tension b broadcasting a statement saying all Ami' wished to do at the meeting was "to thank a the Americans for the excellent work they hav' been doing in Uganda." But in a long and ram bling message to Carter, the 49-year-old Ugan dan leader said the United States shoul' consider its own human rights crimes befor meddling in Ugandan affairs. These, said th' message, "range from racial discrimination an' bombing in Vietnam to the Bay of Pigs invasio' of Cuba, the dropping of atomic weapons o' Japan and the killing of world leaders by th' Central Intelligence Agency."

Amin also warned the Americans against at tempting an Israeli-style invasion of Uganda t' rescue American citizens. He charged that re ports from neighboring Kenya told of 5,000 U.S Marines poised to rescue the American

Anglican Archbishop Janani Luwum was killed shortly after he had been accused of plotting against Amin. The government said he and two others also accused of plotting had been killed in an auto accident

32

Above, Amin talked to American newsmen at the presidential lodge in Kampala. He denied charges that he was exterminating members of the Acholi and Langi tribes. Right, Amin took time out to play basketball with an army team near Kampala

trapped inside the country. But no such mission was possible, he warned, because "Uganda has the strength to crush any invasion."

The Americans immediately denied the claim and the patrolling ships were reportedly not geared for an airborne rescue bid.

Uganda's self-styled field marshal obviously feared a repetition of the successful Israeli raid on Entebbe Airport July 4, 1976, when commandos rescued more than 100 hostages being held by pro-Palestinian hijackers. Amin went out of his way to discount fears that he might be putting the Americans in a similar position by saying he had no intention of holding them hostage.

A spokesman for Amin, quoted by Radio Uganda, said: "This has never crossed his mind. He has never thought of making any of them hostages. It is just the U.S. imperialists putting words into his mouth." All Amin wished to do was to thank the Americans for their work in Uganda and present some of them with medals, the radio said. Carter meanwhile arrived at the presidential retreat of Camp David, Md., to tell reporters: "I think it's going to be all right."

As Amin's latest escapade captured headlines around the world, the West German embassy in Kampala advised Americans contacting it to remain at home and keep a low profile until the meeting. The embassy had been handling American affairs since the United States closed its embassy in October 1973 on the day Amin sent a cable to President Richard Nixon wishing him "a rapid recovery" from the Watergate scandal. Earlier the United States was angered by Amin's expulsion of the embassy's Marine guard and detention of a group of Peace Corps workers for 56 hours at Entebbe on the grounds that they were Israeli spies.

Virtually nothing was heard direct from the Americans in Uganda. But as it was to turn out, there was more concern in the outside world over their safety than among the U.S. community in Uganda. An American nun, Sister Judy Marie Garbacio, contacted by telephone, said that she and other Americans were not "overly fearful" and that they "certainly" planned to attend Monday's meeting with Amin. They had not been threatened and felt no hostility from Ugandans.

Amin's next move, which came Sunday, was to postpone the meeting for two days until the following Wednesday. He said this was being done at the request of the Americans, to give them more time to prepare for the meeting and reach Kampala from remote areas. He also changed the venue from the International Conference Center in Kampala to the main lounge of Entebbe Airport 19 miles away.

The lounge was the only facility in the country large enough to accommodate the 3,000 persons who were to attend. However, there was no indication who would be present besides the Americans and Amin, with a collection of stuffed wildlife carcasses as onlookers. The collection, dominated the second-floor lounge of Entebbe's airport building, which was empty most of the time as the majority of international airlines now bypassed Uganda.

The announcement of the postponment was again accompanied by a warning to the Americans not to try any sort of rescue operation. The official radio told Ugandans to be on the alert for any signs of an invasion. After the Israeli raid on Entebbe, the presence of U.S. naval vessels off the Kenyan coast "must be taken seriously," the radio said. Quoting a military spokesman, the radio said:"In the event of an invasion, the invading force will be disintegrated by the Ugandan armed forces."

But Amin, under pressure from Arab and African governments apparently interceding at the request of the Carter administration, intended to back off completely from any confrontation with the United States. On the eve of the Entebbe meeting he postponed it indefinitely and lifted his ban on the Americans leaving the country.

"They are now free to go anywhere they wish, such as going on holidays or going about their normal business, be it inside or outside Uganda," Amin said. The reason he gave for chang-

ing his plans was that Carter is "still new and young and not familiar with African affairs."

The crisis, as far as the United States was concerned, was all but over. But Amin, through Radio Uganda, continued for several days to claim that some 2,600 Americans, British and Israeli mercenaries were advancing through Kenya to invade Uganda. Kenya, he charged, was aiding the invasion force. Amin gave no details to substantiate his claim.

The United States and Britain promptly denied the charge. Kenya, which so far had remained silent on the affair, issued an unusually harsh statement saying: "hallucinations and shadow boxing are a commonplace thing with the military regime in Uganda. With this understanding you can expect to hear that God has shaken hands with Amin."

What Amin's five-day confrontation with the United States did achieve was to divert attention from a continuing reign of terror in Uganda, reports of which were reaching the outside world from refugees fleeing into neighboring Tanzania and Kenya. The main targets for attack, according to the refugees, were members of the Acholi and Langi tribes, serving in the armed forces, civil service and as academics. The two predominantly Christian tribes formed the backbone of former President Milton Obote's power structure.

Some refugee reports put the number of persons killed in Amin's latest bloodletting at more than 3,000. But independent confirmation was not available. In early February, the 18 bishops of Uganda's Anglican Church, including Luwum, sent a letter to Amin urging him to halt bloodshed in the country.

"The security of ordinary Christians has been in jeopardy for a long time," the letter said. "We have buried many who have died as a result of being shot, and there are many more whose bodies have not been found, yet their disappearance is connected with the activities of some members of your security forces."

One refugee, Geoffrey Mugabi, claimed that hundreds of Langi tribesmen were massacred by Amin's troops in a barracks where he was detained. When he was ordered to carry out bodies he said he saw that "all the heads had been smashed in and the floor was littered with eyes and teeth."

Amin's rule had been characterized by slaughter. Opponents, real or imagined, regularly disappeared. Sometimes their bloated corpses were tossed into the Nile River to be eaten by crocodiles or they were found washed up on the shores of Lake Victoria. Amnesty International, a London-based human rights organization put the number killed at between 50,000 and 300,000.

Kenya's Anglican bishops, responding to the death of Luwum and reports of mass slaughter of Christians in Uganda, called for internationally sponsored armed intervention in Uganda to topple Amin and restore law and order. The in-

ternational "police force," said the bishops, should be created by the Organization of African Unity and the United Nations.

Yet it appeared extremely unlikely that their appeal would meet a positive response. African states in particular were reluctant to criticize Amin or condemn the brutality of his rule. They fell back on the OAU charter which forbade interference in the internal affairs of other African states.

Neither did the United Nations show any inclination to take steps over the situation in Uganda. The world body's Commission on Human Rights overruled a call by Britain and Canada for an international investigation into the reports of atrocities in Uganda. Amin invited a party of American newsmen to visit him in Kampala to explain that massacre reports were being spread by his opponents "who are speaking bad things about me to get money from the newspapers." Amin also predicted Carter eventually would "be one of my best friends" and suggested the United States reopen its embassy in Kampala.

Meanwhile in the nearby East African nation

of Ethiopia another tragedy was also being played out. The nation's socialist revolution, which began with the overthrow of Emperor Haile Selassie's feudal rule in September 1974, was being written in blood.

In February, Lt. Col. Mengistu Haile Mariam, the pint-sized strongman of the shadowy Military Council that had ruled Ethiopia since Selassie's overthrow, consolidated his power in a bloody shootout at the council's headquarters in which at least seven persons died. They included his chief rival for power, Brig. Gen. Teferi Bante, and six supporters, who reportedly wished to start a dialogue with the underground leftist Ethiopian People's Revolutionary Party as part of a move to reduce tensions within the country.

There was armed resistance to the council in at least seven of Ethiopia's 14 provinces. Street assassinations of government supporters by the Revolutionary Party were a regular occurrence in the capital of Addis Ababa, and government opponents received similar "revolutionary justice" in their homes and mass executions. Thousands were believed to have died.

Amin harangued reporters during a news conference at Arab League headquarters in Cairo while attending an African-Arab summit conference

35

Queen Elizabeth II,
who celebrated her
Silver Jubilee Feb. 6,
stood in the Throne
Room of Buckingham
Palace wearing the
imperial state crown

Silver Jubilee Brought Britons Out of Doldrums

The 25th anniversary of the Queen's reign gave the people a needed lift

Britain needed a Jubilee. She needed to dress up a gray decade with a flash of scarlet and a ruffle of drums for a spiritual boost and an economic shot in the arm.

Despite the old hymn exhorting God to save the queen, to keep her "victorious, happy and glorious", there had been little enough to celebrate in the 25 years since Elizabeth II ascended the throne. Political murder in Northern Ireland, economic suicide at home. Swollen prices and withered world influence.

Hanging on: a class system out of the 12th century and labor relations out of the 19th. Going, gone: that old grace and grandeur, that old self-confidence.

So the Silver Jubilee could not have come at a better time.

"We need a new start," said the Anglican Archbishop of York in a Jubilee message. "It would be a pity if we were just to become the repository of the antique, a giant museum for the tourists, a mirror of the past."

As the 1976 bicentennial helped America put war and Watergate behind, the Silver Jubilee presented the British with a reason to do what they still do better than anybody:

"We may not lead the world in motorcycles any more," asserted one Briton, "but by Jove there's still no one who can touch us for pomp and circumstance.

Starting slowly with a seven and a half-hour New Year's Day television replay of Elizabeth's coronation (the TV audience never fell below a remarkable 1.25 million), the year moved into a crescendo of celebrations.

They ranged from a dinghy show to a review of the Royal Navy; from an exhibit of matchbox labels to an international homecoming of Scottish clans, more than 3,000 bike races, ballets, band concerts, fireworks shows and village festivals, embroidery contests, parades, regattas, cricket matches and other events and observances drew a special air from the Jubilee.

The Queen tackled an exhausting itinerary that included state visits to Australia, New Zealand and her South Pacific territories, Canada, the Caribbean, Northern Ireland and almost every county at home. In June the peak: Elizabeth's official 51st birthday and the anniversary of her coronation. London ablaze in crimson and silver. The program featured: A bonfire at Windsor, lit by the Queen. A hundred answering fires, springing up at 30-mile intervals, streaming outward from the home castle like the ribbons on the Union Jack until all Britain glimmered like a jewel.

Next a solemn service of Thanksgiving amid the other-worldly glory of 17th century St. Paul's Cathedral. A Royal Progress up the River Thames, a river pageant splendid beyond the dreams of Cleopatra. A gala birthday parade with gleeming brasses, tossing cockades and high-strung chargers on polished, prancing hooves.

As spring arrived, waves of tourists began surging onto British shores. London hotels were booked solid for months at a stretch as big spenders from countries with sounder economies took advantage of Britain's bargain-rate pound sterling.

Jubilee coffee mugs, Jubilee platters, plaques and punchbowls poured from the heirloom and limited edition mills. Jubilee omelet pans, bookends, postage stamps, tea towels, medallions, keychains. Forty different Jubilee-linked books and magazines more than 2 million copies.

"Whenever I think of Jubilee I think of profit," said the manager of a chain of blue jeans emporia. Several companies with big stakes in the Jubilee insured the lives of the Royal family for millions of pounds.

Busts of the Queen, Jubilee T-shirts and bikinis, a provincial butcher's red-white-and-blue Jubilee sausages.

Jubilee alchemy: a royal crest turned 5-cent plastic shopping bags into 25-cent keepsakes, $10 souvenir cigarette lighters into $15 collectors' items; a bath in gold paint transmuted halfpennies into $5 pendants.

The Lord Chamberlain's office, sold copyrights on the royal coat of arms for $17 a go and tried to keep things genteel. But there was fury on the City Council of Reading at that city's Chamber of Commerce scheme to auction off 200 chamberpots emblazoned with royal insignia.

Besides heraldry and hard-sells, British jubilees are a time when the thoughts of the public-spirited turn to public works: to making parks out of parking lots or vice versa, to cleaning up, or putting up, some civic eyesore. For many a British hamlet a jubilee statue or horse trough is its only local landmark.

Thus it was that Clay Cross, pop. 9,000, and **37**

Much of the Queen's time was occupied with duties of state, such as opening Parliament in this picture where she sat next to her husband, Prince Philip several years earlier

120 miles north of London, got a main street face-lift, a profusion of flowers and a new bench outside the parish church. The coronation clock, which had not worked for several years, was restored.

Like many other Britons, members of the House of Commons were asked to dig into their pockets to pay for a memento of the Jubilee. In their case it was a 12-foot-tall steel statue outside the Houses of Parliament, depicting the symbolic beasts of countries that have adopted British-style Parliaments.

The British capital also gained a 4½ mile walkway from Leicester Square to the Tower of London with special Jubilee pavement tiles and signs pointing out places of interest. An area on the South Bank of the Thames that lapsed from parkhood after hosting the 1951 Festival of

Britain was reinstated, much to the consternation of patrons of the new nearby theater and concert complexes who had been using it as a parking lot.

Hong Kong sent along a 140-foot ritual dragon with silvery scales mounted on sky blue and orange-red taffeta to dance the Queen's health when manned by 24 Chinese-born subjects. Twenty-five of London's bright red double-decker buses got Jubilee coats of silver paint. Producers put together a 75-minute movie of the Queen's life.

Prince Charles, 29-year-old heir to the throne, was mustered out of the Royal Navy as the year began, ending a military career of helicopter piloting and a minesweeper command to take up royal ribbon-cutting duties. His first job was as titular head and star attraction of the

gation of the earth alone in a small sailboat. But they couldn't stop the sun setting on the British Empire.

The realm the Queen toured at age 50 was two dozen colonies smaller and considerably poorer than the one she inherited at age 25. Instead of network of tributaries in Asia, Africa and the Caribbean, Britain has membership in the European Common Market — and as sort of a poor relation at that. And there were demands for autonomy in Scotland and Wales.

The Royal Navy flotilla the Queen reviewed off Spithead was pinched for hardware and scrimping on fuel. It was smaller by almost half than the one that assembled for the last Jubilee, that of her grandfather George V in 1935. The pound sterling, once the foundation rock for international commerce, declined in a quarter century from $2.80 to about $1.75.

The change from crowns, farthings, shillings and other mysterious coins to decimal currency in 1971 helped disguise racing inflation but nothing could cover up the strikes, the stagnant production.

Left, the Queen and her husband walked together at Windsor as she marked the 25th anniversary of her reign. Below, Prince Charles, heir to the British throne, stood with his sister Princess Anne on the grounds of Windsor Castle as the nation celebrated their mother's jubilee.

Silver Jubilee Appeal, a fund-raising exercise in support of projects to encourage community service by young people.

Elizabeth II became Queen on Feb. 6, 1952, on the death of her father King George VI. "A Symbol of Hope," and "People Are Looking to the Throne as Never Before," newspaper headlines read that year. Britain was slowly emerging from the shadow of World War II. On Coronation Day the following year word arrived in London that Edmund Hillary had conquered the unscaled Mount Everest, the world's highest peak. Some, took it is a sign that after nearly 400 years a second Elizabethan Age was at hand. They looked for a Renaissance, for new Drakes and Raleighs to spread Britain's glory and new Shakespeares and Spensers to sing it. It was not to be. The Queen was crowned to preside powerless over profound transformations at home and abroad that wrenched the national fiber.

There were magnificent personal achievements along the way: Roger Bannister's first 4-minute mile, Francis Chichester's circumnavi-

This pretty model added sparkle to a set of gold and silver ingots embossed with the royal coat of arms to commemorate the Jubilee

Labor unions became more powerful. Labor governments set out to demolish the class system that had supplied imperial Britain with some great men and some useless ones. The middle and upper classes screamed that it was not the system but themselves that were being destroyed, and class resentment and snobbery seemed little abated.

Immigrants from former colonies poured in, complicating the class issue. Suddenly Britain had a race problem. In Northern Ireland long-simmering hate burst into religious gang war in August 1969 and claimed the lives of more than 1,700 people in the ensuing eight years. The result was a spiritual and material drain for Britain, which still kept 14,000 troops in the province to maintain some semblance of order.

For all of this, few blamed the Queen, who stood aside from the alarms and excursions of daily politics, a calm, steady figure in tweeds and sensible shoes.

"She has brought continuity in a period of acute change; she has brought the balm of a glamorous tradition to the wounds of lost power," said a columnist in London's Financial Times. The Times of London called her "our best professional monarch for several, or perhaps many, generations."

The Winter of 1977 Brought Widespread Death and Disaster

The National Weather Service called it the coldest since the founding of the Republic

The winter of '77 began in September of '76 when high in the upper atmosphere distorted wind patterns began sending arctic air deep into the United States.

The distortion locked itself in place for four months and the result was a bitter winter that the National Weather Service called the coldest "since the founding of the Republic."

Some of the country's energy supplies were severely strained, people froze to death, schools and businesses closed down and it even snowed in Miami for the first time.

President Carter turned down the White House thermostats and wore a sweater as he worked. With natural gas supplies at critical levels, he urged that homes and businesses keep thermostats at 65.

Ironically, while much of the nation was locked in a deep freeze, Alaska was experiencing one of its warmest winters. The Anchorage Hockey Association canceled games because the ice on the outdoor rinks melted. Instead of

A rotary snow blower slowly chewed through snow 12 feet deep near Tylerville, N.Y., after a five-day storm

His collar pulled over his head and umbrella turned inside out, this Boston pedestrian tried to leap over a pile of slush

skidding on icy sidewalks, urban Alaskans dodged splashes from passing vehicles and swapped mukluks for sweaters.

"There probably isn't any simple underlying reason for all of this," Dr. Donald Gilman, head of the weather service's Long Range Prediction Group, said of the weather distortion. "It's just the very complicated result of a lot of factors acting together in a subtle way. We don't know why and just don't have the means of finding out."

The Utah Legislature didn't wait for a scientific reason. It adopted a resolution asking state residents to pray for relief from the severe winter and also from the drought in the Midwest and far West. Before the winter would end, however, the East and Midwest were severely crippled — 75 people died in weather-related deaths in one week — and other areas suffered disastrous effects.

One city became the focal point of the winter's fury: Buffalo, N.Y. A blizzard ushered in

February and there already had been more than 100 inches of snow on Buffalo when the storm struck.

The Buffalo population was going about its business on streets already reduced to one-lane arteries. As the work week came to a close, cars trying to reach the suburbs were enveloped. Motorists panicked and abandoned their vehicles, clogging up the highways. By Saturday morning, the city was isolated from the rest of the state. The bodies of several motorists were found in their vehicles.

Firemen had to drag hoses by hand along hundreds of feet of narrow streets only to watch as spray flying from the hoses became instant glass. Authorities borrowed civilian snowmobiles and Jeeps and worked 24 hour stretches.

"What I found out these last few days is that there are a lot of wonderful people in our county," said Sheriff Kenneth Braun of his staff and citizens who teamed to help stricken families.

As natural gas supplies dwindled, a Canadian gas company agreed to help Buffalo with emergency gas. Carter declared nine New York State counties disaster areas. He did the same for Maryland, Virginia and Florida. And he declared emergencies in Michigan, Pennsylvania, Indiana and Ohio.

In Florida, the major problem concerned the citrus crop. Gov. Reubin Askew had asked for the federal declaration of emergency aid after officials estimated the freezing temperatures had caused about $150 million worth of damage to the citrus crop and about $50 million damage to other Sunshine State crops.

The U.S. Agriculture Department's Florida Emergency Board estimated that 35 to 40 percent of the citrus crop was lost and perhaps 95 to 100 percent of other vegetables. An estimated 100,000 farm workers were thrown out of work.

Within a week, food prices across the nation reflected the weather's disastrous effect. An Associated Press spot check showed prices zooming on many fruits and vegetables that Florida traditionally sends North in the winter.

In some cases, growers and wholesalers had increased prices early to anticipate shortages.

Florida's plight was a boon to citrus growers in California and Texas. Before the freeze, Florida's citrus crop had been running 15 percent ahead of the previous year's size. Since Florida produced 70 percent of the nation's grapefruit and 45 percent of its oranges, western growers began raising prices.

California shipped 1.2 million 40-pound boxes of oranges out of state before the freeze. The amount climbed to 1.7 million boxes the week after the freeze.

California, however, was struck by a severe drought, which affected the northern part of the state.

But between the East and West coasts was Ohio, an area that seemed to feel the biggest pinch because of the energy shortage. Not only did natural gas supplies dwindle, but transportation necessary to get other forms of energy to the state also had weather problems: frozen rivers.

Barges backed up on the Ohio River after it froze. Fifty-four towboats, each pushing 10 to

The temperatures dropped so low in New York that the Hudson River froze over trapping a ship in the ice, as shown in this picture taken from the New Jersey shore

Layers of ice surrounded the Capitol in Washington

12 barges waited more than a week at inoperative dams. At least half of the barges carried fuel, petroleum, coal or road salt. Much of their cargo—a single barge can carry six million gallons of heating oil—was destined for Ohio and western Kentucky.

Trouble occurred in other waters. A barge carrying 3.3 million gallons of home heating fuel ran aground off the coast of Massachusetts. The Coast Guard was forced to firebomb a 200-yard-long oil slick to keep 100,000 gallons of the leaked oil from killing marine life and fouling Cape Cod beaches.

Typical of problems in Ohio towns and cities was Dayton, reeling under electricity and natural gas shortages. On January 18, the town was nearly deserted as businesses and industry shut down to conserve energy.

"It's kind of eerie really," said Matt Minehart, 18, as he looked around an almost empty shopping mall. "It feels like you're the only one left in town or something." Dayton policeman J.P. Moore said the weather also affected the crime rate. "Crimes of violence are way down," he said.

There would be other odd weather-related effects: electric clocks in eastern parts of the country ran 28 seconds slow during one cold

seizure because of an overload on electric generating capacity.

The City of Miami Beach stopped its ads in New York newspapers inviting tourists to warm beaches because of the snow. The snow fell all over Miami, but it was never officially recorded at the National Weather Service offices.

In Pennsylvania, all of the state's 6,000 schools closed during February to save fuel. About 90,000 people were unemployed, many of them out of jobs because of a shutdown of heavy industry.

In neighboring New Jersey, Gov. Brendan T. Byrne issued an order that allowed businesses to stay open only 40 hours a week, the exceptions being firms that kept thermostats at 50 degrees. New Jersey police drove around using loudspeakers to warn residents that they would be fined if their thermostats were not at 65 in daytime and 60 at night.

A record 104 inches of snow fell in Terra Alta, W. Va., during January. An estimated 30,000 persons had to evacuate their homes. Shell fishermen in Maryland were unable to work for a month.

About 50,000 people were laid off work in Georgia, but some returned to work as mills found alternate fuels.

GUNMAN HELD HOSTAGE IN INDIANAPOLIS FLAT IN 62-HOUR ORDEAL

Friends described Anthony Kiritsas as an outgoing man with a time-bomb personality—quick to like people, but just as quick to turn on anyone who crossed him. That was the unsettling description given police when the 44-year-old Indianapolis man took a mortgage company executive hostage and held him in an apartment he claimed was rigged with dynamite.

Kiritsas kept police at bay with threats to blow up the building unless the company canceled a $130,000 loan and authorities granted him immunity from prosecution.

"I've already lost all my self-respect," Kiritsas told WIBC news director Fred Heckman at one point. "I'm going to be a marked man all my life.

It had all begun three years earlier when Kiritsas borrowed the $130,000 from Meridian Mortgage Co. to purchase 17 acres of land on which he had hoped to develop a small shopping center. But it didn't turn out that way. Kiritsas claimed that the mortgage company tried to steer prospective retail outlets away from the property to force default on the loan.

On Feb. 8, with the deadline for payment of the loan only 20 days away, Kiritsas made his move. He seized Meridian director Richard O. Hall, 42, wired the muzzle of a sawed-off shotgun to his neck and marched him four blocks through downtown Indianapolis. The gunman then forced Hall to drive a commandeered police car seven miles to the west side of town. Finally Kiritsas holed up with Hall in a third-floor apartment in Indianapolis and began issuing his demands.

Throughout the first night police and newsmen kept vigil outside the apartment. Tension mounted as Kiritsas shouted through the door "I'm not going to do any time . . . I'm not going to jail. Don't come through the door. I don't want to hurt anybody."

Meanwhile, the mortgage company announced that it had released Kiritsas from the loan. A spokesman for the Marion County prosecutor said immunity was under consideration.

At this point, Kiritsas made three new demands: a public

and written apology from Hall's firm, payment of an unspecified amount of damages, and a guarantee that Hall's company would pay any damage incurred by Kiritsas because of civil suits that might arise from his actions.

On Feb. 9, Meridian chairman M. L. Hall, father of the hostage, broadcast a statement apologizing for any wrong done Kiritsas. Late that night authorities promised Kiritsas total immunity, provided he freed Hall. But Kiritsas still refused to surrender.

The immunity offer was read over the telephone to Kiritsas by a friend, Wendell "Dutch" Sheffer. His only response, said Sheffer, was "I don't want to see it. I'm not ready. I'm drawn out."

Finally at 10:20 p.m. on Feb. 10, Kiritsas walked his hostage downstairs. After shouting to reporters, he removed the wire that connected the shotgun to Hall's neck. The 62-hour ordeal was over.

Suddenly Kiritsas said "I've wanted to fire this thing ever since I've had it." Breathing heavily, he fired a shot skyward out of the window. Four policeman grabbed Kiritsas and whisked him into the back seat of a patrol car. Witnesses said the gunman stared in disbelief when he was seized.

The Indianapolis police chief was quoted by a bystander as saying "Tony you lied. You said you would let the man go before you came down."

Cursing angrily, Kiritsas told newsmen the mortgage company had swindled him. "I'm a national hero and don't you forget it," he shouted.

Police then began to look for the hundred pounds of explosive with which Kiritsas said he had rigged the flat. They found nothing.

Later Deputy Sheriff Darrell Manners said Kiritsas bragged that he had bluffed police. "I really pulled one over on you," he was quoted as saying. "All I had up here was four gallons of gasoline."

Kiritsas was arraigned Feb. 11 on a list of charges, including kidnapping. He was ordered held under $850,000 bail.

Some authorities said they had never intended to let Kiritsas go free. Said Marion County Sheriff Lawrence Broderick "I would have promised you title to Hawaii if I could have gotten that guy out of there."

"We had to placate him," said Indianapolis Mayor William H. Hudnut. "Everybody thought he had the dynamite."

Anthony Kiritsas twisted Richard O. Hall's neck with the wired shotgun before he released his hostage

Fred Cowan posed for this picture in a physical culture magazine

NAZI-LOVING WEIGHT LIFTER KILLED FIVE IN SHOOTING SPREE

Fred Cowan was a hulking, army-trained sharpshooter who idolized Adolf Hitler and expressed hatred for Jews and blacks, but so far as anyone knew he had never hurt anyone. Then, on Valentine's Day, the 33-year-old Cowan strode into the warehouse where he worked and killed five persons, including a policemen. He wounded five others and finally took his own life.

Cowan was a body-building enthusiast who went in for weight lifting. He had spent 17 months in the army, a career distinguished mainly by two courts-martial; for being absent without leave and for leaving the scene of a highway accident.

Neighbors knew little about the six-foot 250-pounder who lived with his parents in New Rochelle, N.Y., except that he had a mania for guns and Nazi memorabilia. He had tattooed his body with Nazi swastikas, German crosses and bolts of lightning, and he adorned the walls of his room with more swastikas.

And there were the guns. Said a neighbor, "He's got every kind of a rifle that was ever made, and has been collecting them since he was a kid."

About two weeks before the Feb. 14 massacre, Cowan had been suspended from the job he held as a driver's helper for a moving company after getting into an argument with a customer over moving a refrigerator.

Cowan was due to go back to work on the morning of Feb. 14, the date his suspension expired. He arrived, but with his gun blazing. He was said to be bent on revenge against Norman Bing, traffic manager of Neptune Worldwide Moving Co., who had ordered the suspension.

"If I had been 30 seconds later in getting out of my office, I'd be dead," said Bing who had huddled for three hours under a desk in an adjoining office, undetected by Cowan." He kept asking people if they knew where I was. Thank God, nobody did."

46

During his search, Cowan shot to death three blacks and a dark-skinned native of India, all employees of the firm. The fifth victim was one of the first policeman to arrive at the scene.

Other policemen were called in and a 10-hour siege ensued. It finally ended when police cautiously began moving through the building after the last employee trapped inside by the killer had escaped. They finally found Cowan dead from a self-inflicted bullet to the brain.

PRESIDENT CARTER WROTE TO A SOVIET DISSIDENT

It was an action believed to be without precedent: a personal letter of support from President Carter to Soviet dissident leader Andrei Sakharov.

The president's four-paragraph letter on White House stationery, dated Feb. 5 and delivered to Sakharov at the U.S. Embassy in Moscow Feb. 17, was sent in response to a Sakharov letter received in Washington Jan. 28. In that letter, Sakharov, a noted nuclear physicist and winner of the 1975 Nobel Peace Prize for his activities in behalf of human rights, asked Carter to "raise your voice" on behalf of political prisoners in the Soviet Union and Eastern Europe.

Carter's letter, which Sakharov said was the first he had ever received from the U.S. government, said in part:

". . . I want to express my appreciation to you for bringing your thoughts to my personal attention.

"Human rights is a central concern of my administration. In my inaugural address I stated: 'Because we are free, we can never be indifferent to the fate of freedom elsewhere. You may rest assured that the American people and our government will continue our firm commitment to promote respect for human rights not only in our own country but also abroad.

"We shall use our good offices to seek the release of prisoners of conscience, and we will continue our efforts to shape a world responsive to human aspirations in which nations of differing cultures and histories can live side by side in peace and justice . . ."

While Carter had said U.S. statements about human rights in the Soviet Union "were not attacks on the Soviet Union and should not be interpreted as such," the Soviet Union had reacted with irritation to administration statements in support of Soviet dissidents, and Western observers said the president's letter probably would heighten tensions between the two nations on the human rights issue.

Shortly after the Sakharov letter, Carter met briefly March 1 in the White House with Soviet dissident Vladimir K. Bukovsky. Bukovsky, whose civil rights activities led him to spend 12 of his 34 years in Russian prisons, was released from a Soviet jail in December 1976. His freedom was tied to Chile's release of Luis Corvalan, a Chilean Communist who then met with Leonid Brezhnev on the Soviet leader's 70th birthday.

During his 10-minute visit with Bukovsky, Carter told the Russian that he would not be "timid" in his pronouncements on human rights and that the U.S. "commitment to the concept of human rights is permanent." But Carter said he wanted his public statements on human rights to be "productive and not counterproductive." In the face of strong Soviet protests over Carter's human rights pronouncements, the president told Bukovsky that he wanted "to assure that our own nation and countries other than the Soviet Union are constantly aware that we want to pursue the freedom of individuals and their right to express themselves."

Bukovsky's prison terms came as a result of his organizing exhibitions of forbidden art, distributing writings from the West, staging dissident demonstrations, and speaking out about what he believed was a repressive government in the Kremlin. He was in the fifth year of a seven-year prison term when he was swapped for Corvalan.

U.S.-SOVIET COOPERATED IN KIDNEY TRANSPLANT

In a demonstration of Soviet-American cooperation that could have been titled "From Russia With Love," a Brooklyn construction worker with kidney trouble got a new kidney that had been taken from a 16-year-old boy who had been killed in a Moscow auto accident.

Although there previously had been successful trans-Atlantic organ transplants, the one performed Feb. 21, at the New York Hospital-Cornell Medical Center was believed to be the first involving a Russian donor.

Dr. William Stubenbod, the surgeon who performed the kidney transplant on Jose Serrano, 32, said the donation was "indeed a testament to the brotherhood of man." The donation came about through Dr. Albert Rubin, who said he learned during a trip to Moscow that organ procurement was "more advanced" in that country. Rubin said that in late 1976 he arranged with Dr. Valery Schumakov of Moscow's Institute of Organ and Tissue Transplant to try the trans-Atlantic operation. Rubin added that about 50,000 Americans were getting dialysis machine treatment while waiting for kidneys to become available for transplants.

Rubin said a first attempt failed when a kidney from Moscow arrived in the United States infected but that a second try was made when the youth was killed in the Soviet Capital. He said the body of the boy was taken to the institute, his kidneys removed and one was transplanted into a Russian patient while the other was placed in a refrigerated preserving solution and shipped to New York by air.

When the kidney arrived, it had tissue samples taken to see if they matched with anyone on the waiting list for transplants. When this was done, Serrano got a telephone call advising him to come to the hospital and the transplant operation was performed.

CHICAGO TRAIN CRASH KILLED 11, HURT 200

As day drew to a close, workers streaming out of their offices in the heart of Chicago's downtown business district found that a winter storm had dropped nearly four inches of snow on the city to further slow rush-hour traffic. James Kilroy was standing on a crowded street in the area—known as the Loop—chatting with a friend. Suddenly Kilroy heard screams, looked up and saw four cars of the train he usually took home plunge off the elevated tracks.

"I met an old friend on my way to the train station and we got a little carried away. I missed the train, but, man, was I lucky," Kilroy recalled.

He stood only a few hundred feet from where a Chicago Transit Authority train crowded with homeward-bound passengers had crashed into the rear of another train. The impact sent four train cars off the track, causing 11 deaths and injuring some 200 persons.

"We were standing here talking about the good, old times," said Kilroy, "and then we heard a lot of screams and a loud noise—like a big thud—and that was it." The train had left the tracks as it snaked around a sharp curve Feb. 4.

Agnes McCormick was sitting in a restaurant near the window, sipping coffee when the trains crashed. "Everbody jumped up," she recalled. "We thought the train was going to come right through the windows. People fell out of the train and the train fell on top of them. We tried to pull the people out from under the train. There were a lot of dead people."

Three cars of the train, which was headed for the western suburb of Oak Park, plunged from the tracks into the street and a fourth car crashed atop one of them. Paul Bowman, John Williams, Teresa J. Patorelli, and Mary E. Anselmo were among the passengers on the train.

"It was sheer chaos," Bowman said. Recalled Williams, there was a girl screaming "my mother is dead. . .my mother is dead." Said Miss Patorelli, "There were a lot of people pinned under the seats," and Miss Anselmo added, "everybody was flying, seats, everything."

The crash was the latest in a series of collisions and derailments that had hit the aging elevated tracks of the Chicago Transit Authority. On Jan. 9, 1976, 333 persons were injured because of what was termed a signal malfunction. In 1974, there were four train accidents involving the CTA, the worst being a rear-end collision that injured 224 persons. Another 41 persons were hurt in a September 1974 wreck.

Chicago's worst commuter wreck in recent years came Oct. 30, 1972, when 45 persons were killed and more than 320 persons were hurt when one train slammed into the rear of another.

Terrified passengers hung to seats in a dangling car of the Chicago elevated train

Also in FEBRUARY...

FIRE SWEPT WING OF MOSCOW'S HUGE ROSSIYA HOTEL

Since the giant Rossiya Hotel opened on the north bank of the Moscow River in 1970 it had been the pride of the Soviet Union. The huge square structure boasting 3,200 rooms, was said to be the world's largest inn. Seven years later on Feb. 25, the Rossiya's north wing was virtually gutted by a fire that forced guests to leap from windows and killed an estimated 45 persons.

The fire, blamed by the Soviet news agency Tass on "a technical fault in elevator equipment," erupted at about 9 p.m. near the top of the 12-story wing. The flames quickly spread to lower floors, blowing out huge glass windows and filling Red Square, a block away, with heavy smoke. The blaze also extended to a 21-story tower in the center of the complex, damaging several floors.

The fire erupted when the hotel was packed with foreign businessmen and tourists, as well as Russians, but no Americans were reported killed. At the height of the blaze, hundreds of guests fled into the winter night while others trapped by the flames screamed for help in various languages. Some of the injured were carried out of the building on stretchers by firefighters wearing heavy padded uniforms and oxygen masks. Many who fled left behind their belongings, passports and other documents.

"They were loading people onto ambulances on one side of the hotel," said Samuel Hensley of Altus, Okla., a hotel guest. "I saw four people who I know were injured. A couple of them had their faces wrapped in bandages. There were ambulances going off in all directions."

Left, Indianapolis firemen Daniel Gammon, left, and Donald Graston clutched Clarence E. Abbott on a ledge of the Indiana World War Memorial in downtown Indianapolis saving him from a 150-foot plunge

Below, America's Space Shuttle Enterprise, which was roughly the size of a DC9, shown airborne as it rode piggyback aboard a NASA 747

Soviet authorities refused to say just how many were killed or injured in the blaze, but at one point they did identify 11 bodies. Informed sources, however, estimated that at least 45 persons perished. U.S. officials said about 170 Americans were believed to have been staying at the Rossiya. Two Americans were reported treated at the hospital for smoke inhalation.

So vast is the Rossiya (the name means "Russia") that the main restaurant continued to operate normally. People dined, drank and danced while the fire raged in the north wing. One report said several wedding parties were going on during the blaze.

FOR THE RECORD

CONVICTED. Larry Flynt, publisher of Hustler magazine, on obscenity and organized crime charges. Flynt was found guilty of the charges in Cincinnati Feb. 8 and sentenced to 7 to 25 years in prison. He and Hustler Magazine Inc., were fined a total of $22,000. The conviction was being appealed. Flynt had maintained the case was a test of his First Amendment privilege to publish. The prosecution had contended Flynt was exploiting sex for profit by distributing Hustler.

RESUMED. Diplomatic relations between Spain and the Soviet Union. The resumption was announced Feb. 9, and came 38 years after the ties were broken off at the end of the Spanish Civil War. During that war, rebel forces, led by Gen. Francisco Franco, fought against the Second Republic, with the Soviet Union supplying arms to the Republicans. When Franco's armies triumphed in 1939, the Soviet Union's diplomatic presence in Madrid came to an end.

Right, Chimney sweep Charlie Mullins looked like he was walking on air as he jumped from one roof to another in Chatanooga, Tenn., where he pursued a career sweeping chimneys. He got the idea watching chimney sweeps in wartime Germany and adopted the European sweep's tie and tails uniform

Below, this petroleum conduit was the lifeline for oil-rich Qatar in the Persian Gulf

MARCH

Hanafi Moslems Held 134 Hostages During Siege of Washington

They called it the Siege of Washington. Some said it was the most terrifying direct assault upon the capital since the British sacked it in 1814.

But this was no incursion by an enemy nation. It was an act of religious vengeance, stemming from a feud between black Islamic sects, triggered by a man whose injuries from battles past had exploded into violence.

His was a fury whose origins ranged from the streets of New York's Harlem to the holy fires of faraway lands, from the frustrations of personal failure to a father's tragic loss.

On a balmy March 9, Hamaas Abdul Khaalis made his move. The 55-year-old Khaalis and 11 followers emerged from the mansion that housed both the surviving members of his family—many were murdered there four years earlier by Black Muslims—and the headquarters of his own smaller Islamic group called the Hanafi Moslems.

A black reporter was killed. Three buildings were seized. Other men were stabbed, shot or beaten and 134 hostages lay at a point of machetes for 38 hours as he chanted his cause, often incoherently, in the name of Allah.

"Are you listening?" demanded Khaalis, a onetime Black Muslim leader whose breakaway band of Hanafis is believed to number, less than 1,000. "It has not even begun . . . We have wild men out there . . . wild in the way of faith."

Khaalis was determined to have his revenge for seven murders, including six of his sons and daughters, at his house in early 1973.

Three Moslem diplomats went to see Khaalis in an effort to reason with him, to discuss his actions in terms of common faith and especially the Koran, the holy book of Islam. "Don't teach me the Koran," he exploded. "I know it better than you."

The three Moslem envoys were Ardeshir Zahedi of Iran. Sahabzada Yaqub-Khan of Pakistan and Ashraf A. Ghorbal of Egypt.

Khaalis, had declared himself a soldier at war and the Koran speaks of "blood for blood" in time of war. Pakistan's Yaqub-Khan calmly countered: "Our point is, you're not at war." But neither would anyone have suggested that Khaalis had been at peace for a long time.

Americans had known a rash of terrorism in the early weeks of 1977, but nothing to compare with this. In fact, one such episode was at the top of the news even as Khaalis walked out of the Hanafi mansion the morning of March 9. President Carter announced at a 10 a.m. news conference that he would meet the demand of kidnapper Cory Moore in Warrensville Heights, Ohio, by calling him personally if he released his hostage. Moore did release his captive, a police captain, and, later got his call from the president—who simply wished him well. Moore originally had begun his own siege with a demand that all white people leave the earth, or, failing that, burn their money.

Before Cory Moore there were others. They complained, variously, of lost jobs, lost girl friends, of being cheated financially. But none had threatened so many lives as Khaalis.

March 9 began auspiciously for the capital's citizens. A warm front provided a respite from the long winter, and office-workers began to think early of lunch. Israeli leader Yitzhak Rabin was there on a state visit, and Carter, aside from his handling of the Cory Moore affair, made news by lifting travel restrictions to Cuba.

A city council committee was holding a hearing on the fifth floor of the District Building, the city hall, within sight of the White House. A few blocks away, an official of B'nai B'rith was talking by telephone to one of his colleagues in Richmond, Va. And on Embassay Row, about two miles away, students were touring the Islamic Center, headquarters of the city's orthodox Moslem movement.

Then, with no warning, Khaalis' religious vendetta erupted at those three spots. Khaalis and six followers struck B'nai B'rith. At 11 a.m., they strode up to the eight-story concrete building six blocks northwest of the White House with guns out and machetes swinging. They pistol-whipped as they went, rounding up anyone in their path.

"They kept saying they were going to cut people's heads off," said Andrew S. Hoffman, 20, a George Washington University student caught up by the sweep and then released. "They all said they were going to die, but they were going to die for a cause."

Suddenly, the B'nai B'rith official in Richmond heard the telephone drop. Before it went dead, he heard a voice say: "Up against the wall or I'll blow your head off."

To the top floor the invaders went. Office workers tried to hide behind locked doors, but the gunmen shot the locks off. Their leader, Khaalis, ordered windows covered or painted over. The number of captives grew to more than 100.

As police rushed to the B'nai B'rith building seven blocks north of the White House, four

Police and firemen scaled a ladder up the side of the District Building where hostages were being held

"I'm shot," cried Maurice Williams, a 24-year-old reporter for Howard University radio station WHUR. He fell dead.

Two others were wounded. Mayor Walter Washington barricaded himself in his office and awaited rescue. Police were spread thin.

There were conflicting reports. Police tried to log developments as they occurred but gave up in mid-afternoon. So they waited. The day dragged. Dusk came, and they still waited.

Reporters and police talked to the invaders by telephone, getting few clues. But it became clear that all three invasions were part of a common effort on the part of the Hanafi Moslems for a single motive: revenge.

The night produced more tension. The police, who had set up special command centers near each of the three sites, checked and rechecked with relatives and co-workers in an effort to arrive at an accurate hostage count, finally settling on a total of 134—104 at B'nai B'rith, 7 at city hall and 23 at the Islamic mosque. Still others, they knew, were trapped in the B'nai B'rith and City Hall buildings, undetected by the gunmen but unable to leave their hiding places for fear of being spotted. Those with access to phones were advised by police to stay put until help arrived.

A few, including some hostages, did manage to get away. A maintenance crew at B'nai B'rith escaped through an air conditioning duct. A few hostages were released because of chest pains or wounds.

At the Islamic Center, a man answered the phone: "We're all having coffee and tea and a nice chat, but heads will roll and people will die unless we get our demands."

In city hall, hostage Alan Grip told telephone inquirers: "We've asked for cigarettes. They've gotten them. We've asked for fruit for breakfast. They've gotten it. We've asked for a newspaper. They've gotten that." But Grip also relayed this message from his captors: "We are Hanafi Moslems to the death, and if the police have any ideas about storming this room, all lives are in immediate danger."

Police pondered rescuing more than a dozen persons trapped in city hall by ladder, but decided against it because the fifth-floor ledge was slippery with pigeon dung.

And so it was a stalemate. One brave soul, Ben Gilbert, city planning director, entered the building and went to his fourth floor office. He reported the floor above was quiet. He grabbed some papers he needed and left, saying: "The planning process must go on."

The negotiating process went on, too. The three foreign ambassadors became a link to the terrorists, able to communicate through a common religion.

The Carter administration had asked the ambassadors to communicate with the terrorists, at the request of the gunmen themselves. At first, however, their discussions via telephone were simply one-way affairs, with Khaal-

other terrorists struck at the Islamic Center. They rounded up employees and touring students, 23 in all.

More than two hours later, two blacks with rifles marched into the city hall. They took an elevator to City Council offices on the fifth floor. Shots were fired.

"I've been shot," screamed Councilman Marion Barry. He staggered into the council chamber where the economic hearing was under way. Shocked spectators turned toward him as he fell into a chair, clutching his chest. A bullet lodged a quarter-inch from his heart. He lived.

52

is bellowing threat after threat. He was the same with the many reporters who got him on the phone. One threat: meet my demands or we will march the hostages into a "killing room" and drop their severed heads, one by one, out the eighth floor window of the B'nai B'rith building.

The hostages, particularly at B'nai B'rith, were kept in considerable discomfort. Most were bound and ordered to lie face down on a cold cement floor. Many nursed wounds from pistol-whippings suffered during the early moments of the assault.

Hostage Ed Mason, a painter, was ordered to help move some furniture and told his head would be chopped off if he didn't. "If you've got to die, you've got to die," he replied. For that, he was knocked unconscious with a rifle butt. The older men, eight of them, were not tied up. But they were told they would be the first to die in the event of trouble.

By 8 p.m. Thursday, there was new activity at B'nai B'rith. A table was set up under bright lights in the ground-floor lobby. A black limousine arrived. The ambassadors entered the building. The table and chairs were moved out of view, and three hours of bargaining began.

Face to face with Khaalis, the Moslem diplomats sought to mediate a religious war within the United States, one which had triggered at least 20 assassinations over the past decade. Involved were the Black Muslims now known as the World Community of Islam in the West, and their various offshoots, of which the Hanafis were one.

The Hanafis, numbering no more than 100 when they moved to Washington from New York in 1970 to set up shop in a house donated by basketball star Kareem Abdul-Jabbar, had never been known as perpetrators of violence — (As the Muslims had.)

In fact, it was the militancy of the Muslims that had led Khaalis to break with the Chicago-based Church. He had risen to No. 2 in command, next to the late Elijah Muhammad, of the Muslims while advocating a more moderate line — especially with regard to whites — than Muhammad himself. But he failed to engineer the reforms he sought, just as he subsequently failed in attempts to win Muslims over to his new black Islamic sect.

Khaalis was born Ernest Timothy McGhee in Gary, Ind., of devout Seventh Day Adventists who had fled poverty and racism in Alabama farm country. As a young man — and aspiring jazz drummer — he headed for the glitter of Harlem's black clubs in the mid-1940s.

But he lost his taste for professional music the more he saw of the other sides of Harlem society — dope, alcohol, filth-filled streets, poor blacks scraping to deal with white merchants and landlords.

In 1946, he was converted to the Moslem faith by a Pakistani teacher. He soon joined the more radical Black Muslims, who not only taught that the Jew was an enemy, but that all whites were.

The latter doctrine — as well as personal rifts with Muhammad — became intolerable and Khaalis, along with his friend Malcolm X, left the Black Muslims in Chicago to return to New

After it was over, Hanafi Moslem leader Khalifa Hamaas Abdul Khaalis talked to a police officer at the door of his residence

York City. Soon afterwards, on Feb. 21, 1965, Malcolm X was gunned down and Khaalis' disrespect for Muhammad turned to hatred.

But it wasn't until early 1973 that the feud reached its peak.

"Hamaas came in and found four babies stacked up in the tub, foam coming from the mouth," recalled Amina Khaalis, his daughter. In all, seven persons, including six of his sons and daughters, were drowned or shot to death in Khaalis' house.

The government managed only to indict six of Muhammad's followers—not from Chicago, but Philadelphia.

One man was acquitted outright, another got a mistrial. The others received life imprisonment, despite their demand for a new trial after Khaalis stood up in the courtroom and screamed: "You killed my babies! You killed my babies and shot my women!" an outburst for which he was fined $750.

Khaalis had vowed that if the law didn't give him justice, he'd get it himself.

For years, even back to the murder of Malcolm X, Khaalis waited. Meanwhile, he fought to enlarge his sect succeeding only nominally. Then, another blow. Wallace D. Muhammad, the new leader of the Black Muslims, returned from a trip to the Mideast with $16 million in Arab money and a proclamation declaring him "the sole consultant and trustee for all American Moslem organizations."

That, some have speculated, made Khaalis snap. And hence his three-pronged attack in Washington—on Jews, on the government and upon the Islamic Mosque, against believers in his own god. And hence his demands: For the killers of his family and of Malcolm X, presumably so he could execute them himself. For the return of his $750 courtroom fine. And for abolition of a movie, "Mohammad, Messenger of God," financed by other Islamic nations.

Among the Black Muslims he wanted police to deliver to his custody were Wallace D. Muhammad and boxer Muhammad Ali, both of whom, charged Khaalis, were implicated in the earlier murders. By all accounts, the authorities never seriously considered complying. But police did give Khaalis the $750, and the movie premiere was stopped in mid-reel in New York City.

Now it remained for the Arab diplomats to bargain, not for money or movies, but for lives.

"I'm a soldier" Khaalis told them. "In a war, innocent civilians are killed."

But "Our point is, you're not fighting a war," said Ambassador Yaqub-Khan.

And then, as Hamaas Abdul Khaalis listened to a Moslem teacher from Pakistan, he broke into tears after what Yaqub-Khan called "moments of almost hysteric paranoia."

For Yaqub-Khan had read him this verse from the Koran: "And let not the hatred of some people in shutting you out lead you to transgression and hostility on your part; help ye one another in righteousness and piety."

With that, the Siege of Washington was at an end. "We withdrew, remaining brothers in faith, and the police moved in and arranged for the lifting of the 38-hour ordeal," Ghorbal recalled.

Khaalis and his followers in each of the three buildings surrendered quietly. The hostages were bused to a downtown church for a tearful reunion with their friends and families. Throughout the city, the bells of churches of all faiths pealed joyfully.

Khaalis, as part of the surrender agreement, was allowed to return to the Hanafi mansion, free on a bond of personal recognizance. But on March 31 he was jailed along with the others. A judge ruled that he had violated the rules of the bond by uttering a threat of violence during a tapped telephone conversation with a relative.

These three ambassadors met with gunmen in negotiations that ended the siege. They were from left: Pakistan's Sahabzada Yaqub-Khan, Egypt's Ashraf Ghorbal, and Iran's Ardeshir Zahedi

Collision of Two Jumbos Was Aviation's Worst Crash And Took 582 Lives

"Okay," crackled the voice from the control tower through the hum and static, "Standby for takeoff. I will call you."

But everything was not okay:

—Santa Cruz de Tenerife's Los Rodeos Airport in the Spanish Canary Islands was patched with fog, visibility down to 300 yards on the afternoon of March 27. The control tower had an airport apron jammed with diverted planes waiting to get back in the air again. Two of the airport's three radio frequencies were out of order. The central runway lights were not working. There was no ground radar.

—Waiting to take off at one end of the 11,155-foot runway, Royal Dutch Airlines KLM 4805—The Rhine River—did not acknowledge that it was, in fact, holding as requested by the tower. Squatting in the fog, the KLM jumbo could not be seen from the tower.

—Taxiing toward the KLM jet, another jumbo, Pan American's 1736—The Clipper Victor—went by intersection C-3, its crew convinced that the turnoff was not "the third one to your left" it had been told to take by the tower. It could not see, or be seen, by the KLM jet.

Half a minute later, roaring down the runway with takeoff power, the KLM jet smashed into the Pan Am jumbo at more than 160 miles per hour. Both planes exploded and burned, taking 582 lives. More than 60 persons aboard the Pan Am jumbo survived, but all 249 aboard KLM's plane perished.

Ironically, the collision of two jumbos, a nightmare that had haunted passengers and airlines since the jet age crowded the skies, was on the ground.

Preliminary evidence indicated no mechanical failure by either of the giant 700,000-pound aircraft. Everything, instead, pointed to human error, perhaps something as basic as a misunderstanding of words—or failure to hear all of them.

KLM pilot Jacob Veldhuizen Van Zanten, 25 years of experience and a model for KLM's advertisements of "the reliable airline of those surprising Dutch," may never have seen the Pan American jumbo lumbering toward him because his cockpit horizon was changing as the KLM jet lifted. Or, as Pan Am investigators suggested later, he may have tried to leapfrog over the American plane in the 3-4 seconds that both planes came into each other's view just before the crash.

But Pan Am captain Victor Grubbs did see

55

A fireman played a stream of water on the burning wreckage of one of the Boeing 747s

the KLM hurtling toward him, its engines thundering out 2,000 degrees Fahrenheit of heat, its lights winking, its undercarriage still down. Grubbs, also a veteran pilot, tried frantically to wrench his jumbo off the runway.

A few seconds or a few feet difference in either plane's position might have averted disaster.

But the "ifs" were all the other way. At 5:07 p.m., the two Boeing 747 jets collided in the world's worst aviation disaster.

Edward Hess, 39, a Phoenix food broker, traveling Pal Am first class with his wife, recalled they were trapped after the impact—then the fire began.

"We were engulfed in flames. It probably was only minutes but it seemed like months. Then there were several explosions and they blew the flames away. We jumped down. I remember the grass was wet."

Pan Am purser Dorothy Kelly shook off her surprise and looked up at the open sky.

"There was nothing around that looked like anything had looked before, just jagged metal. The only noises I heard were explosions behind me. I heard no people". She jumped to the ground from 20 feet as the jet's floor began giving way. The back of the plane was in flames, she said.

U.S. and Dutch investigators later concluded the KLM jet was barely airborne when it hit the Pan Am jet by the right inboard engine and sheared off part of the fuselage over Pan Am's first class passengers. The survivors were located there.

Out of control then, the blazing KLM jumbo pancaked onto the runway 500 yards from the point of impact and blew apart in a mass of flames and molten metal.

Bleeding, burned, dazed, their clothing in rags, Pan Am's survivors stumbled away from the exploding jumbo. Behind in the Pan Am

inferno, the rest of the occupants of their plane were dying.

Captain Grubbs was dragged to safety by purser Kelly. One month after the crash he was released from a hospital in Fort Dix, N. J., still unable, he said, to bring himself to read about the crash.

For all those aboard the KLM jet, including 48 children, there were no escape stories. Their blackened bodies were placed beside those of the Pan American victims in an airport hangar just a few yards away from the crash scene to await transport home.

Yet most of the dead could not be identified, carbonized beyond recognition. Some human grace tempered the horror of the piles of bodies inside the hangar: a man lay with his arm around a woman, their last touch before death; a baby died in the arms of its mother.

The fact that either of the two planes had been in the Santa Cruz airport at all was an accident.

Flying its vacation-bound passengers away from the cold and rain of Holland, the KLM jet was scheduled to land at Las Palmas airport, another island 40 miles away from Santa Cruz. But Las Palmas airport authorities closed the airport temporarily after leftist terrorists set off a bomb earlier in a flower shop inside the terminal. KLM was diverted to the Santa Cruz airport.

Pan American's jet, also heading for Las Palmas to put its passengers aboard the M.S. "Golden Odyssey" for a 12-day Mediterranean tour, was about one hour from touchdown when it, too, was ordered to land at Santa Cruz. Its flight originated in Los Angeles, refueled in New York and took on 14 more passengers before heading for the Canary Islands.

The Pan American's passengers were people in their 50s and had paid up to $2,500 each for the trip.

With Sunday already a busy air day in Santa

Cruz because of charter flights to the resort island, Los Rodeos Airport apron soon became overcrowded with scheduled and diverted flights.

KLM, due to pick up passengers in Las Palmas for a return flight to Amsterdam, took on 21,000 gallons of fuel while waiting for clearance to leave. It wanted to save time when it eventually reached Las Palmas. Pan Am, on the ground for two hours, tried to get away first, but could not find enough space to taxi by the KLM jumbo.

The countdown to disaster began when the control tower cleared the Dutch jumbo to leave first, taxi up the single runway, make a 180-degree turn and hold for takeoff clearance. Pan Am was to follow the KLM jet up the runway about three minutes behind. "Taxi into the runway and leave the runway third, third to your left, third," said the control tower.

Pan Am investigators said the first taxiway on the left, blocked by aircraft, would have taken the plane right back to the crowded apron and thus was considered "inactive." Taxiway C-3 would be a difficult, abnormal turn for the big jumbo. Taxiway C-4, the last exit, must be what the tower meant by the third intersection, Pan Am contended.

KLM knew that the Pan Am jet was following it and asked the tower to confirm that Pan Am was to turn off at the third taxiway. The tower replied: "The third one, sir. One, two, three, third, third one." The tower asked Pan Am to confirm when it was off the runway. Pan Am confirmed it would.

KLM 747 operational manuals required the pilot and co-pilot to check 10 items as they taxied the length of the runway. Another 12 checks were required before takeoff. The KLM co-pilot did the talking to the tower, as did the Pan Am co-pilot. The plane captains were busy with other tasks.

Heard on tape, the conversations sound surprisingly scratchy, like a bad telephone line, incompatible with an electronic age or the complicated cockpit from where they were coming.

At the end of the runway the tapes showed KLM's Van Zanten had received airways clearance. He repeated back his instructions: "You are cleared to the papa beacon, climb and maintain flight level nine zero, right turn after takeoff, proceed on heading zero four zero until intercepting the three two five radial from Las Palmas V-O-R."

Pilots are required to repeat airway clearance. They are not required to repeat takeoff clearance although it is recommended they acknowledge it. KLM's airways clearance however, was not takeoff clearance, and Dutch government investigators acknowledged it was not.

A Spanish civil guard and Red Cross official sorted through the personal belongings of the hundreds of dead

Above, the coffins of crash victims were loaded aboard a plane for the flight back home

Left, survivor Larry Walker of Laguna Beach, Calif., suffered extensive burns

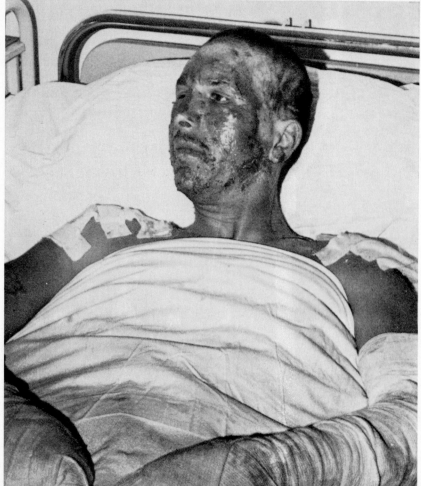

"Without takeoff clearance," said a Pan Am investigator, "the KLM jet still should be sitting on the runway."

The investigation and the tapes from the cockpit voice recorders, the in-flight recorders (the black boxes), the tapes from the control tower and testimony from the surviving Pan Am crew and the Spanish air controllers remained the best evidence.

With the loss of lives, the wreckage of two $50 million planes and lawsuits and insurance claims in the billions of dollars, fixing the blame became important, the cold aftermath of plane crashes after the dead and debris are gone.

The Los Rodeos Airport remained closed for one week. Then it opened again to the jets and the tourists.

Romania Devastated By Quake Which Killed More Than 1,500 Persons

The promise of spring was in the air and a full moon beamed on Bucharest the evening of March 4, luring crowds to restaurants and movie houses. Then something slipped deep beneath the ground and 20 seconds later Romania's capital was falling apart. When the dust finally settled, more than 1,500 people lay dead in Romania, most of them in Bucharest.

There was no warning rumble when the quake, one of Europe's worst in a century, struck at about 9:30 p.m. For the next 49 seconds, buildings in Bucharest swayed violently as the ground undulated like ocean waves. Thirty-two apartment buildings came crashing down into their foundations. Walls in other buildings fell into the street and onto people below. Power failed and lights went out. Only the moon and car headlights penetrated the cloud of dust that rose from collapsed buildings.

One of the first to relay a sketchy account to the outside world was an operator at the Bucharest telephone exchange. "The situation is terrible here. We know nothing but we have heard that many are dead," she said in a voice quivering with emotion when reached by the Associated Press office in Rome.

A Marine guard at the U.S. Embassy in Bucharest told AP's Rome office by phone that first reports indicated the heart of Bucharest, the city's old section, had been almost destroyed. As the hours passed more detailed reports began to pour in.

British salesman John Rix was playing darts at the British Embassy recreation lounge when beer glasses began to shake violently. "When the tremor stopped we could hear the buildings all over Bucharest crashing to the ground," he later recalled. "The air was full of screams and dogs barking. It then went very quiet and people just seemed stunned."

Eduardo Rahn, musical director of Venezuela's Maracaibo Symphony Orchestra, recalled, "I walked through the main square of Bucharest and people were dragging bodies to the side of the road."

Worst hit by the quake was Magheru Boulevard in the center of Bucharest. An army officer was standing on the avenue when the shock hit the Continental and Dunarea apartment build-

A Romanian soldier discovered a dead victim still in his bed beneath the debris of a collapsed home

The wreckage of many apartment houses and office buildings blocked the main streets of Bucharest after the quake

ings, structures about 10 stories high where prominent people lived. "I saw the Continental go. Fft," he said later. "In two seconds it was down. Two seconds later, the Dunarea went."

There seemed to be no real pattern, eyewitnesses said: There would be one building a pile of smoking rubble, the next intact, the next only partially collapsed.

Writer Alexander Ivasiuc, who once worked for the U.S. Embassy, was waiting for a bus on Magheru Boulevard in front of the Scala Cafe when the quake struck. A brick fell on his head killing him.

In Bucharest's Fundeni Hospital, Dr. Dan Setlacec was performing delicate surgery on a woman who had an arterial blockage when the operating room was plunged into darkness. "Don't move," Setlacec shouted. Without light, he and his assistants successfully completed the operation.

Tom Caragiu, a popular actor in Romania, was in his apartment talking with television director Alexandru Bocanets about an upcoming production when the shock came. They were crushed on a stairway trying to escape. The apartment from which they had fled remained undamaged. Drinking glasses stood intact on a table and Caragiu's dog was found alive in the flat.

Far into the first night teams of soldiers and civilian volunteers all over Bucharest worked under flood lights probing for bodies under heaps of rubble from collapsed apartment buildings. A middle-aged man pointed to one

mountain of rubble. "That building fell on a busload of people," he said. "Everyone on the bus was killed."

To prevent fire and explosion, gas mains in the capital were shut off. With no gas for heating, hotel patrons, bundled up in overcoats, sat in lobbies and restaurants. Some families sat huddled with their salvaged possessions outside their abandoned apartment buildings.

On the morning of March 5, lines began forming outside food stores and reports of food hoarding spread. One radio broadcast said the sale of alcohol had been banned.

At the city morgue, long lines of people waited to look for friends and relatives among the bodies brought in by hearse and ambulance. As the situation grew more critical, taxis were pressed into ambulance service while all available trucks carted off debris. A number of United States medical students were reported helping in jampacked hospitals.

The quake originated about 65 miles below the earth's surface, said the U.S. Geological Survey. It started beneath the Carpathian mountains about 120 miles north of Bucharest. A vertical shock hit the Romanian capital and shook other parts of eastern Europe.

The quake caused scores of disasters in neighboring Bulgaria. Casualties were also reported in Yugoslavia. The tremor shook pictures on walls in Moscow, drove Hungarians from buildings into the streets and rattled glassware in Vienna. Greek officials reported five tremors and brief panic in the northern city of Salonica. Tall buildings swayed in Rome, Naples and most of central Italy.

As time passed and rescue efforts continued, stories emerged of people who survived for days without food or water beneath piles of rubble.

A 58-year-old school teacher was plucked from the ruins of her apartment house after being buried for eight days without food or water. A hospital worker said the survivor, Elena Enache, told her rescuers, "I don't need water, I want yogurt." She was reported in shock but otherwise normal condition.

Authorities also told of a 19-year-old youth buried for 10 days without food or drink. Sorin Carinic was in "surprisingly good" condition although suffering from dehydration and shock, said hospital officials. Amazed doctors said it was rare for a human being to last for more than four or five days without water.

Then there was 37-year-old Gheorgh Stoica who was lying in bed when the quake began. "I went to the door of my studio apartment and threw my arms around it," he said. "Then I fell seven stories. They rescued me from the second floor the same night. I only had a few bruises."

Others told stories that were more grim. Stefan Moldovan, 52-year-old construction worker, stood in a doorway of his flat during the quake and survived. His wife, mother and daughter were killed a few feet away. Moldovan said he tried to commit suicide by jamming a shard of glass into his heart when rescuers dug him out the day after the disaster. "But I didn't have any strength left in my arm," he said.

The quake did heavy damage outside of Bucharest. It knocked out some 200 factories, many of them in Ploesti, center of Romania's petrochemical industry. Officials estimated the production loss caused by the disaster at $50 million and the total damage nationwide at about $500 million. The shock killed 26 workers in Ploesti whose oil fields were a prime target of Allied bombers during World War II. Romania has the second largest petrochemical industry in Europe after the Soviet Union.

Three days after the quake, a U.S. Air Force C-130 cargo plane loaded with medicine and food flew into Bucharest. Later that same day, aircraft carrying relief supplies arrived from Bulgaria, Yugoslavia, Switzerland and East Germany, according to Agerpress, the official Romanian news agency. Greek Premier Constantine Caramanlis pledged $300,000 worth of medical supplies and other material.

Romanian President Nicolae Ceausescu who broke off an African tour to inspect the ruins received a message of sympathy from President Carter.

A Romanian couple bade a sad farewell to their daughter-in-law killed in the quake

President Carter chatted with CBS newsman Walter Cronkite before the president began fielding phone calls from people across the nation

Millions called, but only 42 of them got to 'ask President Carter'

The busiest telephone number in the United States March 5 had to have been 900 242-1611.

That toll-free number was spun or punched out on phones across the nation an estimated 9.5 million times that day. The callers were Americans who wanted to speak to their president. And President Carter wanted to talk to them. While the great majority of those who called got busy signals or recorded messages that told them the lines that led to the president were busy, 42 persons in 26 states did manage to get through.

The questions they asked were heard on a two-hour, nationwide radio broadcast produced by CBS News. It was an unprecedented event, a folksy forum in which the president sat in a big wingback chair in front of the fireplace in the Oval Office and spoke into a pair of gooseneck microphones that curled toward his face. Seated in a similar chair near the president was Walter Cronkite of CBS, serving as moderator and followup questioner on the program, "Ask President Carter."

The questions the president answered ranged from Cuba to Idi Amin to taxes to an Indian land claim to a forbidden cancer treatment to a government job. Carter responded to them all and when he had no immediate answer he promised to provide it at a later time. The president sipped tea between answers and told one caller about it as he pointed out that the only way the price of coffee could be reduced was by cutting back on consumption.

The president made no major disclosures in his answers, but he did cover a wide variety of subjects. Among them:

—Moves seeking the restoration of U.S. relations with Cuba would be made soon, Carter said, but added that there would have to be major changes in Cuban attitudes with an end to intervention in Africa and interference in Latin America before full diplomatic relations would be resumed.

—A treaty that would give control of the Panama Canal to the Panamanian government about the year 2000 while guaranteeing American and world shipping access to the waterway would be sought, the president said, adding, "As far as sovereignty is concerned, I don't have any hangup about that."

—The president said he had no plan to revive the military draft. He also said he wanted to explore a new system of military enlistment "to combine it with a much more comprehensive public service opportunity." He indicated that would link military recruiting with recruitment for such programs as the Peace Corps and Vista but did not explain further.

One caller, Nick Kniska of Lanham, Md., wanted to know why Carter's son, Chip, and his family were living at the White House instead of earning their own way. The president said the family paid all its own living expenses, adding, "I want you and the American people to know that we're not mooching off the American taxpayer." Responding to a question from Phyllis Dupere of Rehoboth, Mass. as to whether he'd like to fly the space shuttle, the president said, "I'm probably too old to do that," but he added his sons would like to fly a mission on the shuttle and so might his 9-year-old daughter Amy. Said the president: "She's a very innovative young lady and is always trying new things, and I think she is competent to be a pilot in a space shuttle in the future or to be a member of Congress or even to be president, yes ma'am."

Ronald Fouse of Centerville, Ga., told Carter: "Now that you've pardoned the draft evaders and you propose to pardon the junkies and deserters, do you propose to do anything for . . . the veterans like myself?" Carter told him, "I don't intend to pardon any more people from the Vietnam era" and said there would be no blanket pardon for deserters. He said his administration was offering veterans help in training and job opportunities and by maintaining the GI Bill of Rights without cuts proposed by the previous Ford administration.

When Mike McGrath of Warsaw, Ind., asked "is that there tax rebate supposed to be for $50 or what?" the president explained the proposed rebate would be more than $50 for low income people. He added that his economic program also included a permanent tax cut making it "a pretty good deal for you, I think."

Gerald Anderson of Denver wanted to know why congressmen were getting a $12,900 raise while taxpayers got a $50 rebate. He asked how the raise fit the president's efforts to balance the budget. "That's a hard question," Carter said. Replied Anderson, "That's why I thought I'd throw it at you." The president then said the congressional pay hike was justified, adding that he thought the salary system ought to be changed so that when there was to be another raise it would not take effect until after the following election. That way, he said, the voters could judge the question.

Some of the callers had comments instead of

Left, one of the first callers to talk with Carter was Nicholas Kniska Jr. of Lanham, Md., shown here with his father, Nicholas Sr. Right, Mrs. Richard Nicholson of Ft. Worth, Tex., was one of those who took part in the Dial-the-President show

The last person to talk to the president was 11-year-old Michelle Stanley of North Benton, Ohio, shown here with her parents, Mr. and Mrs. Fred Stanley

questions. One woman suggested the president was violating states rights by urging individual state legislators to vote for ratification of the Equal Rights Amendment. Carter said he was not, repeated his endorsement of the amendment and said he had a right to express opinions "just as you do." A Pennsylvania Republican questioned how a government of affluent Americans could relate to the average or low-income citizen. The president said that was one of the reasons he was trying to keep in close touch with the people and also said his tax reform plan would end "loopholes that do benefit the rich and powerful."

He told an 11-year-old Ohio girl his daughter Amy went to public school because she liked it and because he was strongly committed to the public school system. "It indicates to other parents that I have confidence in the public schools all over the nation," he said. More than once the president said he like his job and was constantly learning, noting the call-in program was part of his learning process. It's an exciting job," Carter said. "I spend about half the time being president and about half the time being a student . . . The number of hours I put in is about the same I put in as governor of Georgia."

After the final call, Carter said he might give a repeat performance some time. "I liked it," he said. "The questions that came in from people all over the country are the kind which you would never get in a press conference, that the news people would never raise . . . . I think it

is very good for me to understand directly from the American people what they are concerned about, in questions that have never been asked or been reported in the news media. So my inclination would be to do this again in the future.

While Carter said he enjoyed the broadcast, Otto Flaig of Milwaukee apparently didn't. Save for the 900 area code, he had the same telephone number as the one set up for calls to the White House—242-1611. "Since six o'clock this morning, he has been getting calls from people who want to talk to me," Carter said, and asked to be careful in dialing to spare Flaig any more wrong numbers.

During the broadcast, the names of the callers who got through were flashed on a television screen so the president would know who he was talking to. A computer determined which calls got through, so as to make sure the questions came from a broad geographical area. Those who did get through were asked for their names, addresses and phone numbers. Operators called them back to verify the information and compile the list of people who would be talking to Carter. Then the operators would call back again for the final connection with the Oval Office. There was a seven second delay between the instant the president or a caller spoke and the actual broadcast of their voices, so that a CBS censor could cut off anyone who got abusive or obscene. CBS' telephone bill for the phone-in program came to $50,000—roughly $1,190 for each of the 42 calls that go through.

64

WHEN SHIPS OF THE U.S. AND THE USSR COLLIDED

The U.S. Defense Department finally released pictures taken when a Soviet ECHO II class nuclear submarine collided with the frigate USS Voge Aug. 28, 1976, in the Ionian Sea

Top, the Russian submarine was shown just before the collision with the Voge. Bottom, the Soviet craft wallowed in the sea after colliding with the American frigate

Exhaustion showed on the face of this miner as he kept vigil during the rescue operation

MINER TRAPPED NEARLY SIX DAYS RECALLED ORDEAL

Anthracite miner Ronald Adley had just finished lunch in the Kocher Coal Co. mine, a mile underground inside Big Lick Mountain near Tower City, Pa. Then he climbed up a ladder, followed by two buddies, to check the result of dynamite they had set off earlier to knock down loose rock and coal.

"The smoke from the blast hadn't quite cleared," Adley said in recalling the chilling events of that March 1 day. "We decided to give it a couple of more seconds when— suddenly—it happened. We felt this terrific gush of air. It was chilling, like the feel of death. It came from somewhere down below us. It went everywhere . . . And then I saw the water. That was something I had never seen in my life . . . Like a gusher forcing its way out of the ground. We watched it for a couple of split seconds, not knowing what to do . . . . The water roared up, and caught me in it, hitting with terrific force. It came so fast. So fast."

The water had broken through a wall of the north-central Pennsylvania mine without warning. It knocked down timbers, blocked tunnels, closed off shafts. Adley and nine other men were trapped by the debris. Adley spent nearly six days lying at a 45-degree angle in a sealed coal hole before rescuers drilled a 50-foot escape tunnel to him. Only he survived the worst mine disaster in the region's history.

"I try to blank it out," Adley said. "But something like that you never wipe completely from your mind. Over and over again, I feel it happening . . . . choking for air, gasping for breath under cold, dirty, smelly mine water . . . . trapped with two dead buddies in a black coal mine."

Kocher's Porter Tunnel is the largest deep mine in the Pennsylvania anthracite fields. It was first opened in 1946, abandoned seven years later, and reopened in 1968. Last year the mine, with some 200 employees on two shifts, produced 121,506 tons of hard coal.

Adley, who had gone into the mine with some 20 other men before dawn on the morning shift, said he was at the farthest end of the tunnel, preparing a new chute for coal removal.

"We drilled test holes to check where they might be water above us," Adley said. "This is always done for safety purposes. Most of the morning we kept drilling. Then we hit rock. We stopped drilling to fire some dynamite near the

ceiling. We wanted to clear away loose rock and coal so it wouldn't fall down on us."

Then Adley and the two other men working with him ate lunch. "We didn't hear any warning when the water came," Adley said. "No alarm bells . . . no sounds . . . no shouting from other men. The water went all the way up to the roof of that shaft, more than 110 feet. It covered everything. I was just floating behind the timber, fighting the pressure, holding my breath as long as I possibly could, searching for an air pocket. I thought the end was there, that it was all over. Then I felt the water going down, and I found a little space at the top, and I could breathe. I was so thankful to God."

Adley found the body of one of his buddies, and he saw the light of the other shining under a pile of broken coal. "I listened for some noise," he said, "but there was only silence, broken by the thump of coal lumps falling."

Adley's battery-operated light went out after a while and he was in darkness for more than 20 hours before rescuers heard his tapping signal on the coal wall the next day. "You can't imagine how I felt," he said. "I couldn't see a thing. Not even my hand in front of me. It was pitch black. But I felt that I could see life again."

Rescuers worked slowly, carefully, cutting an escape tunnel to Adley, just inches an hour through coal and quartz described as hard as iron. It took 108 hours, 4½ days, to make the hole wide enough for Adley to squeeze through, although smaller holes had been drilled into his chute so he was able to get food, dry clothes and a light.

"Every day that passed the waiting got tougher," Adley said of his underground ordeal. "It seems that the closer they got the further away they felt. They couldn't fire any dynamite at all. They couldn't chance shaking anything. They didn't want to loosen anything that might fall on me or them."

When the rescuers finally punched a shoulder-wide hole Adley grabbed the air drill and cut away the final inches of rock so he could squeeze out of his dungeon. "It felt so great, just like being born again," Adley said.

Outside, at the mine entrance, relatives and friends of the other trapped men waited. Two bodies had been recovered before Adley was rescued. And two others were found in Adley's chute.

The final five bodies were recovered nearly a month after the tragedy. They had drowned when caught in the mangled wreckage of the mine tunnel.

OIL TANKER EXPLOSION KILLS CAPTAIN AND NINE CREWMEN

The Panamanian tanker Claude Conway was running a cargo of oil from New York to Freeport, Bahamas, when sparks from a welder's torch blew the ship in two and killed 10 persons.

The 43,000-ton Japanese-built vessel was off the coast of North Carolina March 20 when it happened. "I was asleep and then 'boom!' the back of the ship broke off," said Giuseppe Alotta, one of 27 crew members rescued by the Coast Guard.

Alotta said welding repairs were being made and the sparks apparently touched off gas fumes deep in the hold carrying 536,000 gallons of oil. The captain and nine crew members were killed by the blast.

Word of the disaster did not reach shore until the merchant ship Moss Point spotted the bow floating in choppy seas. The Moss Point flashed a distress call and the Coast Guard cutters Dallas from New York and Conifer from Morehead City sped toward the scene.

Most of the survivors were found huddled on the stern of the shattered tanker which was drifting about two miles away from the bow. Rescue efforts were delayed by darkness, gale-force winds and squalls. But finally, with the aid of lifeboats and a Coast Guard helicopter, the survivors were plucked from the wreckage.

Oil from the torn hull caused a slick 15 miles long and 2,000 feet wide.

VIETNAM RETURNED BODIES OF AMERICANS WHO DIED IN THE WAR

Considering the occasion, the welcome was laconic. "I am prepared to listen to you."

The words were spoken by Vietnamese Foreign Minister Nguyen Duy Trinh March 16 as he met in Hanoi with the first official American delegation to visit Vietnam since the war in that country ended in April of 1975. Responded United Auto Workers President Leonard Woodcock, head of the five-member commission sent to Vietnam by President Carter to seek information about Americans missing in Indochina prior to formally establishing United States relations with Vietnam, "We are very pleased your government is receiving us and we look forward to fruitful discussions."

The following day the committee met with Premier Pham Van Dong, who told them, "You come here with good will. President Carter obviously wants to solve the problems between us in a new spirit. There are no problems about this. We are ready." When Woodcock said he hoped the wounds of the war could be forgotten and a new relationship forged between the two nations, Dong replied that "everything stems from that fact."

After several days of talks aimed at opening friendly relations between the Communist regime and its former battlefield enemy, the commission left Hanoi for Vientiane, Laos, taking with them the remains of what they thought were 12 U.S. pilots turned over by Vietnam. Later, the remains in one of the 12 black steel caskets were found to be those of a Vietnamese. The bodies had recently been dug up from several cemeteries around Hanoi. A Vietnamese official told the commission, "We are checking to see if there are any more Americans in our cemeteries and if there are we will turn them over to you." The Pentagon has listed 795 men as missing in action, and more than 1,700 have been listed as dead with their bodies not recovered.

After leaving Laos, the commission paused for a rest stop in Honolulu before returning to Washington, D.C., with assurances from Vietnam that procedures could be set up to clarify the status of some of the Americans missing in the Vietnam War. Members said there also was hope that Laos would assist the U.S. in its quest for those missing in the Indochina war.

Woodcock said the trip had laid the basis "at the will of the president, for moving toward normalization" of relations between America and Vietnam.

On March 22, the commission returned to Washington, and the following day President Carter said the United States would resume negotiations without preconditions or delay to establish friendship and normal relations with Hanoi. He said the commission told him, "Vietnam is prepared to establish diplomatic relations with us." As to the returned bodies, the president said, "The Vietnamese delivered to the commission 12 bodies. Eleven of them have been identified as American servicemen. One body is not an American serviceman and will be returned. We have notified the Vietnamese government about the error. It was an honest mistake."

Caskets containing the remains of American pilots killed in the Vietnam war lay in a row at Hanoi's Gia Lam airport

CONGO PRESIDENT AND CATHOLIC PRIMATE SLAIN IN SPREADING VIOLENCE

For several weeks there had been rumblings of unrest in the impoverished West African state known as the Congo People's Republic. They reached a sudden climax March 19 with the terse announcement by Radio Brazzaville that leftist President Marien Ngouabi had been gunned down the previous day.

A later broadcast monitored by the British Broadcasting Corp. said 39-year-old Ngouabi was killed by a Capt. Barthelemy Kikadidi, who allegedly led an "imperialist suicide commando" squad in an attack at army headquarters. The president was shot in the jaw, the broadcast said, and died "with a gun in his hand."

Radio Brazzaville said an 11-man military committee had assumed power in the state which lies in a narrow 800-mile strip stretching inland from the Atlantic Ocean. The attackers got away and a call went out to hunt them down.

First hint that something was wrong in the 17-year-old nation came March 1 when a Congolese official said there was a "difficult and dangerous" international situation afoot, brought on by a "vast imperialist sabotage plan."

A dusk-to-dawn curfew was clamped on the country after Ngouabi's death and its borders were closed by authorities who also banned meetings of more than five persons.

Three days after the assassination, the Congo government announced the arrest of former President Alphonse Massamba-Debat who had been overthrown by Ngouabi in a military coup back in 1968. The announcement accused Massamba-Debat of organizing the squad which had assassinated Ngouabi.

Twenty-four hours after his arrest, Brazzaville radio said Massamba-Debat had confessed to organizing the abortive coup that led to Ngouabi's death. Listeners then heard Massamba-Debat say in a flat voice that he had never forgiven Ngouabi for ousting him and denying him the respect due a former chief of state. He read a list of names of politicians he said had been marked for posts in a new government after Ngouabi's government had been eliminated. Informed sources said Massamba-Debat had spent the past seven years living in seclusion in his native village and had appeared to be isolated from political maneuvering.

On March 23, the government made another dramatic announcement—the murder of the Roman Catholic primate

President Marien Ngouabi who was gunned down by an assassin in the Congo

of the Congo and one of the church's eight black African cardinals. The statement said Emile Cardinal Biayenda, archbishop of Brazzaville, had been kidnapped and murdered by three members of the family of slain president Ngouabi. The government said it was seeking the killers of both men.

Finally came the announcement that former President Massamba-Debat had been executed March 25 for plotting Ngouabi's assassination. The government radio declared that the only way to deal with counterrevolutionaries "is to cut of their heads."

Movers were attempting to haul this $40,000 house across frozen Lake Superior when it broke through the ice

This was the scene at the 15th green of the Augusta National Golf Course as the Masters Golf Tournament got under way. Tom Watson won the event

SOVIET REJECTED U.S. ARMS PROPOSALS

When Secretary of State Cyrus R. Vance left Washington on a mission to Moscow his task was to set down new American proposals for a nuclear arms control agreement.

"I see our task as seeking to reach an agreement with the Soviet Union on the framework for negotiations that would follow in Geneva for a SALT (strategic arms limitation talks) agreement," Vance said March 25. "I hope very much, indeed I pray, that we may achieve this purpose because I know of nothing that is more important to not only our country and the Soviet Union but to the peace of the world at large" than an arms agreement.

But on March 30, Soviet leader Leonid I. Brezhnev shattered the latest United States effort to reach a new arms treaty when he rejected American nuclear arms control proposals. Vance, who had waited three days for a Soviet answer to his proposals, said both a comprehensive and a more limited approach had been offered but the Soviets "did not find either one acceptable."

Vance denied his proposals had been rejected because of Soviet unhappiness over American human rights criticism. The Russians rejected both proposals, he said, because "they did not coincide with what they consider to be an equitable deal."

When the Carter administration had stressed its commitment to human rights around the world, Brezhnev had warned that American criticism of internal Soviet affairs could interfere with arms talks and other attempts to improve U.S.-Soviet relations. Brezhnev had told Vance earlier that American criticism of Soviet handling of human rights matters made good relations impossible between the two nations. But Vance said the human rights issue had "not come up" and the SALT proposals "stood on their own feet."

LEADERS OF 60 NATIONS AT FIRST AFRO-ARAB SUMMIT

"When I arrived I was quite pessimistic. Now I leave happy. But we must implement all our decisions. That is the challenge."

The words were spoken by Senegal President Leopold Senghor as he and the leaders of 59 other nations departed from Cairo at the end of the first African-Arab summit conference. The three-day meeting between oil-rich Arabs and poor Africans opened March 7.

Few surprises came out of the summit session, the major one being a decision by Saudi Arabia to allocate $1 billion to African development. That announcement by Saudi Foreign Minister Prince Saud El Faisal resulted in prolonged applause and more clapping followed each detail of the contribution from the Arab world's richest country. The money was in addition to $600 million Saudi Arabia had given to regional African development operations over the past few years. Other oil-rich Arab nations pledged an additional $500 million after Prince Faisal's announcement.

In other action, the 60 nations reaffirmed support for "just struggles against the oppressive racist regimes" of Israel, South Africa and Rhodesia. A document signed by leaders representing 500 million people supported efforts to "find means of increasing the political and economic isolation" of the three nations. The document condemned Israel for "attempts to change the geographic and demographic status of occupied Arab lands."

Most of the leaders who took part judged the conference a success. "The decisions we have reached are bound to make our enemies as angry as we are pleased," said President Kenneth Kaunda of Zambia. Added President Anwar Sadat of Egypt, "The ring that now binds us is the basis for common action for many years. Long live Afro-Arab solidarity."

69

Riot police carried away a wounded colleague during clashes with students outside Rome University

DEATH OF STUDENT LEADER TRIGGERED RIOTS IN ITALY

Italian students had rioted over the years for a variety of reasons, from a poor performance at the opera to an unpopular government reform. So it was not surprising that an alarmingly large segment of the nation's youth erupted in anger when a student was slain during a demonstration in the Communist-run city of Bologna.

It began in February when leftists demonstrated throughout Italy to protest the conviction in Rome of a leftist extremist in the killing of a Greek rightist two years earlier.

Ten days of rioting were climaxed in Bologna March 11 when shooting broke out as police tried to break through barricades set up by students from overturned cars, furniture looted from faculty offices in the ancient University of Bologna and chunks of street paving. During the ensuing struggle, 25-year-old Pierfrancesco Lorusso, a medical student and leader of the ultra-leftist Lotta Continua, was fatally shot.

The following day thousands of aroused leftwing youths battled police in Italian cities from Milan to Palermo. In Turin, 29-year-old police officer Giuseppe Ciotta was gunned down from a passing car as he was driving to work. Callers identifying themselves as members of the "Fighting Brigade" claimed responsibility for the killing and said it was in reprisal for Lorusso's death.

The rioting reached its peak in Rome where some 50,000 youths converged on the city by train and bus from across the land for a mass march that spread terror through parts of the historic center of the metropolis.

Chanting "It's not a crime to kill a policeman," the youths began their march on Rome's Piazza del Popolo. A splinter group threw fire bombs at a branch office of the ruling Christian Democratic Party, and others shouted "idiots, idiots," at the police. In Turin, three youths broke off from the march in that city and attacked a police station with pistols and fire bombs. Demonstrators in Milan also brandished pistols and tossed fire bombs during the march.

The riots caused alarm among authorities. Premier Giulio Andreotti appealed for "moral reaction" to end the disorders. Members of Italy's Communist Party who had openly supported leftist students in the past, warned that the country was "experiencing an antidemocratic provocation."

By mid-March calm appeared restored, but the government warned that it would not rule out a state of national emergency if unrest continued. Observers blamed much of the campus unrest on student frustration over inability to get jobs when they finished their education. About 800,000 of the nation's 1.5 million unemployed were said to be recent graduates searching for their first jobs in a sluggish economy.

FOR THE RECORD

EXPIRED. The longstanding ban on the use of U.S. passports to travel to certain Communist-run nations. President Carter said he would not renew the ban which expired March 18, because of his belief in the need for open borders in international travel. For the first time since 1950, Americans were free to journey anywhere in the world without restrictions on the use of their passports. The order had forbidden use of American passports for travel to Cuba, North Korea, Vietnam and Cambodia. The restrictions were ordered to prevent Americans from traveling to those countries because of their Communist governments. In the case of Cuba, the Havana government had allowed Americans to visit the island without a passport.

GUILTY. Joanne D. Chesimard, a leading figure in the so-called Black Liberation Army. She was found guilty March 25 of first degree murder in the death of a New Jersey state policeman and was sentenced to life imprisonment. The jury found Mrs. Chesimard guilty on all eight counts—two for murder and six for assault and related charges—in the slaying of Trooper Werner Foerster and the wounding of Trooper James Harper during a shootout May 2, 1973.

Right, American actress Farah Fawcett-Majors, pinup sensation of the year, smiled prettily for this picture

Below, these scantily-clad Japanese farmers braved near freezing temperatures to observe the festival of Doronko Matsuri. The aim was to run into a rice paddy pond and pelt each other with mud

APRIL

Indira Gandhi's Talent For Power Politics Proved Her Undoing

With a vengeance she ruled India, and with a vengeance the Indian people turned against Indira Gandhi. In March, after enduring her "national emergency" for 21 months, India's millions quietly unleashed their pent-up fury and turned the world's largest parliamentary election into a stunning rebellion against their once beloved prime minister. The aroused electorate, some 320 million strong and most of them illiterate, impoverished peasants, broke Mrs. Gandhi's 11-year grip on power by electing only 154 members of her Congress Party to the 542-seat Parliament.

The dimensions of the election upset were staggering. After ruling India for 30 uninterrupted years, the Congress Party failed to win a single seat in the nation's two most populous and politically powerful states. All but a handful of Mrs. Gandhi's cabinet ministers suffered decisive defeats, and her son Sanjay lost his maiden bid for parliament by 75,000 votes. Voters in Mrs. Gandhi's own home district added a crowning blow. They defeated the 59-year-old prime minister's personal re-election effort by more than 55,000 votes.

Ironically, when Mrs. Gandhi relaxed the national emergency and called elections in a surprise radio and television broadcast Jan. 18, the prime minister appeared to have pulled off another political masterstroke. Her decision to restore political and press freedom and to release her political opponents from jail would seemingly deflate charges she had become a permanent dictator. And her decision to schedule the poll for mid-March would give India's divided and demoralized opposition parties only eight weeks to marshal an attack on the well-armored ranks of the Congress Party.

On the morning of Feb. 2, however, Mrs. Gandhi's carefully plotted strategy received an unexpected blow. Jagjivan Ram, a powerful Congress Party warhorse and the leader of 85 million Hindu outcasts called untouchables, resigned from Mrs. Gandhi's cabinet and her party. Along with five other resigning Congress leaders, Ram formed the Congress for Democracy Party and joined forces with a group of opposition parties that had hastily come together under the banner of the new Janata— "peoples"—Party.

Almost overnight India's mood appeared to change, and the prospect of ousting Indira Gandhi no longer seemed an impossible dream. A cheering crowd of more than 250,000 turned out for an opposition rally in New Delhi, the capital city, and the newly freed Indian press began reporting signs of a "Janata wave" sweeping the politically decisive northern states. Mrs. Gandhi was thrown on the defensive and spent much of her campaign energy denying she was a dictator.

In the early morning hours of March 21, the election returns made clear India's political genius had run out of magic. Mrs. Gandhi resigned the following day, accepting "the verdict of the people . . . in a spirit of humility." Gracious and stoic in defeat, Mrs. Gandhi indicated she would bow out of the political limelight for a while but said she would continue to work for the nation and her party. Her son Sanjay announced his retirement from politics in favor of "quiet, constructive work."

India's new rulers, meanwhile, set about the difficult task of putting together a government from the disparate groups and ideologies that had buried their long-standing differences to form a united electoral front. After two days of bitter infighting, the party chose as its prime minister an 81-year-old political legend named Morarji Desai.

Considered one of India's most able and incorruptible administrators, Desai had served as a former deputy prime minister and finance minister and had become renowned for fiscal conservatism and his iron-willed rununciation of alcohol and any diet but the strictest vegetarian regime of cheese, fruit and nuts. Like many of the Janata Party leaders, Desai was a former Congress Party member who had crossed swords with Indira Gandhi, lost and had wound up in jail for opposing her authoritarian rule. Accordingly, the cabinet Desai put together read like the previous government's list of public enemies. By April, though, the new government had begun making good its pledge to fully restore individual and press freedom, release all political prisoners and carry forth what Desai called India's "peaceful revolution."

The Indian press and many Western countries wasted no time in applauding the way the huge Asian nation of 620 million people had reclaimed the right to call itself "the world's largest democracy." As soon as the results were clear, President Carter endeared himself to India's new leadership by saying the election should be "an inspiration" to the rest of the world.

Desai, India's fourth prime minister in 30 years of independence, quickly returned the favor. At a news conference moments after taking the oath of office, Desai signaled an end to India's "special relationship" with the Soviet

73

Union and pledged to follow a foreign policy of "genuine nonalignment."

Amid all the rhetoric about the triumph of democracy over dictatorship, the new government and the Indian press fixed much of its attention on exposing and redressing the specific grievances of Mrs. Gandhi's 21-month emergency and trying to come to grips with the many reasons for her fall. Almost daily, the English-language newspapers uncovered new instances of alleged misdeeds by Sanjay and his cronies, particularly in connection with the government's high-pressured sterilization campaign, one of Sanjay's pet projects.

Mrs. Gandhi and her party, on the other hand, did their best to play down the reasons for their rout. At a "soul-searching" election post-mortem, Mrs. Gandhi issued a statement accepting full responsibility for the election results. But the party high command publicly blamed its defeat not on Mrs. Gandhi's authoritarian policies but on their "harsh implementation" by overzealous lower level administrators. The party blackballed Mrs. Gandhi's defense minister, Bansi Lal, for "abuse of authority" and reprimanded her information minister, V.C. Shukla, the architect of the censorship policies.

Both Bansi Lal and Shukla were close confidants of Sanjay. But the Congress high command ignored the allegations against Sanjay and spared him even token criticism. As for Mrs. Gandhi herself, the party command not only excused her for leading it to near destruction but also allowed her to tiptoe from the wreckage with her hold on the party virtually intact. Said party secretary Mrs. Purabi Mukherjee: "She was our leader, she is our leader and she will be our leader."

Such was the political magic of Indira Gandhi, and such was the blind faith she once evoked all across India. From the very start of her involvement in politics, the soft-spoken mother of two seemed to enjoy a special hold on the hearts and minds of her people, for she was the daughter of Jawaharlal Nehru, India's revered prime minister for the first 17 years of independence. During his reign, the Oxford University-educated daughter Nehru called "Little Indoo" quickly distinguished herself at home and abroad as her father's personal aide and confidante. When she herself laid claim to the prime ministership, many Indians responded as if it were her natural birthright.

Soon after taking power, Indira Gandhi proved herself to be a brilliant expert at power politics. Her grasp of ideology, economics or world affairs may not have been exceptional, but when it came to political instincts Indira Gandhi had few equals.

At the peak of her reign, after the Indian army scored a lightning victory over neighbor Pakistan in the 1971 Bangladesh war, Indira Gandhi enjoyed an almost fairy tale adulation. Impressed Western news magazines deemed her "the world's most powerful woman," and her nation's Hindu masses bowed to her as their "mataji," respected mother, Effortlessly she seemed to float from the sophisticated parlors of international diplomacy to the timeless Indian countryside with its bullock carts, mud huts and barefoot villagers. Indians seemed spellbound, and for a time it seemed that Indira Gandhi could do no wrong.

Drought struck in 1972 and 1973, though, and then the jump in Middle East oil import prices came along to deepen India's economic woes and send inflation spiraling. Other burdens included the government's refusal to move ahead with land reforms and the feudal caste system. The Congress Party's 1971 campaign pledge to "abolish poverty" became a forgotten hope, and corruption continued to nibble at the fabric of Indian life.

Two other headaches for Indira Gandhi also started in the early 1970s.

In the Allahabad High Court, a socialist, Raj Narain, filed a court case challenging a 1971 election race that he had lost by some 110,000 votes. Narain accused the victor of corrupt electioneering practices and using government machinery for partisan ends. The victor had been none other than Indira Gandhi.

In the Indian capital, meanwhile, Mrs. Gandhi's government passed over bids by a number of India's leading industrialists and awarded a highly lucrative auto manufacturing license to a young man who called himself an auto engineer on the strength of a brief training course at the Rolls-Royce plant in England. Mrs. Gandhi's political opponents and the Indian press claimed the young man did not have the experience or expertise to fulfill his dream of bringing India a small "peoples' car." But as always the prime minister prevailed, and the young man was allowed to proceed with the project. The car was to be called Maruti, after the son of the Hindu wind god. The young man was Sanjay Gandhi.

In 1973, in impoverished Bihar state in India's northeastern coal belt, frustrated students launched an educational reform movement and turned for help to an aging, quixotic, intellectual named Jayaprakash Narayan. Narayan, a hero of the independence struggle against the British, a friend of Nehru and a follower of the nonviolent teachings of India's Mohandas Gandhi, agreed. Within months the movement transformed itself into a forum for burgeoning anti-government dissent.

On June 12, 1975, with Narayan's movement turned into a potent political force, the economy depressed and Sanjay yet to have his car in production, the Allahabad High Court returned a bombshell verdict. The court found the prime minister guilty of corrupt electioneering practices, declared her election invalid, ordered her to vacate her Parliament seat and barred her from holding public office for six years. Mrs. Gandhi immediately appealed the verdict to the Supreme Court. But Narayan, Desai and other

opposition leaders demanded the prime minister step aside pending the outcome of the appeal.

Step aside Indira Gandhi would not. Instead, two weeks later she stunned her country and the world with a bold power play. Citing unspecified internal and external threats to India's national security, the prime minister declared a national emergency, suspended political activity and civil liberties, imposed rigid press censorship and began rounding up thousands of her political opponents and jailing them under an internal security act.

Then, with the two dozen most influential opposition lawmakers in jail, Mrs. Gandhi had the Congress Party majorities in both houses of parliament take swift action. They retroactively rewrote the Indian constitution to place her emergency declaration beyond judicial review, and retroactively rewrote the election laws to remove those clauses on which Mrs. Gandhi's conviction was based. On November 7, 1975, India's Supreme Court upheld Mrs. Gandhi's appeal on the basis of the retroactive legisla-

tion, and the prime minister's hold on power once again appeared secure.

As Mrs. Gandhi promised it would, the "shock therapy" of the emergency did bring some economic gains to the Indian masses. Fortuitous monsoons brought record harvests and the emergency's crackdown on smuggling and blackmarketeering kept prices even and distribution adequate. The emergency ban on strikes helped boost industrial production, and government pressure on business helped bring inflation to a welcomed halt. Indian trains began running on time.

To help sell the emergency, the government launched a massive propaganda assault portraying Jayaprakash Narayan as an enemy of the state and Indira Gandhi as its savior. "She stood between order and chaos," read the caption on one popular poster of the prime minister. "She saved the republic." In the same way, Sanjay Gandhi was portrayed as India's hope for the future, a charismatic young man with the tough, pragmatic ideas to mold a modern India. Sanjay triumphantly toured India and

Jubilant supporters of the opposition Janata party held up an edition of the Times of India recounting upset victories of the Janata party in the Delhi area

75

enormous crowds gathered to see the young man whom friend and foe alike called India's "crown prince."

Sanjay turned the "Youth Congress" of his mother's party into what appeared to be a potent political force, and he won wide acclaim for his simple five-point program. The plan encouraged Indians to work for family planning, literacy and afforestation and work against the systems of caste and dowry. Sanjay's rightist economic views ran him afoul of the pro-Moscow Communist Party, his mother's allies. But apart from them, all India seemed to be at the young man's feet.

Why Mrs. Gandhi decided to relax the emergency, call elections and unshackle the press might never be known. Parliament had voted to postpone the elections until March 1978, and could have delayed them further. In any case, as soon as she announced the decision the Gandhis' world began to collapse. All the decisions taken and acts committed during the emergency suddenly had political consequences. Indian newspapers revealed instances of political prisoners being tortured and peasants being sterilized against their will. Riots and widespread bitterness touched off by the birth control program suddenly were reported in the Indian press for the first time, though the foreign press had reported them months earlier. The political pressuring and stage-managing of Sanjay's political rise were exposed, and Jagjivan Ram declared Mrs. Gandhi had not even consulted the Cabinet before declaring the emergency.

Nevertheless, until the balloting was finished no one was quite sure just how much political magic Indira Gandhi had left or just how India's silent masses would cast their ballots. When it was over, though, one young Indian journalist watching a triumphant Janata Party victory parade summarized his feelings. "You know what happened?" he said. "We all underestimated our people."

Prolonged Drought Caused Crisis In Much Of California

Brown lawns and three-minute showers became part of the California lifestyle in 1977 as drought shrank the vast system of reservoirs built to make the deserts bloom.

A bizarre weather pattern shielded Northern and Central California from rain for the second straight year, turning rivers into creeks and lakes into mudflats. In 1976, rainfall over the northern half of the state averaged just over half of normal, making it the third dryest year in the state's history. 1977 was even dryer.

As the weeks of California's winter "rainy season" crept by with hardly any rain, cities began to map plans to ration water. Northeast of San Francisco, the mountaintops of the Sierra Nevada jutted brown and green above the clouds, holding no hope for a spring snow melt to refill the state's reservoirs. The huge metropolitan areas of Northern and Central California began to map plans to order city dwellers and suburbanites to cut back their water use.

In 1977 the drought spread north to Oregon and Washington state, where 1976 had been a wet year. Power companies, noting the skimpy water supplies behind their hydroelectric dams, began raising prices for electricity and plan-

ning possible brownouts. In the plains states east of California, dry years—though not this dry—had become almost a way of life. In 1977, cattle ranchers unable to find water for their stock unloaded their herds on a market already depressed by a glut of beef. Winter windstorms obliterated some farmers' unsprouted wheat crops, unprotected by the usual blanket of snow.

Water experts warned the nation might be facing dryer times in years ahead if the growing population continued to pump its wells dry, using up the vast but limited supplies of water stored underground. The huge water systems that moved 13 trillion gallons a year to supply California's cities and irrigate once-arid farmland were designed to make it through one year of scarce rainfall. Never in the state's recorded weather history had a year so dry followed on the heels of another.

"Nobody wants to think it will never rain," said one water official waiting for the rains to start that winter. Some California farmers, who produced 25 percent of the nation's fruits and vegetables, were told their supplies of irrigation water would be cut as much as 75 percent. Af-

Robert Price glumly inspected the dried-up stock pond on his farm near Deerfield in southwestern Kansas. Like many others in the midwest it was the victim of the long drought

ter initial estimates of losses in the billions of dollars, most managed by changing crops, cutting acreage and digging deeper wells to pump more water up from underground. Consumers were told to expect higher prices for a variety of products from wines and fresh fruit to canned tomatoes and rice.

Ironically, Southern California farmers were expecting bumper crops. The south, traditionally the most arid part of the state, received rainfall well above the average. But the reservoirs that were going dry were Southern California's too. Practically the entire state depended for irrigation and municipal water on a system of canals to carry water south from reservoirs placed where they would catch the runoff from the Sierra Nevada.

Los Angeles replaced part of its Northern California water supply from the Colorado River to make more available for the parched northern half of the state. Marin County, home of wealthy suburbanites who commuted to San Francisco across the Golden Gate Bridge, became the first metropolitan area to impose mandatory water cutbacks.

In 1976, the lush green hills of the sunny bayside communities turned brown as tough restrictions were placed on outdoor watering. Years before, "no-growth" interests in the county had voted down proposals to tie into the state's water system. Marin's own local reservoirs depend upon rainfall for replenishment. In 1977, Marin residents were ordered to cut water use by more than half, to live on an average daily allotment of 46 gallons per person.

Across the bay, San Francisco officials pointed proudly to the huge Hetch Hetchy Reservoir, completed in 1935 with capacity enough to withstand the driest year of drought. But as the second dry winter turned into a second dry spring, Hetch Hetchy dropped dangerously low. So did the big Pardee Reservoir, main supplier of water to more than a million residents in Oakland and other cities east of San Francisco. With hardly any snow covering the mountaintops, there would be hardly any spring runoff. Residents and businesses were ordered to cut water use by 25 percent.

Before the summer was over, millions of Californians were under orders to conserve water. Citizens generally responded to the orders with good humor. Bottles and bricks were placed in the backs of toilets; water-saving shower heads were installed, and homeowners tightened up leaky faucets. It became passé to flush a toilet each time it was used. Phrases like "gray water"—water used once and saved for recycling onto plants and lawns or rewashings—crept into the language. Newspapers sponsored contests for water-saving ideas and began drought gardening columns.

A few months after rationing began, officials reported that nearly everyone—even in Marin County, where rations were the smallest—was complying. "What we have to see is whether people will continue to conserve when the novelty wears off," said one state official.

The first discontented grumbles came from businesses in Marin County, ordered like the residential consumers to cut back 57 percent from the amount of water they used two years ago. Those that didn't or couldn't manage that much conservation were billed at rates that accelerated sharply for accounts above the allotments. A few restaurants reported their two-month water bills, which used to run between $100 and $150, had jumped well over $1,000. Laundromats, diaper services and car washes in rationed areas also were badly hurt. The state's huge canneries said they were unable to cut back much on the water used for cleaning and processing farm fruits and vegetables. The timber industry in the Pacific Northwest wondered if there would be enough water to run their mills and make wood into paper.

Economists predicted a "multiplier" effect that would first be felt in farm communities as farmers, uncertain that their crops would flourish in the dry year, put off purchases of heavy equipment. Later, they said, it would be felt in widening circles as jobs were lost and the doomsday mentality began to shake consumer confidence generally. The first layoffs came early in the winter, at the ski resorts that had hired their usual crews to get ready for a ski season that never came. Estimates of jobs that would be lost in all industries, from farm workers to recreation to heavy equipment, ranged into the tens of thousands.

The economists warned that the drought and its economic impact would be felt well into 1978, even if the rains came then. Most of the first rains and snows would be absorbed into the thirsty ground, with little moisture left to run off into reservoirs—certainly not enough for full production of hydroelectric power. Utility bills would remain high, keeping up the costs of producing nearly everything. While resort and boating interests looked toward a slow summer, officials of the 237 state and national forests nervously assessed the fire danger in land parched tinder-dry. Open campfires were almost universally banned, and officials spoke of the possibility of closing down some of the parks.

In 1976, more than 190,000 acres of state and federal forestland went up in smoke at a cost estimated at almost $27 million. The worst year on record was 1923 when, in the midst of another brutal drought, 967,000 acres were blackened. As the camping season approached, the levels of moisture in forest fuel were assessed at between 3 and 33 percent of normal. Like everyone else, forest rangers crossed their fingers and hoped for rain in 1978.

But what of 1978? Most water officials were reluctant to predict the devastation that a third dry year might bring. Instead of electrical brownouts, they said, the severe shortages of

This scene was reminiscent of the Kansas dust bowl of the 1930s. Winds whipped up dust from the parched north central section of hard-hit Oregon to send up gritty clouds

Below, grim evidence of the drought was shown in this picture of Hetch Hetchy Reservoir in the Sierra Nevadas which was one of the main water suppliers for San Francisco. The lake had a normal capacity of 360,000 acre feet but when this picture was taken it contained only 25,000 acre feet

A view of a portion of California's Nicascio reservoir showed the parched land with a small reserve of water in the background

hydroelectric power would mean rationing of electricity as well as water. Farmers would get little if any of their contracted irrigation water. Some would be able to draw still deeper on their wells—if their ration of electricity supplied enough power to pump up the water—but more wells would go dry, more crops would fail, more jobs lost, more household water rations slashed.

Some state officials said 1977's drought was merely a signpost toward an ethic of water conservation that would have to be adopted universally in a few short years. California's governor, Edmund G. Brown Jr., told voters after his election in 1974 that days of unquestioned growth and abundance were nearing an end. He called it an "era of limits" and warned that it would provide new challenges that would call for new lifestyles.

"The drought can be an occasion for learning as well as occasion for suffering," he told an audience in 1977. "It is an era of limits and we have to recognize that. I'm sure we will solve all our problems."

School For Soviet Children Includes Study Of Weapons

School is more than studying history, mathematics and the arts for millions of Soviet children. It can also involve learning how to assemble and take apart a machine gun, care of military uniforms and proper use of a gas mask.

Those are among the courses suggested in an instructor's manual published by the Soviet government for the nation's military training programs geared for teen-agers in schools as well as for young workers.

"The Soviet Union is a peace-loving state," said a textbook for children illustrated with hand grenades, rifles and military tactics. But, added, the book, since "reactionary imperialist circles" are plotting to increase world tensions, "every young person even before his service in the armed forces, must prepare himself for the defense of the Socialist motherland."

Not every school in the Soviet Union has an equally effective military program and some children take the training light-heartedly. But there is apparently some training for everyone.

The training does help pupils prepare for military service. Two years is required for every able-bodied young man without a special deferment and it provides the country with a ready reserve of civilians familiar with military skills in case of war.

By the time of World War II, school programs and other volunteer defense training had prepared a ready reserve of more than 120,000 pilots trained in flying clubs, some 6 million people trained in rifle shooting and 222,000 citizens who could parachute from planes. This was in addition to the Soviet Union's standing armed forces.

Military training in 1977 is carried out in official school programs led by a school "military director" who sometimes doubles as physical education teacher and by the All-Union Voluntary Organization for Assistance to the Army, Air Force and Navy, known as DOSAAF. DOSAAF has chapters in many schools and large clubs in big cities.

Through school and DOSAAF programs, children hear patriotic lectures and visit military installations. They can study rifle shooting, auto mechanics, radio operation, parachuting and plane and ship modeling.

According to DOSAAF, one third of the young Russians called up for military service already have some kind of "military-technical specialty" because of programs for school students.

Western specialists familiar with the school programs say they help make up for the limited opportunities of many Russians to become acquainted with modern technology.

While a complicated radio receiver, automo-

A group of youngsters in a parachute club received instructions from a pilot in the Tula region

The military has long been stressed in Soviet schools as evidenced in this picture of primary school youngsters taken some time ago

bile or plane model is nothing novel to many Western children, such items might not be available to young Russians, if it were not for school programs and DOSAAF.

Since Soviet army recruits are often assigned directly to active military units for training instead of going to specialized basic training camps, the more acquaintance they have with mechanical equipment, the better their adjustment will be.

School programs also stress sports activities and DOSAAF runs 16 national sports federations. Children are encouraged to attain physical standards laid down by the national Ready for Labor and Defense program called GTO.

One set of GTO standards, for instance, requires satisfactory performances in rifle shooting from a distance of 50 yards, the 100-meter freestyle swim, the 1,000-meter run, throwing a hand grenade and automobile skill driving.

The DOSAAF organization, which celebrated its 50th anniversary in 1977, also provides military-related sports and technical training to millions of Soviets who are not students.

The organization claims to have a total of 76 million members, which would be a third of the Soviet population. Many of them are factory and farm workers, organized into 320,000 chapters. The minimum age for joining DOSAAF is 14. Western sources believe that some of the DOSAAF membership figures maybe inflated, however.

Military and military-related training for young students and workers dovetails with the strong positive publicity given to the Soviet Union's armed forces throughout the country. Newspapers, magazines, books and television constantly recite accounts of Soviet heroism in World War II.

The military receives particular attention on such national occasions as Tank Day, Anti-aircraft Force Day, Border Forces Day, Strategic Rocket Day, Army Day and World War II Victory Day. Attempts are made to involve youngsters in all these events.

The result of such work, according to DOSAAF officials, is to create young "patriots of the motherland and active builders and defenders of Communism" who are prepared for military service and who respect the armed forces.

PILOT KILLED EIGHT IN SHOOTING SPREE OVER PHILIPPINES

The Philippine airliner was carrying 34 members of the nation's armed forces back from leave March 31 when the pilot got up and grabbed a rifle. He proceeded to shoot and kill five passengers and a flight attendant and wound 16 others while the rest aboard looked on in horror. Later two more passengers died of wounds.

Stunned officials of Swiftair Inc. of Zamboanga tried to figure out what had caused Capt. Ernesto Abuloc, a veteran pilot to go berserk. One of the most deeply shocked was Capt. Jacob Lim, owner of the airline and father of a slain stewardess. Lim said he knew Abuloc well.

"Our people in Zamboanga said he apparently was normal when he boarded the plane," said Capt. Rudolfo Noel, Swiftair's administrative manager in Manila as authorities sought to explain Abuloc's actions. "His medical record, everything, it was all okay."

Finally, Alejandro Morados, head of the aviation security command at Zamboanga airport, pieced together this account of what happened.

The twin-engine DC-3 was flying members of the Philippine navy and constabulary from rest and recreation leaves in Zamboanga City to duty stations in Tawi-Tawi, a province in the Sulu Archipelago. The plane was approaching its destination about 200 miles southwest of Zamboanga City when Abuloc got up from his seat and changed from his uniform to civilian clothing while still in the cockpit.

Abuloc then walked to a storage bin where the servicemen's rifles had been placed for safekeeping. He picked up an American-made M-16, pushed it slightly through a curtain separating the cockpit from the passenger compartment and opened fire.

At the first flashes of gunfire, passengers began ducking behind their seats. When the rifle magazine was emptied, Abuloc started swinging it wildly. Copilot Rolando Suarez and the flight mechanic jumped the gunman. They were joined by soldiers and sailors who pummeled Abuloc to the floor.

Suarez grabbed the controls and swung the plane back toward Zamboanga City where the dead and wounded were removed.

On April 1, reporters saw Abuloc at the Zamboanga City Hospital. He was reported incoherent and in shock. Bound hand and foot, his face badly bruised, the airman was under heavy guard. Later, the 40-year-old pilot was interviewed on government television from his hospital bed. He claimed he remembered nothing about the shooting.

ETHIOPIA ORDERED 300 AMERICANS EXPELLED

Deteriorating relations between the United States and Ethiopia continued to erode in early 1977.

In February, the Carter administration cut off $6 million in military aid to Ethiopia because of alleged continued human rights violations. In late March, Ethiopia expelled two Americans. Authorities contended the men, both black, were agents of the Central Intelligence Agency and were engaging in espionage activities. However, United States officials said there were no Americans working in Ethiopia under the names supplied by the Ethiopian government.

Then, Ethiopia's leftist military rulers announced April 24 they had closed the consulates of the United States and five other countries in war-torn Eritrea province where guerrillas of the Eritrean Liberation Front had been fighting for 16 years to win independence for the province. That order came a day after the Ethiopians had closed down four other American facilities. The government said they contradicted the ideology of the Ethiopian socialist revolution. The facilities were the U. S. Information Service Center, the Military Assistance Advisory Group program, and the Naval Medical Research center, all in Addis Ababa, and the Kagnew radio communications center in Asmara. The expulsion order affected some 300 Americans.

The closings followed an increase in anti-American statements by the increasingly pro-Soviet military council, which ruled the nation under the leadership of Lt. Col Mengistu Haile Mariam. Under the late Emperor Haile Selassie, Ethiopia had been dependent on the United States for military equipment, but after President Carter halted military aid, Ethiopia reportedly had taken delivery of tanks, armored personnel carriers and anti-aircraft guns from the Soviet Union.

Capt. Ernesto Abuloc, his face badly swollen, was interviewed on government television

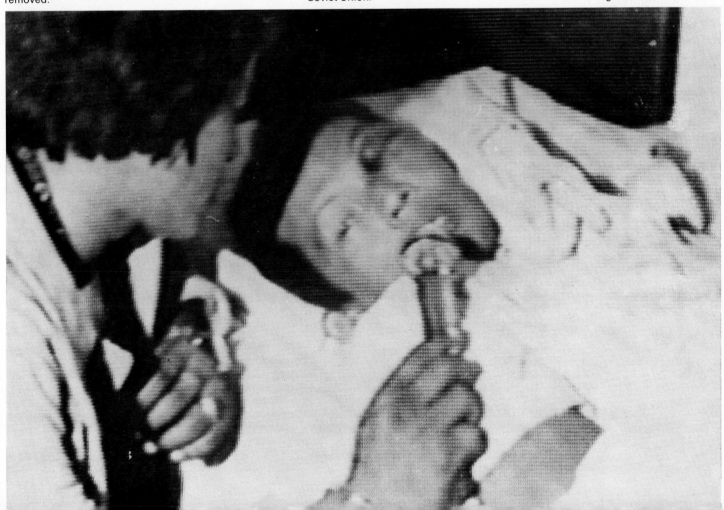

Fire raced through the sprawling clubhouse in Cherry Hill, N.J.

RACE TRACK FIRE CAUSED ESTIMATED $20 MILLION DAMAGE

The sixth race had just been run when fire broke out in the rambling 35-year-old clubhouse at New Jersey's Garden State Park. Fifty fire companies from the surrounding countryside were called in but by the time they had quelled the blaze two hours later the building lay in ruins with damage estimated at up to $20 million.

Authorities said it was a miracle that the firemen and police had been able to evacuate more than 10,000 people from the fast-spreading blaze with so few casualties. One fire captain died of a heart attack fighting the blaze and two track employees were missing. Twenty-two persons were injured, only four seriously enough to be hospitalized.

The fire erupted the afternoon of April 14 in the second floor administrative offices of the clubhouse, a quarter-mile long structure with a maze of passageways in the upper levels.

Bettor Bob Carr of Laurel Springs, Md., said the sixth race had "finished as we turned around and the smoke was unbelievable. We heard cries of 'run into the track' but there was a drop, so we went inside, jumped on an escalator and rode the heck out of there."

Phil Beisblatt of Clifton, N.J., was on the ground floor of the clubhouse watching the race on television when the picture and light went out and water started pouring through overhead fluorescent fixtures. "All the cashiers started to grab the money and run, and then the smoke really started pouring in," he said. Beisblatt saw jockeys throwing clothes and equipment from their dressing room windows about 20 feet above the parking lot. "Some of the jockeys tried to climb down a fire hose and burned their hands," he added.

Earl Ford, a funeral director from Wilmington, Del. was having a drink in the bar when the bartender suddenly grabbed up his cash bag and told everyone to get out. Ford and several others tried to leave by escalator but smoke forced them back. They climbed onto a balcony and shouted to firemen to put up a ladder.

"We were scared to death. As the last man came down the ladder, the flames started licking that section of the building," said Ford.

84

EGYPT'S SADAT, JORDAN'S HUSSEIN VISITED CARTER

Two Middle Eastern leaders—Egypt's President Anwar Sadat and Jordan's King Hussein—journeyed to Washington in April to meet with President Carter and to discuss a variety of subjects, among them the possibility of peace in the Mideast.

Sadat, who arrived April 3, called on Carter to open a dialogue with Palestinian leaders and back a role for them in Mideast peace negotiations. "You would agree with me," said Sadat, "that the Palestinians who demonstrated moderation and a great sense of responsibility are entitled to be heard by you and the American people."

The Palestine Liberation Organization had been excluded from peace talks by Israel, with the backing of the United States, partly because of its commitment to the dismantling of the Jewish state and its refusal to accept United Nations resolutions calling for a peaceful settlement. "The Palestinian cause," said Sadat, "is the core of the Arab-Israeli dispute. Their leadership has established their credentials to be part of the peace process." He said a "dialogue with them will reassure them and stimulate further moderation."

In a windup session April 5, Carter and Sadat surveyed Soviet and Cuban intervention in Africa and joined in an appeal for peaceful settlement of conflicts and territorial integrity there. Carter said he was "perfectly satisfied" with the discussions and said of Sadat: "He's been very helpful to me in understanding the prospects for permanent peace in the Middle East and I'm very pleased."

Jordan's Hussein, who arrived April 25, said after talks at the White House that he felt "more encouraged and more hopeful than I have for a long time." Carter, who emphasized "the difficulties of resolving the historic animosities" that exist in the Mideast, said, however, that 1977 could be a year for significant "strides toward a permanent peace," in part because he felt current Middle Eastern leaders shared a desire to display moderation.

At the conclusion of their talks the following day, Carter said it would be better not to have a Geneva conference on the Middle East "unless we see some strong possibilities for substantial achievements." Hussein said such a conference "would be a disaster without prior planning and without realistic appraisal of all the difficulties and possibilities for making progress in advance of holding the meetings."

KILLER FLOODS SWAMPED FOUR APPALACHIAN STATES

April was the cruelest month in Appalachia.

Early in the month wind and storms swept through Kentucky, West Virginia, Virginia and Tennessee—generating tornadoes which killed 21 persons in Alabama—and then caused floods in the four Appalachian states which killed at least 19 persons, left thousands homeless, and caused millions in damage.

But as the rampaging rivers—swollen by storms which dumped rain on the region for seemingly endless hours—began to return to their banks, those made homeless began to return. Many found nothing to come back to. Said E. T. George, as he looked about Matewan, W.Va., "Ain't nothing left here. This town's completely gone." Lamented another West Virginia resident, "I lost everything, and I don't even know if I want to go back to my house and see what the water did to my life's work. I've lost it all."

In Eastern Kentucky, which had the worst flooding on record from the Big Sandy, Cumberland and Kentucky rivers, damage was expected to top $100 million. "All you can see downtown is mud," said Cindy May of Pikeville, a city where the Big Sandy had spilled more than 15 feet of water into the streets.

As the flood waters abated, cleanup efforts were begun but often they were hampered by looters and curiosity seekers. In Virginia, West Virginia and Kentucky, police blocked off highways and bridges to prevent looting and keep tourists away.

Many of the battered places were declared federal disaster areas by President Carter, and federal-state relief centers were set up in stricken regions to provide information and emergency housing assistance and other forms of aid.

Bound prisoners were put on display in Wuhan, eastern China, as bystanders watched in the foreground. Placards with the prisoners' names and crimes were suspended in front of them

Above, Pope Paul VI, right, and Dr. Donald Coggan, the Archbishop of Canterbury, signed a joint declaration in the Vatican April 29 that study should continue so that the Roman Catholic and Anglican churches "may be led along the path towards unity"

Right, taking shelter from chill winds these people, waiting for a bus in Ottawa, sat on the concrete ledge of a building

TO SPANK OR NOT TO SPANK? THAT WAS THE QUESTION

Does not sparing the rod constitute cruel and unusual punishment?

The question was answered by the U.S. Supreme Court April 19 when it ruled 5-4 that the constitutional prohibition against cruel and unusual punishment did not protect public school students from spankings by teachers. However, it also was noted that students still had the right to sue teachers and school administrators and to bring criminal charges in state courts for spankings and other disciplinary measures.

Justice Lewis F. Powell, writing for the majority, said: "We are reviewing here a legislative judgment, rooted in history and reaffirmed in the laws of many states, that corporal punishment serves important educational interests. This judgment must be viewed in the light of the disciplinary problems commonplace in the schools."

The opinion emphasized that common law and the laws of 21 states recognized corporal punishment in school as a valid disciplinary tool, but the question before the court had been whether such punishment in schools ever could be unconstitutional. Attorneys for two Miami youths who brought the case had wanted the court to decide the Constitution protected students and to tell school officials just how far they could go in punishing students.

The decision was termed "incredible" by a spokeswoman for the National Parent-Teacher Assn. It was greeted favorably at the American Federation of Teachers.

NORTH SEA BLOWOUT SPILLED MILLIONS OF GALLONS OF OIL

Out in the storm-tossed ice-cold North Sea a strong man could die, of exposure in eight minutes if he fell in. In this rugged area, about 11,000 oilmen were tapping vast under-sea reserves of oil and natural gas when disaster struck.

It happened April 22 when an oil well suddenly "blew out" on Bravo 14, a rig of Phillips Petroleum Co. in Norway's Ekofisk Field. It spewed millions of gallons of crude oil into the deep, causing fears that the fish-rich waters might be turned into a dead sea.

The 221-square mile body of water was one of the world's most treacherous. Winds sweeping across the oil platforms often reached a hundred miles an hour and towering waves slammed against the tall offshore structures.

After fruitless efforts of oil workers to stem the surging flow of oil that spurted 200 feet into the air forming a huge oil slick, a team of trouble shooters was called in to deal with the crisis. The team was led by Boots Hansen, right hand man of the legendary Texan, Paul "Red" Adair, who was regarded as the world's top "blowout" expert. Hansen and his team worked in a chamber 45 feet square. They couldn't talk and they had to wear ear protectors to partially drown out the unremitting thunderous roar of the blowout. They were constantly drenched by a spray of oil heated by friction to 240 degrees Fahrenheit.

"It was very confining on the platform," Hansen said later . . . . "and of course the well could have gone up at any time. Anything could have touched it off." Experts agreed a single spark could have ignited a fire of immense proportions in the midsea oil field. To minimize the danger of an explosion, fire boats sprayed a steady stream of water on the rig to cool it down. Damage control teams used brass wrenches that did not cause sparks and power tools that were driven by compressed air rather than electricity.

Tension mounted during the eight-day ordeal as the team made four vain attempts to seal the 10,000-foot deep well. If they were unable to cap it, the alternative would be to dig another well to divert pressure from the runaway, Bravo 14. This would take more than a month to accomplish and damage from the spreading oil slick could prove catastrophic.

Adair flew to the scene to aid his hard-pressed men. At week's end the break came. A one-eighth change in the length of a piston allowed the team to stop the torrent. On April 30 they clamped a four-ton "stopper" over the well head and choked off the week-long spill. They then pumped mud down the shaft to offset the upward pressure estimated at 3,300 pounds per square inch. "I turned to Adair when it was over and said 'let's go home, buddy,'" said Hansen.

FOR THE RECORD

LEGALIZED. The Communist Party in Spain, for the first time since the end of the Spanish civil war in 1939. The government's legal journal published the decree April 9 and officials said the party was registered in the Interior Ministry's book of political associations. Franco, who led a revolution that toppled the Spanish Republic, banned all political parties except the right wing movement during his long tenure that ended with his death in November 1975. His successor, King Juan Carlos, had promised to lead the country to democracy and announced a number of liberal reforms, including the first free elections in Spain in 41 years.

A firefighting boat sprayed water on the blown-out oil rig in Norway's Ekofisk Field in the North Sea

87

MAY

TV Interviews Showed Nixon Still Held Public's Interest

Time had not shaken the nation's fascination with the ex-president and Watergate

President Gerald Ford took office pledging to "put Watergate behind us." President Jimmy Carter took office pledging simply never to lie to the American people. Both men perceived a nation grown weary of the most lurid political scandal in its history and of the man who was at the center of it. Nonetheless, as the cherry blossoms bloomed in the spring of 1977, it was apparent that time had not shaken the public's strange fascination with either the man or the event.

Richard M. Nixon, the only United States President to be forced from office, appeared in four, 90-minute television interviews with David Frost, a British show-business celebrity and entrepreneur. The TV ratings the series received, especially the first of the four shows, were evidence of the nation's continued curiosity. A further irony was that as the fourth and final show was about to be aired, the U.S. Supreme Court refused to hear the appeals of two of the most prominent men to be caught in the Watergate web, John N. Mitchell, the former attorney general, and H. R. Haldeman, Nixon's chief of staff. Thus, even as their former commander in chief again denied to the nation that he had committed an impeachable offense, the two became the 24th and 25th men to go off to prison as a result of actions for which Nixon was named as an unindicted co-conspirator, for which he resigned rather than stand trial in the Senate, and for which he accepted a pardon rather than face possible trial in the courts.

Why did Nixon, then, agree to undergo public questioning? One obvious reason was the fee: $600,000 plus an undisclosed cut of the profits, which likely brought the total to a million dollars. Some veteran Nixon-watchers also opined the ex-president perhaps thought he might somehow change the national perception of himself so that he could once again find a public role. They noted that people who had regarded Nixon down for the count had been wrong in the past.

Only the second show, aired May 11, a sometimes tedious and rather uncontroversial discussion of Nixon's accomplishments and goals, failed to generate wide interest. In the first show, May 4, Nixon admitted he had lied to the public but not in any serious way and only for the best of reasons. In the third, May 18, he said he had had inherent power to order burglaries and other illegal conduct against American dissidents: "When the President does it, that means it is not illegal." In the final installment, May 25, he said life had become "almost unbearable" for him since he resigned the presidency in disgrace and took up a life of isolation at San Clemente, his Pacific coast home.

The May 4 show, 999 days after his resignation, was the nation's first close-up look at the man since Aug. 9, 1974, the day a helicopter lifted him off the White House lawn and out of public view. He seemed healthier than in those final turbulent days of his reign, and generally relaxed, but his voice and his mannerisms were unchanged.

To the surprise of most who watched, interviewer David Frost pursued Nixon tenaciously. In many exchanges Nixon bristled. At times he appeared distraught.

For example, Frost at one point asked Nixon why he hadn't fired his aides as soon as he leared of their involvement in covering up the break-in at Democratic National Headquarters. "Why didn't you pick up the phone and tell the cops?" Nixon said he had been humanely concerned about his chief aides, Haldeman and John Ehrlichman, and about their families, and "I felt that they in their hearts felt they were not guilty." He contended that obstruction of justice required evidence of corrupt intention. "No, I did not have a corrupt motive," he said.

Frost, however, had studied the statute just before questioning Nixon. He informed him that proof of criminality rested solely on a showing that actions had a corrupt purpose whatever the personal motive. Nixon was visibly rattled, but continued to cling to his own interpretation.

Frost kept after him. When Nixon asserted he had never authorized hush money for the Watergate burglars, Frost ticked off 16 Nixon quotations from a tape recording, including: "Get the million bucks; it would seem to me that would be worthwhile." Nixon accused Frost of "reading there out of context" but finally did concede, "It's possible . . . it's a mistake that I didn't stop it." Again, when Frost cited a taped Nixon statement to his top aides: "Just be damned sure you say 'I don't remember, I can't recall.'" Nixon asserted that he wasn't counseling perjury, he was simply counseling his aides not to volunteer anything to a grand jury, just as "every lawyer" does to a client.

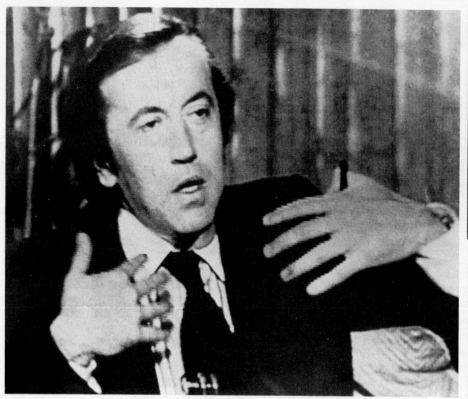

Above, British TV notable David Frost opened the questioning as the series got underway. Top right, the former president listened intently as the probing began. Bottom right, Nixon gestured for emphasis as he recalled the Watergate affair

An emotional high point of the interview came when Frost urged Nixon to admit "wrongdoing" and apologize for it. With moist eyes, Nixon said: "I let down my friends. I let down the country. I let down our system of government . . . . I let the American people down and I have to carry that burden with me for the rest of my life." Later he said: "I brought myself down. I gave 'em [political opponents] a sword and they stuck it and they twisted it with relish. And I guess if I'd been in their position I'd [have] done the same thing."

Wrongdoing he did not admit. He said he had made statements from the White House about the cover-up "that were not true" but did not specify them, and added that anyway "most of them were fundamentally true on the big issues." He repeated time and again that his motives were either political or humanitarian, never criminal. "Technically I did not commit a crime, an impeachable offense," he insisted. "I made so many bad judgments. The worst ones mistakes of the heart rather than the head." In his own view he was guilty of no more than being overly kind in trying to protect his guilty friends.

The first interview actually represented the last of 11 taping sessions between Frost and Nixon. The show's producers felt it should be shown first because of its dramatic impact. Indeed, viewers had to wait for the third show for any drama that came close to matching it.

In that show Nixon likened himself to a latter-day Abraham Lincoln embattled in an ideological civil war. That was by way of explaining an obligation to act forcefully against dissident Americans in order to extricate the nation from the Vietnam War. He chronicled without apology his decisions to use wiretaps, burglary and harassment of political "enemies" as complements to his secret Southeast Asian diplomacy. With a familiar jut of his chin, he said defiantly: "Call it paranoia, but paranoia for peace isn't that bad."

Again in his questioning Frost was tenacious, sometimes openly skeptical. Nixon, in turn, was often sullen and bitter. As the first interview might have served as his defense against a charge of obstructing justice, the third interview amounted to his response to the allegation of abuse of power, another of the findings of the House Judiciary Committee's 1974 report recommending Nixon's impeachment.

The former president's defense, though, which boiled down to "When the President does it that means that it is not illegal," was in marked contrast to his denunciation in 1973, when he was trying to cling to the presidency, of "a few overzealous people" who were to blame. At that time, Aug 15, 1973, Nixon acknowledged in a television address that "Instances have now come to light in which a zeal for security did go too far and did interfere impermissibly with individual liberty."

In his interview with Frost, Nixon claimed his underlying motive in setting government agencies against dissidents had been to convince Hanoi that he would not yield to the protesters and thereby lose the war in Washington "as the French lost in 1954 in Paris rather than in Dien

Bien Phu." He said the North Vietnamese had consented to bargain in earnest in early 1973 because they had decided Nixon was not going to be affected by the protests.

He apparently was, though. When Frost demurred at Nixon's comparison of the ideological split in the country to that of the Civil War, Nixon told his questioner: "Nobody can know what it means for a President to be sitting in that White House working late at night . . . and to have hundreds of thousands of demonstrators around charging through the streets. No one can know how a President feels when he realizes that his efforts to bring peace . . . [are] being jeopardized by individuals who have a different point of view as to how things are to be done."

He said he had been forced to try to plug leaks of sensitive secrets by such extralegal means as creation of the White House "plumbers" unit, development of a master plan to eavesdrop on dissidents, and sanctioning after the fact the burglary by the "plumbers" of the office of Dr. Daniel Ellsberg's one-time psychiatrist. At one point he called Ellsberg a "punk."

Nixon was the one who injected the term paranoia into the conversation and used it more than once. "Am I paranoic about hating people and trying to do them in?" he said. "The answer is, at times, yes. I get angry at people." Among the targets of his wrath, he said, were officials of the Kennedy and Johnson administrations who "got us into the war" and later "turned totally around and they stirred up the demonstrators."

He also said he was being judged by a double standard in the matter of harassing political opponents. He said his predecessors had done it, and even if such tactics were "wrong" they were not illegal.

In the final interview, Nixon similarly contended that politics-as-usual was what brought down his first-term vice president, Spiro Agnew. He also described a plan to start a defense fund for his two chief aides, Haldeman and Ehrlichman, with $100,000 of a secret campaign contribution from industrialist Howard Hughes.

To the very end, Nixon professed his innocence. He said he accepted a pardon from President Ford not because he was guilty but because his lawyers persuaded him that he could not get a fair trial and because he was "so emotionally drawn, mentally beaten down, physically not up to par."

He summed up his ignominy by saying he could understand those who say, "Gee whiz, it just isn't fair, you know, for an individual to be, get off with a pardon simply because he happens to have been president." In mitigation, he offered this self-appraisal:

"I can only say that no one in the world and no one in our history could know how I felt. No one can know how it feels to resign the Presidency of the United States. Is that punishment enough? Oh, probably not. But whether it is or isn't, as I have said earlier in our interview, we have to live with not only the past but for the future and I don't know what the future brings. But whatever it brings, I'll still be fighting."

Above, Nixon sadly conceded that he let down his friends, the nation and our "system of government" but he insisted his offenses were not criminal or impeachable. Top right, in the second interview, Nixon discussed foreign policy carried out during his administration. Bottom right, the former president said he had rejected a Soviet proposal for U.S.-Soviet imposition of a cease-fire in the Middle East in 1973 contending it might have raised "the possibility of a big power conflict"

Supper Club Fire Killed 164 in a Night of Terror

As the fire raged, rescue teams began removing the victims

Most people drove through Southgate, Ky. without realizing they were there. The northern Kentucky town of 3,200 was often merely a blur to cars, whose occupants were intent upon getting to the Beverly Hills Supper Club.

The club sat on a hill outside the main part of town—about five miles south of Cincinnati. It was a magnet for all types of people who wanted to have a "night on the town."

Its clientele often drove up from Kentucky, or down from Ohio or east from Indiana. They were drawn by an ornate decor which outshone other establishments in the area. They enjoyed entertainers whose ranks included the likes of Pearl Bailey, Carol Channing and Liberace.

On the evening of May 28, disaster struck. A fire swept through the club, killing 164 people, and leaving in its wake damage suits totaling hundreds of millions of dollars.

During its 40 years, Beverly Hills claimed to be the "showplace of the nation." In its heyday, casinos flourished and feather-costumed show-girls pranced Parisian style. For a time, it was a national symbol of revelry. The aura dimmed somewhat in 1952, when Sen. Estes Kefauver of Tennessee cracked down on gambling. With betting gone, the nightclub turned to entertainment and presented a dazzling display for its customers.

The swank complex was a labyrinth of assorted rooms to accomodate big and small parties. Its walls were decorated with oil paintings. Fountains bubbled in its lobbies. There was even a chapel for couples who wanted to get married and have their receptions at the club.

It was mainly, however, the kind of place where an average couple could feel rich, if only for an evening. That evening there were hundreds of such people who quickly filled the club's parking lot. A group of teachers had come from a rural school district in Ohio to celebrate the retirement of an elementary school teacher. One guest was the retiring teacher's son, brought in as a surprise from Alabama.

The club's main entertainer that night was John Davidson, and by 7 p.m., the Cabaret Room—where the show was to go on—was already filling.

"We were sitting like sardines," recalled Bernie Doctor, who had come from Columbus, Ohio, for the evening with his wife and aunt.

Eighteen-year-old waiter, Walter Bailey, was unhappy. Already busy, he had been told to place seats in the aisle of the Cabaret Room. It wasn't the first time he was annoyed at the assignment. Bailey, a tray in his hand, watched the comedians who preceded Davidson on stage. A waitress dashed past him in the dark with a whispered message.

He rushed to the corridor where thick black smoke billowed from the Zebra Room, which had been the scene of a wedding party only a half hour earlier.

Bailey raced back to the Cabaret Room. It was 9:02. He went up to the woman in charge. "I asked her if I could go to the stage and tell everybody to get out. She didn't say anything so I did it anyway," Bailey recalled later.

He walked onstage, as the comedy team watched curiously. He tried to disguise the ur-

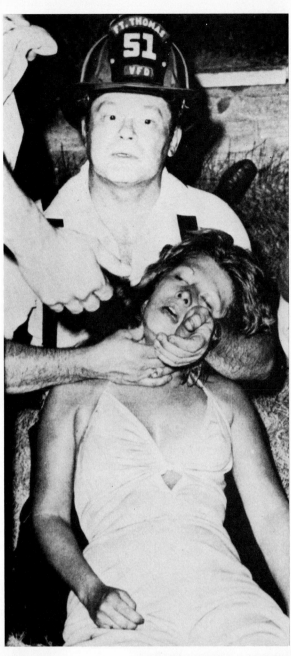

Firemen worked to revive a woman patron

Below, masked volunteers carried out the body of a victim

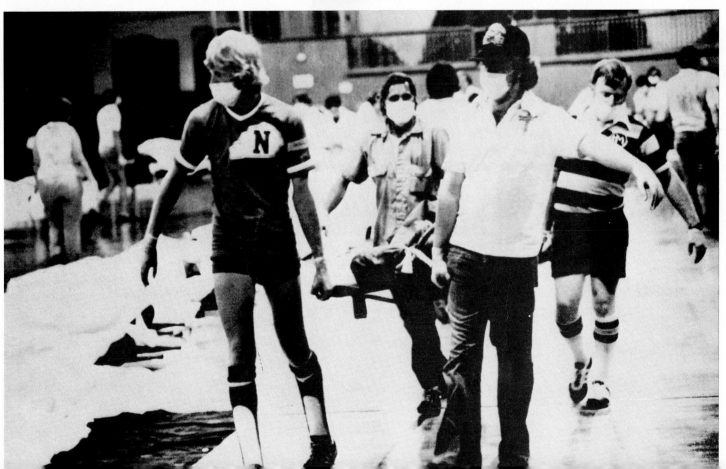

The day after the disaster, a huge crane was used to seek bodies in the wreckage

gency of his mission. He pointed to the exits. He never said fire—until the end.

"Some guys were laughing. They thought I was part of the act," Bailey said.

Doctor remembers hearing a near-chant spread through the room when Bailey was finished. "Everyone was saying, 'Don't panic. Walk slowly.'" Doctor too started to leave.

"We were walking and laughing. But the minute we got into the hall, all hell broke loose."

Preliminary findings by Kentucky officials showed that the fire started in a crawl space around the Zebra Room and was electrical in origin. It burst out of the smaller room and whipped through the halls.

Within minutes, it had swept into the Cabaret Room. Flames engulfed cushioned chairs and elegant evening dresses. A logjam of people crushed toward the exits. The teachers recalled seeing some of their friends trampled to the floor, and others were swept along with the crowd. The lucky ones ended up outside.

A wrong turn meant death. A woman stopped to catch her breath, felt a chair and sat down. Firemen found her body the next day—upright in the chair. She had suffocated.

Paula Neill Jr. made her way outside from the backstage area of the Cabaret Room only to find that her husband Everett, who played in the band, was not with her.

She stood for frantic seconds outside the exit and then went back inside. Everett too had made his way to an exit, then decided that his wife was still inside. He too turned back. They both died in the blaze.

Doctor was twisted around backwards in the milling mob when he reached the exit. He tumbled down the steep stairs, hitting the ground hard as he rolled down the grassy hillside.

All around him were bodies, still clothed in their evening finery. Tablecloths had been draped over their faces. Doctor shouted for his wife and aunt. They answered. He saw Davidson weeping nearby.

For days afterwards, firemen sifted through the rubble of the club to find additional bodies. Volunteers took part in the grim search.

"They were stacked three feet high," said Jim Lanagan, an ironworker helping the fire department with the removal of debris. "Their flesh is welded to those steel beams."

More than a week later, a memorial service was held at a nearby cemetery. Only the shell of the burned-out supper club could be seen through a clearing in the trees surrounding the cemetary knoll where the service was to take place.

By the time the service was held, all of the bodies had been removed from the National Guard Armory which had been set up as a morgue and where the bodies had been placed in long rows for identification.

The elementary school in that rural school district had been forced to close for the week because six of its 18 employees had died in the fire.

The town was in mourning because 14 of the 37 guests of the school teacher's retirement party had died, including the surprise guest, who had come from Alabama to share the evening with his mother. She survived the fire.

During that memorial service, Southgate's young mayor Ken Paul reflected on the emotional torment which had gripped his town.

"Something horrible has happened here," Paul concluded. "We will never be an average American city again. People will always associate Southgate with smoke . . . and fire . . . and death."

94

President Carter's Foreign Debut Made Good Impression

U.S. chief of state was hailed by leaders, public and press

Jimmy Carter was supposed to be a stay-at-home president during his first year or so in office. But in May, only 15 weeks after his inauguration, Carter made his debut in foreign summitry in London. He was, as the British say, a smashing success.

After some somber and disillusioning years, America's allies and friends abroad were longing for a change. And Carter, said host Prime Minister James Callaghan of Britain, was "a breath of fresh air."

"For the first time since President Kennedy died," The Times of London said in summing up what it called "Mr. Carter's Summit," "the Western world can feel that it has a leader — and one who can both arouse the enthusiasm of peoples and inspire the confidence of statesmen."

The summitry itself was overshadowed by Carter's presence. His fellow leaders and their people were anxious to get a closer look at this man who in the preceding two years shucked off the nickname "Jimmy Who?" to become one of the most powerful men in the world.

"I have seen in action," wrote John Knight in the mass-circulation Sunday Mirror, "what the Western world has desperately needed for a heck of a long time: a hero."

It was the little things that people noticed. A London cabbie observed that Carter, wearing an infectious grin, shook hands with a policeman before any of the dignitaries when he stepped off Air Force One at London's Heathrow Airport May 5 to begin his first visit abroad as President. When he got off his plane at Newcastle Airport, on a sightseeing trip to England's industrial Northeast, it was a blue-overalled airport worker who got the first handshake.

Italian diplomats noted that Carter carried his own briefcase to sessions of an economic summit of the noncommunist world's seven strongest industrial nations May 7 – 8 and a subsequent meeting of the North Atlantic alliance May 10 – 11.

President Valery Giscard d'Estaing of France commented that Carter was "a man of simplicity, a man of modesty" who was "ready to listen to criticism."

Carter was the "new boy" in international summitry but he won the respect of more senior statesmen by doing his homework on the complex economic and military issues under

Heads of state posed in front of No. 10 Downing Street; left to right Giulio Andreotti of Italy; Takeo Fukuda of Japan, Valery Giscard d'Estaing of France, Jimmy Carter, Helmut Schmidt of West Germany, James Callaghan of Britain and Pierre Elliott Trudeau of Canada

Below, Carter chatted with Queen Elizabeth II before a state dinner

Trudeau executed a pirouette for photographers at the Buckingham Palace banquet

discussion and saying he had come to London to listen and learn. He traveled an extra mile to accommodate more than one of his fellow leaders.

For Giscard d'Estaing it was exactly 2.4 miles —the distance from Winfield House, the U.S. ambassadorial residence in Regent's Park where Carter was staying, to the French ambassador's residence in Kensington Palace Gardens. Other leaders came calling on President Carter at Winfield House, but the proud and sometimes aloof Giscard d'Estaing balked. So Carter went to him. After an hour-long breakfast tete-a-tete over coffee and croissants, Giscard d'Estaing said he and the peanut farmer from Georgia "call each other by our Christian names."

For Hafez Assad, the equally independent president of Syria and a key figure in the quest for a Middle East settlement, Carter traveled an extra 1,100 miles. Carter wanted to meet in London with Assad, but the Syrian insisted on a get-together on neutral territory. So on a free day between the economic and NATO summits. Carter flew the 1,100-mile round trip to Geneva to meet Assad and got back to London by nightfall.

Like many American visitors to London, Carter seemed a bit awestruck by royalty and all its trappings. At a glittering state dinner at Buckingham Palace the no-frills President and the other leaders ate chicken mousse off gold plates with Queen Elizabeth II.

"It's one of the most beautiful places I've ever seen," Carter enthused to reporters afterwards. "And I think the whole royal family was there. I had a good place to sit—I was between the Queen and Princess Margaret and across the table was Prince Charles and Prince Philip and the Queen Mother."

Carter said it was the "first time I've ever been inside of Buckingham Palace. I was through as a tourist several years ago, my only previous visit to London, and I saw it through the fence."

Carter also employed the common touch in forays amidst his packed schedule of bilateral meetings and formal summit sessions. One of his most eager and adept pupils was Prime Minister Callaghan, whose struggling Labor government had just suffered massive setbacks in local elections around the country. But it was Carter, not Callaghan, who got most of the cheers.

Three little words won over the soccer fans of Newcastle during a pre-summit visit to see—as host Callaghan put it—"a little bit of the backbone" of industrial England. Addressing a huge crowd in front of Newcastle's ultra-modern civic center, Carter gave the city's traditional soccer cheer of "Awa' the Lads," roughly translated as "Up With Our Boys."

"After that there was simply nothing the U.S. President could do wrong," said The Sun, a mass-circulation London tabloid.

"He took a lot of hearts and maybe some minds," said another London tabloid, the Daily Mail, "and when he was gone there was a gap and no one to fill it."

"As a preliminary to the economic summit in London nothing could have fostered good humor and Anglo-American relations better than this leisure-before-business trip," said the Daily Telegraph.

Besides Carter, Giscard d'Estaing and Callaghan, the London economic summit brought together Chancellor Helmut Schmidt of West Germany and Prime Ministers Pierre Trudeau of Canada, Takeo Fukuda of Japan and Giulio Andreotti of Italy.

Meeting around a 14-by-16-foot table in the oak-paneled state dining room at 10 Downing St., home of Britain's prime ministers, the leaders wrestled with such problems as inflation, unemployment, soaring oil prices, nuclear proliferation and how to speed the noncommunist world to economic recovery after its worst recession since the 1930s.

Spokesmen cautioned in advance that no earth-shaking decisions would be made at the Downing Street summit and the final communique bore out their predictions. The 600-word communique said the "most urgent task" of the seven nations—which had total unemployment of 15 million—was "to create more jobs while continuing to reduce inflation." There was dis-

The president and Schmidt seemed amused

Carter addressed a welcoming crowd at Newcastle

agreement over the prickly issue of nuclear proliferation.

But the leaders agreed to an urgent two-month study of how to increase the use of nuclear energy in the world without also encouraging the spread of atomic weapons and the risk of nuclear war.

The Carter administration was seeking to curb the spread of nuclear technology that could result in atomic weapons. But some other leaders at the summit, notably Schmidt, saw the export of nuclear energy as a major source of foreign earnings, and West Germany planned to push ahead with a sale of $4.8 billion worth of nuclear technology to Brazil, despite United States objections.

The leaders also called for a prohibition against "irregular practices and improper conduct" in world business dealings. "We believe." said Carter, who suggested the action, "the time has come for international control and prohibition against illegalities, bribery, extortion, and other actions that have sometimes been condoned in trade, commerce and banking."

At the NATO summit which followed the economic gathering, Carter tried to breathe new life into an alliance weakened by defense cuts and internal squabbles while facing a massive Soviet arms buildup. The President told NATO leaders that Soviet-bloc forces were "much stronger than needed for any defense purpose"

and pledged the United States "to make a major effort" toward improving NATO's strength and urged the 14 other members to do the same.

He also promised "to promote a genuinely two-way trans-Atlantic trade in defense equipment." This was welcome news to European members of the alliance who buy about 10 times as much military hardware in the United States as the United States spends on arms and equipment in Europe.

London's mass-circulation Daily Mirror called the week of speech-making "the long hot-air summit" and The Times noted that "the world has not been changed" by it. But there seemed little doubt that Carter had made a strong and favorable impression on his fellow leaders and the people they lead.

The conservative Daily Mail spoke of a new presence on the world scene and called it "the Carter factor."

"Into this somewhat macabre gathering, politically crippled and, in the case of Giscard rendered politically spiteful by France's domestic insecurity, comes the new American president in the full flush of power," the Daily Mail said.

"Now, close up, he seems more genuine, more thoughtful—a man of infectious charm and unsapped zest, a man from the New World who has dropped in to refresh the staleness of the Old."

A HUMAN FLY AT WORK

New Yorkers forgot their troubles for a while on May 26 and experienced a vicarious thrill when George Willig, 27-year-old toymaker and amateur mountain climber, scaled Manhattan's quarter-mile-high World Trade Center. Thousands lining the streets below held their breath while Willig inched his way up the towering structure.

Right, watchers could barely see the tiny figure slowly ascending the 1,350-foot south tower of the trade center

Below left, as Willig clung to sheer wall, police who rode up the building on a window-washing machine tried to talk him out of completing the climb. He politely refused. Below right, all was forgiven and the city dropped plans to file a $250,000 suit against Willig when he handed a smiling Mayor Abe Beame $1.10, or a penny a floor

Oysterman Butler Flower relaxed a bit after a day on the water

VETERAN OYSTERMAN HAD UNCOMMON FAITH IN CAPRICIOUS SEA

(Editor's note: This feature on the tribulations of an oysterman is taken from one of the Elsewhere In America columns written by AP Special Correspondent Jules Loh)

Butler Flower was an oysterman. He worked aboard a boat with a battered wooden hull and muscular booms on its deck, a working boat. He was a man of uncommon faith in the sea.

You would have thought a hard-working oysterman plying his trade in Oyster Bay, the very waters named for an abundance of those creatures, would never have had a worry about putting food on the family table. On the contrary, "I damn near went broke," Butler Flower said.

That was some time back, a time when the other oystermen on Oyster Bay did indeed go broke. They watched a dependable yearly harvest of 200,000 bushels of oysters dwindle to zero, sold their boats and moved on.

Butler Flower stuck it out. He gambled on a scientific long shot, artificial breeding, and it paid off. Even if good times had not returned, even if Butler Flower had not been able to build back his harvest to 40,000 bushels and climbing, he likely wouldn't have left anyhow. Oyster Bay was his world.

"I live a quarter mile from the house I was born in," he said. "In 75 years, a quarter mile is as far as I've moved."

Flower moored his boats on an inlet in the village of Bayville. It is part of Oyster Bay township and a stone's throw from the bay itself.

There was a continuity to the Flower oyster business too. Butler Flower's father put aside boat-building to take up oystering and a sign on the old building at dockside still bore his name: Frank M. Flower & Sons, 1897.

Butler, the middle of three sons, was the last remaining. He grew up on oyster boats, from sail to deisel, and it was a rare day that he wasn't out on one from dawn to dusk. He was, at 75, still fit and agile on a slippery deck.

"Nobody knows this bay better than he does," said his cousin, Henry Flower, an employee and skilled bayman himself. "He will glance at any three points of land and say 'Hey, the marker should be right there.' Sure enough, look over the side, and there will be the marker."

Oyster Bay was divided into sections, much as a town is divided into lots. The sections, or oyster beds, were leased by the town; small floating markers, anchored, set the boundaries. The map of the beds in use in 1977 was dated 1936, but the practice dated to colonial times.

The Flower family held leases for beds totaling 1,500 acres, more than enough for a prosperous oyster business. Provided, of course, oysters grow on them.

"I can remember when we believed it would be impossible to sell all the oysters in Long Island Sound," Butler Flower said. "A man with a boat could take all the oysters off his beds he could carry. Oysters set in this bay every year as regular as the sun rises every day." "Set" is the oysterman's word for spawn. Oysters spawn every year, in the summer when the water is warm and the months have no R. On Oyster Bay, for reasons no one has explained, the oysters quit spawning in the 1930s.

"For many years I went into Connecticut waters and brought little oysters back and let them grow big in Oyster Bay. Then they quit setting in Connecticut. Connecticut has a set about once every five years now, that's all.

"It was rough. If I hadn't been able to sell a few mussels and clams, I wouldn't have made it."

For half a century, Butler Flower said, scientists had been trying to breed oysters artificially. More than 100 efforts had been made on Oyster Bay. He watched them all fail.

But Butler Flower had faith in his beloved bay and faith as well in Dave Relyea. Relyea had worked on Butler Flower's docks as a teen-ager, unloading boats. He went off to college, learned things about oysters even Butler Flower didn't know, came home and since 1968 worked a few feet from the same dock in a building full of beakers and test tubes and porcelain tanks.

There he mixed male and female spawn. Larvae attached themselves to crushed shells. They fed on laboratory-prepared algae. They grew. Dave Relyea dropped them into the sea. A year later Butler Flower took them out. Would it had been that simple.

"Many, many things can go wrong," the marine biologist said. "But we get better at it every day."

Out on his own laboratory, the Ida May, a boat Butler Flower helped his father build back in 1920 and named for his mother, the old oysterman of Oyster Bay studied the result. "I've never seen better oysters." he said. "Right now they're so fat they're popping out of the shells."

MAY DAY MARKED BY PEACE AND VIOLENCE

May Day: A day of sunshine and flowers, bullets and blood in 1977.

In China, officials marked the day by joining the masses in garden parties that Hsinhua news agency said created "a joyous atmosphere of unity" for the Marxists traditional day of the worker. Politburo members turned out for a two-hour parade in Moscow's Red Square for a two-hour parade of floats, flowers and banners under brilliant sunshine. No arms or military hardware were displayed. In Rome, Pope Paul VI called on the faithful to pray for the world's unemployed.

These peaceful scenes were counterpointed by violence in Turkey, Greece, France, Spain, San Salvador and other nations. At least 33 persons died, 126 were wounded and 200 arrested during a wild gunfight between rival leftist factions in Istanbul. Witnesses said the battle apparently was touched off when shots from the roof of a building sparked a volley of return fire from members of a rally of 100,000 persons in Taksim Square.

Scores of people were injured when riot police in several Spanish cities used tear gas, rubber bullets and clubs on newly legalized trade unionists and others who defied a ban on May Day demonstrations. Eight persons were killed in El Salvador in a shootout between police and alleged terrorists. During a rally in Paris, about 200 anarchists threw stink bombs at Communists, as thousands of persons marched from the Place de la Nation to City Hall.

Violence erupted in Athens after a peaceful rally when 100 leftist youths marched in defiance of an official ban. The clashes left 12 policemen and 20 other persons injured. About 40 persons were hurt when police opened fire on a crowd that was attacking buses headed for a May Day rally in Colombo, Sri Lanka. No disorders were reported in Lisbon, Portugal, where more than 100,000 Communist-led demonstrators marched in a show of strength.

HELICOPTER ACCIDENT ATOP SKYSCRAPER KILLED FIVE

It was 5:22 p.m., Monday, May 16.

A 59-foot-long helicopter, carrying 20 passengers in from Kennedy International Airport, had just settled down atop the 59-story Pan American building in crowded midtown Manhattan. The building rose directly behind Grand Central terminal and straddled Park Avenue in one of the most congested areas of the midtown portion of New York City. In the streets far below the landing site, the evening rush hour was starting to build.

When the inbound passengers had been debarked, the copter began taking aboard 21 others for the next flight to Kennedy, its five bladed rotor still whirling. Then, suddenly and without warning, the landing gear of the copter collapsed, dropping the ship onto its side. The 30-feet long blades of the rotor hit the roof surface, shattered and ripped through the air like scythes. Four persons waiting in line to get on board the ship for the ride to the airport were sliced to bits by the whirling blades, and part of one blade plunged 800 feet from the roof to the ground below where it struck and killed a woman pedestrian.

Robert Levenwood was one of the passengers about to board the craft. "Everyone threw themselves to the floor," he recalled. "There was blood all over everyone." Deputy Chief Medical Examiner Michael Baden showed several paperback books to newsmen. The books had been sliced and had blood on them. Said Baden, "This is what the bodies looked like. They were not transsected, but they had deep lacerations. They died immediately. Their wounds were immediately fatal."

Helicopter flights from atop the midtown skyscraper had been suspended nine years earlier because they were losing money and because of community concern over the safety of the operation. They had been resumed Feb. 1. Following the accident, all flights from the building were ordered halted until further notice.

A new passenger-carrying hydrofoil made its debut off Portsmouth, England. It was capable of doing 50 miles per hour

Also in MAY . . .

Joan Crawford holding award

THE FINAL CURTAIN FOR JOAN CRAWFORD

Joan Crawford portrayed the flaming youth of the 1920s and then went on to become as great an all-around actress as the film industry had ever seen. She also carved a name in the business world and was a leading benefactor before she died in her Manhattan apartment of a heart attack May 10 at the age of 69.

An aura of glamour surrounded the actress throughout her career, and she conformed to that image, once confessing that "If I'd ever been seen on the Sunset Strip with bare feet and my hair uncoiffed, I would have killed myself."

"She believed in the Hollywood legend, and she was a creature of it," said George Cukor, who directed her in three of her 80 films. "She represented the best in the golden period of Hollywood. She started as a personality girl, a dancing flapper and made herself into an excellent actress. She had a wonderful bone structure that made it impossible to photograph her from a bad angle."

In her last years, Miss Crawford remained in virtual retirement both as a performer and as a director of and ambassador-at-large for the Pepsi Cola Co. She had become that firm's first director in 1959 upon the death of her fourth husband, Pepsi board chairman Alfred Steele, whom she married in 1955. But she was a leading benefactor, fundraiser and honorary official for dozens of philanthropies. She explained to an interviewer in 1971; "I've been on the receiving end of so much good that I feel I have to give something back."

Miss Crawford was born Lucille LeSueur March 23, 1908, in San Antonio, Texas, in what she described as "a drab little place on the wrong side of the tracks." Her parents were divorced a few weeks after her birth and her mother married an Oklahoma theater owner. When touring road companies played there, Joan's blue eyes widened with envy and she vowed she would become a dancer.

While still in her teens she landed a chorus girl's spot in a nightclub in Kansas City, moving on as a hoofer to Chicago and Detroit. A Broadway producer saw her in a Detroit nightclub and brought her to New York in the chorus line of the 1924 musical *Innocent Eyes*.

Offered a film contract, she headed for Hollywood in 1926 on a salary of $75 a week. While waiting for a chance before the cameras, she won a number of prizes for dancing the Charleston, the dance craze of the day.

Miss Crawford's first picture was a silent movie *Pretty Ladies* in 1926. She played the then familiar role of a hoofer. The roaring 20s had arrived; the era of hip flasks and bathtub gin. Skimpy skirts were the feminine vogue and Flaming Youth held sway throughout the land. Nobody epitomized the era better than Joan Crawford, as she whirled through one picture after another, her chiffon skirts swirling high to show her shapely legs.

But as time went on, Joan Crawford perfected her talent and widened her scope. In 1945 she won an Academy Award for *Mildred Pierce*. By then few Hollywood personalities were more respected than Miss Crawford.

She married and divorced two of the biggest stars in Hollywood, Douglas Fairbanks Jr. and Franchot Tone. A third marriage to actor Phillip Terry also ended in divorce. But she once declared that "my last marriage to Alfred Steele was a good marriage." He died in 1959.

Joan Crawford summed up her personal life in an interview not long before her death. "Maybe I was the one who gave myself three unhappy endings and untold loneliness," she said. "I'm the sum of everything that ever happened to me, every mistake I've ever made and every tear I've ever shed. And I've tried never to repeat a mistake."

GENERAL RECALLED AFTER QUESTIONING CARTER KOREA PLAN

After President Carter unveiled a plan for withdrawing American ground troops from Korea, a U.S. general stationed there said it would lead to war. He was promptly recalled.

The White House announcement also caused open concern among South Korean leaders and stirred up some thorny questions back home. Were U.S. troops on the divided peninsula a deterrent to aggression or a trip wire to possible American involvement in yet another Asian war? Did peace depend on the Korean antagonists or on their big power patrons?

The President's decision for a pullout over the next four or five years gained wide attention after Maj. Gen. John K. Singlaub, chief of staff at U.S. Forces headquarters in Korea, questioned it in an interview with a reporter for the Washington Post.

"If we withdraw our ground forces on the schedule suggested, it will lead to war," said Singlaub, the third-ranking U.S. Army general in South Korea.

After the general's words appeared in the Post, Carter issued an edict May 19 ordering his immediate recall. The order reminded observers of the action Harry S. Truman took in 1951 when he recalled Gen. Douglas MacArthur as commander of United Nations forces in Korea after that commander took issue with the President over the handling of the Korean War.

On the heels of the White House summons, Singlaub, wearing civilian clothes, arrived in Washington. He refused to comment on the case other than to say that he awaited orders to report to the President.

On May 21, as generally expected, Carter removed Singlaub from his Korean command for publicly criticizing his decision on a phase-out. At a news conferencce several days later, the President defended his plan to move out the 33,000 U.S. ground forces in Korea. He said "we evolved the policy for South Korea over a long number of years. And I finally made a decision after consultation with the intelligence community, the military leaders, a formal meeting of the National Security Council, that we would withdraw our ground troops over a period of four or five years."

Carter also defended his recall of Singlaub, saying "I don't believe that Gen. Singlaub . . . could have effectively carried out this policy when he had publicly been identified as being opposed to it."

Carter made clear, however, the general was not being "fired" or "chastised" but transfered to a position of equal "stature." On May 27, the Pentagon announced that Singlaub would become chief of staff of the U.S. Army Command. The Army's biggest command, it is responsible for assuring combat readiness for 292,000 regular soldiers and 670,000 National Guardsmen and reservists in the United States.

But the dust had not yet settled. Testifying before a House armed services subcommittee, Singlaub said his view that withdrawal of U. S. troops would lead to war was shared by other senior officers, both American and South Korean. The general asserted that the administration had not asked the U.S. military command in Korea for its opinion on the impact of withdrawal.

Two days after relieving Singlaub of his command, Carter sent two top aids to Seoul for consultations on his controversial plan. Dispatched on the mission were the chairman of the Joint Chiefs of Staff, Gen. George Brown, and the State Department's top political officer, Philip C. Habib.

It was by now apparent that the President's decision did no sit well with the Koreans. After consulting with Brown and Habib, President Park Chung-hee said he did not welcome withdrawal, but would accept what he called "established" United States policy.

Former South Korean President Yun Po-sun, one of the few political opposition leaders not in jail, said he agreed with Singlaub that such a pullout would lead to an invasion by Communist North Korea.

Gen. John Singlaub pointed to a map of Korea as Rep. W. C. Daniel (D-Va) watched during testimony before the House armed services subcommittee

Also in MAY . . .

ANNIVERSARY OF AN EPIC FLIGHT

On May 20, 1927, the famed American humorist, Will Rogers, wrote in his newspaper column: "No attempt at jokes today. A slim, tall, bashful, smiling American boy is over the middle of the Atlantic Ocean where no lone human being has ever ventured before." On that day, a single-engine monoplane called The Spirit of St. Louis had taken off on a nonstop flight from New York to Paris. At the controls was a 25-year-old air mail pilot named Charles A. Lindbergh. Thirty-three hours and 29 minutes later, the Lone Eagle, as he came to be known, landed at Le Bourget Field, bringing off a feat of daring and courage that thrilled millions on both sides of the Atlantic. A half century later, the United States paid tribute to Lindbergh and his historic flight with anniversary celebrations across the land.

Left, some time before the flight, Charles A. Lindbergh, posed with The Spirit of St. Louis at Curtiss Airfield on Long Island, N. Y. Lindbergh, an air mail pilot, had smashed all cross-country records on a transcontinental U.S. flight but he was still a dark horse in the race to be the first to fly solo across the Atlantic. Below, on May 20, 1927, Lindbergh took off for the flight to Paris.

Above, suddenly world-
famous Lindbergh
appeared before a
cheering crowd in Paris

A half century after
the flight Lindbergh's
widow, Anne Morrow
Lindbergh sat quietly
on the porch of her
late husband's boy-
hood home in Little
Falls, Minn. as 2,100
persons braved the
rain to attend the
anniversary ceremony

Also in MAY . . .

SLAIN WIDOW LEFT MILLIONS OF DOLLARS HIDDEN AROUND HOUSE

Neighbors of Marjorie V. Jackson said the 66-year-old grocery chain heiress was reclusive, deeply religious and very distrustful. Distrust apparently prompted her to keep millions of dollars in currency stashed away in her home in a swank suburb of Indianapolis and finally led to her murder.

Police were summoned to her house May 7 when neighbors saw smoke billowing from the place. A fire, fed by gasoline, had been set in two spots. The owner, widow of Chester Jackson, son of the founder of the former Standard Grocery chain, was found dead on the kitchen floor. She had been shot once at close range by a .22 caliber pistol. What intrigued police was the discovery of more than $5 million in cash stuffed in trash tins, drawers and tool boxes.

Two 1977 Cadillacs, one unlicensed and partly covered with a blanket were found in the garage and enough food for a banquet was spread on a table although Mrs. Jackson was rarely known to entertain.

The more police probed, the more puzzling the case became. The FBI disclosed that in May 1976 it had investigated a shortage of funds in the Jackson trust. Later an Indiana National Bank vice president pleaded guilty to embezzling $534,000 from it.

As police began rounding up suspects, one told them he and two companions had stolen $817,000 from Mrs. Jackson in January 1977. Sheriff's Lt. Robert W. Kirkman said the woman had refused to press charges against the three saying the robbery "was the will of God."

Mrs. Jackson's three-acre estate, surrounded by homes with manicured lawns, was overrun with weeds, causing neighbors to file complaints. "She said God told her not mow the yard for seven years," recalled Mrs. Betty Miller, a neighbor.

The trail became warmer when police were tipped that a man had paid $13,500 in cash for a new car and then tried to trade it because it was scratched. This information led to the arrest of three persons and recovery of $1.6 million.

Just how much money was still missing remained a mystery. "She had different businesses she was involved in," said Kirkman, "and she had money in all different banks. We're still trying to figure it all out."

A grocery cart contained more than $5 million which was found in the home of slain heiress Marjorie V. Jackson

THE END OF THE LINE FOR THE ORIENT EXPRESS

For a handful of those boarding the tarnished but still famed Orient Express as it prepared to race the 1,900 miles from Paris to Istanbul, it was a sentimental journey. Long romanticized in story and song as a luxury train crowded with the rich and the beautiful, with secret agents and with intrigue, the Orient Express had reached the end of its line.

As the famed train pulled out of the Gare de Lyon on May 20 at 12:13 a.m. — 17 minutes late — a small band of railroad lovers toasted its departure with champagne. Unlike the days of its glory, the last Orient Express pulled only one first class sleeper and three day coaches. The 18 passengers in the first class car were taking a nostalgic trip. The day coaches were crowded with Yugoslavs, Bulgarians, Greeks and Turks going home and apparently unaware of the occasion.

Those taking the trip had to supply their own water, food and refreshments. The luxurious dining cars that once served gourmet meals were dropped from service years earlier.

The Orient Express was established in 1883 with stops in Munich, Vienna, Budapest, Bucharest and a crossing of the Danube River by boat. It later saw modifications in its route to include Sofia and Belgrade. In 1919, the so-called "Simplon Orient" line was established as an off-shoot to run along the Mediterranean coast. That connection eventually became the Direct Orient Express with twice-weekly journeys between Paris and Istanbul.

As the final Orient Express rumbled into the Instanbul's Sirkeci Station May 22, first class passengers leaned out the windows and gulped champagne as the train creaked to a halt. But second class passengers tumbled off and soon disappeared in the throngs on the street. When the train stopped, the 18 first class passengers stepped down and joined hands to sing *Auld Lang Syne.*

Most of the first class riders said the trip was worth the $375 ticket because of the "feeling of camaraderie." They said there was champagne toasts and dancing in the aisles each night during the 60-hour trip. They paid about $50 more than the price of an airline ticket from Paris to Istanbul, a flight that took three hours.

Trying to hold back tears, Vianelle Fauste, a 67-year-old conductor on the train, said: "A piece of good old times goes into history with grace and pride. I'm sure nothing has matched it and no other means of transportation will surpass the exotic atmosphere it created."

The famed Orient Express which made its last run May 19

FOR THE RECORD

CONVICTED. Four terrorists, in the September 1976 hijacking of an American jetliner. The three Croatians and the American-born wife of one of them hijacked the plane from Kennedy International Airport in New York and forced the pilot to fly to Canada, across the Atlantic Ocean to Scandinavia and finally to Paris where they were taken into custody. The federal court jury in New York City May 6 found Zvonka Busic, 30, and his wife, Julienne, 27, guilty of air piracy involving a death, air piracy in which no death was involved, and conspiracy. Peter Matanic, 31, and Frane Pesut, 25, were convicted of air piracy in which no death was involved and conspiracy.

JUNE

Oil Began Moving Over $7.7 Billion Alaska Pipeline

But hardly had the flow started when accidents began to plague the operation

There were shouts of triumph in the control room at Pump Station No. 1 in Alaska's Prudhoe Bay. In Valdez 800 miles away, there was a lone handclap and the traditional thumbs up. Thus was heralded the birth of the great trans-Alaska pipeline, which was to be plagued with accidents soon after it began operating.

On June 20 at 2 p.m. after nine years of controversy and three years of construction the oil began flowing slowly toward the Valdez terminal through the line which cost $7.7 billion to build and was hailed as the world's largest and most expensive project.

The reaction in the Prudhoe control room to the clickity-clickity sound of the oil flowing through the line was like the response to the blastoff of a spaceship, according to one observer.

"There was a big cheer, like at Cape Canaveral," said Martin Rowe of Westinghouse Inc. who was at Prudhoe Bay when the black gold began its journey. But there was no champagne; just coffee and rolls.

At Valdez, when the signal to start the oil flowing was flashed to Prudhoe, a big smile lit up the face of Don Gray, an official of Alyeska Pipeline Service Co., the consortium of eight companies which had spent three years building the 800-mile line. Gray gave an arms-raised thumbs-up signal to 10 Alyeska colleagues in the depot. His engineering advisor, U.J. Baskurt, jubilantly smacked his hands together.

For employees in the field who had been working seven straight 12-hour days to get the oil flow started, there was little sign of excitement.

"For the punchy people up here, it's just another day," said Dave Higgins, a security guard at Prudhoe. "I suppose we will wake up later and realize it's a historic day."

The oil flow actually began when crews at the starting point inserted a 2,000-pound plastic

This view taken from inside a length of pipe showed oil storage tanks at Valdez, terminal of the line

A pipeline worker listened for the sound of the "pig" as it was forced through the line by crude leaving Prudhoe Bay

"pig", a device to clean the line and mark the progress of the crude through the 48-inch tube to Valdez on ice-free Prince William Sound. From there it would be loaded aboard tankers for shipment to the United States West Coast and other areas.

A monitoring crew began walking down the line keeping pace with the oil which was moving at 1.1 miles an hour. Initial flow was said to be 110,000 barrels a day with the volume to increase to 300,000 barrels within 24 hours and 600,000 within a month. By year's end the flow was scheduled to reach 1.2 million barrels daily.

With the opening of the pipeline, America's 49th state was paying the United States back with ample interest for the $7.2 million it had shelled out to buy the northern territory from Russia back in 1867. Oil had made Alaska the richest state in the union on a population basis. It had the highest per capita income in the nation, having grown from $5,162 in 1972 to more than $10,000 in 1976. State Senate President John Rader of Anchorage described Alaska as a big oil company and its state officials as "simply a board of directors."

Alaskans were rejoicing over realization of the dream born in July 1969 when American petroleum companies confirmed discovery of oil in their state. Then trouble began. The oil had just started flowing when workers discovered cracks in the 48-inch pipe near Pump Station No. 8 about 25 miles south of Fairbanks.

That problem had barely been disposed of when an explosion tore through the station on July 8 killing one worker and injuring five. The blast touched off a fire that reduced the multimillion-dollar pump house to rubble. The pipeline did not seem damaged but, to be on the safe side, officials shut it down and began an investigation into what caused the accident.

The Department of Interior blamed "human error" for the explosion and, after a 10-day shutdown, the oil began moving once again. But less than 24 hours later, a front-loading truck rammed into the line about 23 miles south of the Prudhoe Bay oilfield and knocked off a vent fitting on a valve.

Officials shut down the line at once, but oil already in the pipe began gushing forth from the ruptured section. By the time workers managed to drive a wooden wedge into the 1½-inch valve fitting, about 1,000 barrels of oil had sprayed out like a black and brown fan over some 15 acres of tundra. The system was restarted eight hours after the leak had sprung, but by that time some of the escaped oil had seeped into two nearby lakes.

Aware of the possibility of such accidents, the Alaska state legislature had already passed a law setting fines for oil spills along the 800-mile line, but it was not due to take effect until 1978.

Barely 12 days after the explosion at Pump Station No. 8, which would cost an estimated $50 million in repairs, a more threatening incident occurred. At 3:09 a.m. July 20 three dynamite charges were exploded against the pipe, but fortunately the only damage they caused was to rip off the insulation. State troopers arrested three young men on charges of malicious damage to property.

"Quite clearly there are chinks in our armor," said William J. Darch, president of Alyeska.

However, despite sabotage, explosion, fire and accident, oil from the Alaska Arctic finally began pouring into the terminal storage tanks at Valdez July 29. Tankers steamed into Prince William Sound to begin receiving oil bound for refineries in California, Washington State and the Middle West.

This ponderous grizzly ambled along the Haul Road that paralleled the Alaska pipeline

111

Bloody Shootout Climaxed 20-day Hijack in Holland

Dutch troops finally stormed the school and train where Moluccans held hostages

It was 4:53 a.m. when the marines went in amid the crunch of explosions, the scream of jets and the rattle of heavy machine gun fire.

The target: A Dutch passenger train seized by South Moluccan terrorists with dozens of hostages and held for 20 nerve-racking days in the flat farmlands of the north of the Netherlands.

At the same moment 12 miles south in the village of Bovensmilde, another unit of the Royal Dutch marines stormed the local elementary school where South Moluccan gunmen still held four of an original 110 hostages. An armored car smashed through the main doors of the building and the marines raced in guns at the ready. Then four Moluccans were dragged out, spread-eagled, searched and taken away.

The closely coordinated attacks, carried out soon after dawn Saturday, June 11, were over in 15 minutes. Forty-nine hostages were rescued from the train and the four from the school were also saved.

In the wrecked shell of the train, two hostages lay dead and six of nine terrorists aboard perished in a hail of fire poured into the forward area where their command post was located. Moluccan sources said there were 106 bullet wounds in the body of one dead terrorist, a woman, and 300 in the body of the leader, Max Papilaya, 24, a clerk in the provincial administration, said to have been trained by Palestinian guerrillas.

"We hit the deck and stayed there when the planes came over," said Adriaan Dijkman, a 51-year-old businessman aboard the train. "Then a smiling marine tapped me on the shoulder and said 'it's safe to come out now.'"

The 40,000 South Moluccans who live in Holland are a legacy from the Dutch colonial past. The older generation fled there as refugees soon after their home islands were forcibly incorporated in Indonesia (the former Dutch East Indies) in 1949. Ever since, the exiles have unavailingly urged the Dutch to help them in their struggle for an independent homeland.

In the Netherlands, the Moluccans have always refused to integrate with Dutch society. They were settled into old army camps on arrival here and later into tightly knit housing communities, scattered around the country but always standing apart from the Dutch section of town.

The new generation—born on Dutch soil—had been nurtured on dreams that one day the Moluccans would go home and it was the militants among the younger people that had turned to terrorism to enforce this goal.

In 1975, resentment boiled over against Dutch society. A plot by fanatical young Moluccans to kidnap Queen Juliana was uncovered by Dutch authorities and smashed. In December of the same year, Moluccan terrorists hijacked a train and seized the Indonesian consulate in Amsterdam.

In the 1975 attacks, three men were murdered on the train and a fourth died from injuries after trying to escape from an upper window of the consulate. The terrorists held out for nearly three weeks, but eventually surrendered without further bloodshed after the intervention of Moluccan mediators. The seven consulate gunmen got six-year prison terms, the seven from the train drew 14 years.

It was 18 months before Moluccans were to strike again in a repeat of the 1975 train hijacking, coupled with the raid on the Bovensmilde village school.

Traveling north and only 20 miles from where the 1975 hijack occurred, a yellow four-car train of the Dutch national railway system jolted to a halt in open country eight miles north of Assen, a 17th century market town. It was 9:10 a.m. Monday, May 23. Somebody had pulled the emergency cord.

Mrs. Nelleke Ellenbroek, 23, put down her knitting and wondered what was happening. Janneke Wiegers, a 19-year-old student teacher, peeped along a corridor and saw armed men coming in through the doors from the rail embankment. "If you do what we tell you, nothing will happen to you," they told her.

Other passengers said the train's emergency cord was pulled by two Moluccans—a young woman and a youth—who had come aboard at Assen. They pulled guns out of plastic bags and yelled "this is a hijack." The terrorists spread swiftly through the cars. Old people, mothers with children and those who looked infirm were allowed to get off the train.

Others were herded into the first class compartment where gunmen fired warning shots into the roof. With tensions at breaking point, Mrs. Ellenbroek took out her knitting and resumed work. Seven months pregnant, she was

112

Above, Dutch troops stood by as relief supplies were ferried to hostages aboard the hijacked train

Two men wheeled a hand cart crammed with food and supplies toward the train

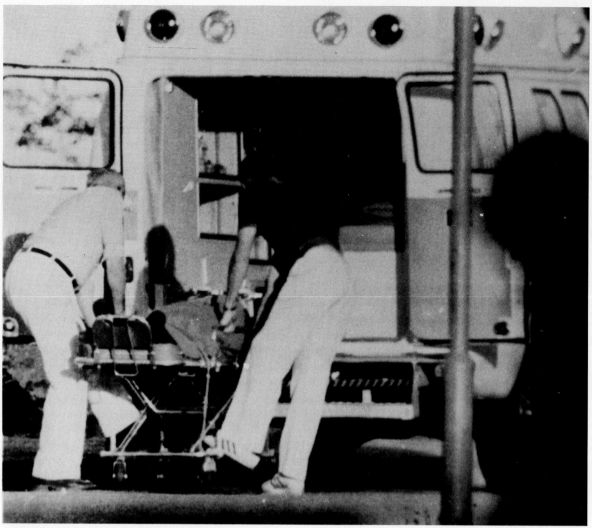

making baby clothes and had been expected that day for a medical check-up in the city of Groningen, a few miles to the north.

The check-up was to be delayed for another 13 days until she and a second pregnant women among the hostages were released in a surprise move by the terrorists. "It was enormously reassuring for us to see her knitting," said Janneke.

At about the same time at the school, other Moluccan gunmen walked in soon after the start of morning classes. They pulled out weapons and told everybody to stay put. Children coming in from a physical education session, in the gym found themselves trapped. Others, still in the gym class, got away.

One of them was Roald, a blue-eyed 9-year-old. "A couple of my Moluccan friends ran over and warned us that bad things were happening," said Roald. He and his friends scampered through a hedge behind the school and ran home. The gunmen themselves immediately released 15 children from the Moluccan quarter of Bovensmilde, a separate housing development attached to the village.

The 105 children they kept were all 6 to 12-year-olds from the Dutch community. Five teachers also were taken hostage.

The nation reacted with shock and horror. Premier Joop Den Uyl went on TV to condemn what he called "a horrible act of terror." The government's first duty, he said, would be to liberate the schoolchildren and the other hostages.

Johan Alvares Manusama, self-styled president of the Moluccan Republic in Exile, also condemned the seizure of the children and the new outbreak of violence. "This will do our cause no good at all," he declared.

A general election was scheduled for May 25, but campaigning was suspended by all the major parties as Den Uyl and key ministers in his coalition government grappled with the crisis. They employed the same patient tactics as in 1975. Teams of psychiatrists were sent into the area to reason with the terrorists over field telephones. A cordon of 2,000 police and troops was thrown around the siege locations.

The terrorist demands—relayed to the government and the national TV system—called for the release of 21 compatriots jailed for previous acts of extremism and a jumbo jet to fly all the militants out of the country together with hostages. The terrorists said hostages would be shot unless their demands were met by 2 p.m. on election day.

Two hours before the deadline expired, the children were brought up to the windows of the schoolhouse and made to chant in unison: "We want to live, Van Agt."

This was a reference to Justice Minister Andries Van Agt, the man most involved along with Premier Den Uyl in handling the crisis and also Den Uyl's leading political rival.

The deadline—one of three as a government report later disclosed—passed without bloodshed and 87 percent of the Dutch electorate turned out to vote in a record poll. Den Uyl's Labor Party picked up 10 extra seats in the 150-member parliament for a total of 53. Van Agt's moderate Christian Democrats finished with 49. The results were seen as a clear endorsement for the country's two leading politicians and the electorate rejected the appeals of extreme right wing factions that Holland should free itself of troublesome minorities such as the Moluccans.

At the train, three hostages were thrust out on to the track blindfolded and with nooses round their necks, but later taken back inside unharmed. The next day came the first break in the sieges when four sick children were released from the school. On May 27—the fifth day of the siege—all the remaining children were freed after a mystery stomach ailment spread through half of them. They came out in a phased release that started well before dawn, many of them huddled in blankets.

Most were sent home after a check, 28 went to the hospital. Members of a crack British anti-terrorist unit, the Special Air Services, had paid a flying visit to The Hague and there was speculation they had put the Dutch up to something. However, Van Agt firmly declared there had been no question of doctoring food deliveries and the children's stomach infections were "exclusively an act of nature." Within a few days, all the children were discharged from the hospital and allowed home.

Government efforts now concentrated on the train where a sophisticated system of electronic surveillance was established. Remote control cameras recorded every movement in the vicinity and the pictures were relayed over closed circuit TV to the security forces. Marines dug into foxholes 100 yards from the train. One night a detachment—with blackened faces—crawled up through the long grass and planted bugging devices on the train's underbelly. In this way, information is believed to have been obtained for the eventual attack but in the meantime the government stuck to policies of patience and persuasion.

Nothing worked however. The stonewalling continued. The sweltering heat let up somewhat. Then on Saturday June 4 Moluccan mediators were brought in for the first time. Mrs. Josina Soumokil, widow of a Moluccan secessionist leader executed in Indonesia in 1966, and Dr. Hassan Tan, a physician, boarded the train for a six-hour session with the terrorists.

Mrs. Soumokil's own son had been jailed in the Juliana plot and was one of the 21 whose freedom was sought. The mediators came off the train bearing messages that brought the sieges no nearer to a conclusion and they did not go back into action until June 9. After another four-hour session on the train, they reported that the militants were standing by their demands for release of prisoners and a getaway plane. They were threatening to kill their hostages unless the government bowed.

On June 11, the government took action. The marines came out of their foxholes and six Starfighter jets streaked in from the south. Ex-

Newsmen and photographers took up vigil near the hijacked train

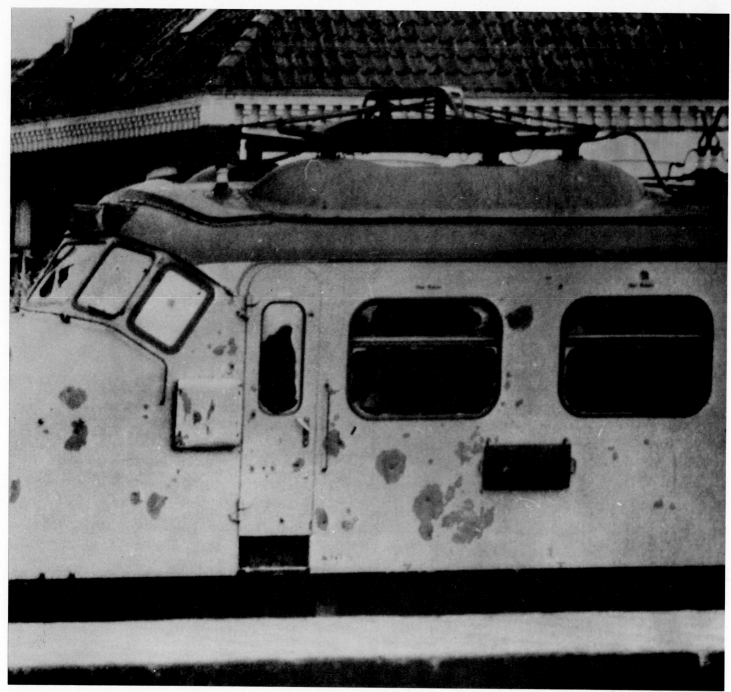

Dutch forces who stormed the train riddled the front part with bullets

plosive devices were detonated on the ground and smoke was laid across the area, while heavy machine guns raked the compartments occupied by most of the terrorists.

The marines stormed aboard the train through holes blasted by plastic explosives. Loud-speakers warned the hostages to lie low. Janneke Wiegers was wrestled to her feet by a terrorist. She screamed, struggled away from him and flung herself back on the floor. Two other hostages—one a girl—died in the shooting.

At about 5 a.m., Dutch reporters heard a crisp message come over the military radio in English: "mission completed." A little later, as the smoke cleared, there was another message, this time in Dutch: "Well done boys."

In the uneasy aftermath of the sieges, Den Uyl said the use of military force was seen as a defeat but he declared it had been "the only way out." Manusama said the government's actions were "understandable" in the circumstances.

The bodies of the six slain terrorists were returned to their families and buried in a common grave on a day of solemn ritual, attended by 5,000 Moluccans from all over the Netherlands. The Dutch turned to the task of repairing relations with the Moluccan community, shocked and bristling in their separate neighborhoods.

Leaders of Moluccan youth groups gave differing assessments of the future.

"The misery will now be endless," declared Etty Apponno, president of the young Moluccan Liberation Front.

Noes Solisa, a 24-year-old militant leader, said however that terror acts on Dutch soil had "little political value."

"If there are to be any more violent actions, they'll have to take place on Indonesian soil," he declared. "that's where the struggle is."

Jailhouse Fire in Columbia, Tenn. Killed 42 Persons

Eleven days later, a blaze in a Danbury, Conn. prison claimed five lives

"These are the only items allowed—cigarettes," said a sign over the doorway of the Maury County Jail in Columbia, Tenn., where 42 persons died in a jailhouse fire June 26.

It was a hot Sunday afternoon as visitors walked into the one-story whitewashed jail, built in 1964 to be escapeproof and fireproof. Nearly 60 prisoners were being held in the jail, most of them awaiting trial. Although each inmate was limited to two visitors, guards didn't have the heart to turn away several families—including five kinfolk of Buck Rowland, charged with armed robbery and attempted murder. But guards did shut the doors shortly before 2 p.m., refusing to let a few latecomers in.

Down the corridor from the cell in which Rowland visited with his wife and her family was the isolation cell in which deputies had housed a troublesome juvenile. Andy Zinmer, a 16-year-old with a history of setting or threatening to set fires, had been picked up the day before as a fugitive from Wisconsin, where he had fled from a home for emotionally disturbed boys.

Deputies placed him in the jail's only padded cell after he flooded his holding cell by stopping up the toilet, then flushing it repeatedly. Just before the visiting hour ended, Zinmer begged for a smoke and a teen-aged visitor passed a lighted cigarette through a slot in the metal door. Moments later, Chief Deputy Bob Farmer heard Zinmer scream, "Help me! I'm on fire!"

Farmer and another deputy ran for the cell, unlocked it, and pulled the juvenile out. Then oxygen hit the smoldering padding. "A sharp torch-like flame came down the hall from the other end," said Garry A. Pillow, who was in the workhouse room at the center of the jail. "It came down that hall like it was gas or something."

Panic broke out. Some visitors standing in the corridor surged for the exit, colliding with the deputy who had keys to unlock the seven main cell doors. The keyring was jarred loose and lost underfoot. As guards pawed frantically for it, inmates in the central workhouse room fought to wet themselves down in two tiny shower stalls.

The bodies of some of the Tennessee fire victims lay in a parking lot awaiting transfer to funeral homes

A guard stood by the padded cell in the Maury County jail

"It got dark and black," said Pillow. "No one answered when we shouted. All I could hear was praying, moaning and screaming. I put a towel over my face and kept laying there in the shower stall and the next thing I knew, I woke up in the emergency room."

By the time guards remembered a duplicate set of keys hanging in the dispatcher's office, the smoke was too thick and the heat too great to get back into the building. Joined by firemen a few minutes later, deputies smashed two man-sized holes through the cement walls and began pulling out the victims.

At the Maury County Hospital, a basement storage room was quickly converted to a makeshift morgue. A delegation of ministers met stunned relatives of the victims near the morgue and took them to private rooms to adjust to grim realities. Ten hearses lined up in a muddy construction field behind the hospital to take the bodies of 34 inmates and eight visitors to funeral homes, once identifications were complete and next-of-kin notified, a process which took only hours.

Officials of the state fire marshal's office immediately launched an investigation of the cell which they had believed fireproof. They found the padding was fire-retardant polyvinal chloride over four inches of foam rubber. Tom Copeland, state fire protection chief, said the padding would be difficult to ignite, "but if it gets a significant amount of energy, it can really take off and be dangerous." Autopsies of some of the victims revealed unusually high levels of cyanide, indicating that the roiling black smoke was laced with the deadly gas.

Later, officials of the Mississippi firm which produced some of the foam rubber told The Associated Press that it had not been treated with fire-retardant chemicals. In Chattanooga, Hamilton County Sheriff Jerry Pitts read about the fire and called for a torch. He went into his jail's isolation cell, ignited the padding, extinguished it, and ordered jailors to replace the padding with a safer material.

After his own investigation, State Fire Marshal Gene Hartsook deplored inadequate fire codes for penal institutions, covered in two pages of the 16-volume set of state regulations. Hartsook said the codes did not require the jail

118

to have sprinkler systems or a smoke detection device. And he said polyurethane mattresses are used in virtually every jail in the country except in Connecticut, where the material was banned after a jail fire similar to Maury County's; state corrections officials said they would consider switching to a fire-retardant cotton mattress.

Maury County officials charged Zinmer with arson and said they would seek to have him tried as an adult. They speculated the youth had punctured the polyvinal padding and ignited the foam rubber. Zinmer, hospitalized with burns, was not told of the deaths for several weeks. His attorney later said Zinmer was "very sorry the whole thing happened but he feels he did not set the fire deliberately."

Two days after the blaze, the first of the mass funerals was held. "This is the greatest tragedy this town and county has known in our generation," said the Rev. Glen Mayfield, looking down at the coffins of Mrs. Herman Anderson, her sons Marvin and Billy Anderson, her daughter Margaret Rowland, and her son-in-law Frank Irwin Jr. They had been visiting Buck Rowland, whose funeral was held separately. After the service, the caskets were placed in five gunmetal gray hearses and driven through the Tennessee hills to two cemeteries.

"I've lost more than anyone," said Carolyn Irwin, standing beside her husband's coffin.

But she didn't comprehend the enormity of her loss until after she came home from the cemetery. "I have four children of my own left without a father and my sister (Mrs. Rowland) had three, including a 2-year-old," she said then. "And I have nothing, no husband and no job, and it's going to take me every penny I'll ever have to pay for the funeral expenses. But I can't break down—I've got seven children to take care of now."

Eleven days after the Tennessee disaster, flames erupted at 1:15 a.m. in a federal prison in Danbury, Conn., killing five inmates and injuring 71 persons. Confusion surrounded the origins. At first officials said arson caused the blaze which sent toxic fumes racing through the prison July 7. But several days later, they said the word arson had been used too loosely. A prison official said the blaze could have been accidental.

Prisoners interviewed in blackened Cell Block G denied that the fire had been set. They expressed belief it had been caused by faulty wiring. One prisoner said a door to their cell block was locked, trapping them for several minutes and that they had to break down the door to escape.

Acting Warden Anthony Young said a key apparently had broken off in a door between cells. He added that he did not know if there had been a delay in evacuating inmates.

Fire left these smoke-stained walls at the prison in Danbury, Conn., where a second jailhouse fire broke out

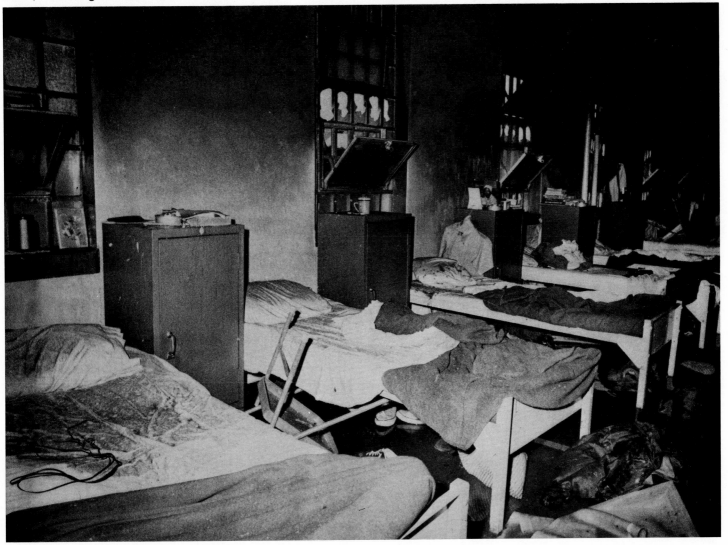

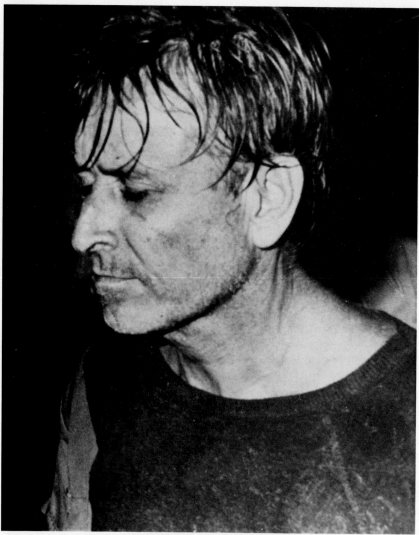

James Earl Ray after his capture

JAMES EARL RAY ELUDED SEARCHERS TWO DAYS AFTER SCALING PRISON WALL

The first reports came from Brushy Mountain State Prison as darkness settled over the hills of eastern Tennessee. Jail break! Six men, four of them convicted killers, had gone over the wall at dusk.

But there was more news from Tennessee on June 10 as authorities prepared one of the biggest manhunts in the state's history. James Earl Ray was among the fugitivies from Brushy, a maximum security prison from which no man had ever successfully escaped. Ray, who confessed — then recanted — to firing the rifle shot that killed Dr. Martin Luther King Jr. Ray, the center of conspiracy theories, rumors and debates for years. Ray, the escape artist.

According to prison officials, there were some 250 inmates in the exercise yard around 8 p.m. They were peacefully enjoying the waning hour of the day: talking, playing basketball. A mock fight broke out without warning, one prisoner feigned a broken leg and in the confusion seven men broke for the wall.

One of the convicts had a ladder made of plumbing hardware that he'd built on the sly in the prison shop. It hooked neatly over the lowest point of the wall — a depression near one corner. One by one, they scaled the two-foot-thick, 14-foot-high stone barrier.

They snaked under a wire charged with 2,300 volts and dropped down the other side to disappear into the rugged country around the prison. The escaping prisoners were aided by approaching nightfall and the fact that No. 8 tower was unmanned, officials said later.

120 Nobody noticed the break until the last man was on top of the wall. Then a guard in No. 3 tower spotted him from more than 100 yards and opened fire with a .22-caliber rifle. Jerry Wayne Ward, a 34-year-old bank robber doing a 40-year stretch, fell, wounded twice but only superficially. Prison guards had no trouble recapturing him. The chase was on for the other six.

The area was sealed off. Roadblocks were set up on all routes from the prison near the Kentucky border. Bloodhounds were put on the trails of the fleeing prisoners. About 125 prison guards, FBI agents, agents of the Tennessee Bureau of Criminal Identification and sheriff's deputies from at least six counties took off after the state's most notorious prisoner and his companions.

In fact, authorities were unsure if the six had escaped together, or if some had just seen the ladder and decided to run for it. They were certain, however, that the other five would soon want to ditch Ray because he was too recognizable. They searched in helicopters, on foot, in cars. Carefully, methodically, they combed the snake-infested woods and rockpiles of the hilly country.

Ray was known among the cons at Brushy as an escape artist. He was, in fact, a fugitive from the Missouri State Penitentiary when King was gunned down on April 4, 1968 on a balcony of the Lorraine Motel in Memphis. He was arrested in London after eluding one of the most extensive manhunts in history.

The 49-year-old criminal tried twice to escape from Brushy Mountain before the June breakout. In May, 1971, he left a dummy in his bunk and tried to get out through a steam tunnel. Then in February of the following year, he was caught trying to cut a hole in a ceiling.

Ray had also attempted other means of winning freedom. He recanted his guilty plea, claiming he was an unwitting part of a conspiracy and had not fired the round that killed King. He appealed his case but was not allowed to stand trial. And he invited members of a congressional assassinations committee to interview him about the alleged conspiracy. Ray's attorney said he was getting desperate in his desire to be free.

Of the five men who broke out when Ray did, three were serving murder sentences. David Lee Powell, 27, was doing 100 years for first-degree murder. Earl Hill Jr., 34, a former cellmate of Ray, was serving two life terms plus 27 years for first-degree murder, assault with attempt to murder and rape. Douglas Shelton, 32, worked in the prison shop and was believed to have been the creator of the escape ladder. He was serving 65 years for first-degree murder, felonious assault and grand larceny.

Larry Edward Hacker was 32, in jail for 28 years on convictions of burglary, safecracking and robbery. Donald Ray Caylor, 24, would be 75 before his term for assault with a deadly weapon, armed robbery and escape ran its course.

About 2 p.m. the day after the breakout, Saturday, June 11, searchers aboard a helicopter spotted Powell crossing a field. He gave up quietly. By 3 a.m. Sunday, five of the six were back at Brushy. Shelton was brought in the next day and joined the others in "administrative segregation," one step short of solitary confinement.

Penalty for the escape attempt would be another five years at most added to each sentence. That would make Ray's term 104 years.

Ray had been sniffed out by a bloodhound named Sandy. Looking "like a pig wallowing in a sty," he was dragged from his hiding place beneath a pile of leaves. When asked later what he had done on the lam, Ray merely replied, "Nothing."

TWO SHOT TO DEATH, MORE THAN 100 HURT, IN CHICAGO FLARE-UP

The temperature was about 97 degrees when members of Chicago's 80,000-member Puerto Rican community finished up a Puerto Rican Independence Day parade.

A celebration got under way that June 4 in the Humboldt Park area, a section centered on a half-mile business strip three miles northwest of Chicago's downtown. Tension began to build and then there was a flare-up between police and about 3,000 persons—most of them youths. Soon there was fighting, burning and looting and by the time the situation had calmed down after two steamy nights two men had been shot to death, at least 133 persons, including 57 police officers, were injured, and 154 arrested.

At the height of the disturbance, thousands of rock-and-beer-can-tossing demonstrators forced about 200 policemen to withdraw for reinforcements and prevented fire trucks from reaching a burning three-story building. Calm finally was restored by club-swinging officers, backed by mounted police.

Humboldt Park once was a Polish and Italian community, and most of the two and three-story apartment buildings in it date to the 1920s. In 1977, the area was mostly Puerto Rican, with blacks making another sizeable group. Unemployment was high—officially 9 percent compared to 6.6 percent for Chicago as a whole. But officials conceded the real figure probably was higher than the statistics indicated.

Said an official at the neighborhood's Roberto Clemente High School: "I don't think enough is being done by the city for a neighborhood as restless as this one. It would be nice if someone listened to them (the community)."

THE PRESIDENT'S WIFE VISITED SEVEN COUNTRIES

"I've got a lot of information for you," said Rosalynn Carter.

The President's wife was speaking to Secretary of State Cyrus Vance at the White House June 13. The information she had she had collected during a two-week tour of seven Caribbean and Latin American countries. In an hour-and-a-half discussion, Vance and Mrs. Carter "talked with great specificity about what she had discussed with the leaders of the countries she had visited," said Mary Hoyt, Mrs. Carter's press secretary. "They went over her entire agenda and a whole range of issues, country by country."

President Carter sent his wife on the trip May 30. Her first stop was Jamaica where she told more than 300 U.S. Embassy employees and Jamaican guests, "I had a very informative and productive session wih Prime Minister (Michael) Manley this afternoon and I can take his hopes and dreams back to Jimmy."

In Costa Rica, she met privately with President Daniel Oduber and other Costa Rican officials, and her press secretary said the topics discussed included human rights, Cuba, Panama and an upcoming conference of the Organization of American States.

Mayor Sixto Duran Ballan gave her the keys to the city of Quito, Ecuador. Later, as she met with members of the Supreme Electoral Tribunal, a group of students threw stones and bricks and shouted anti-American slogans in the first show of hostility on her tour.

After arriving in Peru, Mrs. Carter said she discussed Peruvian arms purchases "extensively" with President Francisco Morales Bermudez, who had bought large amounts of Soviet weapons. She said later that U.S.-Peruvian relations were a "close friendship" and said the Peruvian leader gave her a copy of the government's plan that called for a return to civilian rule by 1980. "Jimmy," she said, "would be very interested to read it."

Three days of her tour were spent in Brazil. Her visit came as university students throughout the country were demonstrating against 13 years of military rule. After meeting with President Ernesto Geisel, Mrs. Carter was asked about human rights at a news conference. She was asked if her failure to talk about government repression and student unrest was a "cop out" and she replied:

"No, not at all. You presume a determination that I am not in a position to make. I have stressed here as well as I have stressed in every other country the deep, deep commitment we have to human rights."

In reply to another question, she said she had "glanced at briefly" a letter from university students which accused the military regime of arbitrary imprisonment and torture. She said she would deliver the letter to her husband, adding, "I'm sure he would be glad to receive the perspective on human rights of the students."

Later she met with two American churchmen who were arrested and reportedly beaten by Brazilian police. After the meeting, Mrs. Carter said, "I have a personal message from them. I have listened to their experience and sympathize with them and have a personal message to take back to my husband."

Moving on to Colombia, Mrs. Carter reviewed U.S.-Colombian relations with President Alfonso Lopez, and then flew to Venezuela where she said the United States and Venezuela "have many things in common, but I believe that that which most unites us is our worry about the individual and for individual liberty and dignity."

During her flight home, the First Lady told reporters her meetings with the leaders of the seven countries were "very, very good." She said no questions "went unanswered or slurred over—even when they knew it was not what I wanted to hear."

On arriving in Washington, she told the President: "They love you in the Caribbean and in Latin America."

Mrs. Rosalynn Carter waved after landing in Kingston, Jamaica

Also in JUNE . . .

VON BRAUN, PIONEER IN ROCKETRY, DIED AFTER LONG CAREER

To Americans, Wernner von Braun stood for triumphs in space. To Germans in the 1940s he stood for victories in rocket warfare.

Von Braun was best known for two achievements: the German V-2 rocket the Allies came to dread and the American Saturn rocket that led his adopted country to the moon. When he died in Alexandria, Va. June 16 at the age of 65, von Braun was hailed by the White House as "a man of bold vision." A eulogy by the National Space and Aeronautics Administration called him "a 20th century Columbus who pushed back the new frontiers of outer space."

The German-born scientist's value lay beyond his ability as an engineer and rocket designer. He also was a leader of men and a super-salesman for the space program.

Perhaps his most valuable contribution was made in 1945 near the end of World War II when he led 129 of Germany's rocket experts away from Adolf Hitler's V-2 rocket base at Peenemunde and surrendered them to the Americans rather than fall into the hands of the advancing Russians. He was then technical director at Peenemunde, and he and his group brought out several truckloads of V-2 parts.

The United States sent von Braun and his colleagues to Ft. Bliss, Tex., where they assembled and fired 70 V-2s in five years. In 1950, they were transferred to the Army's Redstone Arsenal in Huntsville, Ala., to develop America's first ballistic missile, the Redstone. That same year, they launched the first missile, a V-2 with a second stage—from the United States' new rocket base at Cape Canaveral, Fla.

Long before the Russians lofted Sputnik I Oct. 4, 1957, von Braun said his team had the capability to orbit a payload by putting an upper stage on the Redstone.

President Dwight D. Eisenhower turned him down on the grounds that the Redstone was a military rocket and he wanted to stress peaceful uses of space. Eisenhower ordered the development of a completely new rocket, the Vanguard, as a satellite launcher.

After Sputnik was launched, von Braun who had become

a U.S. citizen, pleaded with Defense Secretary Neil McElroy: "Vanguard will never make it. We have the hardware on the shelf. For God's sake turn us loose and let us do something. We can put up a satellite in 60 days."

When the first Vanguard exploded on its launch pad in December 1957, the nation was shocked and the von Braun team got its chance. On Jan. 31, 1958, a modified Redstone propelled Explorer I into orbit.

In 1960, von Braun and his team, now grown to 4,000 engineers and technicians, were transferred to the young space agency. A year later, Alan B. Shepard rode a Redstone and became America's first spaceman. Three weeks later President John F. Kennedy committed America to land a man on the moon and return him safely by 1970. Von Braun was told to build a rocket big enough for the job. The result was Saturn 5, a 36-story-tall behemoth capable of placing 140,000 pounds in earth orbit or sending the 110,000 pound Apollo spaceship to the moon.

Von Braun was in the Mission Control Center July 20, 1969, when Neil Armstrong and Edwin Aldrin planted the American flag on the moon. For the scientist, it was the realization of a longtime dream.

SPAIN HAD FIRST FREE ELECTIONS IN 41 YEARS

It was the first time in 41 years the people of Spain were able to vote in free parliamentary elections and an estimated 80 percent of the nation's 23 million eligible voters turned out to do just that.

Long queues built up outside polling stations in the early morning hours of June 15. Large families piled out of small cars or buses and read newspapers or snapped photographs while quietly waiting in line. There were incidents, however. Four policemen and three civilians were injured in 13 bombings across the nation—most of which took place before the polls opened. And another half-dozen unexploded bombs were found at polling places.

The election was held to name a 350-seat Chamber of Deputies and to pick 207 senators to replace a rubber-stamp legislature appointed by dictator Francisco Franco before his death 19 months earlier. The last free elections were held in Spain in 1936—five months before the nation's civil war. After winning the war in 1939, Franco banned all elections and political parties except his own.

The voters had more than 5,000 candidates from 157 parties to chose from. When the ballots were counted, Premier Adolfo Suarez's moderate coalition was the major victor, garnering 276 seats and 30 percent of the vote.

EXIT OF PODGORNY VAULTED BREZHNEV TO NEW SOVIET POWER PEAK

Nikolai Podgorny, longtime survivor in the Soviet political arena, had pushed his way up from manager of a Ukrainian sugar plant to the presidency of the Soviet Union. Then on May 24, the 74-year-old Communist leader was suddenly on the way out. A month later, the same surprise reshuffle vaulted Soviet Communist Party leader Leonid I. Brezhnev to a new pinnacle of power.

In the best Soviet tradition, Podgorny had come from a working-class family in the small Ukrainian town of Karlovka. A teen-ager during the Bolshevik revolution, he took an active role in Communist Youth League activities, according to his official biography.

Podgorny survived the Stalinist purges of the 1930s, running sugar plants in the Ukraine and rose to deputy commissar of the state's food industry in 1939. Later he moved to Moscow and during World War II directed Russia's Food Industry Institute.

After the war, Podgorny developed an alliance with fellow Ukrainian Nikita Khrushchev then head of the Ukrain's Communist Party. He backed Khrushchev when the latter

Rocket pioneer Wernher von Braun

became national party leader in 1953 after the death of Stalin. Notably he supported Khrushchev's ouster of the "anti-party group" in 1957.

But Podgorny was adept at sensing the winds of political change and reportedly opposed Khrushchev at the 1964 Central Committee meeting that dumped the Soviet chief from power.

Analysts wondered whether Podgorny was elevated to the presidency in 1965 because Brezhnev considered him a threat to his own move to top leadership of the party. But why, they asked, did he suddenly step aside?

There had been no outward signs in the spring of 1977 of political ill health for Podgorny. In March he took a political tour of southern Africa which was well publicized and a week before his stepdown he played an active role in a visit to the Soviet Union of Finnish President Urho Kekkonen.

Then on May 24, the Communist Party newspaper Pravda carried a terse two-line report that Podgorny had been removed from the powerful Communist Party Politburo.

The move touched off a flurry of speculation in Western circles as to the future of the Soviet presidency, an illustrious but largely ceremonious post.

One answer came June 16 when the Supreme Soviet named Brezhnev new chief of state as well as party chief, thus making him the first person in Soviet Russia to hold both posts at once.

The parliament was told that Podgorny had wanted to step down "in connection with his retirement on pension" and he was voted out without further discussion.

It was seen as the biggest Kremlin power shuffle since Khrushchev was ousted as premier and party leader in 1964.

The appointment of 70-year-old Brezhnev to a second high post came as a surprise to some since his health had been a subject of speculation in Moscow for many months. It was also noted, however, that Brezhnev's takeover as head of state was the latest step in a gradual process of aggrandizement since he had become party leader in 1964.

People recalled Brezhnev's designation in 1976 as a marshal, the dedication of a bronze bust to him in his home town of Dneprodzerzhinsk and the public observance of his 70th birthday. All three events were celebrated as major state occasions with splashy press coverage.

Above, exit Nikolai Podgorny

Left, Jockey Jean Cruguet sat in the Belmont winner's circle astride Seattle Slew, winner of the Triple Crown

WINDOWLEDGE RESCUE

This dramatic sequence showing the rescue of an elderly woman teetering on a fourth-floor ledge was taken by Stanley Forman of the Boston Herald American

Above, while 92-year-old Chin Goon stood on the narrow ledge of a building in Boston's Chinatown section, fireman Robert Markey, 51, edged toward her. Bottom left, bracing himself, Markey grabbed the woman as she threatened to jump. Bottom right, the danger was finally over and tensions relaxed as Markey carried Chin Goon to safety

MITCHELL BEGAN SENTENCE AT ALABAMA PRISON CAMP

As the dark blue Cadillac drew up at the minimum security prison at Maxwell Air Force Base in Alabama, a man emerged from the back seat. He was greeted by jeering inmates at the federal prison camp.

"They got you now, Big John. They got you now," several prisoners shouted. Yelled others, "You're nothing but another convict with a number now."

The man they were shouting at was John N. Mitchell, once the nation's top law enforcement officer. Mitchell, who was attorney general under President Richard M. Nixon, had arrived to begin a sentence for his role in the Watergate cover-up. The 63-year-old Mitchell spent about 45 minutes being processed and then was led into the compound, having changed from his dark green pinstriped suit into prison-issued light brown shirt and dark brown pants.

Mitchell, the 25th person to be imprisoned in connection with Watergate, began his 2½-to-8-year term June 22—a day after former White House chief of staff H.R. Haldeman entered a similar institution for the same length of time in California. The two, along with former Nixon domestic adviser John D. Ehrlichman, who already was in prison in Arizona, were convicted for conspiracy to obstruct justice, obstruction of justice and lying under oath.

FOR THE RECORD

CANONIZED. Bishop John Nepomucene Neumann of Philadelphia. Pope Paul VI elevated him to sainthood June 19, paying "honor to the Catholic Church in the United States as it inscribes its first son in the roll of saints." Neumann, born in Bohemia in 1811, went to the United States when he was 25 and worked as a priest among German-speaking immigrants before he was named bishop of Philadelphia at age 41. He died of exhaustion on a city street eight years later. The Pope canonized Bishop Neumann, America's first male saint, before 25,000 people in St. Peter's Square in Vatican City. Among those at the ceremony were two Pennsylvania men and an Italian woman who the church believes owe their lives to the spiritual intercession of Philadelphia's "little bishop."

ELECTED. Tanzanian Bishop Josiah Kibira as president of the Lutheran World Federation. Bishop Kirbira was elected June 24 by delegates—representing 53 million Lutherans—to the sixth assembly of the Federation during a two-week conference in Dar es Salaam, Tanzania. He became the first black president of the assembly, following seven years service as chairman of the LWF Commission for Church Cooperation. He told a news conference after his election that one of his main concerns was to bring about greater church involvement in secular affairs.

WINNER. The Republican People's Party of former Premier Bulent Ecevic emerged June 7 as the winner of Turkey's national elections. With 95 percent of the votes counted, the Republican People's Party had 41.3 percent of the vote and Premier Suleyman Demirel's ruling Justice Party had 37.12 percent. However, Ecevit resigned as prime minister July 3 after his center-left government was defeated on its first vote of confidence in Parliament by a coalition of rightist parties.

AGREED ON. A new pact between Britain and the United States on aviation rights which replaced an agreement in effect since 1946. The new pact was arrived at in London June 22 and gave England valuable route concession while also maintaining the United States' refusal to allow rigid controls which would diminish competition among airlines. The pact averted a possible rupture in air service that would have affected some 3,000 passengers a day on flights between the United States and Britain.

Ben Skora of Palos Hills, Ill. developed a robot which he programmed to serve as a waiter, butler and dog walker among other things

JULY

Blackout Paralyzed New York and Touched Off Looting Orgy

The crisis cost the city millions of dollars and businesses even more

At 9:34 p.m. on Wednesday, July 13, New York City was plunged floundering into a darkness that would not lift for 25 hours.

Before the juice began to flow again, the stores of 2,000 mostly small entrepreneurs in the city's gray ghettoes would be gutted by looters. More than 500 policemen would be injured. With the streets and sidewalks of the city's impoverished neighborhoods carpeted with splintered glass and debris, nearly 4,000 of their residents would be packed into the city's jails.

It proved far more costly to the city than the 1965 blackout which blanketed New York for more than 10 hours and cast a pall of darkness over most of the Northeastern United States and parts of Canada.

The financially-strapped city government would spend millions of dollars in overtime wages to police and fire employees. Businesses would lose tens of millions in profits.

Consolidated Edison Co. later laid the blame on human error and "an act of God." But it began with a muggy, heavy July heat that dropped on New York City like a suffocating quilt.

The generators of Consolidated Edison were already straining to power millions of air conditioners and elevators and refrigerators in the heat of that Wednesday evening when a brooding summer storm moving over the city's norther suburbs loosed two vagrant bolts of lightning that cut the flow of power into the city from upstate New York.

The senior dispatcher of the New York Power Pool in Guilderland, N.Y., called the systems operator in the city. The system can't keep it up, he said, and every option has been exhausted. "Shed some load," he suggested black out a few neighborhoods.

But the New York man didn't know that a line dubbed W93, a major power carrier, had been knocked out of service. He postponed shedding some load.

And at 9:34 p.m., the straining generators shuddered, then failed. Elevators stopped. Subway trains creaked to a halt. Millions of air conditioners sputtered, then died. The lights flickered, failed, and darkness fell on the 8.5 million people who live in New York City and its Westchester County suburbs.

At 9:40 p.m., a cop at the desk in a Brooklyn precinct picked up the jangling telephone. "They're coming across Bushwick Avenue like buffalo," a woman's voice said. The looting had begun.

Thousands of people had fled the suffocating heat of their homes and were on the streets of the city's impoverished neighborhoods when the lights went out. In the darkness, many of them milled together in front of the heavy metal riot gates that protect store windows and doors, then moved to wrench the metal away. Before dawn's light filtered through the ghettoes of Harlem, Bedford-Stuyvesant, and Brooklyn, the mobs would lob bricks through windows of 2,000 stores, carrying away booty in shopping carts, on dollies, in stolen cars.

Police Commissioner Michael Codd ordered all officers to report to the nearest precinct, but at 4 a.m., 10,000 of the city's 25,000 cops had not clocked in. The police who patrolled the ghettoes found themselves nearly powerless before the ransacking crowds. "For every two we can collar, there are forty more waiting for us to drive away," said one cop.

Across the city, store-owners converged on their property. Many pulled their cars up onto the sidewalk, illuminating the shopfront with headlights. Ned Krohn rushed to his furniture store on Harlem's 125th Street, and planted himself, shotgun across his knees, in the doorway. He was to spend all the hours of darkness there.

The ghetto night was heavy with shrill echoing burglar alarms, crashing glass, discordant sirens and a haze of smoke from dozens of fires. Before the dawn flickered over the streets the fire department would respond to 1,500 alarms. They fought 400 fires in the darkness of the night, 40 of them serious.

The darkness was different in the city's more prosperous neighborhoods, though in some ways no better. The blackout there sparked a lively celebration—a demonstration of New Yorkers' renowned capacity to cope. But as the hours inched past, the party faded into a wearying ordeal.

Apartment dwellers poured into the streets. Hundreds of impromptu parties gathered on the stoops of hundreds of streets as the curious shared warm bottles of beer and listened to blackout reports over transistor radios.

127

Radio station WMCA issued an appeal for a car battery to spark an emergency generator and a telephone company supervisor, William McCormick, climbed 14 flights to deliver the battery.

A common first reaction to the sudden darkness was to call a friend, compare notes. While the system never collapsed, the telephone company confirmed that lines were so jammed that some customers had to wait a while for a dial tone. Calls to Dial-A-Joke declined, during the blackout hours, by 25 percent.

Citizens with a penchant for order descended on street intersections to unsnarl the chaos that began when the traffic lights failed. One 10-year-old girl directed traffic with a flashlight and such aplomb that even police cars obeyed her signals.

With refrigerators and ovens out of commission, restaurant and bar owners produced candles and, in some cases, drinks on the house by candlelight.

At Roseland, the orchestra played "Dancing in the Dark" for celebrants who did just that. A harpist at the Metropolitan Opera played the same number as a disappointed audience filed out after the darkness interrupted a performance by the National Ballet of Canada.

Most Broadway theatre patrons were ushered into the streets midway through the second act. At one theatre, where "Otherwise Engaged" was playing, the stagehands formed a flashlight brigade to substitute for the blackened spotlights and the show went on.

Bernice Saks was eating Chinese food with her two children in a restaurant. "We just went right on eating," she said. "You know how New Yorkers are. It's like everything is cool and someone's going to take care of us. We just expected the candles to arrive, and they did."

A dozen policemen and passersby took care of the riders on Coney Island's 150-foot-high Wonder Wheel, cranking the great 200-ton wheel around by hand, slowly bringing the dangling riders back to earth.

City subway dispatchers, meantime, had noticed the erratic current and managed to bring all but seven trains into stations before the power failed altogether. Some commuters, en route to Rye or Yonkers, were less fortunate, as their trains ground to a halt midway between stations.

Cabbies around the city did a bang-up business, sometimes at inflated prices, until the blackout came home to them too: The gas pumps couldn't pump.

Hotels were overwhelmed with stranded tourists and suburbanites begging for a bed at virtually any price. The Hilton had to break through a wall to rescue eight patrons from a stalled elevator; the posh Waldorf-Astoria estimated that it lost $100,000 to customers who walked away without paying their bills.

As the night wore on, adventurous spirits

wore thin. New Yorkers abiding in prestigious luxury high rise apartment buildings found themselves stranded on the 23rd floor, or the 38th, or the 54th. And, along with the lights and the elevator, the water pumps failed.

The American Society for the Prevention of Cruelty to Animals later reported a rash of heat prostration among pampered pets whose owners walked them down endless stairs and then back up again. One woman carried her dog and cat down five flights, then back up again.

At the city's hospitals, the art of coping was elevated to the point of life-saving. At Metropolitan Hospital an alternative generator failed; staffers hauled heavy mechanically operated generators up eleven flights to intensive care. At Bellevue Hospital, the backup system folded, so doctors and nurses used hand-pumped air bags to keep critically ill patients breathing. Babies were delivered by flashlights' glow.

At Radio City Music Hall, 400 patrons slept in the lobby. So it was throughout the city, as the darkness deepened toward morning. In hotel lobbies and stairways, on park benches, in the cavernous railroad stations, people set adrift by the blackout tried to sleep it away.

In Harlem, a cop taking a break from the ebbing and flowing mobs of looters on 125th Street pulled on a cigarette, grinned wearily and said, "Well, it's only a couple of hours now, until dawn."

The precinct stations steadily filled with confiscated booty jewelery, televisions, appliances and such mundane miscellany as diapers. Their lockups were packed shoulder-to-shoulder with looters arrested on the streets.

In the Bronx, 50 new cars in one dealer's lot were hotwired and driven away. Youngsters wrestled with shopping carts loaded with food and heisted goods. In Harlem, an elderly volunteer auxiliary policeman watched as an old woman leaned stiffly through the jagged glass of a store window and emerged slowly, clutching a single shoe. In Spanish Harlem, looters lit a candle on the counter of a shoe store, then systematically rifled the stock.

On 125th Street, a youngster shouted, "It's Christmas in July."

As night edged toward morning, Mayor Abraham Beame issued angry statements from City Hall. He denounced Con Ed, the utility that promised the blackout of 1965 could never happen again; he denounced looters; he praised police restraint; he urged New Yorkers to stay home when dawn finally broke, and they did.

New York was closed for business on Thursday, July 14 — Bastille Day. The thin morning light filtered through a ghost town. The dark narrow streets of the financial district were deserted — except for knots of security guards, who sat on the stoops of the banks and investment houses and played gin rummy. In the residential neighborhoods, New Yorkers emerged again, this time carrying jars, scavenging for water.

And they asked each other when it would end.

In the city's ghettoes, sporadic looting con-

Firemen fought a blaze above a row of looted stores in Brooklyn

tinued as residents picked through the debris strewn over the streets and sidewalks in the night. The weary police shuttled prisoners from the precincts to the crowded jails; when the jails were filled, the city re-opened the Tombs, the cavernous old prison closed in 1974.

Thursday was a weary day, wilted and wrinkled by the heat, tired of the adventure of coping. Con Ed mobilized all its 23,000 employees and waged weary war in its complex underground cable network. Slowly, as the temperature rose and the hours inched past, the juice began again to flow. Refrigerators started, then begun to hum, elevators moved, first in Midtown, the Lower East Side, the Upper West Side.

The last to see their power restored were 44,600 residents of the Upper East Side. One of those residents is Mayor Abraham Beame. It was 25 hours after the blackout began.

The jails were packed, and the overcrowding and heat created nightmarish conditions for 3,800 persons arrested for looting during the hours of darkness. The courts worked overtime to arraign them, but the process was not completed until the following week.

Four agencies—the Federal Power Commission, the New York State Public Service Commission, a panel named by Mayor Beame and Con Ed—all began investigations of the utility to find out what went wrong. Con Ed announced immediately that it would beef up its control center staff, initiate a storm-watch system and explore the possibility of increasing its load-shedding capability.

In Harlem, businessmen picked their way through the debris that was once a livelihood and shook their heads. "I haven't got insurance to cover this," the owner of a gutted pawnshop said. "Harlem is a lousy insurance risk."

The Small Business Administration made loans; Mayor Beame created a grant-fund with donations.

The looting provoked vigorous debate among city residents: The looters are common criminals taking advantage of a crisis, said one side; they are impoverished, unemployed people whose desperation was unleashed by the darkness, said the other.

Nearly a month later, the federal government would give the city $2 million to hire 2,000 temporary workers to clean up the debris and return the ghettoes to commercial normalcy. Police reinforcements had to be called in when more than 8,000 applicants deluged seven city job centers, seeking one of the conveted 30-day jobs. One city official characterized the incident as "a fight over crumbs."

But on Friday, July 15, New Yorkers arose as usual, elevatored down to the street, subwayed to air conditioned offices, dined to piped music in dim restaurant light, and, for a day or so at least, grinned with surprised delight when everything worked.

New York's skyline presented a somber appearance during the blackout

Israel's Socialist Government Defeated By The Likud Group

The election marked a personal triumph for hardliner Menahem Begin after 29 years in the opposition

As June 21 was just a few minutes old, Menahem Begin strode to the rostrum in Israel's Parliament, the Knesset, to be sworn in as prime minister along with his new, strongly nationalist and religious cabinet. For Begin, this was an immense personal triumph after being in the opposition throughout Israel's 29-year history.

For Israel, it was a political earthquake as Begin's Likud bloc, with its free-enterprise ideology, supplanted the socialism of the long-ruling Labor Party. For the rest of the world, Begin was a known hard-liner with little inclination to compromise with the Arabs. His election appeared to be a detour on the difficult path to peace in the troubled Middle East. However, Begin and President Carter sounded a cordial note during talks in Washington in July.

The fine points of the Arab-Israeli dispute, however, were little discussed in the long Israeli election campaign. The economy, corruption and national morale were bigger issues. In December 1976, Prime Minister Yitzhak Rabin had dissolved his ruling coalition after an official welcoming ceremony for three U.S.-made F-15 jet fighters had dragged on past sundown on Friday, thus technically desecrating the Jewish Sabbath. Two cabinet ministers, members of the National Religious Party, abstained in a vote of confidence over the issue. Though Rabin's government survived the confidence ballot, he dismantled his cabinet himself by expelling the NRP for its breach of coalition discipline. Rabin's move looked clever in early political analysis. His Labor Party had an effective machine which would take the bigger advantage from having elections in May instead of in November as scheduled. This would head off budding challenges from new parties headed by war heroes Yigael Yadin and Ariel Sharon. Begin's Likud figured to get its usual 30 percent of the vote.

Or so the analysis went. But Yitzhak Rabin's political world soon began to crumble. His housing minister, Avraham Ofer, committed suicide in January after he was accused in the press of corruption. This was neither the first scandal to afflict the Labor Party nor the last. In October 1976, Asher Yadlin, a key financial figure in the party, had been indicted for fraud and bribery. At the time he had been nominated by Rabin to head the Central Bank of Israel, a position akin to that held in the United States by the head of the Federal Reserve Board. When Yadlin was convicted in February, he said he had helped the Labor Party gather illegal contributions—an accusation which did not lead to further criminal charges but still tarnished Rabin's party in the eyes of the electorate.

In March Rabin went to the United States for consultations on Mideast peace with President Carter. A Tel Aviv newsman learned that Rabin's wife, Leah, had visited a bank in Washington, and soon a new scandal touched Rabin personally. It was illegal for Israelis to hold bank accounts abroad without permission, and it turned out that Yitzhak and Leah Rabin were co-holders of a Washington account which contained as much as $21,000. Rabin resigned his party leadership three weeks later and paid a small fine. His wife, as the actual operator of the account, was fined $26,000.

Defense Minister Shimon Peres, who had lost a close party leadership contest with Rabin in February, assumed the top position in the Labor Party and tried to revive the flagging campaign. But things had progressed to a point where a Likud figure could say, "Voters here are beginning to realize that a Likud government is not unthinkable."

This feeling was fueled partly by electoral events outside Israel—Jimmy Carter's outsider victory, Indira Gandhi's defeat in India and the Socialists' loss in Sweden. Israel's economic situation also was conducive to thinking that a change was in order. Labor unrest was high. Inflation was 38 percent in 1976. Personal incomes also went up exactly 38 percent, according to official statistics, as the government pumped money into the economy and refused to allow any unemployment; the traditional cure for inflation.

"We live for today," a Tel Aviv housewife said, exemplifying the attitude which can develop after three years of inflation topping 30 percent. Her husband had fought in two of Israel's four wars and now her eldest daughter was drafted into the army. "If the Arabs don't get us, the prices will be out of sight next year, so we do as much as we can with our money—now," she said.

A Likud voter for many years, she was happy with the election result. A Haifa woman, a war

The new prime minister, Menahem Begin

widow, had voted Likud for the first time. "I did it to punish Labor," she said. "But I certainly didn't expect Likud to win. My son is in the army, and he said his buddies believed the Likud was more likely to bring war, but they voted Likud too. We just couldn't go on the way things were going."

Analysts felt the election was more of a defeat for Labor than a victory for Likud. Labor had had 51 seats in the outgoing 120-seat Knesset, and plunged to 32. The Likud edged up from 39 to 42 seats, while the new Democratic Movement for Change won 15 seats in its first electoral try. The NRP rose from 10 seats to 12, and two ultrareligious parties stayed steady at five seats.

The election could not be described as a ringing endorsement of Menahem Begin, but it made his Likud the largest of the dozen parties in the Knesset. With 35 percent of the voters behind him, Begin started to change the face of Israel. The day after the election he did what no member of the defeated Labor government would have done: he traveled to a technically illegal Jewish settlement in the heart of the occupied West Bank of the Jordan River and proclaimed it "liberated land of Israel."

This brought wintry comment from Washington, which held that the West Bank should be returned to Arab rule in a Mideast peace settlement. Washington also viewed Jewish settlements in the occupied territories as obstacles to peace. Begin told the settlers his view: "Let there be many more settlements like this."

Meanwhile he formed a slim majority of 63

seats in the Knesset with his Likud, the NRP, an ultrareligious party, and a handful of independents. The new cabinet gave early attention to the economy. Planned government spending was reduced and there were cuts in subsidies that resulted in 25 percent hikes in controlled prices of basic commodities such as bread, dairy products, frozen chicken, gasoline and electricity.

The price increases (a gallon of gasoline, for instance, rose from $1.71 to $2.10) met with hardly a murmur of protest. The public's attention happened to be riveted on the prime minister, who was in Washington in Mid-July holding important talks with President Carter on the Middle East situation. Observers in Israel had nothing but admiration for Begin's sense of timing with the potentially troublesome economic moves.

Begin's party had lost eight parliamentary elections before his 1977 upset. Indeed, he had been the opposition leader for so long that some had difficulty in taking him seriously. But Begin was a serious man. His life story was jammed with incidents which, if taken individually, would be enough to crush many people.

His book, "The Revolt," the story of the role played by the Irgun Zvai Leumi (National Army Organization) in Israel's fight for independence, opened with Begin, a man of 28 in 1941, under interrogation by Soviet secret police. Deemed a "danger to society" for his Zionist views, he was soon at hard labor in a Siberian work camp.

Begin's youth in Poland had not been easy.

132

Left, Begin's predecessor, Yitzhak Rabin, was still chief of government when he greeted a crowd in Philadelphia during a visit to the United States. Below, Rabin's wife, Leah, appeared in a Tel Aviv court where she pleaded guilty to charges that she held two illegal bank accounts in the United States

Poverty and anti-Semitism were constant companions. Their impact, however, was lessened by his warm family life and by his early fixation on the idea of Palestine as a homeland for the Jewish people. The German invasion consumed his parents as two of the Nazi holocaust's six million victims, but Begin was by then in Siberia, far from the Nazis. His Polish citizenship won him his freedom in 1942, and he went to Palestine, then ruled by Britain.

Begin quickly became commander of the Irgun, whose underground fighters attacked British troops and police stations. Begin aimed at driving the British out of Palestine, even though the mainstream of Jewish thought at the time favored cooperation with Britain during World War II. The British responded by calling Begin the "number one terrorist" and posting a reward of 10,000 pounds sterling for his capture.

Helped by his modest, clerkish looks and sometimes disguising himself as a rabbi, Begin stayed underground and avoided arrest. He emerged from hiding in 1948 with the proclamation of the Jewish state, and his Irgun fighters joined their former rivals, the Hagana, in Israel's regular army.

Soon came an incident for which Begin was still remembered in the Arab world. An Irgun detachment attacked the Arab village of Deir Yassin and 250 Arabs were killed. Foreign investigators claimed many of the deaths were wanton murders, but Begin said all the deaths came in justifiable combat actions.

The toll in Deir Yassin contributed to panic among Palestinian Arabs, many of whom fled. Today these Arabs are the Palestinian refugees; with their children and grandchildren they number some 1.6 million and are one of the toughest factors in the Middle East equation.

While Arabs remembered Begin as "the man of Deir Yassin," many Israelis recall the "Altalena Affair" when they thought of Begin's role in the fight for independence. The Altalena was a ship loaded with arms bought by the Irgun. It arrived off Israel's coast soon after the Irgun merged with the Hagana, and Irgun men began to unload its cargo. Many Israelis believe the weapons were to be used in a Begin-led putsch against David Ben-Gurion, Israel's first premier. Begin vehemently denied this, saying he wanted much of the weaponry to go to Irgun units in the regular army. Gunfire broke out between a Hagana force on shore and the Irgun men unloading the ship. There were some casualties, and more followed when the ship, with Begin on board the next day, was grounded and set afire by Jewish troops.

This was the stuff of which Begin's reputation was born and grew in the first 29 years of Israel's independence. But he showed, at age 63 when he took over the government, that he had forgiven some of the old differences with his fellow Israelis. He named war hero Moshe Dayan of the Labor Party as foreign minister. Dayan, during part of the Altalena affair, commanded the Hagana force attacking Begin's men.

Demonstrators stood outside Begin's home protesting his plan to name Moshe Dayan as foreign minister

134

Ten-Week War In Zaire Sent Reverberations Throughout Black Africa

The 10-week long war in a faraway corner of Zaire produced few deaths and little destruction, but reverberations and political implications from the mini-conflict rippled into the statehouses of most black African nations.

The concepts of territorial integrity and foreign intervention, of concern to many African leaders, were at issue in Shaba Province, formerly Katanga, in southern Zaire, when an unknown number of ex-Katanga gendarmes launched an attack March 8 from camps in Angola. The invading force was estimated at less than 2,000 men.

The invaders, primarily from the Lunda tribe which predominates in Shaba, overran one-third of the copper-rich province before their drive stopped some 12 miles from the mining center at Kolwezi. Poorly trained and disciplined government troops fled in panic as the ex-gendarmes approached. Few government deaths were reported. Most casualities came from mines. No rebel bodies were produced. Diplomats estimated less than 50 government troops died during the war.

The attack caught President Mobutu Sese Seko with his popularity at a low ebb in the former Belgian Congo. Early in the conflict, pro-Mobutu rallies in Kinshasa were poorly attended and during one spectacle a large portion of the crowd left as the president was speaking. From that low point, Mobutu rallied Western and African support for his drive to oust the rebels and keep Zaire's boundaries intact.

With the help of 1,500 Morrocan troops, 55 Egyptian Air Force technicians and a French airlift of equipment and arms, Mobutu and his 40,000-man armed forces repulsed the rebels. The United States speeded up delivery of military supplies already on order from Zaire, but did not provide new arms aid. The Kinshasa government claimed there was major fighting, but journalists, barred from the conflict area unless on a tour with Mobutu, could not substantiate those claims. The government offered several times to fly reporters to view rebel bodies but in each case the 1,000-mile trip from Kinshasa to Shaba was cancelled.

At the town of Kasaji, a Canadian medical missionary said he saw 200 government bodies but reporters visiting the town in mid-May, a day after it was captured, reported almost no signs of fighting. A government communique issued in August said 219 military men were

An officer of the Zaire army, right, held a captured document as two wounded men, left, described as rebels were put on display along with confiscated weapons at a news conference in Kinshasa

dead or missing as a result of the war. No figure was given for rebel dead.

Morrocan and Egyptian intervention established the principle of one African nation going to the aid of another in order to preserve its territorial boundries. No African nation criticized the intervention. Zaire claimed the ex-Katangans, who fled to Angola in the early 1960's after an abortive revolt, were supplied and supported by Cuban advisors based in Angola. Angola denied the claim saying the conflict was an internal matter between the government and dissident refugees.

Most African nations watched silently as the conflict went through the stages, of rout, inter-African intervention and counter-offensive ending with Mobutu's personal prestige in Zaire and Africa greater then before the war. After the victory, Mobutu felt secure enough to call for presidential elections in October, the first since he seized power in a coup in 1965.

In August Mobutu began a purge of civilian officials and had his number two man, Foreign Minister Nguza Karl-I-Bond, a Lunda, arrested for treason. While most African nations declined comment on Zaire, moderate states in French-speaking West Africa supported Mobutu. In Africa, tribalism and liberation groups formed along ethnic lines threatened a number of countries. During the Organization of African Unity, conference in Gabon in July, some Afri-

can leaders criticized the Soviet Union for its policy of arming insurgent groups and not providing economic or development aid. The Cubans were blamed in private by some Africans for supporting the Katangan rebels at the OAU conference. Others said Angola backed the attack as a way to get even with Mobutu for harboring anti-government insurgents in Zaire.

During the Angolan Civil War, which ended in March 1976 when 12,000 Cuban troops arrived, Mobutu supported one of the losing factions. Some observers thought the Angolans were getting even by supporting the Kantangans.

The roots of the Shaba conflict went back to 1960, shortly after Zaire gained independence from Belgium. Zaire, with an estimated 25 million people in 47 major tribes and few educated people, was unprepared for independence.

Moise Tshombe, the Lunda chief in Katanga at independence, attempted to secede but the revolt was put down by United Nations troops and white mercenaries. The Katangans fled to Angola. Tshombe died mysteriously in Algeria several years after his revolt.

"Every country in Africa has its Katanga," a European ambassador in Kinshasa said. Mobutu sent emisarries to various neighboring states with the message that it would set a dangerous precedent if African nations supported exile or rebel movements against neighboring states.

The conflict had its light moments when the government announced it had sent several hundred "elite pygmy bowmen" into the fray. Later, a government spokesman said the pygmies were withdrawn because their training was "not right." At the same time, Zaire asked the United States for military aid to include $60,000 worth of Coca Cola. The U.S. State Department said it would not provide the drink that Zaire could buy it on the commercial market.

While American efforts were limited to speeding up delivery of already committed non-lethal military gear, France provided air force transport planes to ferry Morrocan troops to Shaba Province. It also sent about 20 advisors and logistic technicians to iron out supply and transport bottlenecks. The strong stand was apparently a signal to other French-speaking African nations that France would aid countries threatened by insurgents or by Soviet or Cuban meddling. That view was reinforced in Paris July 14, Bastille Day, when President Valery Giscard d'Estaing reviewed a military parade that highlighted units that had served or were serving in Africa or were connected with the Zaire conflict.

While Mobutu won the war, the battle for the economy lay ahead. His country owed other nations or international banks nearly $3 billion because of spending and policies in the early 1970's when the price of copper, the principal export, was high.

During July in Paris, 11 countries that had loaned money to Zaire held a meeting and agreed to stretch out Zaire's debt repayment schedule.

Under an agreement reached in 1976 creditor governments agreed to reschedule over a 10-year period 85 percent of Zaire's repayment debts falling due in 1975–76. The July meeting, according to a French banking source, offered Zaire "easier conditions" but did not elaborate.

Uganda's President Idi Amin who reportedly offered Mobutu military aid was a luncheon guest of the president of Zaire

137

Johnstown and Other Pennsylvania Areas Hard Hit by Floods

The rains came to Pennsylvania with a vengeance in July.

"The radio was just forecasting heavy rains," recalled Rita Jo Searle. "I didn't think anything of it because it had rained four or five nights without a letup." But then the radio station began to warn motorists to stay off the roads.

Then, after an hours-long rainfall which dumped up to 7.75 inches of rain on seven western Pennsylvania counties, disaster struck

Johnstown's city hall was reflected in the flood waters

July 20. It was especially bad at the city of Johnstown, where a heavy storm seemed to sit over the city of 41,000 for several hours without moving.

Triggered by the seemingly endless flow of water, dams in several areas wore away sending a tide of rushing water and debris plowing into communities. Johnstown—which became a synonym for disaster after 2,200 persons died in an 1889 flood when a dam burst and nearly wiped out the city—was buried under eight feet of water in some places before the flood waters began to recede.

Rita Jo Searle and her finance Richard Stantz were watching the *Rookies* on television in an apartment in the Solomon Homes project in Johnstown when the power went off. The clock stopped at 11:52. Rita switched her radio to battery power. Richard went to the window. "I said, 'My God, look at the cars floating down Solomon Street. There are people screaming for help.' They were going so swift no one could help them." By 12:30, cars were tumbling down Solomon Street, a slight incline.

Ray Stantz, Richard's brother, and his wife, Deborah, who also lived in the same apartment complex, went out to see if they could help anyone. Across Solomon Street, water swept away a house, taking a man and his son with it.

"We couldn't get across the street," Ray recalled. "Boulders were rolling down the river and Solomon Street. The water was washing telephone poles and trees down. After one boulder the size of a house came down, half the highway collapsed. The water changed course and started washing other buildings out."

As dawn broke, the floodwaters began to recede. A photographer who had been in downtown Johnstown as the waters began to pull back said, "There are cars on top of cars. There are cars with their rear ends stacked up on parking meters. Police are riding around in the back of four-wheel drive trucks with shotguns on their laps and the streets are just covered in about a foot of thick mud."

Johnstown—which had been hit by another flood in 1936 that killed 20 people—was without roads. They had been washed away. Communication and powers lines in the town also were blacked out. Days after the flooding, the death toll was placed at more than 70 persons and damage was estimated at $200 million.

Thousands of persons were evacuated from their homes as rescue operations got under way. Many others were stranded because res-

cuers could not reach them, although some eventually were plucked from rooftops by National Guardsmen in helicopters.

Lee Hospital, one of three in Johnstown, had no electricity and food stored in the basement was flooded. Patients were taken from the first floor to higher levels. Life support machines were run on batteries and dry ice was used to keep blood supplies chilled. Doctors broke into the coffee shop to get patients bread and orange juice.

As sun broke through the clouds the afternoon of July 20 and the water continued to recede, cleanup operations moved forward. Remarked a reporter, "There's mud and slime everwhere. The miserable part is that, now that the rain is over, the cleanup comes next, and it's going to be a mess." Many residents who had been evacuated returned home, wading through muck, past heaps of broken furniture and other debris, surveyed the damage and then returned to emergency housing. In the sky, helicopters flitted busily back and forth

bringing in supplies of water, fuel and medicine and taking out flood victims. And in some areas, police grimly poked billy clubs into waist-high mud the consistency of pudding in the search for bodies.

Recovery was hampered by a lack of drinking water as the temperature climbed into the 80s. "My little girl is crying for water," said one man. "Everybody said not to give her the flood water, but I did anyway. She had to have something to drink." John Comey, a spokesman for the state Council for Civil defense, said emergency water equipment, pumps and pipe were brought in. He remarked that "in two days, it's ironic that you go from the most serious pressing problem—an excess of water—to a very critical shortage of usable water either through contamination or because the water works have been knocked out."

The flood brought out the best in most, but as in any disasters there were predators. Wrote reporter Toby Sweeney in the Johnstown Tribune-Democrat: "I watched as eight young peo-

A youngster, standing amid the remains of his flood-ravaged home, waved an American flag

139

ple ransacked the windows of United Jewelers, loading up their confederates with items as if on a Christmas shopping spree." And even as water swirled waist-high in the street, looters systematically cleaned out a camera shop. A jewelry store window was shattered by a thrown brick. A woman charged three stranded women $10 each to drive them to safety and said she was sorry her son was not around to take advantage of the money to be made.

Associated Press writer Harry F. Rosenthal surveyed stricken Johnstown and wrote:

"After the flood, there is mud. Mud in the streets, mud in cars, mud in stores and houses and churches. Mud is everywhere. The flood is gone. But the mud that rushes down hillsides with flood water and debris remains to be cleaned up. The business district of Johnstown, a day after the flood, is deserted, except for the workers shoveling mud and the store owners and their employees come to see for the first time what the water wrought.

"Donald Szabo, owner of the Burger King on Main Street, looked over his devastated business and shrugged his shoulders. 'We have insurance, of course, but not flood insurance. It was available, but in a flood-free city you don't need it.'

"Johnstown got the name of flood-free city after the dams were built—a sloganized assurance to the people that the devastating waters of 1889 and 1936 could never again engulf the city."

On July 21, President Carter declared the region a federal disaster area and soon after representatives of the Federal Disaster Assistance Administration were setting up machinery to get help for flood victims. It was not long before life-saving efforts in the ravaged area turned to rebuilding activity.

Johnstown's Central Park Square looked like a battlefield after the flood waters surged through town

KU KLUX KLANSMEN WERE ROUGHED UP AT TWO RALLIES

It was sunset on July 2 in President Carter's hometown of Plains, Ga., and the Ku Klux Klan was holding an outdoor rally. Imperial Wizard Bill Wilkinson was addressing a crowd of about 250 when a gray Jaguar sports car hurtled through the crowd and slammed into the speaker's platform. The impact injured 32 persons, 19 of whom required hospital treatment, many for broken bones.

The incident caught the crowd by surprise. Said Wilkinson later: "I was on the speaker's stand, speaking when I heard someone shout. I heard a car engine roar, accelerating very rapidly. The next thing I knew, I was lying on the ground. People were covering on the car, of course, and about this time, my security people hustled me away."

When the dust had settled, police arrested the driver, Buddy D. Cochran, a 30-year-old mechanic, living in Americus, about 10 miles from Plains.

"He said he had a lot of black friends and was going to get even with Wilkinson for what he was saying about the blacks," said Sheriff Randy Howard.

Cochran was arraigned before Justice of the Peace John Southwell who called the incident "one of the most uncalled-for offenses I've ever seen." Said he, "It's just a miracle that 10 or 15 people didn't die."

Authorities said Cochran who reportedly admitted having had "three, maybe six beers," was judged legally drunk at the time of the incident and had apparently been aiming his car at the imperial wizard. Officials estimated that the car had been racing at between 50 and 60 miles an hour when it struck the stand.

Arraigned on 19 charges of aggravated battery, Cochran said only "Yes sir" when asked if he understood them. Each charge carried a maximum penalty of 10 years imprisonment.

Two days after the Plains incident, the Klan ran into more violent opposition, this time in Ohio. In the state capital of Columbus, Klansmen were beginning a rally on the steps outside the Statehouse. The local imperial wizard, Dale R. Reusch, was launching into his speech when a man in the audience called out "You talk sick." By this time about 100 protestors were massed in front of the speakers' platform atop the steps. Those in front taunted Reusch and his bodyguards. Klansmen responded by swinging flagstaffs like baseball bats.

"We will go on with the rally, regardless of the agitation." said Reusch. That is as far as he got. He was drowned out by a chant of "Ku Klux Klan, scum of the land."

Reusch was hit and hurled to the ground by fist-swinging demonstrators. Stripped of his purple hooded uniform, he was spat upon and hit by eggs. He was treated at the scene for facial lacerations. Highway Patrol troopers moved in and ended the melee. They arrested three persons.

Asked what his message would have been had he been able to make himself heard, Reusch said "The Klan will fight. We will kill. We will have to rebuild."

Dale Reusch, Ohio Imperial Wizard, was rushed by a demonstrators during a Ku Klux Klan rally in Columbus

141

Fan Yuan-yen, Communist Chinese air force squadron commander, after he defected to Taiwan

COMMUNIST CHINESE PILOT DEFECTED TO TAIWAN WITH MIG-19

Squadron Cmdr. Fan Yuan-yen of the Communist Chinese air force took off in his MIG-19 from Chintsiang military air field in Fukien Province at about noon July 7, ostensibly to make a routine inspection flight. But the 41-year-old airman had other ideas.

Once airborne, Fan headed his jet fighter toward Taiwan. Streaking across the 100-mile Formosa Strait, the airman landed safely at Tainan on the southwest coast of Taiwan and requested asylum.

The Nationalists welcomed the news of Fan's defection; the first by a Red Chinese pilot since 1965. Radio stations played martial music between special news flashes and people set off firecrackers in the streets.

Some Nationalist leaders said privately they found it ironic that the defection should occur just when the United States was pursuing a new China policy which aimed at normal relations with Peking.

The day after his defection, Fan appeared at a news conference and renounced his Communist Party membership. He claimed that the 800 million people on the Chinese mainland led "a very miserable life." The Chinese hierarchy, he asserted, was "unstable" and the purged "gang of four" still wielded some influence.

Fan declared that there had recently been unrest in Fukien province's Chintsiang and Potien areas and that the army had been called out to quell the disturbances.

Fan claimed that many tenant farmers were resisting the government and that there had been a number of outbreaks in Fukien. He said farmers were especially hard up with "nothing much to eat or put on."

Fan told newsmen he had fled to tell the world about true conditions in China. Said he; "there is no freedom, no democracy on the Chinese continent. What foreigners have seen in mainland China was untrue . . . you will never know how many people were slain by the Communists."

Fan, who left a wife and three children behind, brought Chinese defense information with him, according to military sources. Asked by newsmen whether he carried "important documents," the flier would only say he had brought material he needed for his flight. The MIG-19 he escaped in was an outmoded craft that offered little to Western intelligence.

Whatever Fan brought was apparently gratifying to Nationalist authorities. Informed sources said the defector would collect a government reward of $560,000.

NINE SLAIN IN THE WORST MASS MURDER IN CONNECTICUT'S HISTORY

The first hint of trouble in the wood frame bungalow in Prospect, Conn., was the smell of smoke and the snap of flames at about 4 a.m. July 22. But by the time neighbors were aroused, it was too hot to enter the blazing house where Mrs. Cheryl Beaudoin lay with her seven children and a young cousin.

It took firemen 10 minutes to cool down the inferno enough to venture inside. What they saw horrifed them—charred bodies, some bound, some hit on the head. Authorities described it as the worst mass murder in the history of Connecticut.

The only survivor in the immediate family was the father, Frederick Beaudoin, 33. He had been working the midnight to 7 a.m. shift at a plant in nearby New Haven when the fire broke out.

Neighbors remembered Beaudoin, his 29-year-old wife and their brood of children as a happy, loving family.

"What could they possibly done wrong to deserve this?" said Joseph Paolino, who lived across the street and discovered the fire. He said flames were already shooting from the little one-story house in the pleasant suburb of Waterbury when he reached the scene.

"I opened the back door and got driven back by a blast of heat," he recalled. "Then the picture window blew out."

Mrs. Paolino said the Beaudoins were friendly and polite to neighbors and caused no trouble. Another neighbor, Theresa Bainer, recalled that the mother was always with the children. On Sundays at St. Anthony's Roman Catholic church "You'd see her in church with the whole pew filled with her kids."

Police said they were questioning 50 persons in connection with the fire. Then a day later they made an arrest. Lorne Acquin, a 27-year-old ex-convict who had been reared with Frederick Beaudoin as a foster child, was picked up and charged with nine counts of murder. He had been a frequent guest and baby sitter at the house where the bodies were found.

Acquin was a Canadian Indian. His foster mother, Mrs. Marion Beaudoin, said he had been born out of wedlock. "We loved him," she said. "He was part of our family." She said he had turned to crime after their own home was devastated by fire 14 years earlier, perhaps because of fear that the financially depressed family would turn him out. Then began a string of arrests for robbing the homes of neighbors, she recalled.

Mrs. Beaudoin described Acquin as a reflective sort who "was like a shell into himself." She added reflectively "He just liked to think and you don't know what was on his mind."

Hong Kong City at night as viewed from the island's peak took on an air of oriental mystery

VETERAN CORRESPONDENT WAS JAILED IN THE CENTRAL AFRICAN EMPIRE

What had been intended as a pleasant evening out to dinner instead marked the beginning of "four weeks of hell" for veteran Associated Press foreign correspondent Michael Goldsmith while on assignment in the Central African Empire.

Goldsmith was arrested July 14 and during the 30 days he was imprisoned he was beaten and shackled hand and foot at times. As Goldsmith later recalled, after his release Aug. 14, "On the way to dinner with Grant Smith, deputy chief of mission at the American Embassy in Bangui, capital of the Central African Empire, I stopped off first at my hotel. . . . As I entered the hotel lobby, four plainclothes policemen, all armed, arrested me. Thus began four weeks of hell . . . that included six days of agony handcuffed and often chained in a windowless cell, with wounds over my body untreated and badly infected, clothed only in underpants, and with a rough concrete slab for a bed."

The 55-year-old Goldsmith, a British subject said he was told he had been arrested on suspicion of being a spy for white-ruled South Africa and had been sent to the Central African Empire, formerly French Equatorial Africa, as contact man for a South African agent there. He said the accusation apparently resulted from his filing a dispatch from Bangui to Johannesburg which dealt with Emperor Bokassa I, ruler of the country since taking power in a military coup in 1966, and his plans for his coronation Dec. 4.

The AP man said that during his imprisonment he was not aware that Jonathan Randal, an American citizen and correspondent for The Washington Post, had been arrested at about the same time as he but was released a week later.

Shortly after he was picked up, Goldsmith said, he was taken before Bokassa, "Who, without any warning or explanation or attempt to interrogate me, struck me across the forehead with a heavy stick, causing a severe wound. This was at the royal palace in Berengo, about 70 miles southwest of Bangui, in the presence of at least one of his sons and several members of his entourage. After I was struck, I was kicked unconscious by members of his group." He said he was then returned to Bangui and kept handcuffed and chained in a small cell while his wounds went unattended for several days and became seriously infected. Goldsmith said his treatment improved after about a week when he got medical attention, his fetters were removed and he was given satisfactory meals.

On Aug. 12, Goldsmith was taken before Bokassa who "told me of an exchange of messages he had had with my wife, Roxanne, in Paris, and said he had been touched by her appeal that he release me on humanitarian grounds. He said he had ordered that I leave the country on the next plane, Sunday, Aug. 14, shortly before midnight. I spent the rest of Friday and all of Saturday in Bangui under close police surveillance. . . . On Sunday, I was once again taken back to Berengo, for a final three-hour confrontation with the emperor, who then permitted me to leave the country for France."

143

CWO Glenn Schwanke, copter copilot (left), was turned over to the Americans at Panmunjom

U.S.-NORTH KOREA KEPT COOL DESPITE ATTACK ON HELICOPTER

The U.S. Army Chinook helicopter was ferrying construction materials to an observation post south of Korea's buffer zone when it strayed about 3½ miles into North Korean territory. Within minutes the chopper had been shot down, with three crewmen killed and a fourth captured.

In previous years, such an incident would have prompted the Americans to scramble fighter plans and start positioning warships. But this time, both the United States and South Korea went out of their way to keep tensions low.

The official North Korea News Agency called the shooting down of the chopper an "unhappy incident". It said northern troops had been "compelled to fire" because the Americans had tried to evade capture. The last time an American aircraft had been shot down over the North, the North Koreans had termed it "a provocation by U.S. imperialists."

President Carter matched the moderate tone of the Communists. He said the helicopter had crossed into North Korea by mistake and added that "our primary interest" was to prevent confrontation.

Later, at a meeting of the U.S. and North Korean negotiators on the Military Armistice Commission, the Communists said they had decided to settle the incident "leniently" to "avoid a complicated situation."

Three days after the incident, the North Koreans released the surviving co-pilot, Warrant Officer Glenn M.Schwanke, who was described by a U.S. millitary spokesman as in "excellent condition", with minor scratches on his face. It also released the bodies of the three victims, identifed as CWO Joseph A. Miles, the pilot; and Sgts. Robert C. Haynes and Ron Wells.

During the 24 years since the end of the Korean War, there had been five reported incidents involving U.S. military planes and North Korea. In previous cases, North Korea had often waited weeks before even informing the U.S. that there were survivors. And it had taken as much as one year to negotiate the release of the dead or the survivors.

North Korea's response this time was seen as an attempt to soften the image of rock-hard militancy at a time when Carter had said he would withdraw 33,000 U.S. ground troops from Korea. The United States announced July 26, however, that the bulk of the American troops would remain in Korea until the final year of the planned withdrawal, scheduled for 1982. Washington said that it had acted in response to a plea by the South Korean government.

GUNMAN HIJACKED BUS, KILLED TWO HOSTAGES IN A NINE-HOUR ORDEAL

The regular afternoon run of the sleek Vermont Transit liner began peacefully enough on July 4, as the 47-foot silver bus pulled out of New York City's Port Authority terminal and headed north. By that night two persons aboard would be dead, two wounded and nearly two dozen others shaken by a nine-hour ordeal.

The bus was proceeding through the Bronx when the violence began. Suddenly Luis Robinson, a 26-year-old seaman from Panama, jumped up in the aisle and pointed a gun at John McGavern, 50-year-old librarian at the University of Hartford, Conn. He fired and the bullet passed through McGavern's neck. The rest of the passengers sat in mute terror, as Robinson ordered bus driver Norman Bozick to head for holiday-jammed Kennedy Airport.

The gunman told McGavern to lie down on the first row of seats, saying "if you live until we get to Kennedy, you can go."

On arrival at the airport, the gunman ordered Bozick to ram the bus through a security fence. The big vehicle careened onto the runways, where McGavern was dumped onto the tarmac.

A woman passenger tried to subdue Robinson with a karate chop. He responded by firing a shot which killed Mrs. Nettie Blassberg of Greenfield, Mass. Bozick, the driver, then jumped at the gunman and was killed with a second bullet. Both bodies were hurled onto the airport pavement.

Robinson ordered 17-year-old Bruce Deboer of East Hartford to take over the wheel of the bus, the largest thing the youth had ever driven.

Finally the bus was parked behind a terminal and for more than five hours, the hijacker negotiated with authories. He demanded $6 million in cash and a plane that could fly him to Cuba.

Some of the children aboard were released in small groups during the long hours of waiting in small groups.

At around 7 p.m., Jimmy Lo, a Hong Kong businessman aboard the bus apparently decided to make a break for freedom. He was felled with a blast in the chest and taken to the hospital in serious condition.

The final hours of the bizarre drama were enacted with the bus roaming from one end of the field to the other, with Deboer behind the wheel. Twice that day, the airport was closed and planes were diverted or told to circle above.

After nightfall, the hijacker ordered Deboer to back the bus up. He did not know how to and the result was another trip across the airport. This time police maneuvered the bus toward a corner and proceeded to ram the front end with an armored vehicle.

For nearly 10 minutes no sound came from the bus. When police tried to open the door, Robinson fired a single shot, but no one was hit. Seconds later, the doors burst open and sobbing hostages poured out gratefully embracing their rescuers.

Finally, at 11:30 p.m., Robinson walked off the bus with hands in the air.

FOR THE RECORD

SENTENCED. Two of the Croatian nationalists who hijacked a Trans World Airline jet Sept. 10, 1976. Zvonko Busic and his wife, Julienne, were sentenced in Federal District Court in New York City July 20 to mandatory terms of life imprisonment for air piracy resulting in a death. Three others involved in the hijack were sentenced the following day to 30-year terms for air piracy and conspiracy. They were Petar Matanic, Frane Pesut, and Mark Vlasic. Brian Murray, a New York police officer, was killed while trying to defuse an explosive device the hijackers left in a subway station locker.

APPROVED. Vietnam's admission to United Nations membership by the Security Council. The council approved admission without a formal vote July 20. The action was expected since the United States had announced earlier in 1977 that it no longer would veto Hanoi's entry, following a Vietnamese promise to provide additional information about American servicemen listed as missing in the Vietnamese War. A Vietnamese representative said of the decision: "We consider that it is our right, long overdue, to be a member."

Mary Hemingway, widow of novelist Ernest Hemingway, made this expression as she listened to Cuban Prime Minister Fidel Castro. Mrs. Hemingway was in Cuba to assist in production of a movie about her late husband

145

AUGUST

Mother Nature Socked It To Americans Again With A Blistering Heat Wave

Still recovering from the coldest winter in memory, state after state began drying up

Mother Nature zapped weary Americans again only months after meting out the worst winter in memory. As summer got under way, state after state across the union began to dry up under a blistering sun. The heat wave began in July and was still baking the nation in August.

Heat joined with drought to drain the moisture from trees and pastures and reservoirs in Kansas, in California, in Alabama and many other states. A dry, windy heat whipped solitary sparks into raging forest fires.

In some areas, the drought had begun as long as three years ago. But the heat began, for most Americans, on July 11; in some areas it continued well into August.

The heat and lack of rain parched pastures and woodlands across the nation. Steadily, from the Pacific Northwest, across the Great Plains and down to the panhandle of Florida, America dried up.

On July 23, the National Weather Service's Palmer Index, designed to evaluate the scope and severity of unusually dry or wet weather, revealed that parts of 41 of the 48 contiguous states had drought conditions: Colorado's Rocky Mountain peaks were bare of snow.

In New York City, the heat on July 13 bred a demand for power that combined with a summer storm to knock out electrical power for 25 hours; in the corn and wheat fields of the Midwest, it sucked the last juices of life from the crops; and in California, where water was already being rationed, it dried up vital reserves.

In Thermal, Calif., it was 106 degrees on July 18. It was 102 degrees in Roanoke, Va., and 100 degrees in New York City.

And nearly everywhere, the heat created the perfect fuel—brittle trees and brush. Forest fires rampaged through millions of acres of cedar and pine, oak and ash.

By July 18, a fire racing through Utah's Ashley National Forest had killed three men. Flames decimated woodlands in Montana and Wyoming. Two fires in Maine's Baxter State Park chewed steadily through 2,000 of the park's 200,000 acres over a 10-day period.

Two days later, President Carter declared a drought emergency in 26 Alabama counties.

Two teenagers found relief from the heat by sitting in an ornamental fountain in New York City when the thermometer stood at 102 degrees

147

The coolest man in Newark during the hundred-degree spell was truck driver Les Jon who perched atop cakes of ice in an ice house as he waited for his truck to be loaded with the frosty blocks

The prolonged dry spell was killing moist pasturelands, and stock was wilting away. Beleaguered farmers battled a heavy outbreak of marauding insects.

Drought slowly turned the vast Okefenokee swamp on the Georgia-Florida border from a water wilderness into a wasteland, crisscrossed with shallow streams.

On July 21, authorities in California warned of "great danger" of fires because of the prolonged drought.

The weather gave weary firefighters a break on Monday, July 24, as rain and shifting winds helped them battle flames in the forests of Maine, parts of California and New Jersey. But new flames began to course through the woods of North Carolina. Within days, more than 950,000 acres of Alaska would go up in flames.

Fires in New Jersey had blackened more than 4,500 acres of pine, oak and cedar trees in three counties. The fires, said firefighters, were set by arsonists.

In the nation's cities, the searing heat created other problems.

Still reeling from the blackout, New York City suffocated under a damp, windless heat that held the city nearly motionless for more than a week. Children accustomed to frolicking in streams of cool water flowing from open fire hydrants were told there was not enough water any more.

New York City's death rate rose 10 percent during the hottest five days of the heat wave. In Long Island, a mental patient died after running a 107-degree fever without any sign of infection in a psychiatric hospital where the ward temperatures averaged 99 degrees.

Authorities said road service calls nearly doubled in the heat; health officials warned of the dangers of heat prostration; the city's utility company begged citizens to do without air conditioners and other conveniences as power demand reached record highs, then surpassed themselves.

The U.S. Geological Survey reported that water flows in some rivers and streams reached record lows during the month. Flows were reported at less than one-fourth of the normal amount at 23 of the survey's long-term monitoring stations. Nearly all streams west of the Mississippi River were down. The same thing was happening in Georgia and South Carolina. Total flow into the Chesapeake Bay dropped 11 percent during the month.

The Small Business Administration in Washington, already busy handing out disaster aid to victims of the winter's ravages took on extra help in August. The droughts and fires and a disastrous flood in Johnstown, Pa., overloaded the SBA system.

But farmers and ranchers were hardest hit. In the West, the worst drought since the dustbowl days of the 1930's hit first and held on longest. In the eight-state area that lies between the Rocky Mountains and the Missouri River, more than 13 million beef cattle had been sold off in drought sales by the end of 1976; 1977 was to be worse.

In the marginal land of the dustbowl, in Oklahoma, Kansas, Colorado and Nebraska, the subsoil moisture on which corn and soybeans and wheat depend was sucked away under the steady glare of the sun.

The Federal Reserve Bank in Kansas City,

148

which oversees lending institutions in the Great Plains states, reported that more than 65 percent of the farmers and ranchers in the area were asking for extensions or renewals of loan payments they were unable to make.

But, paradoxically, as July matured in to August, many major grain crops had not yet been severely affected by the parching heat. The Agriculture Department, in estimates disputed by some farmers and private forecasters, predicted a record corn crop and a near-record wheat harvest. The rains that fell, said the feds, came at the right times, and in the right places.

Low rivers halted barge traffic on the Willamette River outside the main channel in Portland, Ore. and the Oregon Water Resources Department reported an increase in drownings because people were wading farther to reach the water in rivers and lakes, then falling off into deep channels.

In Utah, the search for Big Foot, a giant man-beast believed to haunt the area, was suspended. Hikers in Utah's High Uintas Primitive Area reported seeing a beast they believed could be the elusive monster; but they couldn't find prints from the creature because the parched ground was too dry to carry a good imprint.

In California, the enduring drought turned to nightmare. The official warnings came true on July 27, when a kite wafting over the picturesque community of Santa Barbara touched a power line and set off a capricious blaze that was to destroy 234 homes.

Driven by winds of up to 60 miles an hour, it was a blaze that moved hungrily down one side of a block, then hopped erratically away, leaving some homes untouched alongside charred shells.

"You could see the fire leap a quarter of a mile at a time as it swept up Eucalyptus Hill, dotted with homes worth $250,000 and more. The tall eucalyptus trees, dried out after months of drought, exploded into flames, as though they were touched with small bombs," reported Wes Gallagher, who moved to Santa Barbara last year after retiring as President and General Manager of the Associated Press.

When the flames turned toward their home, the Gallaghers joined their neighbors and fled: "We encountered 30 or 40 more autos, loaded with children, clothing, dogs and cats. One little girl was leading her horse out of the fire area."

When Gallagher returned to his home by the early light "I found my neighbor's house 50 feet away burned to the ground, but mine was intact. The fire had swept around the knoll of the hill behind us and on the right side as well, but somehow, it left our house untouched."

Though California authorities asked for help, the beleaguered Federal Disaster Administration turned down their request for disaster relief in Santa Barbara. Damage was estimated at $35 million, but the FDAA said 90 percent of the fire victims were adequately insured.

By August the fires had spread throughout much of the West. On Aug. 8, nearly two million acres of forest and grassland were ablaze in an area covering every state west of the Rockies from Alaska on south.

At about this time, however, the heat began to break. The National Weather Service said a rare stagnant high pressure weather system had been at fault, stretching from the Mediterranean across the Atlantic to he Rockies, it eventually had to move. And finally it did.

In Santa Barbara, Calif., Mrs. Bettie Serena wept as she sat by the ruins of her home.

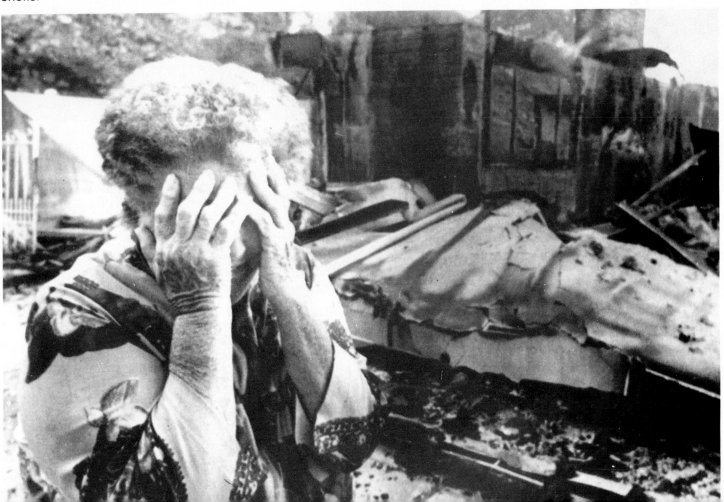

Nations Set Own 200-mile Limits As Fish Stocks Dwindled

When diplomats from 150 nations gathered late in May in New York for the long-running United Nations Law of the Sea Conference, they found that many countries had been busy writing their own laws of the sea, acting to regulate econom- ic activity on the oceans within 200 miles of their shores.

The scope of the new sea laws varied but stating who could fish within the new zones was an element common to all of them. Nine nations

A U.S. Coast Guard cutter stalked the Soviet trawler Taras Shevchenko off the coast of Nantucket in its first impoundment of a Russian boat under the U.S. 200-mile fishing limit

had passed such laws when the conference began in 1974; by mid-1977 more than 40, including the United States, had decided to go it alone. It was because of such a decision that the U.S. Coast Guard on March 1 began policing foreign fishing in a vastly expanded area half the size of the country's land mass and four times as big as its old 12-mile-limit jurisdiction.

There was never a question about the need for regulation. New England haddock, a staple of fish markets since colonial days, had become so scarce by the early 1970s that Americans were forbidden to seek them anywhere off the East Coast; the California and Maine sardine fisheries were commercially extinct; and many other fisheries were being depleted rapidly. One species, the herring, a fish that attracted many foreign fishermen to North American coastal waters, had virtually disappeared from the North Sea and the Atlantic Coast of Europe. Fishermen had learned all their migration points in that part of the world and had systematically fished them out.

Over-fishing emerged as a worldwide problem with the development after World War II of large ocean-going fleets able to go anywhere and haul out fish from any depth. Among the largest, most agressive fleets were those of Japan and the Soviet Union. The Russians were largely blamed for the sharp decline of haddock off New England and the Atlantic coast of Canada in the late 1960s. Experts say that only in its tuna fleet does the United States compare with these nations. Among the American fishermen, tuna fishermen, not surprisingly, have shown little enthusiasm for the new 200-mile limit.

The new American law's aims were to cut back drastically the harvest of fish threatened with extinction, replenish the stock of others depleted by overfishing and regulate strictly any ocean fishing within the 200-mile zone by the fleets of other nations.

The law gave priority to American fishermen out to 200 miles and established eight regional fishing councils to set quotas for various species of fish. The councils could also ban fishing in certain zones to permit depleted stocks to replenish themselves. Foreign vessels, after receiving a permit from the State Department

A Soviet trawler was photographed from a Royal Air Force plane as Britain began an aerial patrol after she declared a 200-mile limit

151

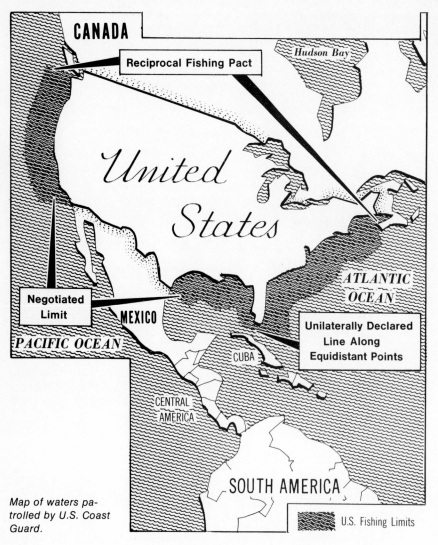

Map of waters patrolled by U.S. Coast Guard.

and paying a fee of up to $5,000, were to be allowed a fixed portion of the "optimum yield" not reserved for American fishermen. The regional councils also were to recommend quotas for foreign ships based on past records.

To handle its new responsibility, the Coast Guard was given one moth-balled seaplane tender, built in 1942, and eight long-range aircraft. It also got 41 new medium-range jets, but the extra ship and planes joined an aging hand-me-down fleet that included a number of seaplanes no longer able to land at sea.

With men and equipment thinly stretched, the Coast Guard approached its new mission, first of all, by relying on the good will of nations that had signed agreements to abide by the new 200-mile limit. But there was some doubt as to how well this would work when it became clear to the signatory nations just what they had agreed to. If cooperation failed, however, the service was prepared to act.

The first attempt to enforce the law came on March 29, during Secretary of State Cyrus R. Vance's visit to the Soviet Union, when the Coast Guard sought permission to seize the Soviet trawler Geroy Eltingina for illegally taking cod and pollock, both protected fish. The State Department blocked the seizure, fearing harm to the arms talks then under way in Moscow. In the next few days, Coast Guard

boarding parties found the Soviet trawler Yahan Sutiste carrying prohibited fish and the Sovremenny, a supply ship, lacking the required license, but State Department objections again prevailed when the service sought permission to seize the vessels.

The matter was taken to the White House, but the National Security Council only backed the State Department.

Then, on April 10, the Coast Guard, in quick succession, seized the 275-foot Soviet stern trawler Taras Shevchenko and a refrigerator transport, the Antanas Snechkus. The State Department then sent a stiff note to the Soviet Embassy complaining of "the number and seriousness of Soviet fishing violations."

On May 2, Alexander Gupalov, master of the Taras Shevchenko and the first man prosecuted under the new law, paid a $10,000 fine for catching more than his vessel's limit of river herring. Three days later, his government paid a $240,000 penalty to release the vessel and its 370-metric-ton catch of hake, herring and squid.

In diplomatic terms, the new 200-mile limit yielded perhaps its most positive results when the United States and Cuba, only 90 miles off the Florida mainland, announced on April 28 an agreement on fishing rights in their overlapping fishing zones as a result of their first direct negotiations in 16 years. Carter administration officials said they regarded the accord, which drew a boundary midway in the Straits of Florida between the two countries, as a limited step toward normal relations between Havana and Washington.

Negotiations with another neighbor, Canada, over rights in the 12,000-square-mile Gulf of Main proved much stickier, however, and it appeared that the boundary dispute might have to be decided by a third party to avoid severe diplomatic friction. The stalemate was caused by U.S. refusal to apply the Cuban formula to Canada and to set high seas boundaries equidistant from the shores of the two countries. The American argument the Canadians refused to accept was that Georges Bank, one of the world's richest fishing grounds, was an undersea extension of Cape Cod.

Together, negotiations with Canada and Cuba demonstrated two things: that fishing rights are only one consideration among many in the development of a United States policy on a law of the sea and that rational and politically workable methods of assuring future supplies of this fundamental source of food would be difficult for one nation to achieve, acting alone.

The initial U.S. rules under the 200-mile limit legislation, adopted by Congress in 1976 under heavy pressure from New England congressmen, might turn out to be short-lived. The possibility was widely noted that many of the new 200-mile limit laws might really be bargaining tactics for the U.N. sea law conference, which had been bogged down by controversies over undersea oil and mineral exploration and high seas freedom of navigation for naval vessels.

The fishing towns in Maine, California and other coastal areas of the United States that had seen better days also had to be viewed against a background of towns just like them all over the world. One sign of the times could be seen in Japan, which with the United States consumed 40 percent of the annual worldwide tuna catch. Fish prices there more than doubled in the months after the new fishing zones were established.

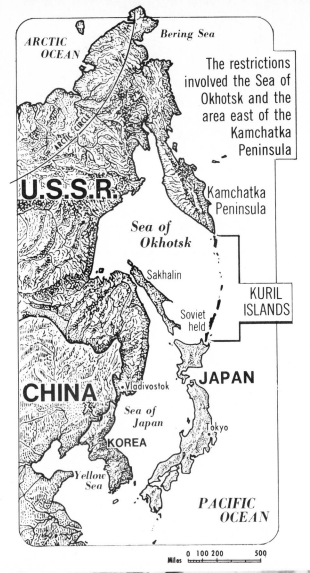

Map of Soviet 200-mile limit

The dispute over fishing limits had been going on for a long time. Here Canadian inspection officers prepared to board a Russian trawler several years ago.

Elvis Presley, Rock Superstar, Bowed Out at 42

The country boy with the swivel hips made millions of fans and millions of dollars

Elvis Presley, the one-time truck driver who became known as the *King of Rock 'n Roll,* was denounced by preachers as a tool of the devil. But millions of fans across the nation idolized him.

When the swivel-hipped, throaty baritone died of a heart ailment in his million-dollar mansion in Memphis, Tenn. on Aug. 16 at the age of 42, radio stations all over the country began playing nothing but old Presley records.

For 20 years, Presley had been an indelible part of the country's musical consciousness and for many of those years the object of teen-age adulation. His songs were tough and driving in the 1950s, a time when American popular music was still based on the tune smithing of Tin Pan Alley.

Presley's beginnings were inauspicious.

Elvis Presley performed in Philadelphia in 1957 in the gyrating fashion that shocked many and earned him the nickname "Elvis the pelvis"

Inducted into the Army, Elvis shouldered his duffle bag like any other G.I.

Upon graduation from high school in Memphis, he got a job as a truck driver for $35 a week. In 1953, he recorded his first song and paid $4 for the privilege. Other songs followed. Then in 1955 he walked into Sam Phillips' office at Sun Records to record *Blue Moon of Kentucky*. The recording became a hit and Presley was on his way. *Heartbreak Hotel* released in January 1956 was Presley's first big hit. It was one of 45 records he made that sold more than a million copies. Others included *Hound Dog, All Shook Up* and *It's Now or Never.*

From the soles of his blue suede shoes to the tips of rakish, hair-oiled sideburns, this long-haired Mississippi country boy with the pro-

vocative sneer became the first shellburst in a revolution of American folkways.

He proceeded to combine country-gospel and rhythmn and blues into an unbeatable combination and a million bobby-soxers begged to just let them be his teddy bear. And a million boyfriends, jealous and admiring, imitated Elvis' look. They grew ducktail haircuts and sported black leather jackets and tried to talk like the sons of Mississippi tenant farmers.

The changes were more than superficial. What Elvis did was bring sexuality into the open. Maybe parents wondered about some of the lyrics he sang, but their children didn't need to be told. He took the raunchy beat of the

155

Presley and his wife, Priscilla, posed with their new baby, Lisa Marie, in Memphis in 1968 before the couple broke up

blues and made them top 40 fare with enough whitewash to give them respectability.

Above all, the key to his success was sex. He would stride into the spotlight at arenas packed with screaming fans, a tall, handsome man with a shock of dark hair, full mouth and heavy-lidded eyes. He would swing his hips and pound his guitar as he tore into *Hound Dog, Blue Suede Shoes* or some other Presley favorite. The screams of the fans drowned out his voice. Nurses would stand in the aisles to catch fainting women. Battalions of police were called out to avert riots.

Booming record sales and overflowing audiences at personal appearances made the entertainer one of the world's wealthiest entertainers.

When television brought *Elvis The Pelvis* into millions of homes, church and parents' groups denounced the raw sexuality of his performances as a bad influence on children. His gyrating hips were only mildly suggestive compared to many of the rock performances of the 1970s. But on the Ed Sullivan Show, Presley was shown only from the waist up.

Elvis' career was largely the creation of a promotional genius, Col. Tom Parker. Presley made his appearances on the Ed Sullivan Show after Parker became his manager.

A television rating service gave Presley 82.6 percent of the nation's television audience for his first Sullivan appearance in 1956, to 78.6 percent for President Dwight D. Eisenhower's acceptance speech on three networks.

"When I found Elvis, the boy had nothing but a million dollars worth of talent," Parker said once. "Now he has a million dollars."

Despite the high ratings he scored on the Sullivan show, Presley shied away from television after he had made it big claiming that it restricted him.

"The music moves me and that's why I jump as I do." He said, "Anyone who sees me on television isn't getting their money's worth like they are in person."

Elvis preferred lucrative appearances in Las Vegas and singing in the movies. His popularity soon made him a film actor and he appeared in about 25 movies, including *GI Blues* and *Love Me Tender.*

When Presley was drafted into the Army in the 1960s, Col. Parker capitalized on it, issuing a record album with the soldier-star's picture in uniform. He let photographers record the Army shearing off the famous locks, a major event that generated front page publicity in America and abroad.

Elvis was still wowing audiences in 1973.

Above, a long line of vehicles including the hearse carrying the singer's remains moved down Elvis Presley Blvd. en route to the cemetery

Left, youthful mourners gave way to grief as they kept vigil outside Presley's mansion.

Presley's fan club had thousands of members in the United States, Canada, Mexico, Cuba, England, France, and Australia.

In Germany, the entertainer met Priscille Beaulieu, the daughter of an Air Force officer. They were married on 1967 and divorced six years later.

In the last years before his death, Presley rarely emerged from the grounds of his estate, except to give performances. His weight was said to have ballooned from the 175 pounds he weighed as a young man.

After news of Presley's death spread, some 80,000 fans jammed the streets outside his Memphis home, hoping for a view of the body. About 30,000 persons were admitted to the house. While dozens of mourners fainted or passed out from the heat outside the mansion gates, two of them were killed when an automobile plowed into the crowd.

AFTER 50 YEARS, CASE OF SACCO AND VANZETTI STILL STIRRED EMOTIONS

Shortly after midnight on Aug. 23, 1927, two Italian-born anarchists named Nicola Sacco and Bartolomeo Vanzetti were executed in connection with a robbery that ended in murder. The case raised a furor then. Fifty years later the controversy still went on.

The story began on April 15, 1920, three years after the Bolshevik Revolution, two years after World War I and at the height of a national scare about radicals. Tension ran high between immigrants and old white Anglo-Saxon Protestant stock. The United States would soon pass laws sharply limiting immigration from such countries as Italy.

On that April day, the Slater & Morrill Shoe Co. in South Braintree, Mass. was robbed of $15,776; a paymaster and a guard were shot to death. A few weeks later, Sacco, an edge trimmer in another shoe factory, and Vanzetti, a fish peddler, were picked up carrying pistols.

In Dedham, Mass., a year later, they went on trial for first degree murder. Both had been active among Italian anarchists in the Boston area. Sacco had been arrested when one group assembled without a permit, and he had helped bring food to strikers in Lawrence, Mass. Vanzetti, who had read widely of radical literature, had recently gone to New York to help another anarchist arrested in Justice Department raids. As anarchists, both men had opposed World War I.

Amid disputed evidence about a bullet and the whereabouts of the defendants, their anarchist views were discussed before the jury. The judge was accused of prejudice.

The alibis of the two defendants rested largely on the testimony of immigrant Italians. The prosecution said they were lying for their countrymen and presented witnesses who placed Sacco at the scene.

Two points that told heavily against them were that the defendants were armed when arrested, and that they changed their story during questioning.

Eventually, the accused said they were hiding anarchist literature that day out of fear of federal raids, and that they lied because they feared deportation as aliens if their views became known.

The prosecution said their lies proved Sacco and Vanzetti had "consciousness of guilt," a major point. Their views led to testimony about Sacco's feelings about the United States and about their flight to Mexico during World War I to avoid the draft. Their partisans said that kind of testimony poisoned the trial.

The case of Sacco and Vanzetti stirred a worldwide controversy over justice in Massachusetts. In Boston, thousands of persons were arrested for taking part in protests. They included such literary notables as Katherine Anne Porter, John Dos Passos and Edna St. Vincent Millay. Demonstrations and bombings broke out in Paris, Lisbon and Montevideo.

Communists attached themselves to he cause and were accused by other sympathizers of being more interested in creating martyrs than in saving the lives of Sacco and Vanzetti.

Felix Frankfurter, later to become a Supreme Court justice, wrote critically about the Sacco-Vanzetti trial. But other distinguished Americans held different views. When appeals on behalf of the two defendants were exhausted, a three-man committee headed by Harvard's President A. Lawrence Lowell, reviewed the trial and found it fair.

Fifty years after the execution of Sacco and Vanzetti virtually all the principal characters in the case were dead. Harry King, 91, the last surviving juror, said he still thought the two were guilty. Katherine Anne Porter, 87, wrote in a new book on the case: "I did not know then and still do not know whether they were guilty, but I still have my reason for being there to protest the terrible penalty they were condemned to suffer."

Bartolomeo Vanzetti (second from right) and Nicola Sacco (third from right) photographed as they left the court under armed guard

Also in AUGUST . . .

London theatergoers enjoyed a new experience when they attended this display of light from laser beams. The audience was free to stroll around the arena enjoying the surrealist effects of light and music

Spectators stood by and watched as this house burned out of control on Dayton, Ohio's West Side during a strike by local firefighters

ARCHBISHOP MAKARIOS WHO SURVIVED ATTEMPTS ON LIFE FELLED BY HEART ATTACK

Archbishop Makarios survived plots against his life and against his leadership during 17 stormy years as president of the divided island of Cyprus. But a heart attack finally felled the controversial 63-year-old Greek Orthodox prelate on the morning of Aug. 3.

To his devoted followers, Makarios the island's first and only president, was a powerful figure, a father image who symbolized the strength of the Greek Cypriot majority in its centuries-old conflict with the Turkish minority.

But to most Turkish Cypriots, Makarios was a clever enemy who had worked to diminish their rights and to emphasize the island's ties to Greece ever since 1960 when Cyprus gained independence from Britain.

The bearded archbishop's strength lay in the support of the vast majority of Greek Cypriots who made up three quarters of the island's population of 647,000. He won 95 percent of the vote in the last contested presidential election in 1968.

The unique position Makarios held as religious and political leader was the basis of his seeming invincibility. As archbishop elected for life by universal suffrage he was guaranteed massive electoral backing, and he was able to rule like a benevolent dictator.

The island was wracked by bloody Greek-Turkish sectarian strife in the 1960s leading to the intervention of United Nations peacekeeping troops.

Makarios may have been hated by the Turks, but many believed his most dangerous enemies were the rightwing military junta that ruled Greece in 1967–74 and its allies on the island. Makarios stood for nonalignment in the East-West struggle and had friendly relations with Communist countries.

The threat of violent death hung over Makarios constantly during his political career. He once told a supporter "I am careful but the evil deed may happen." He survived four assassination attempts, the last in July 1974, when he was ousted by a coup staged by the rightwing Greek Cypriot underground and the Greek junta. He fled the island.

The coup triggered a Turkish invasion, and the Turks seized a third of the island before a cease-fire took effect. They backed up their occupation of the northern part of Cyprus with 25,000 Turkish troops. The rightist government that had replaced the archbishop soon resigned and within five months Makarios had returned from exile to resume the presidency.

On his return, the prelate was confronted with the problem of reuniting the war-divided island. He entered negotiations with his Turkish Cypriot counterpart, Raouf Denktash, and indicated his willingness to allow a formal division of the island as a two-state federation in exchange for return of some of the land held by the Turks.

Archbishop Makarios photographed during an appearance in Sri Lanka in 1976

COMIC GROUCHO MARX DIED AT THE AGE OF 86

"There'll always be a Groucho," cigar-chomping comedian Groucho Marx once quipped, "just as there will always be an England — although lately, England hasn't been doing so well."

But, considering the special place in their hearts that Americans hold great comics, Groucho's prediction about himself might very well be true. Marx died in a Los Angeles Hospital Aug. 19 at the age of 86, but the comic legacy he left behind might continue on and on.

Groucho — it was hard to call the funny man with the bushy eyebrows and leering grin who endeared himself to two generations of Americans anything else — first made his mark teamed with his brothers — Harpo, Chico, Gummo and Zeppo — in a wise-cracking, zany comedy style which sent vaudeville and movie audiences into laugh convulsions for nearly 40 years. Later, Groucho — the most famous and long lasting of the Marx Brothers — continued to break up audiences as he starred as quizmaster on his own radio and television series after his brothers either retired or went into other businesses.

Groucho's humor took many forms although one of his favorite characters was the lecherous Professor Hackenbush — a wise-cracker with raised eyebrows, false mustache and a stooped walk like a tiger stalking a water buffalo. He excelled as an insult comic, but wasn't averse to making himself the butt of the joke, noting once that, "I wouldn't belong to any club that would have me for a member."

Groucho, whose real name was Julius, was born in New York City in 1890, the son of Sam and Minnie Marx. Although the family was poor, the mother managed to save enough to give her sons music lessons. In 1910, the mother organized a group which included Groucho, a tenor and a girl. Harpo later joined the group. After countless whistle-stops, tank town theaters and other similar outlets, the act became the Marx Brothers.

The brothers were a smash in vaudeville and musical comedy hits during the 1920s, and they made their first movie *The Cocoanuts* in 1929. Other hits that followed included *Animal Crackers, Monkey Business, Horse Feathers, Duck Soup, A Night At The Opera,* and *A Day At The Races.* It was in the early pictures that Groucho played such outrageous roles as J. Cheever Loophole, detective Sam Grunion and Wolf J. Flywheel. In the 1950s he moved on to become quizmaster on the successful radio and TV series *You Bet Your Life.*

A mourner at Groucho's funeral summed up his enduring wit when he said, "I think Groucho must still be around somewhere because I don't think he'd leave without a good exit line."

Groucho Marx posed with an honorary Oscar he received from the Motion Picture Academy in 1974

Scuffles broke out during a basketball match between the United States and Cuba at the World University Games in Sofia, Bulgaria

ESCAPE OF A NAZI WAR CRIMINAL CAUSED FUROR IN ITALY

Most Italians had heard of former Nazi SS Col. Herbert Kappler, serving a life term for ordering the shooting of 335 Romans in the Ardeatine Caves in March 1944. The massacre was still a horrible memory for thousands, so when Kappler escaped from a Rome military hospital, it raised a furor.

Angry Italians demanded to know how the 70-year-old ex-Gestapo officer, wasting with cancer, was able to flee Celio military hospital and apparently make his way across the border into West Germany. Someone scribbled on a hospital wall, "who are the accomplices?"

As embarrassed authorities tried to reconstruct the getaway they came to the conclusion that the principal accomplice was Kappler's 54-year-old wife, Anneliese. A nurse who had married Kappler in 1972 prison ceremony, Annaliese had paid a routine visit to her husband's fourth floor room on the night of Aug. 14, according to three military policemen guarding the corridor.

Officials said Mrs. Kappler left about 1 a.m. Aug. 15, first posting a note on the room door, saying "Do not disturb until 10 o'clock." The wife then walked down the corridor, officials said, dragging a heavy suitcase, loaded it onto an elevator and took it downstairs. She then placed the suitcase in the trunk of a red automobile she had left in the hospital parking lot three days earlier, and drove off.

The suitcase apparently concealed her husband, Italian Defense Minister Vito Lattanzio told a news conference. He said this was possible because cancer had reduced Kappler's weight to 105 pounds.

Lattanzio said guards had checked the room as usual through a peephole during the night, but suspected nothing because a dummy made of pillows and a wig had been left behind to simulate Kappler sleeping.

The escape was not discovered until shortly after 10 a.m.,

said the minister. He offered no explanation of how Kappler and his wife slipped through hospital security.

Later Italian investigators said they had recovered the red car apparently used by Mrs. Kappler to take her husband from Rome to a point near the Austrian border. They said the couple apparently switched cars there, aided by two male accomplices who were traced to a train station in the northern city of Bolzano.

The escape strained relations between Italy and West Germany prompting the two governments to postpone a summit meeting set for Aug. 19. West German police staged a brief search for Kappler in response to a request from Interpol the International law enforcement agency. Then they announced they were calling the hunt off since the German constitution barred the war criminal's extradition to Italy. West German officials acknowledged that Kappler was in the vicinity of Lueneberg, southeast of Hamburg, somewhere near his wife's home.

Before Kappler's escape, the West German government had called on Rome several times to release the prisoner on humanitarian grounds. Kappler had often said he wanted to die in Germany, but Italian authorities, under pressure from former resistance fighters and Jewish and leftist groups, had blocked his release. In November 1976, a military court did order Kappler freed, but the order was overruled a month later by Italy's supreme court.

Meanwhile, Italian Premier Giulio Andreotti branded Kappler as a "symbol of the cruel Nazi occupation of Rome" and insisted that Italy's ambassador to Bonn go ahead with extradition proceedings.

Italian officials released an emotional letter from Mrs. Kappler to Italian president Giovanni Leone, pleading with Italians to understand why she had helped her husband to escape.

The Italian news agency ANSA quoted Leone as commenting "Even the personal feelings of the chief of state cannot be dissociated from the severe condemnation expressed by the nation" against Kappler.

163

Also in AUGUST . . .

EVOLUTION OF THE PIGGY-BACK FLIGHT

When the U.S. space shuttle Enterprise made its first free flight after being launched from the back of a 747 jet, aviation experts recalled earlier piggy-back attempts going as far back as the 1930s

Top, the Enterprise riding atop its 747 jumbo carrier took off from Edwards Air Force Base in California. Bottom, the piggy-back method was tried out in England during the 1930s as a means of getting a heavily loaded seaplane airborne

Bottom, during World War II in 1944, the Germans tried controlling an unmanned Junkers 88 bomber carrying 7,700 tons of explosives with an ME 109 fighter plane mounted on a pylon atop the big plane which released the JU88 over the target area. Left, the French tried the piggy-back method to launch a ram jet powered Leduc 010, but their program was abandoned in the 1950s

Also in AUGUST . . .

Argentinian tennis star Guillermo Vilas triumphantly held the victor's cup aloft after beating the defending champion, America's Jimmy Connors, at Forest Hills, N.Y., on Sept. 11

Seventeen-year-old F. C. McCollister, Jr. of Evanston, Ill., wore a sandwich board and held a metal cup in downtown Chicago as he solicited passersby for funds to attend college. He said he averaged $8 an hour

NEW JERSEY SNIPER KILLED SIX MEN

Young Emil P. Benoist was described by friends as a quiet person.

"He was a quiet, regular sort of guy," said one about the 20-year-old Hackettstown, N.J., resident. After graduating from high school, Benoist signed up for a hitch in the Marines, but he was discharged from the corps after three months.

"The Marines really made a change in him," said one youth. "He wasn't as bottled up before he went in. He came out of the service something crazy." Said another, "Something had to set him off."

On Aug. 26, Benoist, armed with a powerful, magnum-load .44-caliber rifle, ambushed and killed six men along a path next to the railroad tracks near his home. Warren County First Asst. Prosecutor James Courter said Benoist would spring from bushes lining the seldom-used railroad tracks, fire the rifle, and then drag his victim from a path along the tracks.

The dead were: David Galvin, 14, Stephen Werner, 20, Robert Visconti, 35, William Nagle, 37, Jeffrey L. Gianquitti, 19, and Clifford Sowers, 38.

Police began a manhunt for the sniper, using helicopters and dogs. It was dark when they surrounded their quarry in a cornfield. Hackettstown Police Sgt. John Seabeck found Benoist lying on the ground on the side of a road. "I pointed my shotgun at him," Seabeck said, "and a second or two later he shot himself." Benoist was pronounced dead at a nearby hospital.

167

SEPTEMBER

Legislators and Public Split Over Canal Treaty

Debate over the Panama accord has cut across party lines

After 13 years of negotiations conducted under four American presidents, the United States and Panama agreed to terms of a new treaty governing the Panama Canal. Seventy-four years after being granted the exclusive right to build and perpetually operate a canal across Panamanian territory, the United States consented to eventually turn over control, management and maintenance of the 50-mile waterway to Panama.

The treaty, signed by President Carter and Panamanian leader Omar Torrijos Herrera Sept. 7, grew out of Panamanian demands for an end to U.S. jurisdiction over the 533-square-mile canal zone, considered by many Panamanians as a "U.S. colonial enclave" in their country. But many Americans saw the treaty as a giveaway of U.S. property, a challenge to America's stature in the world and a threat to future operation of the canal.

The treaty would not take effect unless it was ratified by the U.S. Senate, by a two-thirds vote. Even strong supporters of the treaty predicted that ratification would be an uphill struggle. "It's not going to be easy," President Carter acknowledged. Sen. Frank Church of Idaho, a senior Democrat on the Foreign Relations Committee, predicted a "bloody battle" in the Senate over the treaty. The Foreign Relations Committee held three weeks of hearings on the emotional issue, but a Senate vote was put off until 1978.

The new canal agreement is actually two treaties. Under one pact, Panama would assume a gradually increasing role in the operation and defense of the canal until Dec. 31, 1999, when Panama would assume full control of the canal operation. Panama, which now receives about $2.3 million annually from the canal operation, would receive up to $70 million a year — perhaps more — all of it derived from canal revenues. Under another treaty, the United States would have perpetual rights after the year 2000 to defend the neutrality of the canal and ensure that it was open to ships of all nations. (Since the canal was opened Aug. 15, 1914, some 500,000 ships have saved about 7,000 miles each on east-west voyages by using the waterway.)

By the end of the treaty year 2000, the United States would withdraw its 9,000-man military force from the zone and close its 14 military bases there. The 3,500 American civilian employees in the zone could continue in U.S. government jobs until retirement. But within three years of treaty ratification they would be subject to Panamanian law instead of American law.

The signatures on the treaties were barely dry before conservative opponents opened a campaign to block Senate ratification. Former California Gov. Ronald Reagan, who made the canal a major issue in his GOP primary campaign against President Gerald Ford, said that once the United States agreed to relinquish sovereignty of the canal, there was nothing to prevent Panamanian leaders from ignoring the treaties and immediately seizing control of the waterway. He also said Carter's treaty negotiators were forced into concessions under threats of violence by leftist radicals in Panama. Other critics questioned whether Panama, with its long record of political instability, could be trusted to run the canal.

Treaty supporters said U.S. ownership of the canal antagonized Panamanians, and that Senate rejection of the agreement would raise the risk of guerrilla warfare and mob violence in the canal zone. Arguing that use of the canal was more important than ownership, supporters said a cooperative agreement with a friendly Panama would reduce security risks to the canal and lessen the chances of a Panamanian takeover. In addition, the administration argued the treaty would let the United States "divest ourselves of the last appearances of colonialism" in Latin America.

It was an anti-colonialist demonstration that led to the negotiations which produced the canal treaty. On Jan. 9, 1964, Panamanian students entered the canal to protest American jurisdiction in the zone. What began as a peaceful protest soon turned into the worst incident of mob violence in canal history, leaving 21 Panamanians and three Americans dead and many more wounded. Sensing that Panamanian grievances about the exclusive U.S. control over the zone might have been justified, then-President Lyndon B. Johnson ordered renegotiation of the original canal treaty.

One of the sharpest controversies over the new treaty was triggered by the public release of a confidential State Department cable by Sen. Robert Dole R-Kan., Ford's running mate in 1976. The cable quoted a Panamanian treaty negotiator as disagreeing with U.S. statements about interpretation of the agreement and saying that U.S. officials should stop claiming the pact gave the United States the right to "intervene" in Panama. Dole said the cable proved that Panama did not accept the right of the United States to send military forces to

169

Above, a pair of steam shovels cleared away the last pile of rock completing a deep cut along the canal route in this picture taken back in May 1913

This picture taken at 12,000 feet in 1936 showed the 50-mile waterway with Panama City in the foreground

defend the canal's neutrality. State Department spokesmen criticized Dole for releasing the cable, but acknowledged that some parts of the treaty were open to differing interpretations.

As U.S. negotiators Sol Linowitz and Ellsworth Bunker met with Panamanian Ambassador Gabriel Lewis to clear up the issues, there appeared to be growing skepticism on Capitol Hill about administration claims about the treaty. In mid-October, Torrijos flew to Washington and conferred at the White House with Carter about the problem. They emerged from the meeting with a "statement of understanding" which Carter said resolved the major differences of interpretation.

The unsigned statement said the United States would be allowed to defend the canal against any threat and that U.S. warships could pass through the canal ahead of others in any crisis. At the same time, the statement said there would be no U.S. intervention in the internal affairs of Panama nor any move against Panama's "territorial integrity or political independence."

A day later, Senate Majority Leader Robert C. Byrd said he personally remained uncommitted on the treaty but believed the Carter-Torrijos statement would win support for the agreement. Dole and other critics weren't satisfied. They said the statement should be incorporated into the language of the treaty, a step that would require reopening negotiations. The administration strongly opposed reopening the talks. Ambassador Linowitz argued that the statement of understanding had become part of the legislative history of the treaty and was on the record "so there can be no mistaking what both parties intended by the language that was used."

Another controversy was fueled by allegations of bugging and blackmail during the course of the negotiations. Sources were quoted as saying U.S. agents bugged the home and office of Torrijos, and that the Panamanian leader learned of the surveillance and threatened U.S. officials with exposure unless they made key concessions on the treaty. Torrijos supposedly was given transcripts of the bugged conversations by an American Army sergeant, and there were reports that as many as three soldiers were involved in the matter.

Both the U.S. and Panamanian governments denied that any threats of bribery or blackmail figured in the treaty negotiations. After two days of closed-door hearings, the Senate intelligence Committee said it "found no evidence or reason to believe or conclude that U.S. intelligence activities in any way have affected the final results of the Panama Canal treaties." Even so, the issue had put the administration on the defensive once again over the treaty.

The debate over the treaty cut across party lines and split some traditional allies. Ford, the titular head of the GOP, supported the treaty but the Republican National Committee opposed it. The Joint Chiefs of Staff said the agreement would enhance U.S. capability to defend the canal; Adm. Thomas Moorer, a former joint chief, disagreed.

What did average Americans think of the treaty? In the first nationwide survey conducted after Carter and Torrijos signed the agreement, an Associated Press public opinion poll found that 50 percent of the persons questioned opposed Senate ratification of the treaty. Only 29

The first boat to pass through the canal was this little steamer

President Carter and Panama's chief of government, Omar Torrijos chatted before signing the canal treaty

percent favored the pact while about 21 percent expressed no opinion. The findings of widespread opposition were similar to figures from other polls.

The White House launched a campaign to change that sentiment and create a groundswell of public opinion for the treaty, thereby putting pressure on the Senate for ratification. The centerpiece of the campaign was briefing sessions for "opinion leaders"—more than 800 political, civic and business leaders who came to Washington at their own cost and were armed with arguments to counter treaty opponents.

But treaty opponents were busy, too, mar-

172

shaling a campaign they estimated would cost more than $1 million. It included an avalanche of anti-treaty mail, a television documentary, "fact sheets" on the Panama Canal, protests against the treaty and "truth squads" of prominent treaty opponents traveling around the country to mobilize opinion against ratification.

One requisite of implementing the treaty already had been met. Panamanian citizens, in a plebiscite held Oct. 23, voted by a two-to-one margin in favor of the treaties. While the margin fell below the 85 to 95 percent approval predicted earlier by the Torrijos regime, the Panamanian government hoped the outcome would improve the treaty chances in Washington.

America's Ability To Wage Conventional War Hampered By Shortages

Associated Press survey shows that it will take up to six years to balance the scales

America's ability to fight a major conventional war on land and sea and in the air had been seriously weakened by 1977, according to an investigation by The Associated Press. It found that the United States suffered from shortages in key weapons and ammunition and other deficiences.

The survey showed that the Pentagon had begun corrective actions, but it would take from two to six years to cure most of the main shortcomings.

"Stated frankly and simply, our Army is outgunned and inadequately equipped," said one Army official. "We have had to live with under-equipped tactical fighter units, shortfalls in airlift capability, an austere . . . air defense force . . . and persistent shortages of aircraft spare parts and some types of munitions," said Gen. David Jones, Air Force chief of staff.

Describing the condition of the Navy, the Defense Department said "it will take at least five or six years of concerted effort before the materiel condition of the entire fleet attains a sustainable satisfactory level."

On the other hand, America's strategic nuclear striking arms appeared to be in good shape. These long-range missiles and bombers and missile submarines were designed to deter any Russian nuclear attacks on the United States. They had been receiving top priority.

In 1977, however, the Pentagon and Congress began showing mounting concern about the readiness of U.S. forces to deal with a possible Soviet attack on Western Europe.

This concern grew from a belief that Russia, after more than five years of intensive modernization, might have developed enough hard-hitting, fast-moving ground and air power to attack Western Europe with little warning.

Readiness problems also undercut U.S. ability to use its forces effectively in the Far East and Middle East.

A check with Pentagon sources and senior commanders in the field showed these shortcomings:

—The Army had only 7,000 of the nearly 15,000 tanks planners believed it should have to defeat Soviet armor and replace battle losses.

—The Army's War Reserve stocks of tanks, antitank missiles, self-propelled artillery, armored troop carriers and ammunition were low, particularly in Europe.

—The Air Force was short about half of the advanced air-to-air missiles it needed to duel with Soviet fighter planes for control of the skies. It would also need twice its current long-range air-transport plane capacity to rush vital weapons and other equipment from the United States to the war zone.

—The Army National Guard and Reserve had few units rated ready for deployment. The Reserve manpower pool dropped from 1.5 million in 1972 to 429,000. Because the draft was dead, the Individual Ready Reserve would be the main source of replacements for battle casualties in the first stages of a war.

A U.S. Marine crossed a ravine on a rope bridge during training exercises in South Korea

A U.S. Navy jet fighter took off from the deck of the USS Constellation in the South China Sea as another lined up for takeoff

—Shortages of spare parts grounded warplanes and delayed overhauls severely cut the operating effectiveness of warships.

U.S. military men complained that the size of the armed forces had dwindled to a far greater degree than their responsibilities in protecting America's global interests. In 1977, the U.S. military services had about 2.1 million men and women in uniform—or 1.5 million less than tne Vietnam War peak and the smallest number since before the Korean conflict in 1950.

The 486-ship U.S. Navy was close to the smallest since before the 1941 attack on Pearl Harbor. The fleet had been whittled away by the retirement of older ships for economy reasons.

On the plus side, Gen. Frederick Kroesen, chief of the Army Forces Command, which supervised readiness, said most of the 11 regular divisions in the United States were classed as ready to deploy. The Air Force's Tactical Air Command which was responsible for preparing U.S.-based fighters for deployment, claimed it could about double the nearly 600 U.S. fighters based in Europe in 96 hours.

Despite Congressional criticism of the all-volunteer military concept which replaced the draft, military professionals generally praised the quality and performance of the new breed of enlisted men and women.

With Western Europe the focus of about 75 to 80 percent of its mission, the Army set in motion a $4.7 billion program to strengthen its "warfighting" resources over the ensuing few years.

A new defense directive issued after months of study reiterated the main thrust of U.S. military policy—to defend Western Europe as close to the Communist territory as possible without yielding any more German soil than necessary.

In its annual report to Congress, the Defense Department said that, for the first time, Russian ground and air power "may coincide with the longstanding Soviet doctrine of rapid offensive thrusts reminiscent of German blitzkrieg tactics in World War II."

The report stressed that a conventional Allied defense "must be based on the assumption that an attack with little or no warning by in-place Warsaw Pact forces is possible. . . ."

The AP survey found that the European war reserves stocks contained only about 25 percent of the tanks required, about one third of the ammunition, no armored personnel carriers, and no long-barreled, self-propelled artillery which division commanders said was vital to match the longer ranges of the Soviet field guns. The Defense Department was said to be making an effort to correct that situation.

The Carter administration added $400 million to the fiscal year's budget to speed over-all readiness improvement, including more steel and concrete shelters for U.S. aircraft and ammunition stocks in Europe.

U.S. commanders said they expected the Soviet Union to finish re-equipping its army divisions and air force squadrons with powerful new weapons and planes by 1981–82. Thus American military leaders set 1979–80 as the goal for recovery from weaknesses in firepower, shortages, poor location of vital ammunition stocks and other shortcomings.

Efforts were being made to get West Germany, Belgium, Netherlands and other Allies to provide major, wartime, rear-area support for U.S. forces in transportation, ammunition handling, repair of bomb-damaged roads and bridges and traffic control among other things.

Military experts said in the event of war, the Soviet military theory called for a short conflict. The Russians envisioned Warsaw Pact forces overwhelming Western Europe and reaching the English Channel in eight days.

The United States took a different view. Said one top American general: "I know we have a good capability to slow them. . . . I believe we have the capability to stop them." But, as for

Right, the nuclear submarine Henry L. Stimson attached to the U.S. 6th Fleet, entered the harbor at Rota, Spain, to undergo repairs

Below mudcoated U.S. Marine undergoing special underwater training at San Diego Naval Base

Soviet border guards were shown during winter training exercises on the extreme eastern end of the USSR

driving the attackers from NATO territory, the general said: "I don't think we have the capability without reinforcements from the outside."

Half a world away in the Pacific and Indian Oceans, U.S. military power patroled an area covering nearly half the surface of the globe. But military men feared that these forces were less effective than in the past because of the Pentagon's preoccupation with Western Europe. Informed sources said plans provided for about half of the 218-ship U.S. Pacific Fleet and part of its attendant ground forces to be switched to the European theater, if hostilities with the Soviet Union broke out there. Not only would this leave America's forward-deployed forces vulnerable to Soviet flanking action, it would also, in the words of one observer "mean writing off the western Pacific."

In the 1960s the U.S. 7th Fleet patrolling the South China Sea averaged around a hundred ships. In 1977, the total was down to about 50 ships.

The men who made up the U.S. armed force in 1977 were a different group from the draftees of earlier years. In the All-Volunteer Force of the late 1970s, the motivation for most enlistments was economic, not patriotic. Many men and women signed up to further their educations through military service.

The Army which had trouble attracting quality recruits in the years just after the draft ended in 1973 was doing better in 1977. But it was still having trouble getting enough of them.

In an effort to make life attractive for recruits, the Army made some marked changes in the barracks. New air-conditioned brick buildings began springing up at many Army bases in the United States replacing the old wooden World War II huts. Gone too were the old fashioned mess halls with crowded prison-like tables replaced by airy, color coordinated "dining facilities," with widely-spaced tables and chairs.

Soldiers had choices of egg styles at breakfast, homemade pastries, fresh vegetables and three kinds of meat on the dinner menus.

This was in sharp contrast to the life of the typical Russian soldier, a young conscript who stolidly endured a prison-like existence and repetitious, often dangerous training under rigid discipline. He was paid $3 a month, less than one percent of the $374 received by the rawest U.S. recruits.

A composite of the average Russian serviceman emerged from reports by U.S. officials with access to intelligence sources and by military specialists who had observed the Soviets close-up.

"The two-year conscript is housed in barracks which are surrounded by barbed wire," Army officials told Congress. "He is fed a carefully calculated ration of food, much like a farm animal, and undergoes rigorous physical training and hours of political indoctrination."

In one outpost, Americans were still very much on the alert for trouble. In South Korea, the sons of the men who fought the war a generation earlier were kept in a state of combat readiness, even though President Carter said he intended to withdraw all U.S. forces from the divided peninsula within five years. Because of serious incidents in the Demilitarized Zone including the murder of two U.S. army officers in 1976, tensions remained high in that theater.

American officials had no doubts that should North Korea attack, it would be sudden and massive. "They would try to win a lightning war, probably try and take Seoul within 90 hours," said Maj. Gen. Maurice Brady, commander of the 2nd Infantry Division.

"Let's face it," said Brady, "if the worst happens, if the North invades again, there'll be a lot of Americans killed. We'll lose an infantry battalion right off. I want my men to remember that."

Leopold Stokowski Died After A Career That Spanned 70 Years

The flamboyant conductor helped shape the musical tastes of America for two generations

Leopold Stokowski had a musical career that spanned more than 70 years, and in his heyday he was the most famous and most controversial conductor in the United States.

When he died Sept. 13 at the age of 95 at his country home in England, he was still active, conducting for recordings under a contract that would have kept him in harness until he was 100.

Stokowski was a flamboyant figure who enchanted audiences but often enraged critics with the way in which he altered the works of famous composers. He was also a glamorous figure who held attention, not only through his talent for getting incredible color from an orchestra, but because of his arresting personal appearance. When he was on the podium, lights played around his long mane of blond — later white — hair and his expressive hands he used to direct instead of a baton. The public

The maestro limbered up in preparation for a concert of the New Philharmonic Orchestra in London's Royal Albert Hall in 1968

watched entranced as he shaped interpretations with motions that were both graceful and forceful.

But despite criticism of his showmanship and unorthodox methods, it was generally felt that Stokowski had done as much as any man to mold the taste of two generations of Americans.

Born in London of Polish and Irish parents, Stokowski moved to the United States when he was 23 to become organist at St. Bartholomew's Church in New York. He was naturalized as a U.S. citizen 10 years later. And that brought up another mystery about the man. Despite his London upbringing and the fact that he spent most of his life in America, Stokowski had a foreign-sounding accent that defied identification. Presumably of his own devising, it added somehow to his aura of glamor.

At the age of 27, Stokowski took over the Cincinnati Symphony and began touching up the scores of the masters. The result infuriated some critics. He only remained with the symphony for three years.

In 1912, Stokowski took over the Philadelphia Orchestra and over the ensuing 29 years molded it into one of the world's greatest.

Some musicologists sneered at Stokowski's transcriptions of Bach and other composers, but the criticism did not phase him. He told a Time magazine interviewer in 1962 "You must realize that Beethoven and Brahms did not understand instruments. Composers like Ravel, Debussy and Mozart did."

One of the most lingering controversies that grew up about the conductor had to do with the many orchestral transcriptions he made of Bach's organ works. He gave them 20th century treatment and argued that Bach would have done so himself had he lived to see the development of the modern symphony orchestra.

The most sound-conscious of conductors, Stokowski made records as far back as 1917, experimented with stereophonic sound before its commercial production and worked with engineers on technical advancements to bring orchestral music to home listeners.

He appeared in four Hollywood pictures in the 1930s and '40s and collaborated with Walt Disney in the film classic *Fantasia* which set animated cartoons to classical music and gave the music a popularity it never had before. One highlight of the movie was a photographic study of Stokowski's expressive hands in action.

Despite his early fame and the fact that he was responsible for the first staged performances in the United States of Stravinsky's *Oedipus Rex* and other works, Stokowski had to wait a long time for recognition in some quarters. He did not appear at the New York City Opera until 1959 and it was not until 18 months later that he made his conducting debut at the Metropolitan Opera at the age of 78.

Stokowski's career lost some of its luster in the 1940s. He organized the All-American Youth Orchestra in 1940 and took it on tours of the United States and South America, but it

One of the conductor's wives was Gloria Vanderbilt, who was 42 years younger than he.

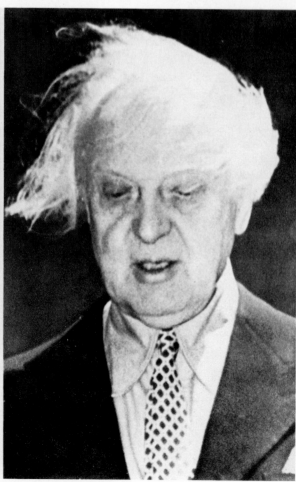

178

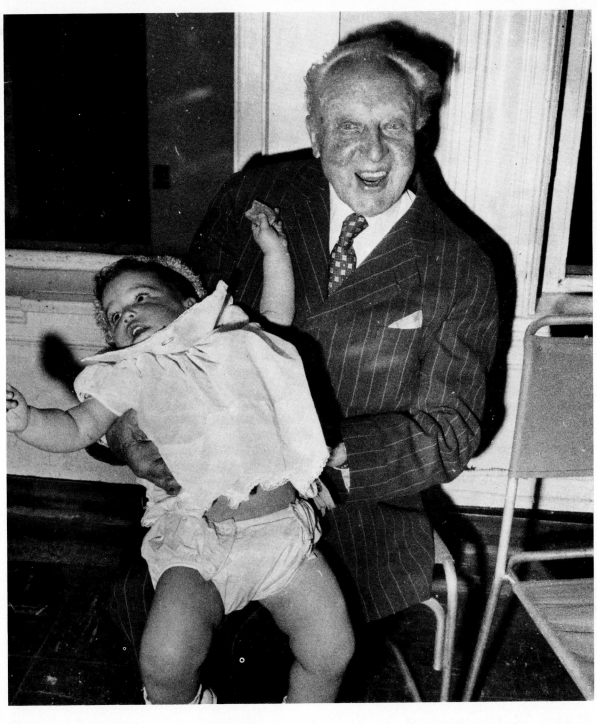

Stokowski shown with a shy youngster at a party at Carnegie Hall in 1967 for musicians' children

went out of existence in 1942, perhaps due in part to World War II. In 1944, he took part in organizing the New York Symphony at the City Center of Music and Drama, but he did not stay with it very long.

In 1949 and 1950, Stokowski shared direction of the New York Philharmonic but it was not a lasting attachment. In 1955, he became musical director of the Houston Symphony and remained there until 1960.

Stokowski seemed to get along well during his sojourns in Hollywood. While there he established a close friendship with one of its most beautiful and mysterious stars, Greta Garbo. At one point, the conductor and actress whetted the interest of the public by spending several months following each other around Europe. Stokowski's marriage, to Evangeline Brewster Johnson, ended in divorce, as did his other two unions. He also married Olga Samaroff, an American pianist and teacher, and heiress Gloria Vanderbilt, when he was 63 and she 21.

Stokowski was feted with an elaborate 90th birthday party at a New York hotel, attended by his three daughters and two sons.

Then, in 1972, he returned to England to live in the Hampshire village of Nether Wallop. He gave up the concert platform with a final, unscheduled appearance in the southern part of France July 12, 1975, but he continued recording.

When the legendary conductor died, he received tributes from many leaders of the musical world. One from violinist Isaac Stern, said that Stokowski "had that rare ability to put his personal stamp on a performance that always is the sign of an original musical mind. He was a very special man, and with him goes a kind of era . . . the time that the giants walked the earth."

G. Gordon Liddy arrived in handcuffs at a Pennsylvania court where he swore he was a pauper and unable to pay his $40,000 fine

FREED FROM PRISON, LIDDY HAD LITTLE TO SAY ABOUT WATERGATE

Throughout the 52½ months he spent in prison, G. Gordon Liddy had observed a code of silence about the Watergate burglary he devised and directed. When he was finally released, he still refused to talk about the break-in except to say he'd do it again, if his president asked.

Bombarded with questions by newsmen as he emerged from the federal prison in Danbury, Conn., Sept. 7, Liddy had virtually nothing to say. He was more expansive the following day when he invited reporters to his Washington hotel suite, but still he ducked key questions about Watergate.

Asked if he'd do it again, Liddy said "When the prince approaches his lieutenant, the proper response of the lieutenant is 'fiat voluntas tua.'" that was Latin for "Thy will be done."

Asked whether he could tell newsmen why he went into the Watergate, he retorted "I can, but I won't." He also refused to tell questioners what the burglars were looking for.

The years in prison had softened Liddy's voice, shrunk his physique and made him less cocky. His manner was almost deferential where before it had been condescending.

Liddy became free one day short of the third anniversary of Richard M. Nixon's pardon by Gerald Ford.

Others linked to Watergate wrote, talked and testified about their roles in the scandal, some of them making a lot of money. Only Liddy held the answer to the central question: what were the burglars looking for? He never talked, however, and he paid for his silence. Liddy got the stiffest sentence of any Watergate figure—six to 20 years plus a $40,000 fine. Later 18 more months were tacked on to his sentence for refusing to answer a grand jury's questions. Liddy's neighbors in Oxon Hill, Md., had banded together in a petition drive that may have played a part in President Carter's decision to commute the 20-year sentence to eight years. Now these same neighbors had launched a fund drive to help him pay his debts.

To win parole and get his $40,000 fine deferred, Liddy had to declare himself a pauper with less than $20 to his name. He said he owed $337,500, most of it to his attorney and former law partner. Peter Maroulis, who had fought his case to the Supreme Court.

AP EXECUTIVE EDITOR BOCCARDI SUMMED UP CHINA IMPRESSIONS

"If we look back we have made great progress. If we look ahead, we have a long way to go."

This comment by a provincial official in China's Hunan province summarized for Louis D. Boccardi, executive editor and vice president of The Associated Press, much that he and a group of AP executives and directors saw and heard during a 16-day visit to China in September. The trip took them the length of the country, from Inner Mongolia in the north to Canton in the south.

Summing up his impressions of the visit, Boccardi wrote, in part:

"We saw a nation working. The scenes were replayed everywhere. Men, young and old, pulling carts laden with mounds of cabbage, or boulders or oil drums or pipes. . . . And in all the cities we saw much construction, primarily apartment houses. All this in a country poor by Western standards but held together by a philosophy that puts the good of the state first. Once a visitor accepts this central premise—that the state comes first and every means is used to spread the state's message—then impressions fall more clearly into place.

"By all the available evidence, this system is providing adequately for its 800 million plus people—not lavishly perhaps by American standards, but, as the Chinese frequently remind visitors, 'Your standards are not ours.'"

As for the "long way to go" remark made in Hunan, "China-watchers seem to agree that the new leaders are more practical, that they will take China into increasing contact with the rest of the world, that the rigid ideology of the late Chairman Mao is being relaxed."

A highlight of the visit was a 90-minute meeting between Chinese Vice Premier Teng Hsiao-ping and the AP executives and directors.

Teng said President Ford promised to break diplomatic relations with Taiwan if he was elected, but the Carter administration offered only to reduce the American Embassy there to a liaison mission in exchange for full ties with Peking. He said President Gerald Ford and Secretary of State Henry Kissinger, during a visit to Peking in 1975, pledged that if they remained in office they would resolve the Taiwan problem the same way the Japanese did—by breaking diplomatic relations with the Nationalists while maintaining nongovernment contacts, including trade.

(Ford said later he had suggested to Chinese leaders the "possibility" of cutting U.S. diplomatic ties with Taiwan in order to have normal relations with Peking. But, the former president said, he had made no commitment to the Chinese and that he had discussed the approach known as "the Japanese formula" only as a possibility.)

Teng also said U.S.-Chinese relations suffered a setback during an August visit by Secretary of State Cyrus R. Vance.

Left, Associated Press President and General Manager Keith Fuller chatted with Chinese Vice-Premier Teng Hsiao-ping during the visit to Peking

Below, Billy Graham, wearing a sheepskin coat sampled some native goulash during the evangelist's trip to Hungary

He said reports of progress resulting from Vance's trip were wrong but added that the talks were cordial and a useful exchange of views.

The meeting with the visiting Americans was Teng's first interview since he returned to office in July. He said that after he was purged from the nation's leadership in 1976 by the Radical "Gang of Four," led by Mao Tse-tung's wife, Mao personally ordered him protected against harm. After Mao's death in September 1976, his widow and the three other leading radicals were arrested a month later. Teng was rehabilitated in July and restored to his previous position by the new Communist Party chairman, Hua Kuo-feng.

The AP officials at the meeting with Teng were President and General Manager Keith Fuller; Boccardi; Jack Tarver, publisher of the Atlanta Constitution and Journal and chairman of the AP board of directors; David R. Bradley, publisher and president of the St. Joseph, Mo., News-Press and Gazette; Frank Batten, chairman of the board of Landmark Communications, Norfolk, Va.; Stanton R. Cook, chairman and publisher of the Chicago Tribune; Katharine Graham, chairman of the board of the Washington Post Co.; William H. Cowles 3rd, publisher and president of the Spokane, Wash., Spokesman-Review; Robert L. Taylor, Chairman of the Philadelphia Bulletin; J. M. McClelland, Jr., president and publisher of the Longview, Wash., Daily News; Daniel H. Ridder, editor and publisher of the Long Beach, Calif., Independent Press-Telegram; Arthur Ochs Sulzberger, chairman, president and publisher of the New York Times, and Robert M. White II, editor and publisher of the Mexico, Mo., Ledger.

Following the group's departure from China, Fuller said Chinese officials, citing a lack of progress between the Chinese and United States governments, said the time was not ripe for an AP bureau to open in Peking. Fuller said the principal discussion on this subject was held with Chu Mu-chih, head of the official Chinese news agency Hsinhua. Chu said he looked forward to the time when the AP could establish a bureau in Peking but said the absence of progress between the governments of the two nations made the time "not yet right."

WHAT A FLASH FLOOD CAN DO

While much of the country was recovering from a withering drought, Kansas City was hit by a flash flood on Sept. 12 that sent water surging through the streets, upending cars and killing nearly a score of persons

Above, as the waters rose, automobiles floated through the stricken city's Country Club Plaza area

Right, after the waters subsided the crisis remained. Here firemen fought a blaze in one district where a fire was touched off by a gas leak

Right, a woman stood on the bank of Brush Creek while rescue teams with spotlights peered into stranded cars looking for victims or survivors

Below, the day after the flood, people walked to work paying little attention to a car left perched at a bizarre angle by the rampaging waters

GOLDEN VOICE OF MARIA CALLAS WAS FINALLY STILLED

Maria Callas was famed mainly for three things; her magnificent lyric soprano, her fiery temperament and her marathon romance with Aristotle Onassis.

Her golden voice brought fame and fortune to the New York-born diva. The Onassis romance kept her frequently in the headlines and added to the aura of glamor that surrounded her. But the Callas temperament often got her into hot water.

In recent years, the flamboyant image faded, however. When she died Sept. 16 in her Paris home at the age of 53, she had not appeared on stage in three years, limiting her singing to recordings.

In parting tribute, Carlo Maria Badini, superintendent of Milan's La Scala Opera where Miss Callas first gained renown, said: "Callas enters by right into the legend of opera."

It was not always thus. Born in New York City to Greek immigrants, Maria spent what she later described as a miserable childhood; a fat, ungainly girl. When she was 14, her mother took her to Greece where they were stranded by the outbreak of World War II. There she won a scholarship at Athens Conservatory and begain a serious study of music. A year later she made her debut in Mascagni's *Cavalleria Rusticana*.

Callas continued studying in New York following the war and after two years the Metropolitan Opera offered her the role of *Madame Butterfly*. But she turned it down because of her weight and went instead to Verona, Italy, where she met Giovanni Battista Meneghini. The wealthy Milan indus-

trialist was enchanted by the magnificent soprano of the stout, near-sighted girl and guided her to stardom. He married her; a stormy union that finally broke up.

Meneghini, spent vast sums on the aspiring lyric soprano and her career began to flourish. The breakthrough came in 1951 with a masterful *Aida* at La Scala followed by a contract with the opera house. At the same time, Maria slimmed down and became a shapely style-setter and finally left Meneghini for Onassis.

Soon the dark-eyed diva gained fame as "opera's bad girl." She battled with managers—including well-publicized duels with the Met's Rudolf Bing. She walked out of performances, one time cutting short a gala performance of Bellini's *Norma* attended by the president of Italy. And she fought with fellow performers.

"Of course I am difficult," she once said. "An artist who tries sincerely to meet the demands of operatic music must work under extraordinary tension. But I know—and my friends would say this for me—I am not a monster."

Maria's nine-year romance with Onassis continued until the shipping magnate married Jacqueline Kennedy in October 1968. Miss Callas claimed she harbored no ill feelings against Jacqueline, but she never met her and continued to see Onassis until his death in March 1975. "He is my best friend," she said. "He is, he was, and he always will be." She said she never married Onassis because "I think love is so much better when you're not married."

Miss Callas retired from concert singing in 1965, claiming ill health. She returned to the stage nine years later, in February, 1974, to the cheers of a packed house in Philadelphia's Academy of Music. But critics found some of the magic gone. "The impression remained that for all her appeal and charm, her voice is probably something to be recalled from recordings of the '50s," wrote one music critic.

Below fiery soprano Maria Callas singing one of her more famous roles, that of Medea, in 1958

SINGER-ACTRESS ETHEL WATERS DEAD AT 80

For many, Ethel Waters was a song. A song her grandmother had taught her. It was called *His Eye Is On The Sparrow*. It was hard to imagine anyone but her singing: "I sing because I'm happy, I sing because I'm free. His eye is on the sparrow, and I know He watches me."

Now only the song remained. Miss Waters died Sept. 1 in Chatsworth, Calif. She was 80-years-old. It brought to an end a career that had begun with an amateur night appearance and had grown to encompass the Broadway stage, Hollywood films and the world of gospel music.

She was born in Chester, Pa., in 1896. Her career began when, working as a $4.75 a week chambermaid in a Philadelphia hotel, she made an amateur night appearance and got a job singing and dancing that earned her $9 a week. She made appearances in numerous clubs and got a reputation for singing *St. Louis Blues*.

She moved on to sing in clubs in New York City's Harlem and was heard singing in one of them by Irving Berlin. Berlin signed her for *As Thousands Cheer*, and she had her first Broadway triumph in 1933, although she had previously appeared on Broadway in other plays.

After *As Thousands Cheer*, Miss Waters appeared in her first dramatic role on Broadway in *Mamba's Daughters*, but a year later appeared in a musical, *Cabin In The Sky*, for which she was much praised. Her greatest triumph came in 1950 when she appeared in a dramatic role as a maid in a Southern household in *The Member Of The Wedding*.

Miss Waters appeared in the same role when a movie was made of *The Member Of The Wedding*, and was nominated for an Academy Award for best actress in 1952. Other films in which she appeared included *Cabin In the Sky* and *Pinky*. She also appeared on television. In 1959, Miss Waters attended a Billy Graham revival meeting and began a new career as a gospel singer, joining his crusades and recording several gospel albums.

One of the songs she often sang, and which also was the title of her best-spelling autobiography, was *His Eye Is On The Sparrow*.

An unusual picture of Pope Paul VI as he stood on the balcony of the Papal summer palace and shouted a farewell to a youth group

Also in SEPTEMBER . . .

Above, Contender Ernie Shavers followed through after landing a right to the head of champion Muhammad Ali during the heavyweight title bout in New York's Madison Square Garden. Ali retained his title.

Poet Robert Lowell in a picture taken 14 years before he died

FAMED AMERICAN POET ROBERT LOWELL DIED AFTER SUDDEN ILLNESS

Many critics regarded Robert Lowell as the best English language poet of his generation. His talent for the natural affinities of words won him the Pulitzer Prize for Poetry in 1947.

The 60-year-old bard's unexpected death after he was stricken while riding in a taxi from John F. Kennedy International Airport in New York Sept. 12 shocked the literary world.

Born in Boston, Robert Traill Spence Lowell Jr. was a member of a prominent New England literary family that included two other famous poets, Amy Lowell and James Russell Lowell.

Lowell's mother, Charlotte Winslow, also came from an upper crust family, but the poet once told an interviewer that he felt comfortable in the "Jewish age" of American literature because he was one eighth Jewish himself.

Educated at St. Marks School in Southboro, Mass., Lowell went on to Harvard but switched to Kenyon College in Ohio after two years, primarily to study poetry.

By 1942, Lowell was devoting most of his time to poetry, but the following year he was jailed as a conscientious objector. He served six months in prison for refusal to bear arms in World War II, an experience he later described in verse.

Lowell's early works drew from his Roman Catholicism to which he converted, then later renounced, from his pacifism and his New England Calvinist tradition.

Lowell achieved full recognition in 1947 with the publication of his second volume of poems *Lord Weary's Castle* which won him the Pulitzer award. Critics said the work revealed the author's nonconformist New England temperament and the adopted Catholicism which enriched it.

In 1959, Lowell published *Life Studies* which included *91 Revere Street* and some of his best poetry. The last of more than a dozen works by Lowell, *Day by Day* was published in early 1977.

MARK RUDD BIG IN 1960s, BUT NOW FORGOTTEN

For seven years he had been one of the most sought-after fugitives in America's radical underground, but now he was all but forgotten. When Mark Rudd, leader of the 1968 Columbia University student revolt turned himself in at the Manhattan District Attorney's office Sept. 14, he faced only a handful of misdemeanor charges and was paroled on his own recognizance.

Rudd looked much the same as when he led the student takeover at Columbia nine years earlier and engaged in bloody street fighting with Chicago police a year later. But his demeanor was much more subdued.

Rudd refused to talk to a milling crowd of reporters and photographers as he arrived at the Manhattan Criminal Court building with his lawyer Gerald Lefcourt.

His appearance made the turbulence of the 1960s seem far away. At Columbia, few of the students lounging around the campus sundial—once the center of radical speeches and the launching point of the 1968 demonstrations—even knew who Mark Rudd was.

It was different story nine years earlier. As a Columbia junior in the spring of 1968, Rudd was campus president of Students for a Democratic Society, the major organization in the activist "New Left" of white, middle class college radicals that largely grew out of the civil rights movement of the early 1960s.

Rudd and his group had billed themselves as revolutionaries and terrorists but the charges against the 30-year-old defendant were relatively light; unlawful assembly, obstructing governmental administration, criminal trespass and criminal solicitation.

In Chicago, authorities said Rudd faced charges of mob action, aggravated battery and resisting arrest stemming from the "Days of Rage" demonstrations in the fall of 1969. In both places Rudd also faced bail-jumping charges.

At the height of the protests against the war in Vietnam, Rudd and other members of the radical Weatherman organization went underground, vowing to act as "vandals in the mother country."

In 1970, three members of the underground group were killed when a bomb they were making exploded prematurely in the cellar of a New York townhouse.

In the early 1970s, the Federal Bureau of Investigation set up special squads to track down the Weather underground, but they were not successful. Rudd's surrender came about eight months after reports circulated that the radical band had become torn by internal strife.

FOR THE RECORD

SENTENCED. Twelve Hanafi Moslems, on Sept. 6, to lengthy prison terms for seizing three buildings and 149 hostages during a 38-hour reign of terror in the nation's capital in March. D.C. Superior Court Judge Nicholas S. Nunzio Jr. ordered each defendant to serve minimum sentences ranging from 24 to 77 years; the maximums ranged from 72 years up to life for the two men who took over Washington's city hall and killed a radio newsman. Hamaas Abdul Khaalis, the group's leader, was sentenced to 41 to 123 years in prison.

Mark Rudd shook hands with an unidentified man as he arrived at the Manhattan District Attorney's office to surrender

OCTOBER

Bing Crosby, Whose Breezy Baritone Charmed Millions, Felled After 50-Year Career

Bing Crosby's crooning voice and relaxed humor entertained millions around the world for half a century. And his business acumen made him a fortune far up in the millions.

When the entertainer was stricken with a fatal heart attack after a round of golf while vacationing in Spain on Oct. 14, his death shocked fans the world over with the intensity of losing a member of the family. No show business figure was believed to have reached so many persons in so many ways.

For nearly half a century, Crosby's breezy baritone was heard throughout America, first as a member of the jazzy Rhythm Boys with Paul Whiteman's Orchestra, then as a soloist who made crooner a household word.

Crosby made more than a score of records which sold more than one million each. The most widely known hits included *White Christmas* which became his best drawing card, selling a staggering 39,110,000 by the end of 1976.

For many years, Crosby was credited with selling more records than any singer in history. He was overtaken finally in the 1950s by Elvis Presley, who died a few weeks before he did.

Crosby, known variously as *Der Bingle* and *The Groaner* seemed to be at home in almost any medium. He made more than 70 films and won an Oscar as best actor in 1944 in *Going My Way* in which he played a priest. His film credits ranged from the "Road" comedies with his longtime friend, comedian Bob Hope and Dorothy Lamour to *The Country Girl* in which he played an alcoholic.

Bing never had the driving intensity, on the surface at least, of Bob Hope. But his on-screen nonchalance was not reflected in his private life. His first marriage to actress Dixie Lee was rocky. When they were first married she was a bigger star than he was as she assumed the role of Mrs. Bing Crosby and mother of their four sons.

Dixie Crosby died in 1952 and five years later he married starlet Kathryn Grant who was 30 years younger than he. They had a daughter and two sons and moved out of the Hollywood scene to Hillborough just south of San Francisco. A family friend said she was a good influence on the singer.

"She got him out of his shell, and the kids kept him young too," he said.

For a while after his second marriage, Bing seemed content to play golf and fish off Baja California. Then he decided to reactivate his career, singing at concerts in Los Angeles, New York, London and elsewhere, usually joined by his wife and one or more of their children.

Asked once why he didn't retire, Crosby said "A man in my position has a tiger by the tail. He just can't let go any old time. So many people become dependent on him for their livelihood. If he quits, scores of jobs go down the drain. Each job represents a family."

Crosby contributed heavily to charities. He also put up the funds each year for a pro-amateur golf tournament at Pebble Beach. Proceeds went into youth recreations centers and other charities. Crosby donated every cent he earned in British appearances in 1976 to youth charities in London, a municipal official in the British capital disclosed.

During World War II, with the Crosby Camp shows, the singer traveled more than 50,000 miles entertaining the troops.

His business enterprises which brought him a fortune estimated at between $40 and $70 million, included oil wells, distribution rights for a frozen orange juice, a 25,000-acre cattle ranch near Elko, Nev., and the far-flung Bing Crosby Enterprises which marketed everything from television films to toy dogs.

A sports enthusiast, Crosby owned 15 percent of the Pittsburgh Pirates baseball team and about 5½ percent of the Detroit Tigers. He raised race horses and at one time had a stable of 21.

But show business was his first love until the end. His last major hit song was *True Love* a number from the movie *High Society* which he recorded with Grace Kelly. "That song came out of nowhere and was a huge seller," said an RCA spokesman "It sold maybe four or five million copies."

Among Crosby's most popular songs were the Christmas tunes he recorded with the Andrews Sisters. Displaying an unparalleled versatility, he also did Irish ballads, country songs and Hawaiian songs through the years.

In one personality poll, Crosby was rated most popular, beating out Gen. Dwight Eisenhower, President Harry Truman and the Pope. For five straight years, from 1943 to 1945, he was voted the top money-making star in an annual poll of theater owners.

Crosby's trademarks included pipes, his race horses and his lurid sports shirts. His smooth ballads were often interspersed with a familiar "bub-bub-bub-boo" and his choruses, particularly in the early days, were varied with whistling.

189

Above, Bing Crosby with Dorothy Lamour and Bob Hope in the 1942 film "Road to Morocco," one in a long line of "road" pictures that brought him fame and fortune. Right, Crosby shook his finger at Barry Fitzgerald in this scene from the 1944 film "Going My Way" which won the singer an Oscar for acting.

190

This picture of the singer swinging at the ball on the Moraleja Golf Course near Madrid was taken shortly before he died. He collapsed after completing the 18-hole course

Probably the most remarkable thing about Crosby's popularity was that it never waned. He made easy transitions from recording artist to radio star to movie star to television performer.

In March 1977, Crosby suffered a ruptured disk in his lower back when he fell 20 feet from a stage into an orchestra pit at a theatre in Pasadena, Calif., where he was taping a television special. He had lost his footing while acknowledging a standing ovation from the audience.

He was hospitalized for more than a month.

He called his October tour of Britain which included a sell-out performance at London's Palladium a "trial run" for a planned European tour. "I'm still a little limpy, but I want to find out if I can still function after the accident."

Shortly before his death, Crosby was planning his first movie in 11 years, hitting the "Road" once more with Hope and Dorothy Lamour.

Viet Cong Tunnels Played Key Role In Vietnam War

The underground tentacles extended 150 miles and took 30 years to build

For 12 years, Associated Press Pulitzer Prize winning photographer-writer Horst Faas covered the war in Vietnam. In 1977, he returned to that country, a little more than two years after it had fallen to Communist forces. The following is Faas' report of his visit to a former Vietnam battlefield.

As Lt. Col. George A. Eyster lay dying from Viet Cong sniper bullet wounds on a jungle trail, he said to me, "Before I go I'd like to talk to the guy who controls those incredible men in the tunnels."

Eleven years later I met that man and he showed me the inside of the fantastic tunnel octopus that took 30 years to dig and stretched 150 miles, with tentacles sometimes winding right under the chairs of U.S. commanders as they sat in their headquarters.

Eyster, a tall West Pointer from Cocoa Beach, Fla., died in a field hospital while his battalion, the 2nd of the 28th Regiment, 1st Infantry Division, was trying to fight its way through the vast underground complex 20 miles northwest of Saigon.

The now peaceful tunnels were on the itinerary of a German tourist group I traveled with on a rare two-week trip to Vietnam.

One of the briefing officers at district headquarters was Capt. Nguyen Thanh Linh. Dressed in an olive drab North Vietnamese uniform and Ho Chi Minh rubber tire sandals, he said, in answer to a question, that he had commanded the Cu Chi Liberation Battalion during 1966.

That was the unit the American colonel's "Black Lion" battalion had opposed. The slightly-built, 45-year-old Capt. Linh looked quizzically as I pursued my questioning. Yes, he said, intelligence reports had informed him at the time that the opposing American battalion commander had been killed.

As he recalled those days for our tourist group, the horror of a war I had witnessed from only one side became vividly real. Capt. Linh spoke in French with grudging respect and almost without hatred about his former enemies, the Americans. The death of Eyster and many other Americans in those early war years

shocked the American public, but as the captain talked it was evident the battles had not been one-sided. Of the 600 men in the Cu Chi battalion that fought Eyster's Black Lions in January 1966, only four survived the war, two officers and two non-commissioned officers, Linh said. The battalion itself "was wiped out several times," he said. "Each time we reconstructed it. In the whole sector we lost 12,000 men in the course of the war."

The former battlefields looked lush and sleepy as our group drove from Saigon northwest along the river bearing the city's name. Some deep B-52 bomb craters were still visible, retained as fish ponds or wallowing holes for animals. Youth labor gangs were widening a road, and occasionally a reminder of the war would appear. A rusting armored personnel carrier with 1st Infantry Division markings and "Little Rose" painted on its side loomed out of a bamboo thicket. The wreck of a U.S. helicopter was overgrown with elephant grass.

The battleground we were being taken to lay beneath our feet, at one, two and three levels underground. It was a twisting octopus of tunnels and caverns stretching from Cu Chi toward Saigon and the surrounding provincial capitals. The tunnels were marked in black lines on a 12 by 12-foot map hanging from a briefing room wall.

The slippery, humid corridors, about two feet wide and two feet high, blocked with wooden trapdoors at underground intersections, spanned the history of the whole Vietnam War, starting from the days when Communist agents hid from the French police. But it was during the American phase of the war, Linh said, that the system was truly tested.

"As more and more American soldiers arrived to occupy the surface above, the more we extended our system below," said a senior officer at the briefing, Col. Duong Long Sang. "At the end we had a three-tier tunnel system and everything was underground—the toilets, the hospitals, all our soldiers, many civilians and even water buffalo." The colonel continued, "We literally dug for 30 years, usually in the dark, squatting down. We carved out about a meter every eight hours, and women distributed the earth on the surface, hiding it under fallen leaves."

The tunnels crept under some U.S. positions. "Several times we knew the American field commanders would sit like this on their metal chairs directly above us," Linh said with a grin.

192

Left, as he lay mortally wounded by a Viet Cong sniper's bullet, Lt. Col. George Eyster told AP photographer Horst Faas "Before I go I'd like to talk to the guy who controls those incredible men in the tunnels". Below, a diagram showed a typical cross section of the tunnels used as fortifications by the Viet Cong

Breathing Hole

Upper Chamber

Supply Cache

Eleven years later Faas did meet the tunnel expert, Capt. Nguyen Thanh Linh shown standing at one of the thousands of wooden trap doors leading to the vast underground complex.

The Vietnamese took our group for a visit, and as noisy swarms of mosquitoes buzzed around our heads we pushed ourselves through the narrow corridors, obviously built by and for slender Vietnamese. "We always move in the dark, saving our candles and torches for emergencies," Linh said, "Our amputees lay in the dark, sometimes for months."

But eventually the Americans figured out the counterattack. First they used hunting dogs "and we battled them underground with rifle butts, mines and knives," said Linh. Then somebody had the idea of using American toilet soap and the Vietnamese started smelling the same as the GIs. "That stopped the dogs," Linh said.

Next came the "tunnel rats — small, tough Americans, like us," Linh said. "They crawled into the tunnels with exposives and gas to blast us out. We installed more escape routes, more tiers, but sometimes we were cornered and tried to kill them with bayonets so as not to give our positions away.

"Many Americans died in the tunnels. They wasted much time pulling their dead back. That gave us time to regroup. The more we killed, the fewer problems we had," Linh said.

The Americans tried flooding the tunnels "and we lost many men until we constructed upper tier escape levels," Col. Sang said.

Finally, said Linh, came the "scorched earth" policy that from 1968 on saw regular B-52 bombing of the tunnel complexes. Only direct hits killed, Linh said, but he described the awesome experience of a near miss: "Fire would be everywhere, the body would be thrown back and forth in the tunnel, shirt and pants would be ripped apart by the suction of the air blast."

Sang stated: "The Americans used to say that as long as there were soldiers of the Liberation Front in the Cu Chi tunnels, Saigon would be in danger. They were right.

"We planned the 1968 Tet attack against the U.S. Embassy in Saigon from here. And it was also from here that details for the final, successful liberation of Saigon on April 30, 1975, were drawn up."

Linh said, as we climbed back into our vehicles for the drive back to Saigon, "The greatest pleasure in those days was to stick one's head out to the surface and just breathe air."

I watched him take a gulp of the heavy, humid and undisturbed air that hangs over peaceful Cu Chi today.

Reggie Jackson Clinched Victory For Yankees In '77 World Series

After a successful road show with stops all over the baseball map, the World Series staged a return to its most popular matchup when the New York Yankees and Los Angeles Dodgers met for the 1977 world championship.

In a simpler, more serene time, when the Dodgers played in Brooklyn and rooting for the Yankees was like rooting for General Motors, the series seemed reserved for an annual showdown between the two teams. Seven times between 1941 and 1956 they had collided in World Series confrontations that captured New York. Together, they had supplied some of baseball's most memorable October moments.

—There was Yankee Don Larson's perfect game, the only no-hitter in World Series history, pitched in 1956.

—There was Sandy Amoros' desperate, running catch that saved the 1955 Series and their first world championship for the Dodgers.

—There was Floyd Bevens' near no-hitter spoiled by Cookie Lavagetto's pinch double that won the fourth game of the 1947 Series for Brooklyn, and a circus catch by the Dodgers' Al Gionfriddo that robbed Joe DiMaggio of an extra base hit two games later.

—There was Mickey Owen's dropped third strike with two out in the ninth inning of Game Four in 1941 that gave the Yankees a lift and eventually the victory.

The Dodgers left New York, moving to Los Angeles in 1958 and after one more World Series meeting in 1963, the matchup went into moth balls. The Dodgers won three more National League titles—in 1965, 1966 and 1974—but each time, when they reached the World Series, the Yankees were nowhere to be found.

Baseball's most successful franchise had slipped into a 12-year slide—a decline that did not end until 1976 when new management, headed by principal owner George Steinbrenner and President Gabe Paul, engineered some

Yankee slugger Reggie Jackson slammed his third consecutive home run in the final game

clever trades that returned New York to the top of the American League.

But in the 1976 World Series, the Yankees were wiped out in four straight games by NL champion Cincinnati—an embarassment that did not sit well with the front office. "We went to work the very next day to make sure that never happened to us again," said Steinbrenner.

His method was money. Baseball's free agent revolution had put some of the game's top names on the marketplace and all it took to get them was money. Steinbrenner, never shy when it came to opening his wallet, lured two of the best ones to New York, signing slugging outfielder Reggie Jackson and ace pitcher Don Gullett at a cost of $5 million.

The move was considered a major coup in the free agent war and seemed to cement New York's position at the top of the American League. But winning wasn't quite that easy.

In a tumultuous 1977 season that included countless intramural squabbles, the Yankees were engaged in a three-way battle with Boston and Baltimore to win their division. Only a sizzling September enabled them to nail down the division crown and even then, their margin of victory was a slender 2½ games, down from the 10½ by which they had won the year before.

In the best-of-five AL pennant playoff against West Division champion Kansas City, New York seemed permanently perched on the edge of elimination. Constantly clawing from behind, they reached the eighth inning of the fifth and final game trailing 3-1. But they scrambled back, scoring a run in the eighth and three more in the ninth to swipe a pennant that the Royals seemed to have wrapped up.

Meanwhile, the Dodgers under new Manager Tom Lasorda, dethroned Cincinnati in the National League West, beating the Reds by a fat 10 games, the same margin by which they had lost to the Reds the year before.

In the pennant playoffs, the Dodgers and Philadelphia Phillies split the first two games. Then in Game Three, trailing by two runs with two out and none on in the ninth, Los Angeles staged a sudden rally which won that pivotal game and turned the series around. Playing in a rain storm the next night, the Dodgers won again and headed into the 1977 World Series.

Gullett opened the first game for the Yankees and carried a 3-2 lead into the ninth inning. But Dusty Baker singled and after the Yankees let him escape on a pickoff play, he moved to second on a walk. Sparky Lyle, hero of the playoffs with victories in the last two games at Kansas City, relieved and pinch hitter Lee Lacy hit a single that scored Baker with the tying run.

The Yankees threatened in both the 10th and 11th innings but each time brilliant plays by backup catcher Jerry Grote on attempted sacrifices shortcircuited the New York rallies. In the 12th, that bunting failure paid off in victory.

Willie Randolph, who had homered earlier, opened with a double. The Dodgers chose to walk Thurman Munson, who already had a single and double. The situation screamed for a bunt and Paul Blair, a defensive replacement, tried to oblige. But he had no more success than his teammates had and Manager Billy Martin finally took the sacrifice off, freeing his batter to swing away. Blair did that much more successfully, slapping a single to left that scored Randolph with the deciding run.

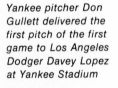

Yankee pitcher Don Gullett delivered the first pitch of the first game to Los Angeles Dodger Davey Lopez at Yankee Stadium

Dodger Dusty Baker dove to avoid a tag by Yankee first baseman Chris Chambliss

Game Two belonged to Dodger power. Strapped for pitching, Martin tried to finesse a start out of onetime ace Catfish Hunter, who had fallen on hard times and had not pitched in over a month. The maneuver failed dismally with Hunter shelled from the mound in less than three innings after surrendering five runs on homers by Ron Cey, Steve Yeager and Reggie Smith. Steve Garvey added another homer in the eighth. Burt Hooton, meanwhile, limited the Yankees to five hits and the Dodgers had an easy 6-1 victory that tied the series.

Bored by the game, New York fans turned ugly. Several jumped on the field and one youngster ran the length of the foul line from left field to home plate and then executed a perfect hook slide while catcher Munson and Umpire Ed Sudol looked on, a little dumbfounded. Debris was strewn over the field at game's end and many expressed happiness at leaving New York and the raucus rooters behind as the series moved to Los Angeles for the next three games.

The trip west took 5½ hours by air, more than enough time for the Yankee cauldron to start bubbling again. Jackson, embroiled in much of the year's controversy, questioned Martin's decision to start Hunter in Game Two. The manager snapped back, suggesting his slump-

ing right fielder had enough other problems without trying to manage the team too.

Before Game Three, the griping was so hot and heavy that Paul called a news conference to try to calm things down. It was becoming a routine job for the Yankee president, who had presided over the season-long soap opera.

With peace restored before Game Three, strong-armed Mike Torrez mowed the Dodgers down 5-3, beating Los Angeles ace Tommy John. Mickey Rivers, hitless in the first two games, ripped two doubles and a single to lead the nine-hit Yankee attack but Torrez was the key, allowing only two hits after Baker's three-run homer in the third had erased an early Yankee lead.

For Game Four, Martin called on Ron Guidry, a pint-sized left-hander who was the Yankees' most dependable pitcher all season. In a year when more expensive arms failed the Yankees, Guidry won 16 games.

The Dodgers went for Doug Rau, who won 14 games but had been idle since the final day of the regular season because of a sore arm. And, just as Martin's second game gamble with a rusty Hunter had backfired, so did Lasorda's decision to start Rau.

Doubles by Jackson and Chris Chambliss sandwiching Lou Piniella's single built a three-

197

Fans mobbed the field after the Yankees won the Series

run second inning that kayoed Rau. Then Jackson tagged a sixth inning homer.

Guidry overcame a two-run homer by Davey Lopes and got a boost from Piniella, whose leaping catch at the left field fence robbed Cey of a certain homer that would have tied the score. After the catch, Guidry coasted to a brilliant 4–2 victory, allowing just four hits to give the Yankees a 3-1 lead in the series.

In Game Five, the Yankees went for the clincher with Gullett, who had pitched so well in the opener. The Dodgers came back with Don Sutton, who matched Gullett through most of Game One.

Los Angeles scored one run in the first inning and then knocked out Gullett in a four-run fourth capped by Yeager's three-run homer. Smith added a two-run homer later and before they were through, the Dodgers had stayed alive with an impressive 10-4 romp. Almost overlooked in the rash of runs were consecutive eighth inning homers by Munson and Jackson. They didn't matter particularly that day but turned out to be significant two nights later when the series returned to New York for Game Six.

In the hours before the next game, the Yankees saw fit to call another of their frequent news conferences "to clear the air." This time it was to bury once and for all the rumor that Martin would be fired after the Series, win or lose. Five times by his own count during the tumultuous season, Martin had come within a whisker of being cut loose by the Yankees. Now the club confirmed that the axe was no longer hanging over him, for the moment at least.

Game Six became a virtuoso performance for Jackson, the controversial slugger, whose seesaw season matched the ebb and flow of the incredible Yankee year.

"Love me or hate me, you can't ignore me," Jackson liked to tell writers who chronicled the season's ups and downs. And in the final game of the year, it was impossible to ignore him because Jackson rewrote the series record book.

Three times he walloped huge home runs, each of them on the first pitch he saw. The first two were low line drives into the right field stands and the last one was an enormous blast into the center field bleachers that sealed the 8-4 championship clinching victory.

He became only the second man in 74 years of World Series history to hit three homers in a single game and the first to connect five times in a single series. The only other three-homer games belong to the legendary Babe Ruth, who did it in 1926 and 1928. But even Ruth didn't hit the first pitch for each of his homers.

Jackson scored four runs and drove in five in the wrapup victory and set a host of records, easily becoming the most valuable player in the series.

In the dressing room, the right fielder embraced the manager as both men celebrated the end of the tumultuous season and the Yankees' 21st World Championship. There were some who said that Jackson and Martin would never make it through the year together but they had made it and when it was over, they were champions.

198

HIGH COURT TO DECIDE WHETHER CONSTITUTION IS COLORBLIND

Hundreds of spectators, many of whom had waited in line more than 12 hours to assure themselves a seat, packed the majestic courtroom of marble and mahogany as the U.S. Supreme Court began its working day Oct. 12.

For 90 minutes, those spectators sat silently as the nine justices of the nation's highest court listened to lawyers' arguments and posed questions in a case entitled *University of California Regents v. Allan Paul Bakke.*

Along with the crowds and national attention, the controversy had brought to the court one of the most profound and sensitive questions ever to confront it—is the Constitution colorblind? Many civil rights leaders predicted the court's answer would dictate the future course of the country's race relations. Some said it would decide the future role racial minorities would play in American society. Even before October's oral arguments, the court decision that would not come until sometime in 1978 was talked about in terms of "landmark" and "historic."

Allan Bakke, 37-year-old engineer with the government's space program from Sunnyvale, Calif., decided rather late in life to become a doctor. He sued the California regents in 1974 after twice being rejected for admission to the state's medical school at Davis. Bakke, who is white, said he had been made the victim of racial discrimination by the school's special minority admissions policy. He charged that an affirmative action program which reserved 16 of the 100 openings in each med school entering class of disadvantaged minority students accepted less qualified black, Hispanic and Asian-American applicants ahead of him.

"Reverse discrimination" is what the admissions policy was called. Bakke, whose application to 10 other medical schools had been rejected, never actually had to prove that any of the minority students admitted to the med school at Davis in 1973 and 1974 were less qualified than he. The university conceded it could not prove Bakke was not excluded because of the affirmative action program.

The California Supreme Court ruled in favor of Bakke, saying that a 109-year-old amendment to the Constitution could not tolerate a premise "that some races may be afforded a higher degree of protection against unequal treatment than others." The 14th Amendment cited by the state court had been passed by Congress and ratified in 1868 to hold out to recently freed black slaves the promise of full membership in American society, ordering all states not to "deny to any person . . . the equal protection of the laws."

Once learning of Bakke's victory and the university's intention to appeal to the Supreme Court, civil rights leaders feared the worst—a striking down of most or all of the thousands of affirmative action programs begun in the 1960s to give racial minorities an extra helping hand as compensation for past discrimination in education and employment.

They feared that even a victory for Bakke on narrow legal grounds would leave a psychological residual which could subject many affirmative action programs to challenging and costly lawsuits. Civil rights activists called such programs necessary "artificial instruments," much like the busing of schoolchildren to racially integrated schools, in order to get a democracy to practice what it preached. But many persons, although sympathetic to the cause of racial justice and equality, viewed many affirmative action methods as kin to the quotas used in the past to hold down minorities. The intense national interest was reflected in the number of "friend-of-the-court" briefs submitted by individuals and groups interested in telling their views to the Supreme Court.

Not since 1954 had the court received so much reading material on one case. It was then the court outlawed racial segregation, and changed the way America lived.

Shortly after doctors told Sen. Hubert Humphrey he had cancer, this building in Washington, D.C., destined to house the Department of Health, Education and Welfare, was named after him. Mrs. Humphrey stood next to her husband

HUBERT H. HUMPHREY BUILDING

Marcel Breuer, Architect

This building is dedicated to Senator Hubert H. Humphrey in recognition of his contribution to the health, education and welfare of this Nation

Dedicated November 1, 1977

Jimmy Carter
President
United States of America

PRESSURE SUITS FOR
YOUNG BURN VICTIMS. . . .

Three young boys, badly burned in an explosion in a methane-filled storm sewer, were able to return to school in Denver, Colo., after doctors fitted them with special pressure suits to help the slow healing process. The youngsters said their classmates accepted them but some adults made rude remarks.

Juan Salazar saluted the flag at Ora Oliver Elementary School

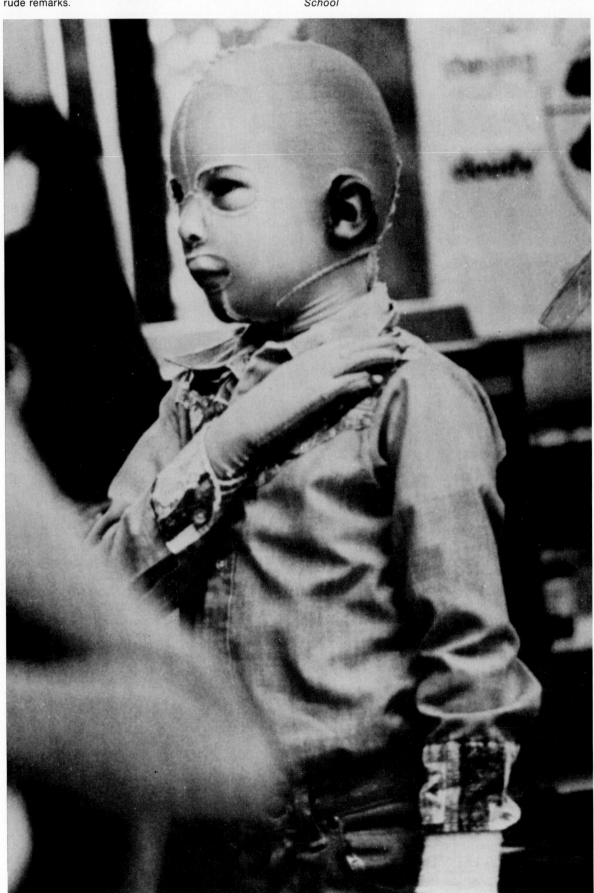

Above, the three burn victims became used to their bizarre-looking suits as they walked along a school corridor. Left, victim Robb Hall managed to play soccer with his classmates despite the special suit which covered the upper part of his body with holes for eyes, ears, mouth and finger tips

SUPREME COURT CLEARED WAY FOR CONCORDE TO LAND

After spending a year and a half in a holding pattern, the supersonic Concorde jetliner finally got its chance to fly in and out of New York City's John F. Kennedy International Airport.

The U.S. Supreme Court cleared the way for the big plane to land Oct. 17 when its justices turned down, without comment, a request by the Port Authority of New York and New Jersey that they order a delay to all Concorde operations at the airport until a formal appeal could be filed with the court. And so the long ban on the use of the field by the British-French plane ended Oct. 19 when the Concorde, after dissipating its sonic boom well out to sea, touched down at Kennedy for a maiden landing.

"Loud!" said a policeman and covered his ears as the needle-nosed plane came in for a graceful 160-mile-an-hour landing. He was one of many officers on duty against possible anti-Concorde demonstrations that never came about. But Bill Gradiska, whose home was near the airfield, declared, "I'm here 46 years and I've put up with 707s and 747s and they're twice as loud as this plane was today. I heard nothing. It was unbelievably soundless and beauti-

ful." Another area resident, Joe Albergo, agreed but with suspicions: "It sure sounded like the guy cut out his engines or was gliding in. I think Air France was duping us." Said Capt. Brian Walpole, who rode the maiden flight as a passenger but was slated to pilot the inaugural run for British Airways in November, said, "We finished deceleration and leveled out below the speed of sound 50 miles from the coast. That was to ensure an adequate margin from the sonic boom."

Although regularly scheduled Concorde flights to the United States had been landing at Dulles International Airport near Washington, environmentalists and families living near Kennedy had fought to bar the SST. They appealed through the courts and through the Port Authority of New York and New Jersey, which operated Kennedy. Opponents contended the plane's noise and vibration would reduce the value of homes and affront and possibly injure the human ear while its exhaust emissions would further pollute the atmosphere near the airport.

By Oct. 22, the Concorde had made six takeoffs and landings at Kennedy, and its rumble never approached the 112-decibel limit in effect at the airport. Opponents, however, called the test flights "a farce" and said if a noise standard wasn't imposed at JFK to keep the SST out, they would reinstate the protests which earlier had paralyzed traffic at the airport a number of times.

The controversial Concorde as it touched down

A Lebanese father lifted his crippled son to kiss the statue of Charbel Makhlouf, a Lebanese saint. Pilgrims to his tomb have been cured of different diseases

Also in OCTOBER . . .

THE CAR THAT TOOK FLIGHT

Americans got a lesson in daring when a Japanese stunt driver raced his sports car off a ramp at Marina del Ray, Calif., and sailed through the air in a sequence for a Japanese movie

The car, a modified Porsche 911 sailed off the ramp at 100 miles an hour

Left, the airborne vehicle and its driver traveled more than 300 feet through the air. Below left, going into a dive, the car came down near a buoy (left) placed there to locate the auto should the driver get into trouble. Below right, the car slammed into the water with a huge splash. Divers quickly removed the driver who was reported okay, but as a precaution he was taken to a hospital for a checkup

Thai newsboys did a brisk business as newspapers headlined news of the coup

THAILAND SEATED EIGHTH GOVERNMENT IN FOUR YEARS

Thailand had switched governments seven times in four years, so uprisings were no novelty in that Southeast Asian nation. But when a bloodless coup unseated the year-old regime of Prime Minister Tanin Kraivixien Oct. 20 marking change No. 8, many observers were surprised by the explanation.

Defense Minister Sangad Chaloryu said he was deposing the Tanin government because it had been taking too long to restore democracy.

First sign of a coup came when Radio Thailand announced that a *Revolutionary Committee* composed of both military officers and civilians headed by Sangad had taken power. Soon after that Sangad came on the air to announce that a general election would be held during 1978.

Meanwhile, soldiers armed with machine guns and rifles, ringed Government House, Tanin's official compound, as well as other key government and military facilities in Bangkok. Armored cars moved into the supreme military compound and jeeps patrolled the streets of the capital.

Sangad, a 61-year-old retired admiral, said that in addition to holding elections, a constitution would be promulgated and martial law lifted in 1978.

The new leader said Thailand would make an effort to improve relations with Communist Indochina, an apparent reference to the border fighting which had been going on with Cambodia. He also told reporters, however, that there would be no major changes in the country's policy which had been oriented toward the West.

The deposed Tanin who used to lecture newsmen on the evils of communism, was accused of causing a stalemate in Thailand's political situation. He had banned most labor unions, censored the press and clamped stern controls on the universities frequent centers of disruption. Tanin had taken over following a previous coup a year earlier. But he had soon alienated the military which found him too conservative and felt that he did not consult with Thailand's military leaders often enough.

STORMING OF HIJACKED PLANE GAVE TERRORISM A DRAMATIC SETBACK

At a time when assassinations, kidnappings and hijackings were horrifying people around the world, terrorism suddenly suffered a setback.

The dramatic turn came when the West German government refused to bow to the demands of an armed band of four who had comandeered a Lufthansa jet and set out on a 110-hour odyssey of terror. When it was over in the pre-dawn hours of Oct. 18, three hijackers lay dead and one wounded, while 83 passengers and four crew members were rescued.

It began Oct. 13 when the Lufthansa jetliner took off from the Spanish resort of Majorca filled mainly with West German vacationers returning to Frankfurt. When the big Boeing 737 became airborne, two Arabic-speaking men and two women pulled out pistols and grenades and ordered the pilot to change course for Dubai.

For two and a half days the plane sat on an airstrip in the Persian Gulf sheikdom while the kidnappers fired off an ultimatum to Bonn. Release from West German prisons 11 guerrillas including Andreas Baader, cofounder of the Baader-Meinhof gang. Also free two Palestinian guerrillas from Turkish jails and pay $15 million in ransom, plus $43,000 for each of the 11 guerrillas. If these demands were not met, said the message, it would mean the death of Hanns-Martin Schleyer, West German industrialist who had been held captive by West German terrorists since early September.

A second ultimatum, sent to the Paris newspaper Ce Soir, said "any attempt on your part to delay or deceive us will mean immediate execution of Hanns-Martin Schleyer and all the passengers and crew of the plane."

Taking off from Dubai, the hijacked plane was flown to Aden after being refused permission to land in Oman. There, the hijack leader who called himself 'Walter Mahmud" suddenly flew into a rage and gunned down the pilot, Capt. Jurgen Schuman.

A day later, the plane pushed on to Mogadishu, Somalia. When it landed, Schuman's body was dumped through the emergency exit chute and the vigil resumed.

It was learned later, however, that as soon as word of the hijacking reached Bonn, chancellor Helmut Schmidt had summoned West German leaders and they had agreed that the only solution was an Entebbe-type raid. Tapped for the job was the elite Border Guard Group 9, which had been formed after the Munich Olympic massacre of 1972. This marked the first anti-terrorist deployment of the 175-man group.

Two squads of 32 commandos took off on the trail of the air pirates, reportedly trailing the plane first to Dubai. On Oct. 17, the plane carrying the commandos, but ostensibly loaded with medics and technicians, touched down under cover of darkness at Mogadishu, not far from the hijacked jetliner.

At 3 a.m. on Oct. 18, airport officials managed to lure all four hijackers into the cockpit of the captive plane supposedly for negotiations. Meanwhile, three commandos slipped up to the rear door of the plane. Suddenly the commandos swung open the door and exploded new-type flash grenades whose loud noise and flash could immobi-

206

lize a person for up to 10 seconds. This gave the three attackers time to spring into the plane while 25 comrades opened emergency doors over the wings. The first commandos to enter the cabin shielded hostages with their bodies, shouting "lie down. Don't panic." Passengers slid quickly under their seats as other commandos surged forward gunning down the four hijackers, killing three.

The jubilation that swept West Germany with news of the rescue was soon muted when word was received that Andreas Baader and two other imprisoned West German terrorists had committed suicide and a fourth wounded herself. The terrorists presumably hoped the deaths would turn them into martyrs for their cause. The news did touch off bombings in three Italian cities and demonstrations in Paris, Athens, Vienna and London.

At this point, West German Walter Scheel went on television to plead with Schleyer's abductors to free him. But 24 hours later, Schleyer's body was found in the trunk of an abandoned car in the French town of Mulhouse. Searchers were guided to the spot by a telephone call to the Paris daily Liberation. The caller identified himself as a member of the Red Army faction that had claimed responsibility for Schleyer's abduction. This was followed by a message to Liberation from the terror group with the blunt warning, "The battle has just begun."

FOR THE RECORD

SENTENCED. Maryland Gov. Marvin Mandel, to four years in federal prison. Mandel, who was sentenced Oct. 7, and five codefendants were convicted of mail fraud and racketeering Aug. 23 in a retrial of a case involving his attempts to help friends obtain legislation favorable to a race track they owned. Mandel, a Democrat who followed Republican Spiro T. Agnew to the Maryland statehouse in 1969, was suspended from office immediately after the sentencing. However, he did not resign and could regain office if his conviction was overturned before his term was up in 1979.

Two young people attended the funeral of Andreas Baader and two other terrorists, keeping their faces carefully covered

NOVEMBER

Son Of Sam Struck Eight Times And Left Six Dead

The series of killings set off one of the biggest police manhunts in history

He struck eight times, the killer known as "Son of Sam," and left six of his victims dead. Five were women, the sixth a male companion of one of the women. When a pattern emerged — each of the female victims had long, dark hair and all six were shot with the same .44 caliber gun — fear seized New York, the nation's largest city. Young women took to tucking their long hair into buns or wearing head scarves, couples avoided parking in secluded places, parents worried for daughters abroad at night, and police mounted one of the largest and most publicized manhunts in history.

When the hunt was over and a 24-year old suspect named David Berkowitz taken in custody, the "Son of Sam" case still refused to vanish from the headlines. After tedious psychiatric studies and hearings a judge in Brooklyn ruled by November, that Berkowitz was mentally fit to stand trial, but lawyers for the accused slayer protested that he could not receive a fair trial in that borough because of the publicity the case had received.

Publicity was not limited to Brooklyn, nor to New York City, nor even to the nation. The killer's notoriety reached the front page of the Vatican's staid L'Osservatore Romano and the Soviet government journal Izvestia, which could not resist the comment that such mass horror was not unusual in a city with a huge rate of crime and mental illness. On the day of Berkowitz's arrest, all three television networks saturated their newscasts with the story. In New York, the Daily News sold 350,000 more copies than usual, the New York Times 50,000 extras.

It was as though the killer expected to be captured ultimately, but not before a plan for one last act of terror, a machine-gun slaughter in a discotheque in the fashionable Hamptons on Long Island. He said the police "would be all summer counting the bodies."

Instead, on Aug. 11, police waited patiently as David Berkowitz walked out of his Yonkers, N.Y., apartment, a seventh-floor room littered with pornography and smeared with graffiti, and approached his cream-colored Ford parked outside. Inside the Ford, police had glimpsed a machine gun and a .44-caliber Bulldog revolver. As Berkowitz turned the ignition key, suddenly the barrels of 15 guns were leveled at him.

"Police. Don't move."

"Okay," David Berkowitz said, "You've got me." Then he smiled.

After his arrest, Berkowitz was cooperative with police, describing shooting exploits as calmly as he might have described his job at the Bronx post office where he worked sorting mail. He used many of the same phrases that Son of Sam had used in his taunting letters to police, including one in a note that had never been made public: "I only shoot pretty girls."

The first pretty girl was 18-year-old Donna Lauria. It was a quiet summer's night, July 29, 1976, and she sat outside her Bronx apartment house chatting with a girlfriend, Jody Valenti, 19, who had just driven her home from a discotheque. The time was 1:10 a.m. Suddenly the windless night calm was shattered by the repeated sharp crack of a gun. Donna Lauria collapsed in death, Jody Valenti, wounded in the thigh, later recovered. Both had long, brown hair.

The killer struck again under a new moon at 2 a.m. nearly two months later, on Oct. 23. Carl Denaro, 20, was shot and wounded as he sat in a car in a residential section of Queens with his girlfriend, Rosemary Keenan. Denaro wore his hair at shoulder length. Police surmised that he might have been mistaken for a woman.

Another month passed. Then on Saturday, Nov. 27, at 12:40 a.m., Joanne Lomino, 18, and Donna DeMasi, 17, were shot and wounded on the porch of Miss Lomino's home in Queens. The gunman approached the two young women and asked directions. Without warning, he drew his gun and fired. Miss Lomino was left a cripple, paralyzed from the waist down. Both had long, brown hair.

New Yorkers celebrated the New Year without knowledge that the three shootings were somehow connected. Police had not yet put together the pieces. Neither did they link the next shooting with the previous ones. It happened on a Sunday, Jan. 30, when Christine Freund, an attractive 26-year-old with long hair, was shot to death as she sat in a car with her boyfriend, John Diel, outside the railroad station in Forest Hills, one of Queen's better residential sections. Diel was not injured.

On Tuesday, March 8, within a block of Miss Freund's murder, Virginia Voskerichian, 19, a Columbia University student, was shot in the face and killed at 7:45 p.m. as she was walking along the street. Her hair, of course, was long.

Now, for the first time, homicide detectives were able to announce that the series of shootings were the work of one person. They de-

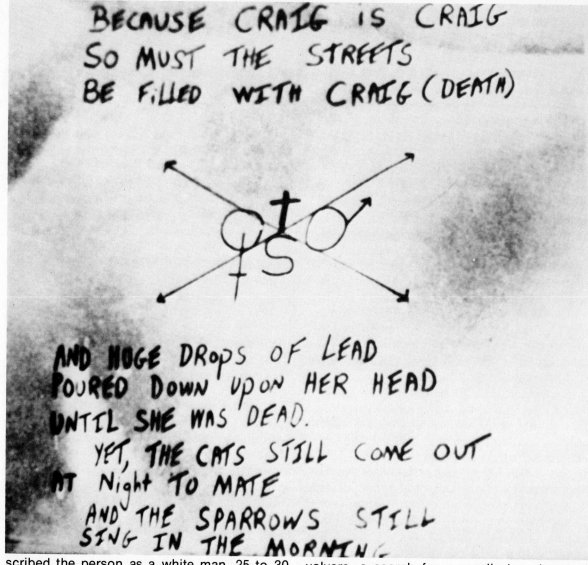

scribed the person as a white man, 25 to 30 years old, between five-feet-ten and six-feet tall, with mod-styled dark hair. The description said he was clean shaven, clear-skinned, had a pale complexion, that he was right-handed and wont to shoot combat style, from a crouched position, holding the pistol with both hands. They based the description on fleeting glimpses by witnesses and on the significant ballistics discovery that the shootings were done by the same .44-caliber weapon.

The next month, on April 17, the killer struck again. Valentina Suriani, 18, and her boyfriend, Alexander Esau, 19, were shot dead as they sat in a car in the Bronx, five blocks from the scene of the first murder. By now the killer had grown bold. In the car where the young couple died he left a note, taunting the police and vowing to "do it again." He signed the note "Son of Sam."

In reply, the police department issued an appeal that read: "Son of Sam: We know you are not a woman hater and know how you have suffered. We wish to help you and it is not too late. Please let us help you." Appended were the telephone number and the address of the 109th Precinct in Flushing, Queens, where the hunt for the gunman was by now centered.

The police had little to go on. First, they sought to trace the owners of .44-caliber re-

volvers, a search for a needle in a haystack that involved contacting 2,000 gun dealers throughout North America. About 28,000 of the weapons had been produced since their manufacture five years previous, and the task was monumental. Other detectives quietly checked out persons named Sampson or Samson—Son of Sam. Mental hospitals were contacted for escapees. Decoy police teams, each with a man and a woman, were positioned throughout the Bronx and Queens. The killer ignored the bait. More police were assigned exclusively to the hunt for the killer—50 detectives, then 100, finally 300, working around the clock.

As the search mounted to a manhunt seldom if ever matched in New York City, the brash killer mailed a letter to Daily News columnist Jimmy Breslin. It began:

"Hello from the gutters of N.Y.C. which are filled with dog manure, stale wine, urine, and blood. Hello from the sewers of N.Y.C. which swallow up these delicacies when they are washed away by the sweeper trucks. Hello from the cracks in the sidewalks of N.Y.C. and from the ants that dwell in these cracks and feed on the dried blood of the dead that has settled into the cracks." Strangely, he spoke affectionately of his first victim, Donna Lauria, as though he might have known her. "She was a very sweet girl, but Sam's a thirsty lad and won't let me stop killing until he gets his fill of blood."

On June 26, near a Queens discotheque, the gunman, his macabre thirst unquenched, struck again. Badly hurt, the victims lived—and the public clamor for his capture reached a crescendo.

Meanwhile, David Berkowitz lived his own tormented life in a world of demons and fantasies.

He was born June 1, 1953, the son of Betty and Tony Falco, parents he never knew. When he was 17 months old he became David Berkowitz, the adopted son of Nat and Pearl Berkowitz. When David was 14, Pearl Berkowitz died. David often wondered, in later years, about his real mother, but never tried to find her; when his adoptive mother died he wept openly at her funeral.

Indeed, David Berkowitz had few known complaints about his adoptive upbringing. He was raised as a Jew and did wonder about his true religious roots but not enough to investigate them.

He left high school in his senior year, a shy type, with few friends. He lived in the Bronx with his father, in an apartment building where his father's mother also lived, and spent a good deal of time with his grandmother. He seemed fascinated by uniforms, and with an acquaintance organized an unofficial volunteer fire department in the apartment complex. He wore the uniform almost constantly.

Soon he chose another uniform. He volunteered for the auxiliary police in his precinct, the 45th in the Bronx, and absorbed the police jargon and procedure that later evolved in notes from Son of Sam. Soon he traded in his auxiliary police uniform for another one. In 1971 he enlisted in the Army. The next year, writing home from Korea, he signed his letters "Doughboy Dave" and, later, "Master of Reality." When he returned from Korea he joined the Baptist Church and became what one of his friends described as a "Jesus freak."

Meanwhile, Nat Berkowitz remarried and moved to Florida. David, discharged from the Army, moved into a Bronx apartment. In the rooms below him an elderly woman watched television with the sound turned on too high, apparently, for David's taste. She began receiving notes with crude drawings. One said: "I'm going to kill you." The woman turned down her television, tore up the notes, and soon David moved away, to an apartment in New Rochelle, N.Y. He stayed there only a few months, just long enough for the landlady to notice that he went "beserk" over barking dogs.

David Berkowitz's new residence was the seventh-floor apartment in Yonkers. The apartment offered a panoramic view of the Hudson, a treat for others in the building, but David Berkowitz covered the windows with blankets. By that time, as police reconstructed the activities of Son of Sam, the killer had struck twice, and soon would pour gunfire on the two girls sitting on their porch in Queens. Neither was killed, and from then on Son of Sam changed his style. The next time he shot he held the gun with both hands—and killed Chris Freund.

That was one fatality; there was another. A Christmas Eve party, in 1976, at the home of some neighbors of Berkowitz, was interrupted by gunfire. The guests ran outside. On the porch their dog lay dead. Later, on April 19 and again on April 22, another neighbor received threatening notes complaining about his barking dog. The neighbor was Sam Carr. The notes, from "A Citizen," said "People like you should not be allowed to live in this planet." Five days later the dog was shot and wounded—Sam's dog. Only a few days earlier the police received their first notes from Son of Sam who kept referring to his "master sam." By this time five young people were dead and four injured.

By now, Berkowitz had passed a civil service postal exam and was hired at $6.18 an hour. On March 17, eight days after Son of Sam had pumped a bullet directly into the face of Virgin-

Four of the six persons who were slain by the 44-caliber killer

ia Voskerichian, David Berkowitz began sorting mail. During the breaks at the post office, he often joined in conversations about the city's number-one topic—Son of Sam. He was an average postal clerk, said the postmaster, Frank Viola. "The average ones never stand out."

Sam Carr, however, did not consider threatening notes average behavior. He took the notes to the Yonkers police and told them he thought they might have come from a fellow who behaved rather strangely in the neighborhood, a fellow named David Berkowitz. Another neighbor, Craig Glassman, also had received two wildly threatening letters ("Spit on you and your mother," one said) which bore, oddly enough, the return address of Sam Carr. To police, nothing made much sense but at least there were some amazing coincidences to work with. Yonkers police notified New York City police. The name "David Berkowitz" joined a growing list of "Son of Sam" possibilities.

On July 31, two days after the one-year anniversary of the first Son-of-Sam killing, Stacy Moscowitz and Robert Violante, both in their early 20s, were enjoying themselves by playfully using the swings in a Brooklyn playground. Violante noticed a man sitting on a bench nearby, staring at them. He and Stacy decided to get in his car.

A short distance away Cacelia Davis was walking her dog. She, too, noticed a man who made her uneasy, a man with a strange smile. She hurried to her home and bolted the door. As she turned the lock she heard a loud report, perhaps a shot. Next morning she read in the newspaper that Stacy Moscowitz was dead and

Robert Violante partially blinded by a bullet. Frightened, Cacelia Davis waited four days to notify police, and even then asked a friend to do it for her. When detectives questioned her, Miss Davis recalled that the man she had seen had held a metallic-looking object in his hand. Questioned further, she also recalled that she had seen policemen putting tickets on illegally parked cars in the neighborhood.

A long shot, perhaps, but worth checking into. Detectives consulted their computer for a list of the tickets issued on the morning of July 31 in the Bensonhurst section of Brooklyn. Ironically, the policemen who had written the tickets had completely forgotten about them in the rush to get the shooting victims to the hospital. On one of the tickets was the name David Berkowitz. He had parked next to a fireplug.

Ten days later, police located the car, license number 561-XLB, parked in front of the apartment in Yonkers. A detective peered through the window and saw the butt of a machine gun protruding through a gunny sack, a road map of Suffolk County, and an envelope addressed to Suffolk and New York police and the press. The handwriting, the detective noticed, was in the same handwriting as that of Son of Sam. He would learn later that the note told of Son of Sam's plan of slaughter at the discotheque in the Hamptons, in Suffolk County.

After the stakeout and the arrest, on the way to the Yonkers police station, detective Ed Zigo, who had spotted the car and its contents, spoke to the handcuffed man beside him.

"Dave," he said, "I'm Detective Zigo."

"I'm Son of Sam," the man replied.

1977 Saw China Embark On The Long, Hard Road To Industrialization

China in 1977 was like a patient emerging from a long and debilitating illness. Still shaky from the ravages of the disease—an acute case of political radicalism—the nation embarked on an ambitious project which could have daunted a healthier and more powerful country: industrialization by the year 2000.

The ChineseCommunist Party's 11th National Congress, convened in Peking from Aug. 12 to 18, elected a moderate new post-Mao Tse-tung leadership, drummed the radical "Gang of Four", headed by Mao's widow, Chiang Ching, out of the party, and laid down the blueprint for China's second Great Leap Forward in two decades.

The closing communique described it as a congress of unity and victory. It also could have called it a congress of change. For what the 1,510 delegates did was bury Mao's more revolutionary and Utopian concepts and resurrect those which more closely fitted their own moderate, pragmatic ideals. The era which opened up before a reborn China was patterned less on Mao's soaring theories than on the no-nonsense line of his long-time chief lieutenant, the late Premier Chou En-lai.

Meeting in Mao's long shadow 11 months after his death, the congress veered away from the personal brand of leadership which had marked his 42 years at the party's helm. Instead it named a five-man top echelon in which new party chairman Hua Kuo-feng, 56, evidently was the first among equals, sharing his power with two vice-chairmen, old Marshal Yeh Chien-ying and senior vice-premier Teng Hsiao-ping, and to a lesser extent, with two other vice-chairmen, Li Hsien-nien, the economist, and Mao's old bodyguard, Wang Tung-hsing.

Twice disgraced and twice rehabilitated, the 73-year-old Teng clearly was expected to supply the spark which would ignite the prairie fire of China's just-beginning modernization of industry, agriculture, national defense, science and technology.

Against a backdrop of red flags, Chinese demonstrators beat gongs to show support for the appointment of Hua Kuo-feng as prime minister

Purged by the radicals during the 1966–69 Cultural Revolution, Teng had been brought back by his old friend and mentor, Chou En-lai in 1973. Two years later, caught up in the power struggle for the dying Mao's mantle he was personally cashiered by the Old Helmsman himself. With Mao's death in September 1976, the emergence of Hua Kuo-feng as compromise choice to succeed him, and the arrest of the radicals, Teng's fortunes again looked up. After an excruciating delay of 15 months, the new moderate leadership called him back in July to administer the program which he and Chou had spelled out in January 1975.

That plan called for a sweeping away of what the moderates called the malign influence of the radicals on the economy, the party, the defense forces, scientific advance, education and culture.

Since the proclamation of the People's Republic in 1949, China had been battered by the ebbing and flowing tides of leftism and rightism. Sitting at the political center, Mao waged purge after purge against what he regarded as the extremes of the party spectrum. On a national scale, they were intended, he said, to cleanse the body politic of capitalist, bourgeois and Soviet influences. Whether by coincidence or not, these high-sounding ideological movements trapped and destroyed a succession of Chinese dissidents, those who dared question the Maoist line and leadership. Old comrades who had shared Mao's revolutionary road awoke one day to find themselves branded ultrarightists and consigned to the rubbish heap of Chinese communist history.

Chiang Ching and her associates seemed fated to escape the doom which had overtaken Mao's rivals thanks to the support the old chairman—now more radical than the radicals in his old age—gave them during the cultural revolution and in the decade which followed.

Brandishing Mao's name and thoughts, they purged their moderate enemies, among them Teng and former chief of state Liu Shao-chi, turned savagely on Mao's designated successor, Marshal Lin Piao, after his death and denunciation as a traitor in 1971, then set about remaking China in their own image.

If the subsequent charges against them were to be believed, everything they touched turned to dross. Wedded to a radicalism which put Marxist-Maoist theory ahead of practical common sense, they were charged with having: (1) crippled the education system, (2) banned pure research in the natural sciences, (3) diminished the quantity and quality of literature, the arts and drama, (4) severely damaged the economy, (5) subverted the militia and (6) plotted to overthrow Hua Kuo-feng.

How much Chiang Ching and her associates actually were to blame for all this may never be known. Had they been allowed to talk—they were not—the guilt might be more widely distributed. But whatever the source, the moderate regime undertook to set matters right. It saw clearly that a modern state could not be built on such foundations. A series of national conferences tackled the problems and set out the goals to be achieved.

They decided that if China was to create the vast reservoir of technicians, skilled workers, scientists, modernized peasants, and intellectuals needed for the giant leap forward, some-

Secretary of State Cyrus Vance, left, and Chinese Foreign Minister Huang Hua got down to the business at hand at a dinner for Vance in Peking

thing more than communist fervor was required. Material incentives, long condemned as heresy by the radicals, were invoked. On Oct. 1, 46 percent of the work force got their first pay raises in 10 years.

Handed out to the worst hardship cases, they did little to raise the level of urban poverty. But more were promised.

The problem of what to do about the 700 million peasants, on whose already burdened shoulders the Great Leap would fall, was not so simple. They were encouraged to exploit their tiny private plots of land still further. The bait of farm mechanization and a greater supply of the consumer goods which would lighten their lives was dangled before them.

For workers and peasants, the examples of the little model agricultural community of Tachai and that of the big industrial complex of Taching were drummed into the consciousness. Their message: work hard, be frugal, overcome all obstacles through daring and inventiveness.

It would take more than words, however, to achieve modernization in 23 scant years. The strides made by the communists since 1949 were enormous. But China still was, in Mao's words, "poor and blank." And as the planners set to work they discovered that the economy had been savaged in 10 years of fractional quarreling more than they had suspected. Some analysts thought the time frame for modernization too short. Others said that, given the vagaries of weather and human error, the regime would be doing well just to keep 900 million people fed, clothed and sheltered.

What China needed most was a climate of confidence. That meant a long armistice in the ideological conflict which had raged since communism took over in 1949. Knocked about in one purge after the other, millions of Chinese survived by their wits. Confronted with movements now anti-rightist, now anti-leftist, some were not nimble enough. Terrified at the possibility of saying the wrong thing at the wrong time, many chose to say nothing, or to parrot the words of the faction currently in power. The result was sterility of thought, banality of expression and an absence of initiative.

The new leadership proclaimed China a more open society than before. Frank speaking was encouraged. Teng Hsiao-ping, twice disgraced and twice resurrected for his candor, was held up as a model. Intellectuals were urged to give full play to their genius. Writers, artists, composers and performers were brought out of political purgatory and told to start living again. Scientists were invited to return to their research laboratories. Foreign works of music, literature and art became respectable once more.

The atmosphere obviously had improved. But it was not surprising that some, remembering the fleeting periods of freedom of the past, still looked anxiously over their shoulders.

The new liberalism—the Chinese disliked the word, preferred to call it socialist freedom—spilled over into foreign affairs. Huang Hua, the new foreign minister—his cashiered predecessor had too many close ties to the radicals—had been educated in an American missionary college in Peking and had a knowledge of the West. He launched two initiatives, the first to achieve full normalization of relations with the United States, the second to draw closer to Japan.

Neither move had smooth sailing. U.S. Secretary of State Cyrus Vance journeyed to Peking

Young girls in costume beat drums as they paraded through Peking to mark the windup of the 11th Congress of the Chinese Communist Party

215

in August, but he might have done better to stay home. Despite his cautiously optimistic statements of progress, the question of full recognition appeared to have advanced little. In fact, Teng Hsiao-ping told a group of visiting Associated Press executives and directors the process had been set back. Vance, he said, offered to establish a liaison office in Taipei and an embassy in Peking. The Chinese curtly refused. Teng said former President Ford had promised during his 1975 visit that, if returned to the White House, he would cut relations with Taiwan and recognize the People's Republic. Ford said this was more of a suggestion than a pledge.

Whatever the case, Chinese conditions for full relations remained unchanged: severance of diplomatic ties with the Republic of China on Taiwan, withdrawal of the remaining 1,200 U.S. troops from the nationalist island and termination of the U.S.-Taiwan Security Treaty.

Besieged by other problems—the Panama Canal treaty, the Middle East, disarmament talks with Moscow—President Carter, to Teng's annoyance, put China recognition on the back burner.

What followed was a typically Chinese ploy. Suddenly, a torrent of American visitors appeared on the mainland as guests of the government. That they were largely in favor of recognition was no accident.

The Japanese question revolved around conclusion of a long-delayed peace treaty. Initially regarded as routine, negotiations broke down

after the forced resignation of Japan's then prime minister, Kakuei Tanaka, architect in 1972 of Sino-Japanese rapproachement. Successive Japanese governments were shackled by domestic problems and the realization that Tokyo-Peking relations weren't going to produce the economic bonanza many had expected. The voices of the pro-Taiwan, anti-Peking faction in the Liberal Democratic Party grew stronger.

With a year of his two-year term to go, Japanese Prime Minister Takeo Fukuda picked up the ball and gave every evidence of being willing to run with it. He hoped, through conclusion of the treaty, to divert attention from more serious internal problems and win enough popularity to guarantee his re-election. The sticking point, as it had been for five years, was China's insistence on including a clause frowning on hegemony by any power in the Pacific. The Soviet Union interpreted this as aimed at Moscow. Unwilling to offend the Russians, the Japanese hung back. But Fukuda hoped, through some judicious re-phrasing, to mollify everyone. The critical moment would come early in 1978.

The Chinese also re-emphasized their long commitment to Third World countries, among which they classed themselves. In doing so, they endorsed Chou En-lai's line that China should cooperate with all developing countries, whether socialist or capitalist. It even should lend encouragement to Second World nations such as Japan and those European countries

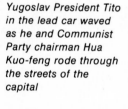

Yugoslav President Tito in the lead car waved as he and Communist Party chairman Hua Kuo-feng rode through the streets of the capital

which it said were, in many ways, exploited by the superpowers, the Soviet Union and the United States.

This policy won favor with Yugoslavia and to show his pleasure that country's 85-year-old leader, President Tito, made his first voyage to Peking where he was received with extraordinary honors. The Chinese expressed admiration for Yugoslavia's staunch resistance to Moscow. It was the tie which bound Peking and Belgrade. As a Third World leader, Tito also was useful to China's own plans in that area.

Less pleased was little Albania, long China's chief ally in Eastern Europe.

Yugoslavia and Albania were historic enemies. They also disagreed over Marxist ideology. Tito's visit was like waving a red flag at a small bull.

The Albanians had cooled in their affection for Peking on other grounds. They resented China's accommodation in the 1970s to Washington and the promotion of Moscow to the position of it's No. 1 enemy.

More serious than this, perhaps, was China's indiscriminate treatment of the Third World. The Albanians said it made no distinction between the real anti-imperialist revolutionaries and the pro-imperialist, reactionary powers. This, they said, was opportunism.

Gunning for bigger game, the Chinese kept to their course. Toward Moscow, the new Chinese regime turned a bland but impassive face. It responded to Soviet overtures by saying that improvement in government to government relations was possible but that the Russians obstinately refused to take the step — withdrawal of a million troops on the Sino-Soviet borders — which would clear the way. In any case, the Chinese said, there was little prospect of a meeting of the minds on their ideological differences. Asked whether they would renew their 30-year mutual assistance pact when it expired in 1980, the Chinese said it had long been a dead letter.

The Kungtsui Hydro-Electric power station neared completion on the Tatu River in China's Szechwan Province

217

Europe's Economy Wound Down in 1977, But Things Looked Better in Britain

The steady slump of the U.S. dollar raised havoc in the foreign exchanges of Europe

The year 1977 started off bravely in what some economists called the "aftermath of the worst depression since the 1930s." But in western Europe it soon looked like a prelude to more bad times.

By early fall, the International Monetary Fund in Washington was telling its 130 member countries: "Economic growth rates are generally subnormal in a setting of high unemployment, excess plant capacity and lagging investment. Inflation is also a widespread problem. . . The scope for improvement in the present unsatisfactory economic situation is thus limited."

The IMF, the Organization for Economic Cooperation and Development and the European Common Market joined in predicting worse to come in 1978. They and other international bodies warned of the dangers of protectionist curbs on free trade. The General Agreement on Tariffs and Trade said such action threatened "the peaceful coexistence of nations."

Everyone seemed ready to blame somebody else for undermining what was to have been the final escape from the depths of the worldwide depression that followed a four-fold increase in the price of oil in 1973.

Some blamed Japan and West Germany for piling up huge reserves of foreign currency, proceeds of their booming export trade, instead of boosting business at home so others could sell to them.

And some, like Belgian Premier Leo Tindemans, said a steady, yearlong slide of the U.S. dollar was creating a turmoil "that could lead tomorrow to a commercial war."

Nearly everybody agreed, though, that a root cause of what was looking more and more like a new recession was fear—anxiety, apprehension, lack of confidence.

U.S. Federal Reserve Chairman Arthur F. Burns said: "the specter of serious inflation continues to haunt the entire business community." Olivier Long, director-general of the GATT, however, said there was more to it than just fear of inflation. "In all countries and at all levels of development." he said in a speech in Zurich, "long-term structural changes in national economies are taking place."

Long was supported by a survey in the British newspaper, The Times, which showed that in the Common Market, only did West German industry still hold first place as the most important source of national income. Elsewhere, marketed services like retailing, transport and finance displaced industrial activity.

In addition, the decline of traditional industries, textiles, shipbuilding, steel, further added to the uncertainty of businessmen over the future.

There were also fears, in France, Portugal, Spain and Italy over possible leftist political victories.

Factories operated below capacity; workers

An elderly news vendor, Mrs. Mary Liston, tacked a pound note on her billboard as she displayed a story of the pound's 7 cent leap against the dollar

Britain became a nation of amateur fire fighters as firemen went out on strike over a pay dispute

were laid off, and retrenchment set in. The economy wound down in western Europe in 1977.

The steady slump of the dollar raised havoc in European foreign exchanges, forced Sweden to abandon the seven-nation exchange rate system known familiarly as "the snake" and made European exports more and more expensive in the United States, the biggest single market for Europe's goods.

The state banks of Britain, France, West Germany, Italy and others were forced to buy up billions of unwanted dollars in a vain effort to hold their monetary rates steady. An estimated $2 billion were bought up in this way in the two-week period between Nov. 23 and Dec. 6 alone. Such amounts added to the amount of money in circulation and thus fed inflation.

Worse, the "snake" — a first step in a bid to tie European currencies more closely together with the aim of an eventual single monetary unit — had been seriously undermined. Sweden, no longer able to stand the strain, had to drop out on Aug. 28, leaving just five currencies clustered within the system around the powerful German mark. They were the Belgian and Luxembourg francs, the Dutch guilder and the Danish and Norwegian crowns.

The six currencies floated in relation to the dollar but were tied tightly to each other within a band 4.5 percentage points wide. That meant they could only fluctuate 2.25 points above or below a mid-point within the band. So when the mark moved higher and higher in relation to the dollar, it dragged the others up with it. Weaker currencies within the snake had to be supported and governments were forced to spend their dwindling reserves to keep their currencies above the lower limit of the snake.

As a result of declines, the American trade surplus with the Common Market increased steadily. That surplus amounted to $8.98 billion in 1976 and was expected to reach 10 billion by the end of 1977.

Talk of raising barriers against American goods was widespread late in the year.

There were a few bright spots, however, notably in Britain, almost prostrate at the end of 1976, and Italy.

Britannia who once ruled the waves, was borrowing so she could stay afloat. Then a $3.9 billion line of credit from the IMF and the promise of North Sea oil put British finances back on their feet. By July, it was the dollar, to which the Labor government had tied the pound, that was holding sterling back.

219

British soldiers who replaced the striking firemen climbed a fence to fight a blaze at a paper factory in East Kilbride near the Scottish city of Glasgow

Foreign currency was pouring into the country to feed inflation. The pound was freed and began climbing. It approached $1.85 in value by year's end.

Oil production from the North Sea was rising fast to reduce the need for fuel imports. Production rose from 528,000 barrels a day in January to 840,000 barrels a day in October.

With the drop in fuel imports, a small trade surplus began building and a record balance of payments surplus was forecast for the year. Britain's reserves of gold and foreign currency soared above a record $20 billion, only topped in Europe by West Germany.

Financially, Britain was in the pink. But economically, the country was in the doldrums: growth was hovering just above zero for the year; industrial production was only slightly above the 1970 level; unemployment reached postwar records of more than one million, and investment in industry was stagnant — a record mirrored in country after country across the continent.

Inflation in Britain, Italy and elsewhere in Europe was coming down. Tourists were flocking back to Italy to the benefit of the balance of payments, in surplus again compared to a $2 billion deficit late in 1976. Industrial production

was climbing, even though the political turmoil of radical leftists still gripped the country. Industrial output in Greece, a candidate like Portugal and Spain for Common Market membership, was climbing also, up 8.8 percent as the Greeks went all out to reach the economic community's standards.

But with Portugal and Spain the situation was different. Both were moving toward democracy after years of dictatorship. Inflation was rampant in both countries with rates of 30 percent or more. Portugal had gone through extremes of radicalism until national elections in 1976 made Mario Soares' moderate socialists the largest single party and Soares formed a government. Industry was at a standstill, unemployment was above 10 percent, the national finances were in catastrophic shape. Late in the year, Soares was defeated on a motion of confidence in parliament and his government fell. Who succeeded him was an unknown quantity.

Spain moved more gradually toward democracy and avoided the political turmoil of Portugal. The centrist government secured the backing of all major political forces, including the Communist Party, for an austerity program that, with the help of income from tourists, could get the economy moving again.

Both Spain and Portugal devalued their currencies during the year, Portugal by 15 percent in February and Spain by almost 25 percent in July. The following month, the Portuguese escudo was set free to find its own level in the market place.

Sweden devalued its krona by 6 percent April 1 and by 10 percent at the end of August. Both Norway and Denmark cut the value of their crowns by 5 percent in Scandinavian solidarity. All three countries suffered from declining industrial production, low investment, relatively high unemployment and inflation.

France was beset by record high unemployment, 10-percent inflation and a flight of capital in fear of what the 1978 elections might bring.

Germany and Switzerland faced the same problem: everybody wanted their currency. Foreign funds poured in, searching for marks and Swiss francs despite stringent restrictions to curb the inflationary inflow. Both countries concentrated on fighting inflation, even though they had among the lowest rates in the world- 4.3 percent for Germany, 1.5 for Switzerland. But the price in Germany was rising unemployment, approaching the million mark at the year's end. Switzerland met that problem by getting rid of many of the foreign workers in the country in what some called another form of protectionism.

Unemployment was the curse of the Common Market during 1977 and it soared to a record six million; 25 percent of the jobless being below the age of 25. Growth in the nine-country community was running at around 2.5 percent, far below the four percent target set at the start of the year.

West German Chancellor Helmut Schmidt was finally forced by flagging production to boost his economy by 10.1 percent in the 1978 budget.

Economists at home and abroad feared Schmidt had acted too late.

President Carter and British Prime Minister James Callaghan exchanged views on the economic situation when the U.S. chief of state went to London for a summit meeting

221

WOMEN CONVERGED ON HOUSTON FOR NATIONAL POLITICAL CONFERENCE

Throughout America, champions of the Equal Rights Amendment kept watch on Houston, Texas, Nov. 19, when 2,000 delegates and 12,000 observers jammed the coliseum there for the biggest political conference of women ever assembled in the United States.

For three days, the National Women's caucus pondered the question: what do women want today? Before the parley was over, they had come up with some answers.

The feminist pep rally and strategy session drew fire from 15,000 other women who gathered in Houston for a counter-convention called the Pro-Family, Pro-Life Coalition. This group was spearheaded by anti-feminist leader Phyllis Shafly, an Alton, Ill. housewife and law student. The rival group denounced many of the proposals of the caucus taking place in the coliseum.

The idea for the caucus was conceived in 1975 as an expression of the International Women's Year declared by the United Nations. Congress provided $5 million for the conference and the preliminary sessions that led up to it. Some 2,000 delegates were elected from 56 state and territorial meetings.

Delegates to the convention included women from all professions and persuasions. They ranged in age from 25 to 55. There were seven male delegates.

Three presidential wives, Rosalynn Carter, Betty Ford, and Lady Bird Johnson, attended the opening session as delegates waved handkerchiefs and colored balloons. Betty Friedan, Gloria Steinem, and former New York Congresswoman Bella Abzug, were among the noted feminists in attendance.

The convention went relatively smoothly. A majority of the delegates voted in favor of resolutions for government funding for day care, shelters for battered wives, accessible and safe abortion, and a host of other measures they hoped would promote greater social and economic equality for women. There was a moment of uncertainty before passage of a resolution to recommend that the states have more time to pass the Equal Rights Amendment. The current deadline was March 1979. To date, 35 states had approved the amendment. Three more states were needed. One resolution — demanding a Cabinet-level women's department — failed to win approval.

The 38-page "National Plan of Action" also contained resolutions on ways to end sexual discrimination in employment, education, marital property relations and other areas. Proposed suggestions ranged from greater compensation and government-supported counseling for rape victims to a federal timetable for adding female managers to the government bureauacracy.

The proposals were sent to the President and Congress as recommendations for new women's laws, programs and policies. A minority report, that would alter all 25 of the conference's proposals, was called for by the anti-feminists who attended Mrs. Schafly s rally. They shouted opposition to abortion, publicly-funded day care centers, ERA, and homosexual rights.

Another minority point-of-view, from among the Women's Convention delegates themselves, occurred in the closing minutes of the conference. About 300 delegates, who opposed most of the agenda, walked off the convention floor singing, "God Bless America." These delegates had worn ribbons during the convention that read "Majority," because they claimed they represented most American women. The walkout occurred when the chair decided to extend the last session two and one-half hours. Delegates on both sides of the political fence rose to complain they had plane reservations and could not stay. The anger of the "Majority" delegates was heightened by a refusal of the chair to act on their submission of a minority report. And they walked out. The presiding officer adjourned the meeting soon afterward.

The delegates returned home vowing to implement the "National Plan of Action" in their own states and communities.

Applauding the presentation of the colors to open the women's conference were, left to right, Bella Abzug, who presided, first lady Rosalynn Carter and two former first ladies, Betty Ford and Lady Bird Johnson

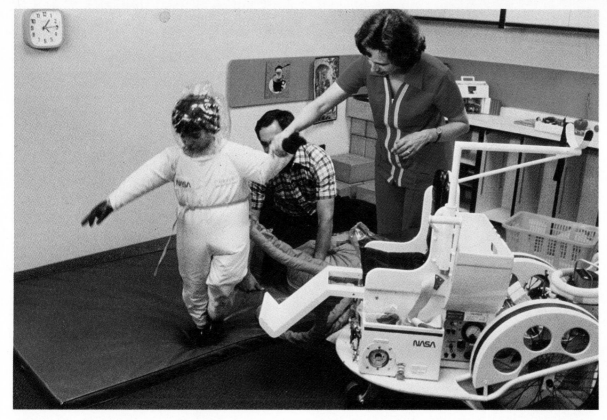

With the help of his parents, David, the six-year-old "bubble baby" walked for the first time outside the isolation he had lived in all his life. David was fitted for a germ-free suit to offset his lack of resistance to infection. David's full name has not been released

ANGRY SOMALIA OUSTED RUSSIANS AND CUBANS

Since 1968, Somalia had been the USSR's chief ally in East Africa, but by 1977 the government in Mogadishu had become increasingly resentful of the fact that Moscow was funneling arms into rival Ethiopia while denying them to the Somalis.

Matters came to a head Nov. 13 when Somalia ordered all Soviet advisers out of the country within seven days and expelled the Soviet Navy from its chief bases on the Horn of Africa. On the heels of this came a second edict giving the Cuba embassy staff 48 hours to get out.

Radio Somalia said the Marxist government of President Mohammed Siad Barre was breaking diplomatic relations with Havana. It also renounced the 1974 friendship treaty with the Soviet Union and ordered a reduction in the Soviet Embassy staff in Mogadishu.

The action brought a quick response from Moscow. The official Soviet news agency Tass issued a terse dispatch declaring that "chauvinist expansionist moods" had prevailed over common sense in the Somali government.

Observers said the Somali action should have come as no surprise since anger had been growing in Mogadishu over Soviet support for Ethiopia in the four-month-old war in Ogaden, eastern region of Ethiopia which Somalia claimed.

Somali Information Minister Abdulcadir Salad Hasan charged that both the Soviet Union and Cuba had "brazenly interfered" in the Ogaden war. He stressed a government charge that the supplying of "military assistance and personnel" to Ethiopia heralded an eventual attack against Somalia.

Somalia asserted that between 7,000 and 15,000 Cuban troops were in Ethiopia, but both Addis Ababa and Havana denied this. Western diplomats in Ethiopia estimated that there were 200 to 400 Cuban military advisers in the country.

Somalia in turn denied that its army was fighting in the Ogaden desert, but admitted arming and aiding the rebels who were Somali tribesmen.

Siad Barre called on the United States, Britain and France as well as the anti-Communist regimes of Saudi Arabia and Iran for arms.

The turn of events had reversed the alignment of the superpowers in Ethiopia and Somalia. In April of 1977, Ethiopia ended its 24-year military dependence on the United States and turned to the Soviet Union. And Somalia had now severed its three-year-old friendship treaty with the Russians and turned to the West.

PRESIDENT PULLED UNITED STATES OUT OF THE ILO

In 1975, the Gerald R. Ford administration filed a notice of withdrawal from the International Labor Organization.

In 1977, President Carter decided not to lift that notice and on Nov. 1 the president pulled the United States out of the ILO, a move that marked the first time the U.S. had withdrawn from a United Nations agency since the world organization was founded in 1945.

The ILO, Carter said, was no longer committed to its original purpose—to improve the lot of workers around the world. "The U.S.," the president said, "remains ready to return whenever the ILO is again true to its proper principles and procedures."

When the ILO was formed in 1919 under the League of Nations, government, labor and employer representatives from each country were independent delegations. But since the ILO became the first specialized agency of the United Nations in 1946, communists and some Third World states had blurred this distinction.

Labor Secretary F. Ray Marshall gave four reasons for Carter's decision to pull out of the ILO:

—The ILO had not applied labor standards equally among all of the nations of the world.

—It frequently issued condemnations "without adequate investigation."

—Politics often entered ILO considerations and nations were condemned for "extraneous political" reasons.

—ILO delegations originally contained representatives of labor, industry and government, and each represented its own constituency. But now too many delegations represented "governments almost exclusively."

The president's decision probably would weaken the ILO since the American contribution to it had been $20 million a year, about a quarter of its budget.

223

AMERICA'S RELIGIOUS CULTS

Pollster George Gallup says that more Americans believe in some form of religion than any other people in the world. We all know the recognized faiths, but AP Special correspondent Eddie Adams in a photo survey of "other" religions, discovered some little-known facts. At least one cult of witches, for instance, has a tax-exempt religious status. There is a 10-year-old evangelist who has several thousand followers convinced that he can cure most anything from sick minds to ailing marriages. And a sect in Tennesse handles deadly snakes and drinks poison as part of its demonstration of faith.

Zsuzanna Budapest, high priestess of the witch coven, Pamis, in Santa Monica, Calif., led her group in a ritual dance on a hilltop near her home

Hare Krishna cult members portrayed the ages of man from birth to death in this tableau in Los Angeles staged by the Society for Krishna Consciousness

Michael Lord, 10-year-old singer, preacher and faith healer, during a prayer meeting at the Evangelism for Christ Church in Miami

A believer worshipping a venomous snake at a meeting of snake-handling sects held at the Holiness Church of God in Jesus Name, Carterville, Ga.

RAINS BURST GEORGIA DAM AND A RAGING TORRENT KILLED 38 PEOPLE

For four straight days, heavy rains had pelted the north Georgia town of Toccoa. Then at 1 a.m. on Nov. 6, an earthen dam on the outskirts of town burst and a 30-foot wall of water smashed through the campus of a small bible college, killing 38 persons.

The rising waters had filled 80-acre Kelley Barnes Lake to capacity when the 35-year-old dam gave way and sent tons of water over 186-foot Toccoa Falls and onto the campus of Toccoa Falls Bible College where about 250 people lived in dormitories, houses and mobile homes at the foot of the fall.

"When the water started coming down, it sounded just like a tornado," said Jim Conaway, a sophomore at the college who was doing a turn as a night watchman at the time. "You could hear the cars banging and bouncing against each other and the trees."

Some of the victims were married students and their families. Others were faculty members and administrative personnel. Also lost were several volunteer firemen, trying to move people out of the path of the onrushing flood.

"One moment the water was inches deep and the next I was swimming for my life," said Eldon Elsberry, a college maintenance worker who managed to escape by hanging onto a floating tree.

Dave Hinkle, a student from Syracuse, N.Y., said a wave 30 feet high and about 40 feet wide poured into the second story windows of the men's dormitory. The four-story building was extensively damaged, and eight or nine permanent faculty houses in the area were destroyed.

The waters that rushed through the collapsed dam and over the falls, turned Toccoa Creek, normally a placid stream only inches deep, into a destructive torrent. Bodies were found as far as two miles from the dam. Water-logged mattresses, battered window frames and dozens of uprooted trees littered the banks of the swollen creek.

About 20 mobile homes occupied a trailer park inhabited mostly by married students at the college and perhaps a dozen other families. Only one trailer remained the day after the dam broke.

Bill Ehrensberger, a 28-year-old volunteer fireman and student at the college, tried to warn trailer park residents of the oncoming flood. He was killed when he was swept from a jeep. His wife and three children also perished.

Fireman Ron Ginther was saved by clutching a tree, but he was to learn that his wife and four children were dead.

President and Mrs. Carter were informed of the disaster in their home state before they entered the Sunday morning worship service at the First Baptist Church in Washington. They decided then that Mrs. Carter would fly to the scene. Later she said the disaster was "indescribable . . a terrible tragedy."

Gov. George Busbee, who also inspected the stricken area, said the dam had been declared a high-hazard dam by the U.S. Corps of Engineers. A corps spokesman said this designation did not mean the dam was unsafe but that if it broke it would carry a high potential for destruction.

Officials inspected damage after the dam burst at Toccoa, Ga.

President and Mrs. Carter and their visitors, the Shah and Empress of Iran, reacted as tear gas fumes interrupted welcoming ceremonies. The fumes drifted onto the White House grounds when demonstrators for and against the royal visit clashed outside the fence and police intervened.

AP reporter Jane See White (with note pad right) spotted this nude stroller crossing New York's Fifth Avenue. Despite his fleshy attire, he turned few heads

LONGTIME BAND LEADER
GUY LOMBARDO DIED AT 75

For nearly 50 years, one of the fixtures of New Year's Eve —
along with the noisemakers, the balloons, the champagne — was Guy Lombardo.

For millions of Canadians and Americans, no New Year's
Eve was complete without Lombardo leading his band of
Royal Canadians in *Auld Lang Syne,* something he had
done since 1929. But 1977 marked the end of the Lombardo
era. The noted bandleader, creator of "the sweetest music
this side of heaven," died Nov. 5 in Houston's Methodist
Hospital of a breathing problem associated with the pulmonary artery trouble for which he had been admitted Oct. 27.
He was 75.

Lombardo had led a band for 63 of those 75 years, having
started out at the age of 12 when he and four other youngsters played for women's clubs in London, Ontario, his
birthplace. The eldest son of musically inclined parents of
Italian descent, he was named Gaetano after his father and
learned to play the violin.

Lombardo and his brothers, Victor, Carmen and Lebert,
moved their band to Cleveland in 1925, Chicago in 1927,
and after that it was a continuing success story.

The band made its first network radio broadcast in Chicago, and then went to New York in 1929 to play at the Hotel
Roosevelt Grill. His orchestra broadcast from the grill and
eventually no New Year's Eve was considered complete by
many until Lombardo and his Royal Canadians had played
Auld Lang Syne at the stroke of midnight.

Lombardo sold over 400 million phonograph records and
for the past 40 years had never made less than $1 million a
year. During the summer of 1977, his revival of "Finian's
Rainbow" took in $1.55 million to spark what rapidly was
becoming a record financial year even for the most successful big band in musical history.

The Royal Canadians had a bland style which irked many
lovers of pure jazz and most critics of popular music, but
Lombardo and his band remained a perennial favorite.
Lombardo once remarked, "We're giving the public what
they want. We don't force bad songs on them. We play music people like to hum while they're dancing." He admitted
that not all people loved his music all of the time, but added
"We lose 'em in their teens, but we catch 'em up later.
Sooner or later we get 'em all and when we get 'em, we
keep 'em." Some of the bands biggest hits were: *Little
White Lies, Boo Hoo, You're Driving Me Crazy, Easter
Parade,* and *Seems Like Old Times.*

As for *Auld Lang Syne,* it was the band's theme song long
before it became a New Year's Eve symbol. Explained

Guy Lombardo at services for Louis Armstrong in 1971

Lombardo, "Western Ontario, where we started, was heavily Scottish, and every dance ended with the playing of that
song."

The Royal Canadian's played every New Year's Eve at the
Roosevelt for more than 30 years before moving to the
Waldorf-Astoria.

In the mid-50's, Lombardo started producing summer
extravaganzas at the Jones Beach theater on Long Island.
He was an astute businessman who was involved in many
enterprises and his total wealth was estimated to be in the
millions.

THOUSANDS KILLED IN
WORST STORM TO HIT
INDIA'S ANDHRA PRADESH
STATE IN A CENTURY

The cyclones that struck terror along the Indian Ocean
coast each year were equivalent to the hurricanes that
plagued the Western world. The one that slammed into India's Andhra Pradesh state Nov. 19 was described as the
worst to hit that storm-lashed country in more than a century. Death estimates ranged from 10,000 up to 50,000 persons.

The storm, packing hundred-mile winds, roared in from
the Bay of Bengal leveling about 100 villages, some of them
little more than clusters of mud huts. In its wake came a
wall of muddy sea water more than 20 feet high. It surged in
over 100 square miles of land, leaving untold thousands of
persons homeless and damaging an estimated 38 million
acres of crops.

As the seas receded, they left stricken areas littered with
human corpses and the bodies of animals.

The first reporters to reach the scene Nov. 23, saw about

200 bloated bodies, turned black by the sun, floating in
muddy waters that had once been fields of grain. Crewmen
of an Indian air force helicopter told the newsmen they had
seen thousands of such corpses earlier in the week, but
that most had been buried or burned on huge pyres.

As the helicopter dropped 44-pound sacks of rice and
vegetables in the Divi Taluk district, dozens of villages were
seen flattened or submerged. In some villages what had
been solidly-built brick structures were mounds of rubble.

Farther in from the coast, the devastation was less severe, but there were miles-long stretches of fallen telephone poles and collapsed rooftops as far as 50 miles inland.

Survivors brought to refugee camps told of their ordeal.
Kadrakollu Saraswati said she grabbed her two children
and ran outside as her hut collapsed. With one child on her
hip and another clinging to her back, she climbed a tree
and lashed herself to its trunk with her cotton sari. The 20-year-old farmer's wife said the flood waters rose during the
night and before daylight the tree was blown down. The
woman was found unconscious by her brother who swam
across flooded fields from a neighboring hamlet. Her children were unhurt but sick from drinking salt water brought
in by the tidal wave.

FORMER CIA CHIEF AVOIDED PRISON AFTER PLEA BARGAINING

Richard Helms said he regarded his conviction as a "badge of honor." But District Judge Barrington D. Parker who sentenced the former CIA chief took quite a different view.

Fining 64-year-old Helms $2,000 and placing him on a year's probation for misleading a Senate committee about covert CIA activities in Chile, the federal jurist said the defendant stood "in disgrace and shame." Helms could have received two years under the charges and Parker made it clear he thought little of the plea bargaining as a result of which he agreed to the Justice Department's strong recommendation that Helms not be imprisoned.

It was a classic case of the conflict that could result from the demands of ordinary justice and the need for extraordinary secrecy.

In 1973, when Helms testified before the Senate Foreign Relations Committee, the CIA was engaged under direction of then-President Richard M. Nixon in activities against the Marxist regime of Salvador Allende in Chile.

At the time, Helms was on his way to confirmation as U.S. ambassador to Iran following a career in the CIA of which he had spent seven years as director.

Faced with a court trial, Helms agreed after extensive bargaining to plead nolo contendere or no contest to two misdemeanor counts of failing to testify "fully, completely and accurately" before the Senate. Explaining his action, Helms said "If I were to contest these charges, I believe that grave and perhaps irreparable damage to the United States would result."

In court, Helms' defense attorney, Edward Bennett Williams pleaded for mercy on grounds that, while the CIA director had technically violated his oath to the Senate panel, he was obligated as well to uphold his separate oath—and statutory duty—to protect CIA secrets. Williams declared that had Helms testified fully, American lives would have been imperiled.

Williams' explanation did not sit well with Parker.

"It is indeed unfortunate," he said, "that there are those in public office who are so divided in their loyalties. You gave your solemn oath to testify truthfully. You, however, failed. You dishonored your oath and you stand before this court in disgrace and shame. There are those in the intelligence community . . . who feel they have a license to operate outside the law."

Williams told the court just before sentencing that his client would "bear the scar of a conviction the rest of his life." But outside the courthouse the lawyer's tone appeared to change considerably. Turning to newsmen he said that Helms "will wear it like a badge of honor . . . I'm proud to stand beside a man who still believes in honor."

Asked if he agreed with the "badge of honor" assessment, Helms replied "I do indeed. I don't think it's a disgrace at all. If I had done anything else than withholding . . . answers to the Senate it would have been a disgrace."

Helms went on to declare that it was "high time" that the executive and congressional branches reach clearcut guidelines for testimony by officials holding national secrets, and added that he hoped his case would bring that about."

The Justice Department seemed satisfied with the outcome. Attorney General Griffin B. Bell said disposition of the case "confirms the important principles contained in the plea agreement. It vindicates the law and upholds the rights of Congress."

Former CIA director Richard Helms (right) and his attorney, Edward Bennett Williams, left U.S. district court in Washington

Also in NOVEMBER . . .

To the accompaniment of flutes and drums, a member of a group formed to preserve the 300-year-old Kiba log-rolling festival performed acrobatic feats on a square log in a pool in Tokyo

A replica of a Sumerian reed boat which dated back 6,000 years was launched at Qurna, Iraq. The craft was built for explorer Thor Heyerdahl

FOR THE RECORD

FREED. Greek Catholic Archbishop Hilarion Capudji. Israel freed the 55-year-old prelate from prison Nov. 6 and deported him to Italy following a plea by Pope Paul VI for release of the convicted weapons smuggler. He had served nearly three years of a 12-year sentence after being convicted of running weapons, explosives and ammunition across the Lebanese border in his limousine to Palestinian guerrillas in Israel. Arrangements for the release were worked out during the three weeks of talks between Prime Minister Menahem Begin's government and the Vatican.

EXPLODED. Thirty tons of dynamite aboard a boxcar at Iri, South Korea. The blast Nov. 11 killed 58 persons, injured 1,343 persons, destroyed or seriously damaged 1,955 buildings, damaged another 7,566 buildings and wrecked a mile of railroad track and 105 freight cars. Damage was estimated at $10 million to $20 million.

BORN. A 7-pound, 9-ounce boy to Britain's Princess Anne. The birth Nov. 15 gave Queen Elizabeth II her first grandchild and crowned the queen's Silver Jubilee year. The queen spent half an hour at her daughter's bedside, seeing the baby and chatting with Anne's husband, Army Capt. Mark Phillips. It was the first time in history that an English monarch's grandchild was born without a title. The princess and her husband did not want traditional courtesy titles passed onto their children.

KILLED. At least 48 persons, three of them Americans, in a fire at the Hotel Filipinas in Manila, Philippines. The fire broke out Nov. 14 on the fifth floor of the seven-story hotel while the city was being lashed by 50-mile winds and heavy rains from Typhoon Kim. The storm caused power failures in Manila, and one theory was the fire started from a candle that was being used during one of the blackouts.

DECEMBER

Sadat's Journey To Jerusalem Transformed Mideast Diplomacy

The Egyptian president's dramatic act set off a reaction that shook Washington, Moscow and the Arab world

In one breathtaking leap, President Anwar Sadat of Egypt went to Israel and by that one dramatic act transformed Middle East diplomacy.

Cairo to Jerusalem. Only 265 miles, a 40-minute jet flight. But psychologically a vast distance along a path strewn with the barriers of 30 years' war and hatred. Sadat's historic pilgrimage set off a reaction that shook not only Cairo and Jerusalem, but also other Arab capitals, and Washington and Moscow. The November journey set in motion a process that shattered a long stalemate and promised at least a glimmer of hope for the war-torn Middle East. Israelis were talking to Egyptians and by year's end the magic word "peace" became thinkable.

There were, however, side effects. Many of the Arab states and the Palestine Liberation Organization were outraged by Sadat's initiative and the Kremlin was angry. The rejectionists saw the specter of a separate peace between Israel and Egypt.

During 1977 a new American president, Jimmy Carter, probed, nudged, cajoléd and issued a barrage of statements designed to get the Geneval Middle East peace conference reconvened. But as the year dwindled, so did hopes for Geneva.

Israel, a major player in the drama, went through a year of political shocks that brought to power a rightist government headed by Menahem Begin, a slight, steel-willed former guerrilla fighter who seemed too unyielding to be an effective force for peace. Then President Sadat, the 59-year-old former army officer who ruled Egypt, launched a series of dramatic moves. He gripped the diplomatic initiative and, aided by Begin, everything changed overnight.

On Nov. 9 Sadat told the Egyptian parliament he was willing to go to Israel in the cause of peace. In the context of the rhetoric of the Middle East, there was no immediate certainty he meant it or that Israel would seriously respond. But Israel welcomed Sadat. It had been a key element of Israeli policy to gain recognition from Arab leaders and to get face-to-face talks, and suddenly a Sadat visit was a real possibility. Israel issued an official invitation and by Nov. 17 Begin was able to make the stunning announcement that Sadat would be in Israel in two days. The announcement touched off a frenzy of activity. More than 2,000 journalists poured into the country, Ben-Gurion Airport sent its red carpet out for cleaning, flag makers started stitching Egyptian flags and the Army band wrestled with learning the Egyptian national anthem.

The first of a series of "firsts" was arrival of the Egyptian airliner with an advance party of Sadat's officials and security men, who got an excited welcome on Friday. Israel quickly mobilized more than 10,000 police and military personnel to clamp a security cordon around Sadat. On a crisp Saturday night, after the end of the Jewish sabbath, Sadat's white and blue Boeing 707 wheeled to a stop at Ben-Gurion Airport and was bathed in the lights of the world's television cameras. The door opened. There was a long, long wait and then the familiar face of Anwar Sadat appeared. The first Arab leader to set foot on the soil of the State of Israel.

Sadat, keenly aware he was making history, looked a bit unsure and stiff in the initial moments as the national anthems of each country sounded across the tarmac. Suddenly, the formal atmosphere dissolved. There was Sadat shaking hands and talking with Begin, with President Ephraim Katzir. Israelis, eyes fixed on their television sets, gave a collective quiver at the jolting emotional impact of what they were witnessing. Many wept. There was Sadat on Israeli soil. Was it a first step toward peace? Sadat, under tremendous pressure to avoid any false steps, set the tone: "Is Ariel Sharon here?" he asked. Sharon was the dashing general who led Israeli forces across the Suez Canal in the 1973 Yom Kippur war.

A smiling Sadat told the white-haired Sharon: "I was hoping to trap you over there." Sharon replied with a grin, "I'm glad to be welcoming you here instead." Within minutes Sadat was shaking hands, talking and laughing with Israel's past and present leadership. There was Begin, Sharon, Yigael Yadin, deputy premier and chief of staff in the 1948 war; Moshe Dayan,

233

Israeli soldiers kept Jerusalem under tight security for the historic visit of Egyptian President Anwar Sadat

the defense minister who was chief of staff in the 1956 Sinai campaign, and defense minister in the 1967 war; Yitzhak Rabin, former premier and chief of staff during the six-day war, and there was 79-year-old Golda Meir who led the nation during the dark hours of the 1973 Yom Kippur war. Sadat bent down to Mrs. Meir to say, "I have waited a long time for this." Mrs. Meir beamed and replied: "But you didn't come."

It was unbelievable—a moving scene, so packed with portent and emotion, and somehow so natural, that many found themselves wondering why such a meeting of neighbors should have been so difficult. An Israeli veteran was reminded of a day in 1973 after the cease-fire when a group of Israeli and Egyptian soldiers spontaneously started kicking around a soccer ball in the Sinai desert. "We didn't talk much. But it was so nice it almost made me cry," he said. "And I felt the same when Sadat came off that plane."

The nationwide welcome Sadat received in Israel was not organized. It was a natural outpouring of feeling from people who had borne their share of suffering and allowed themselves for a few delirious days to hope that Sadat's visit meant no more war. When Sadat's motorcade snaked up the road to Jerusalem, people lined the highway to shout "welcome" and "peace" and to try to catch a glimpse of the Egyptian president. He went to the King David Hotel where the sixth-floor royal suite was ready. Outside in the street Israelis danced the hora and a one-armed man chanted, "no more war, no more war."

By one of those tricks of history, Begin as a guerrilla leader in 1946 gave orders to blow up a wing of the hotel that housed the British occupation staff. The explosion claimed 95 lives and was one of the acts that caused Britain to brand Begin a "terrorist." Now, 31 years later, Begin was prime minister of Israel and meeting the president of Egypt in the King David. Following the initial meeting, Begin could pronounce: "We like each other."

That Sadat was in Jerusalem was significant. After the 1967 war Israel annexed the entire Holy City in the face of Arab outrage and declared it would never again be divided. Such countries as the United States have never recognized Israeli control over the entire city. For many Arabs, Sadat's presence in Jerusalem was another offense. Some radical groups cried for his blood.

Official Syrian newspapers and radio stations branded Sadat a traitor to the Arab cause. Denunciations and demonstrations swept the Arab world and for Sadat it was in many ways a lonely mission.

"Coming to Jerusalem, that means recognizing the Israeli annexation," said Raymunda Tawil, a Palestinian activist from nearby Ramallah.

Sadat was aware of the risk. And so was Begin who said, "We Jews appreciate courage and we will know how to appreciate our visitor's courage." At every step Sadat set precedent, each action was historic, the very words became inadequate during the 44 hours he spent in Israel. On a bright Sunday morning, Sadat was up for dawn prayers at the Al Aqsa

234

Mosque, the third holiest Moslem shrine after Mecca and Medina. As he listened to prayers and touched his forehead to prayer mats in the marble-columned mosque, Sadat abandoned a 1967 wartime vow by Arab leaders that they would never pray at the mosque until it had been recovered from Israel.

King Hussein of Jordan, who did not join in the general Arab denunciation of Sadat, found the sight of Sadat praying under the protection of Israeli guns disquieting. King Hussein's grandfather, King Abdullah of Jordan, was assassinated at the mosque in 1951 by a Palestinian extremist when the area was under Jordan's control.

Sadat, tightly surrounded by security guards, walked 100 yards to the blue-tiled Mosque of Omar, the Dome of the Rock, and then down the twisting streets of Jerusalem's Old City to the Church of the Holy Sepulchre. A group of Palestinian youths, kept well away from Sadat, shouted, "Oh, Sadat, don't sell us out." Then the Egyptian leader went to the newer part of Jerusalem for a visit to the stark horror of the Yad Vashem monument to Jews killed in the Nazi holocaust. His guide was Gideon Hausner, who prosecuted the Nazi war criminal Adolf Eichmann. Hausner explained how Yad Vashem showed the reasons Israel could never forget. "I understand, I realize that," Sadat said. Sadat also laid a wreath at the tomb of the un-known Israeli soldier, another action that added to the outrage of many Arabs.

A high point was Sadat's appearance before a hushed and expectant Israeli Knesset and he told the parliament of the Jewish nation, "we welcome you to live among us in peace and security." Reading his speech, scarcely looking up, Sadat pointedly referred to Egypt as "the biggest Arab state," underlying the fact that it would be almost impossible for the Arabs to make war against Israel without Egypt.

Sadat was firm on the basic points: Israeli withdrawal from captured Arab land, no separate peace agreements and creation of a Palestinian state. He called the Palestinian cause "the crux of the entire problem," but did not mention the Palestine Liberation Organization. The speech was a shock to many Israelis caught up in the euphoria of the Sadat visit — it was as if they had forgotten the difficult problems that remained, problems that could not be solved or erased in a few days. Israelis watching the speech on television in a crowded Jerusalem cafe cried "no" and "never" at the TV set when Sadat spoke of complete Israeli withdrawal. Begin's reply, low keyed, and somewhat rambling, was an almost perfunctory response to Sadat.

There was general disappointment that the two speeches really broke no new ground. And yet Sadat was in Jerusalem and he had specifi-

Sadat also conferred with Israeli Foreign Minister Moshe Dayan, Egypt's arch foe during the 1967 war

سالوم

Many Arabs did not share in the enthusiasm over Sadat's visit as evidenced by this poster put up in the Moslem sector of Beirut decorating Sadat with Uncle Sam's hat and Dayan's eye patch

cally recognized Israel's existence as a state in the Middle East. For Israelis, who seemed to live on an emotional roller coaster, it was the downslide of the Sadat visit. In Sadat's private conversations with Israeli leaders things seemed to get better. Deputy premier Yadin reported Begin and Sadat talked about their health. Begin, who had had heart trouble, asked Sadat how he felt. "I must say, you look much better than I was led to believe," Sadat replied. "You too," Begin said. "My wife mentioned it at the airport. She said you look much better than we thought."

Yadin and Sadat, both pipe smokers, discussed favorite tobaccos. For Defense Minister Ezer Weizman, Sadat was a man who "speaks short and to the point, looks a person straight in the eye — a real man."

In the private talks Sadat told Begin "there must be no more war between us," a pledge he repeated over and over the following day. On Monday there was the remarkable confrontation between Sadat and parliament members, highlighted by an exchange with Mrs. Meir who sternly told Sadat there could be no separate Palestinian state on the West Bank. There should be peace, she added with a glint in her eye, "so that even an old lady like me . . ."

Sadat's laugh interrupted. "Yes, I have said this," Sadat said in reference to his 1973 words branding Mrs. Meir "that old lady." "Yes, you always called me an old lady," Mrs. Meir insisted, and Sadat's rich, deep laugh boomed. Then she presented him with a gift for Sadat's new granddaughter. "From a grandmother to a grandfather," she said, "Marvelous, marvelous," Sadat chuckled. Seeing the exchange Israelis were again elated at the good atmosphere.

At a joint news conference that afternoon it became clear that Begin wasn't getting an official invitation to Cairo right away. But both leaders pledged to work for peace and Sadat raised the slogan: "Let the 1973 war be the last war."

Then, again at Ben-Gurion Airport. "Goodbye, Moshe," Sadat said to Dayan. Mrs. Meir, as if bidding a neighbor goodbye at the back door of her house, said, "Do come again." And Sadat's "Egypt No. 1" was aloft, etched against the twilight sky and trailed by an honor guard of four Israeli Kfir jet fighters.

Sadat made a triumphal return to Cairo, although there were some indications trouble lurked under the surface. When he announced the trip Foreign Minister Ismail Fahmi resigned and Mohammed Riad refused to take the job. Some Arab countries continued to denounce "the visit of treason" and Moscow regretted the blow to "Arab unity." Sadat seemed unconcerned at the storm raging about his head and promptly played another card. He said Cairo was willing to host a conference to prepare peace and invited the Israelis, the United States, the Soviet Union, Syria, Jordan, Lebanon and the PLO. Syria and the PLO promptly rejected the invitation and Syrian President Hafez Assad announced he was ready for reconciliation with his arch-enemies in Iraq to forge a united front against Cairo.

Moscow called the conference "a coverup for a bilateral Tel Aviv-Cairo deal" and even accused the United States of "cooking up" the entire affair. Both Washington and Moscow, superpowers with major interests in the Middle East, were suddenly cast in secondary roles on the sidelines. But Begin, aware that America was Israel's main backer, took pains to reassure the Carter administration. He flew to Washington to brief the American president on his peace plans.

Diplomats and heads of state ricochetted around the world like electric-charged table tennis balls in a drum. U.S. Secretary of State Cyrus R. Vance embarked on a six-nation Middle East tour to emphasize American interest in the Cairo conference, the Americans sent an envoy to Moscow to try to calm the Russians, King Hussein visited Arab capitals, Begin briefed the British, and the key word as far as Sadat and Begin were concerned was "momentum."

Sadat, meanwhile, conducted dozens of

news conferences, puffed his pipe and talked peace. He also expelled a group of Palestinian officials from Cairo. In Tripoli, PLO leader Yassir Arafat, Libyan leader Moammar Khadafy and the leaders of Syria, South Yemen and Algeria met to conduct a rejectionist summit. The Iraqi delegation walked out, but the rest agreed on a military and political front to isolate Egypt.

Sadat's response was quick: He broke diplomatic relations with Syria, Libya, Algeria and South Yemen and called the rejectionists "stupid and ignorant dwarfs." Egypt's relations with the Soviet Union deteriorated with Sadat blaming the Soviet Union for the "rubbish" at Tripoli and the Soviet Union accusing Sadat of "dancing to the tune of imperialist circles."

The Cairo preparatory conference opened in the shadow of the pyramids on Dec. 14—the first time face-to-face negotiations had been undertaken. Included were representatives of the United States and the United Nations.

While they talked procedure, Begin jetted off to the United States to explain his "peace plan" to Carter in an effort to win endorsement.

A second meeting between Sadat and Begin was held Christmas day near the Egyptian town of Ismailia on the Suez Canal. Begin brought with him a detailed peace proposal, elements of which were revealed when the Israeli leader went to Washington earlier in December. Those elements, including a return of the Sinai desert to Egypt, civil home-rule for Palestinians on the West Bank of Jordan, but a continued Israeli military presence, fell considerably short of Arab demands even after they underwent some revision.

The meeting in Ismailia did not produce a declaration of principles for a comprehensive settlement or even the outlines for Israeli withdrawal from the Sinai. Sadat, who claimed he was negotiating for all the Arabs, could not accept the return of the Sinai without Israeli concessions on other fronts.

However, the two men did agree to set up two committees, a "military" group headed by their respective defense ministers to discuss the Sinai and a political one headed by the foreign ministers to try to resolve other issues, such as the fate of the West Bank of Jordan and the million Palestinians who lived there.

President Carter in an interview before setting out on a trip abroad praised the Begin plan as a "long step forward" and strongly reaffirmed U.S. opposition to creation of an independent Palestinian state. Carter insisted that he was only expressing a "preference" and not trying to dictate terms of a settlement. But the president's remarks gratified Begin while they embarrassed Sadat.

The Sadat-Begin negotiations took place before a backdrop of sporadic violence that continued in Lebanon where a bloody civil war that claimed about 37,000 lives was brought to an uncertain close in late 1976.

Syrian troops were still in Beirut maintaining the sole guarantee that full-scale bloodshed would not erupt again.

But political factions of the left and right continued to build up their private armies and fighting still sputtered in southern Lebanon in an area caught in the overall dispute between Israelis and Arabs.

Sadat received an ovation upon his return to Cairo from the mission to Jerusalem

U.S. Economic Year Almost An Exact Replay of 1976

Despite a major change in the cast, the economic scenario for 1977 in the United States was almost an exact replay of 1976.

The big change was the replacement of Gerald R. Ford as president by Jimmy Carter. But if the voters who elected Carter the nation's 39th president had hoped he would be able to work miracles with the economy those hopes slowly faded as the months of 1977 slipped by, and it began to seem that Carter probably had promised too much when he pledged a balanced budget, low inflation, and low unemployment by the end of his current term in office.

But, as it had been in 1976, so largely was it in 1977. Strong economic growth early in the year led to overly optimistic predictions, and when this was followed by a mid-year slump this called into question the administration's economic policies. Critics faulted the president for over-promising and then vacillating in his economic policies. This confused both consumers and businessmen and was blamed—justly or not—for a decline in business confidence. Crit-

Shipping containers lined the docks in Weehawken, N.J., as the result of a dock strike

ics cited Carter's proposal and then withdrawal of plans for a $50 a person tax rebate. They also pointed at his pullback on a pledge to develop a forceful wage and price program to restrain inflation.

In addition, there were major changes in a comprehensive tax reform program that Carter pledged to send to Congress during 1977 to close many of the tax preferences and so-called tax loopholes that he contended benefited wealthy taxpayers. As 1977 drew to a close, the tax reform program was being retooled to mostly a tax cut program of $25 billion and still had not been sent to Congress. President Carter said at a press conference Nov. 30 the program included some tax reform, but that some of his controversial proposals probably would be delayed.

Nearly a year after Carter assumed the presidential office, the economy looked like this:

—Unemployment was 7 percent of the labor force, compared with 7.3 percent in January. Early in December, Jody Powell, the White

House press secretary, told reporters it would appear to be impossible to reach the administration's target of reducing unemployment to 6.6 percent by the end of 1977. An administration economist said it was conceivable the target could be hit but the long stagnation of the unemployment rate made that unlikely.

—Consumer prices were pushed up nearly 6.5 percent by inflation, compared with 4.8 percent in 1976.

—Economic growth—as measured by the gross national product (GNP)—was about 5 percent, down from 1976's 6.2 percent.

—The president was considering a budget deficit of about $40 billion for fiscal year 1979, the first complete budget of Carter's presidency. While the figure was down from the estimated $59 billion deficit for fiscal 1978, it still was a far cry from the balanced budget Carter had promised by 1981.

—United States trade with other nations was in deficit by a huge $30 billion. This included a one-month deficit of $3.1 billion in October alone, the first month in which the excess of the nation's imports over its exports was $3 billion.

In addition, the administration got pleas from steel producers and other industries who asked for protection from lower-priced imports that were contributing to plant shutdowns and job layoffs across the nation.

The nation's trade problems were highlighted in October when Zenith Radio Corp. said it was laying off 5,000 workers, about a quarter of its domestic labor force, because of competition from color TV imports from Japan. In the steel industry, there were several major plant shutdowns and some 20,000 workers were laid off because of imports of lower-priced steel from Europe and Japan. All told, an estimated 300,000 workers were getting federal aid because of the loss of employment to rising imports of all kinds. Special help for the steel industry was in the works at the end of the year. The administration was preparing to set minimum prices below which imports would not be allowed. It also arranged help for the television and shoe industries.

—The American dollar—partly because of the trade deficit—tumbled to new lows against several major currencies such as the West German mark and the Japanese yen—although it did gain against some others, notably the Canadian dollar.

—Prices on the New York Stock Exchange—apparently discouraged by all of the above factors—declined steadily most of the year, with the Dow Jones industrial average even slipping below the 800 mark on several occasions. That compared with a reading of 999.75 on Jan 3, the first trading day of 1977.

—Strikes also affected the economic picture. One strike by dock workers paralyzed container shipping from Maine to Texas for 60 days. And early in December, the United Mine Workers

union went on strike and ordered out 130,000 coal miners.

The discouraging economic statistics had less to do with President Carter and his policies than they did with over-all economic conditions, including conditions in other nations. Much of what was happening to the U.S. economy in 1977 was a continuation of a world-wide economic slump that hit the industrialized nations in 1973 and 1974 when the oil-exporting nations raised world oil prices to four times their previous levels.

Although there was much depressing economic news in 1977, there also were rays of sunshine. For example, despite the high cost of housing, many people still found the money to buy their homes and more than 2 million homes were started during the year. The auto industry churned out its new models at a near-record pace, and production through October came to more than 7.4 million units, a 7 percent gain over 1976. The spendable per capita income of Americans increased nearly 10 per cent—well ahead of the inflation rate—and consumer spending was strong.

One of the best pieces of news came as the year drew to a close when Saudi Arabia and Iran—the major oil-exporting nations—indicated they opposed an increase in oil prices in 1978. If the oil-using nations were to have a full year without an oil price increase, it would give them a chance to repair the damage caused by the earlier price hikes. The 1977 U.S. oil import

At Norton, Va., striking coal miners picketed the entrance of a coal company

NEW YORK SPOT
1·9112
NEW YORK FORWARD
1·9138

13 00

employment with price stability." The president said Burns had "earned our respect and gratitude" for doing what Carter termed "an outstanding job" of defending the dollar, maintaining the integrity of the monetary system, and upholding the independence of the central bank. Burns' tenure as head of the board—he had been chairman of the central bank since 1970—often had been marked by controversy. Among his chief critics were George Meany, president of the AFL-CIO, and Sen. Hubert H. Humphrey, D-Minn. Both said he was largely responsible for the continuing high rate of unemployment by keeping the money supply tight and interest rates high.

Among the economic forecasts for 1978 was one made by the Conference Board, a leading business research group, which projected over-all economic growth for the United States of 4.2 percent, barely enough to keep unemployment from getting worse.

The board said inflation probably would push prices up another 6.2 percent, while unemployment would average about 6.7 percent. Calling for an even-handed approach to the economy in 1978, Albert T. Sommers, the board's chief economist, said, "We seem to be painfully aware that in our recent experience very liberal policies have not accelerated growth, while very conservative policies have not reduced the rate of inflation."

Arthur F. Burns talked with G. William Miller and his wife, after Miller was appointed to succeed Burns as chairman of the Federal Reserve Board

Traders at the London Stock Exchange took it easy while the indicator board showed the value of the United States dollar against the Pound Sterling

bill was projected at $45 billion, and that took wealth from the nation that might otherwise have been spent on jobs and production. In addition, the administration and Congress were working on an energy bill that aimed to reduce American dependence on oil imports.

One of the important economic decisions facing President Carter was whether to reappoint Arthur Burns, 73, to a new term as chairman of the money-managing Federal Reserve Board when his term expired. On Dec. 28, the president personally announced he was replacing Burns in the post with G. William Miller, chairman of Textron Inc. and a director of the Boston Federal Reserve Bank. If confirmed by the Senate, as expected, Carter would appoint him to a four-year term as chairman.

Burns, whose term as chairman was to expire Jan. 31, 1978, stood with Carter and Miller as the announcement was made and told reporters, "I think this is a good day." Miller, who would earn $57,500 a year in his new job, said he intended to "continue the policies of Dr. Burns and President Carter" to achieve "full

240

Bert Lance conferred with President Carter in the Oval Office before the budget director resigned his post

How Carter Fared During First Year In The White House

Achievements were dimmed by the Lance affair and failure to put through an energy bill

Jimmy Carter began his administration jauntily, strolling with his family from the Capitol to the White House on Inauguration Day, and confidently, telling a caller on a phone-in radio show: "I would say that the number of hours I put in and the difficulty of the job is about the same as it was when I was governor of Georgia, but in addition it is more interesting because you have the foreign affairs question to address." By year's end, as with most freshman American presidents, the education of Carter had come a long way.

The man who had run against Washington discovered that the virtues he brought to his office—decency, simplicity, optimism, energy and a belief that governmental problems could be solved by hard work—were not enough to master that political city. As for the difficulty of the job, new age lines etched in his face attested to the realities of the presidency.

Asked in a year-end television interview for his view of the office now that he had held it for 12 months, President Carter readily conceded he had had moments "when I'm not sure that I can deal with problems satisfactorily," and, with newfound modesty, he used phrases like "I'm learning," "my newness," and "my biggest mistake."

On balance, the first president in the nation's third century of independence ended his inaugural year with some achievements, some new initiatives, and also some failures and fumbles in working toward his announced goals. As one Carter staff member put it in an interview with Time magazine, "We haven't done as well as

241

Carter registered surprise during a news conference in Washington

we'd hoped but we've done better than what we're being given credit for." If headlined disappointments did seem to overshadow his successes, the one that plagued him from front pages the longest was the one that came to be known as "the Lance affair." After four months of bit-by-bit exposure and mounting pressure, the president was forced to accept the resignation of his close friend and adviser, Bert Lance, an amiable Georgian who directed the Office of Management and Budget.

Even so, Jimmy Carter could point to substantial achievement. He signed a pair of economic-recovery bills authorizing $4 billion for public works projects such as schools, libraries and city halls, and appropriating $20 billion to pay for that program and other public service employment aimed at developing job opportunities for young people and Vietnam veterans. He signed a bill designed to save low and middle-income taxpayers more than $5 billion as part of a $34.2 billion federal tax cut spread over 28 months and simplifying most filing procedures. His administration worked to make food stamps easier to use by the very poor and to avert the collapse of the Social Security sys-

tem. And he established a new Department of Energy.

Carter gave highest priority to his energy proposals. In April he called upon the nation to wage the "moral equivalent of war" in response to dwindling energy supplies by accepting his program, which was based on stringent conservation of fuels, higher energy prices and penalties for waste. Three months later, though, he felt compelled to scold the public for "not paying attention" to his pleas for voluntary conservation. Later, in October, he accused the oil industry of being uninterested in solutions and intent on staging "the biggest rip-off in history." A month after that, he postponed a tour of nine foreign countries so he could be in Washington personally to battle for his legislation. At year's end, though, it appeared that public indifference and congressional intransigence had won out, at least temporarily: Congress adjourned without passing an energy bill.

If that was disappointing to Jimmy Carter, it was as nothing compared to the series of shocks that culminated Sept. 21. That was the day he received, and read to the nation, a letter from his closest friend and adviser, Thomas Bertram Lance.

"My Dear Mr. President:

"I am convinced that I can continue to be an effective Director of the Office of Management and Budget. However, because of the amount of controversy and the continuing nature of it, I have decided to submit my resignation . . ."

His eyes moist, his voice constricted, Carter called Lance "a good and honorable man" and added, "Although I regret his resignation, I do accept it." Next day, Lance boarded a chartered plane and flew home to Calhoun, Ga., where a crowd of 2,000 greeted him with rebel yells and "Welcome Home" banners, a demonstration equal to the president's own show of loyalty.

Lance was far more than Jimmy Carter's friend and confidant. He won friends and influenced legislators for Carter on Capitol Hill, was the administration's most effective ambassador to the business community, and one of the few people in the country who could say "no" to Carter and have him listen. He was also Jimmy Carter's pal. A big, unassuming bear of a man (6 feet 4 inches, 235 pounds), Lance loved to swap jokes with the president or simply kick off his shoes, sit back and chat in his rumbling voice about whatever was on Carter's mind. In many ways they seemed to be an odd pair— Carter the introvert, Lance the extrovert—but there were many similarities between the two. At 46, Lance was closer in age to the 52-year-old Carter than most of the younger men who made up the White House inner circle. Like Carter, Lance took his religion seriously. Both were tireless workers, at their desks up to 12 hours a day. Both knew what it was like to climb from small-town Georgia to financial and political eminence. After Carter's election, it came as a surprise to no one that Lance was the first man he named to cabinet rank.

Lance was born in the small, north Georgia town of Young Harris, where his father was president of a tiny Methodist college, and later moved to Calhoun, slightly larger at 5,000 population. One of his sixth-grade classmates at Calhoun was LaBelle David, granddaughter of the president of the Calhoun First National Bank. LaBelle and Bert were married when they were both 19. Just before graduation in 1951, Lance had to drop out of the University of Georgia to find work; the first of their four sons was on his way.

He found work easily enough. LaBelle's grandfather gave him a $90-a-week job as a teller at the bank. By 1963 he was the bank's president, and a dynamic one. To stimulate the local economy he gave high-risk loans to people willing to start small businesses, bought purebred bulls to lease to local farmers, all the while increasing the bank's assets and his own local esteem.

When Jimmy Carter ran unsuccessfully for governor in 1966, Lance was there to help,

Lance testified before the Senate Governmental Affairs Committee

rallying businessmen to Carter's cause. He was on hand when Carter ran again in 1970, this time successfully, and won his reward. Carter first put Lance in charge of the highway department, which Lance quickly streamlined, then put him in charge of wheedling the legislature into passing Carter's governmental reforms. In 1974, Lance himself ran for governor with Carter's backing. He finished third. The following year, Lance and two associates raised $7.4 million to buy controlling interest in the National Bank of Georgia. In two years, under Lance's presidency, the bank's assets doubled to $400 million, making it Georgia's fifth largest bank.

His very success, as a banker, a backstairs political cajoler, and a political candidate, returned to haunt Bert Lance when Jimmy Carter summoned him to Washington.

Not, however, at first. At first, at his confirmation hearings before the Senate Governmental Affairs Committee, Lance sailed through with flying colors. There was one minor problem. Lance held a great deal of stock in the National Bank of Georgia that would have to be disposed of to avoid even the appearance of con-

flict of interest. "I believe I can work that out," Lance said. He put the stock in a blind trust with instructions that it be sold by a date agreed upon by the committee.

Then the trouble started. Unfortunately, the bank's stock went down in value as the date approached, and it appeared that Lance would have to sell it at a substantial loss. That seemed unfair to Carter as well as to Lance. On behalf of his friend, Carter, in a letter, asked the committee to grant Lance an extension. The committee convened to consider it. At the hearing, some allegations about irregularities came up. Lance explained them to the committee's satisfaction and, once again, the committee gave Bert Lance, as one member put it, its "Good Housekeeping seal of approval." Lance got his postponement.

To certain members of the Washington press corps, however, Lance's explanations seemed insufficient. Reporters began to dig. Bit by bit, matters began to surface concerning Lance's

Left, Carter held two-year-old Cecily Baskir during a picnic on the South Lawn of the White House. Below, the president chatted with Woodrow Diehl and his family during a visit to their farm home in Indianola, Iowa

These two car salesmen in Clarksville, Ind. did not care for Carter's energy proposals, especially the one encouraging people to buy small cars

former banking practices that seemed, if not illegal, at least irregular. Under pressure, the committee reluctantly reopened hearings to investigate.

In question was whether Lance had improperly maintained "compensating balances" of interest-free deposits made by the National Bank of Georgia at other banks in exchange for personal loans from the banks; whether large overdrafts by him and his family at the Calhoun National Bank, which he headed, purportedly used to finance his political campaign, constituted an abuse of his position as a bank executive; whether he had used collateral due to one New York bank to secure a loan at another bank; whether he had complied promptly with bank examiners' demands for reform; and whether he had improperly used a bank airplane for personal reasons while he was running for governor.

Lance defended his name before the committee, responded to every allegation, but in the end the heat seemed too much to bear for Lance to remain an effective budget director. At year's end he was still under investigation by the Justice Department, the Securities and Exchange Commission, the Federal Deposit Insurance Corp., the Internal Revenue Service, and the Federal Election Commission.

Even the Lance affair, for all its rumors and speculations, seemed to make almost no dent in the popular perception of President Carter's probity. In a year-end poll taken for Time magazine by the opinion research firm of Yankelovich, Skelly & White, Inc., a telephone survey of 1,050 registered voters, the public remained at least as confident of Carter's integrity as when he took office.

The poll-takers asked another question perhaps more revealing of what Americans thought of Carter's first year. They asked what if, knowing what they know now, voters could choose again between Jimmy Carter and Gerald Ford. Asked that question, 44 percent chose Carter, 41 percent Ford, and 15 percent were not sure. It meant the voters would elect Carter with just about the same plurality they gave him when they sent him to Washington. The supposition was that Jimmy Carter would settle for that.

245

South Africa Faced A Stormy New Year

But Rhodesia's Ian Smith appeared hopeful of reaching agreement with black leaders

South Africa's white government faced a stormy new year, bracing for further ostracism and hostility over its widely condemned race policies. Beset by a United Nations arms embargo—with little immediate practical impact but a clear warning of possible future oil and trade sanctions—South Africa's 4.5 million whites adopted a defiant stance. They gave overwhelming support in year-end elections to Prime Minister John Vorster, who vowed to step up implementation of the ruling National Party's policy of apartheid or separate racial development. Vorster said his mandate was a firm rejection of outside interference in his nation's affairs. The arms embargo followed world anger at South Africa's nationwide security crackdown in October on black and white dissidents, two black newspapers and 18 civil rights organizations.

Despite widespread protest over the death in security police detention of black activist Steve Biko, 30, Vorster promised the nation stern measures to safeguard white rule and maintain law and order. More than 700 others, mostly blacks, were still in detention without trial, including editor Percy Qoboza of the white-

Left: Adults tried to help this terrified youngster who had been overcome with tear gas during a disturbance in Soweto, South Africa's largest black township. Right, a mourner at the funeral of Steve Biko held up this poster of the dead leader

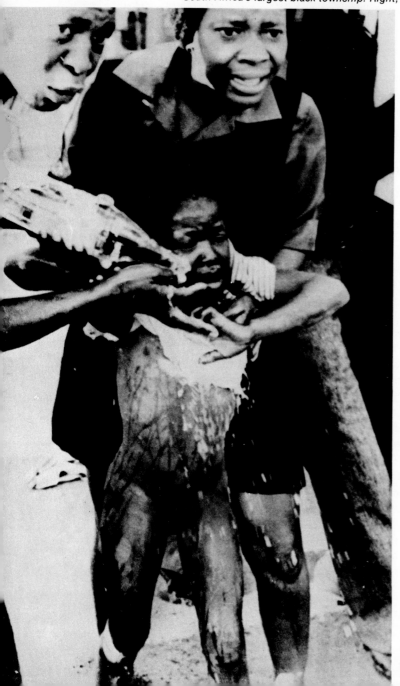

BIKO AND SOLIDARITY

BLACK PEOPLE'S CONVENTION
TRIBUTE TO THE LATE
HONORARY PRESIDENT
BANTU STEPHEN BIKO
One Azania: One Na

owned newspaper for blacks, The World. Another anti-government editor, a white, Donald Woods of The East London Daily Dispatch, fled the country in late December after he was banned in October. Banning is tantamount to house arrest, a system used to silence domestic critics.

The government was expected to begin plans announced in 1977 to create a tri-partite parliamentary system, under the ultimate control of whites, with separate parliaments for the nation's 4.5 million whites, 2.7 million mixed-blood coloreds, and 270,000 Asians.

The 18-million black majority was expected to find political expression in the rural tribal homelands set aside for them. Two of the nine homelands, Transkei and Bophuthatswana, had already opted for independence but others, including Kwazulu, the home of South Africa's five million Zulus, had rejected independence and demanded full political participation in the central government.

Urban terrorism emerged as a real threat in 1977. Black terrorists armed with communist-origin weapons gunned down two whites in downtown Johannesburg, several bombs exploded at a major shopping center and at least one police station, and authorities warned further violence was possible.

More trouble was expected at South Africa's segregated black townships, where youths

Donald Woods, a newsman banned in South Africa posed in Lesotho where he had fled

Rhodesia's Prime Minister Ian Smith seemed confident at this news conference in Salisbury

were demanding reforms in the black education system and an end to apartheid. But with virtually all militants behind bars it appeared South African authorities might have the continuing unrest generally under control, although grievances over backward conditions in Soweto and elsewhere ran deep.

In war-torn Rhodesia, Prime Minister Ian Smith appeared hopeful of agreement with moderate black nationalist leaders on a new constitution leading to a black government with safeguards for whites. Smith agreed to give all adult blacks the vote in exchange for ironclad constitutional guarantees for the safety of white interests.

But as black negotiators in Salisbury sought to reach agreement with Rhodesia's white minority government there was no sign black

247

The Rhodesian Information Ministry released this picture which purported to show guerilla commander Josiah Tongogara training women recruits

guerrillas—operating from bases in Mozambique and Zambia—intended to halt their five-year war of liberation.

The guerrilla leaders—Robert Mugabe and Joshua Nkomo—refused to become involved in the talks between Smith and Bishop Abel Muzorewa, the Rev. Ndabaningi Sithole and Jeremiah Chirau. Britain and the United States had maintained that an "internal settlement" ignoring the guerrilla leaders would not be acceptable. Britain, Rhodesia's former colonial ruler, must legally approve any new constitution for Rhodesia's 6.4 million blacks and 268,000 whites.

The prospect of a civil war loomed between the moderate blacks, who claimed the political support of 70 percent of the black population, and the guerrilla leaders who ran the war against Smith's government.

The future of South West Africa or Namibia, the disputed, mineral-rich territory ruled by South Africa, was also in doubt as the year drew to a close.

Under pressure from the West, South Africa had agreed to internationally supervised elections in the territory, leading to independence by the end of 1978. But the South-West Africa People's Organization, fighting a hit-and-run war against white rule from bases in southern Angola, insisted on a full withdrawal of South African forces in Namibia before elections. South Africa had agreed to a partial withdrawal but SWAPO leader Sam Nujoma had been insisting on a total removal of South African troops.

South African authorities had made it clear they would make no more concessions and would hold elections and grant Namibia independence with or without SWAPO participation. That option could lead to a prolonged conflict between SWAPO and the multiracial government that emerged in Windhoek backed by South Africa.

Charlie Chaplin – The Famed Little Tramp Of The Movies – Died At 88

The props were deceptively simple: baggy pants, battered derby, outsize shoes, frayed cutaway coat, and a jet black mustache. But when worn by Charlie Chaplin they became a symbol: the Little Tramp.

For millions of moviegoers Chaplin always was and always would be the Little Tramp, a battered but dignified Everyman who made people laugh as he stumbled through life, in Chaplin's words, "forever seeking romance, but his feet won't let him."

Chaplin died Christmas morning 1977, but the symbol he had created and which was to identify him for a lifetime lived on in the heart and memory of the many who had seen and still would see his movies.

He was 88 and, his family announced, had "passed away peacefully" in his sleep at his secluded 18th-century mansion at Corsier-Sur-Vevey, Switzerland. He had spent the last quarter century of his life in the small Swiss town—about 35 miles east of Geneva—and rarely left his 37-acre estate.

Born into a theatrical family in London on April 16, 1889, Charles Spencer Chaplin made his debut when, as an infant, he was carried onstage in his mother's arms. By an earlier union, Chaplin's mother had a son, Sydney,

Charles Chaplin made ready to face his fans as he left an airliner bringing him to Paris to receive a movie award

Chaplin as he appeared in the movie "Gold Rush"

who later was to become his half-brother's business manager.

Chaplin's parents separated shortly after he was born. The family's fortunes declined and eventually the mother and her sons entered the Lambeth workhouse, then the two young boys were sent to an orphanage outside London. "Although we were well looked after, it was a forlorn existence," Chaplin was to recall in later years.

Mother and boys eventually were reunited and Chaplin became a clog dancer and then, at 12, he got a small stage part. Other parts followed, and Chaplin, who had decided to become a comedian, studied hard in his highly successful effort to learn how to make an audience laugh.

In 1914, Chaplin was touring the United States with an English comedy troupe and was discovered by producer-director Mack Sennett. It was at Sennett's request that Chaplin created the Little Tramp character. It was then that he put together the costume and the splayed shuffling walk that was to become his symbol as

well as the international signature of a legend who rose from vaudeville trouper to become the toast of Hollywood.

The Little Tramp character was catapulted to fame in such films as *The Gold Rush, The Kid, The Idle Class,* and *Modern Times.* Chaplin was to say later of the tramp's popularity: "One cannot do humor without great sympathy for one's fellow man. As the tramp I think I endeared myself through his terrific humility—the humility which I am sure is a universal thing—of somebody without money. As a youth, I was

very unhappy, soulfully unhappy, not so much from being deprived or hungry . . . there was always plenty of bread and butter around. It is the humiliation of poverty which is so distressing. I had to go through the streets with my mother, who was insane, and so weak, staggering from one side to the other as though she were drunk. Those sorts of things."

As the tramp, he took the side of the underdog, evoking a note of sympathy from most Americans by portraying himself as a victim of the system beset by overbearing policemen,

Chaplin was clad in his famous props in the film "Dog's Life"

251

Chaplin, right, and
Winston Churchill in a
1931 picture taken
when Chaplin was on a
tour for the start of one
of his films

snapping dogs, and Yukon blizzards. "I never thought of the tramp in terms of appeal," Chaplin said in 1966, "He was myself, a comic spirit, something within me that I said I must express."

Chaplin helped give birth to the Hollywood film industry of the 1920s. He had his own studio and later joined Mary Pickford, Douglas Fairbanks and D. W. Griffith in founding United Artists. The film industry was electrified in 1919 when these four biggest luminaries of movies joined forces. Chaplin was involved with the firm for years but he sold his 25 percent interest in 1955.

Among Chaplin's best-loved films were *The Gold Rush, City Lights, Limelight* and *A King In New York.* During his 43 years on the screen, Chaplin appeared in 10 feature films and a host of comedy shorts. In 1914, for example, he made an astounding 35 one and two-reel shorts, plus the six-reel *Tillie's Punctured Romance.* In addition to acting, he often wrote the scripts and directed the films as well. He shunned sound movies when they debuted in 1927, in-

sisting that pantomime was what made his audiences laugh. But he later relented somewhat, and movie fans got to hear him sing in *Modern Times* in 1936 and finally to speak in his 1940 satire on Hitler, *The Great Dictator.*

Off-screen, however, conflicts developed and Chaplin eventually found himself alienated from some of his public's graces following certain private and political incidents. The estrangement began in the 1940s when he made several speeches proclaiming the Russians, then U.S. wartime allies, as "comrades." The House of Representatives' Committee on Un-American Activities suggested in 1947 that Chaplin was associated with communism—a change the comedian denied as "vicious propaganda and lies." Chaplin once explained, "I'm not touting for any ideology. I'm for the progress of the human race. I'm for the little man."

Chaplin had married and divorced three times by 1943 when he was charged with transporting a young actress across state lines for immoral purposes. He was acquitted but later judged to be the father of her daughter.

252

At the age of 54, Chaplin married the former Oona O'Neill, then 18, over the objections of her American playwright father — Eugene O'Neill — who disinherited the young bride. The couple had eight children. Chaplin had two sons by his third wife, the former Lita Grey, and no children with his second wife, actress Paulette Goddard. His first wife, Mildred Harris, bore him a son who died a few days after birth.

In 1952, Chaplin returned to his native London on vacation. Although he had lived in the United States for 40 years, Chaplin remained a British subject and while in England he was barred from re-entering America. Chaplin established a new home in Switzerland and did not leave there for 20 years until 1972 when, just before his 83rd birthday, Hollywood awarded Chaplin a special Oscar citing "the incalculable effect he has had in making motion pictures the art form of this century." Chaplin returned to America to accept the award and was feted by friends and followers on both coasts.

Further honors were to follow. On New Year's Day, 1975, he went to Buckingham Palace to be knighted by Queen Elizabeth II.

Too weak to kneel before the queen, he was dubbed "Sir Charles Chaplin" while seated in a wheelchair.

Praise for Chaplin poured in after his death. Comedian George Burns, 81, summed it up, perhaps, when he said:

"Not only was he the funniest, not only could he make you laugh, but he could make you cry, too. He left a real impression on the world. He made everything up, the Little Tramp, the costume, the cane, hitting his hat and turning around, all the little comedy routines that everybody's been doing for years and will be doing as long as there's comedy."

The famous comedian held an honorary Oscar presented to him in 1972

British troops took shelter behind anti-riot shields during an outbreak on Belfast's Falls Road

VIOLENCE ABATED IN STRIFE-TORN IRELAND AMID GUARDED HOPES

The violence that had torn Northern Ireland for more than eight years, killing nearly 1,800 people, diminished in 1977 raising hopes that the bloodletting might be nearing an end.

But no one was taking bets that the conflict between the British province's million-strong Protestant majority, who wanted to remain under the British crown, and the 500,000 Catholics who sought eventual union with the Irish Republic to the south was over.

The conflict was rooted in the traditional hostility between the Protestants, descendants of predominantly Scottish "planters" used by England to colonize Ireland 500 years ago, and native Catholics.

The feuding erupted in August, 1969, out of a grassroots Catholic civil rights movement determined to end the minority's second-class citizen status and the political, economic and social discrimination that had long been practiced by Protestants in Northern Ireland.

Soon after the first clashes and Protestant attacks on Catholic ghettoes, the outlawed Irish Republican Army, standard bearer of the Irish Catholic independence movement that won freedom from Britain for most of the Emerald Isle in 1921, launched a campaign to end British rule and Protestant domination of Ulster, the ancient name for Northern Ireland.

The level of violence dropped by about half in 1977—109 killings compared to 297 in 1976, 300 wounded against nearly 700 the year before, 320 bombings against 620 in 1976, and about 1,100 shooting incidents against nearly 1,800.

The British government appeared satisfied. The violence seemed to have been reduced to the "acceptable level of violence" that cabinet ministers and civil servants had hoped for.

This optimism was not shared by Mrs. Betty Williams, a 36-year-old Belfast Catholic housewife who won a delayed 1976 Nobel Peace Prize with Mairead Corrigan for their peace crusade in Ulster. Mrs. Williams noted grimly when she received the award in Oslo Dec. 10: "It may take 100 years to stop the violence."

Provisional IRA commanders reinforced that view in clandestine interviews with The Associated Press in the bleak Catholic ghettoes of Belfast and Londonderry. "We fight on." they declared.

"We're in a no-win situation," said a senior British Army officer. "They can't beat us and we can't beat them. We can kill or capture a lot of gunmen and bombers but that isn't going to stop the movement."

The Provisional IRA certainly was less effective in 1977 than in any other year since the guerrillas launched their anti-British campaign in February, 1971.

But the bombs went on exploding almost daily and gunfire still crackled in the leafy lanes of County Antrim and the backstreets of Catholic Belfast. IRA bomb damage totalled more than $62 million.

More than 100 known IRA men were captured, convicted and jailed. Several hundred more extremists, many of them teenage boys and girls linked to IRA factions or their Protestant rivals were arrested for offenses ranging from murder to post office holdups and possessing illegal firearms.

Down south, in the Republic, scores of IRA men were arrested and jailed.

As the IRA's campaign fizzled and security improved, Protestant extremists cooled it too. One of the most significant developments of 1977 was the almost total halt to random sectarian assassinations by Catholic and Protestant death squads that had kept the province in turmoil in previous years. The Protestant organizations had been formed to combat the IRA because they claimed the government was not hitting the guerrillas hard enough.

But that changed in 1977 under Britain's Northern Ireland Secretary, Roy Mason, a bluff-spoken ex-coal miner from Yorkshire. Mason intensified military operations. Several agents penetrated the IRA's cellular network and more than 100 soldiers of the Special Air Services Regiment, Britain's crack counter-insurgency specialists, combed trouble spots in civilian cars with some success.

But the undercover war had its casualties. At least two British agents were killed by the Provisionals.

Mason also declared he would never talk with the IRA as his predecessors had done, a move that reassured many Protestants that the British did not plan to make any concessions to the IRA or push the province into some kind of union with the Republic.

Northern Ireland's police force remained predominantly Protestant but its image had changed drastically from the days of 1969–70 when it was little more than Protestantism's sectarian strike arm. Catholic distrust of the police appeared to have begun to fade—one of the more hopeful signs of 1977.

The crunch point for the Protestants was the failure of Rev. Ian Paisley's attempt in May to force the British to return Protestant rule to the province by staging a general strike.

The IRA's credibility had also been weakened by its failure to carry through a vow to wreck a two-day Silver jubilee visit by Queen Elizabeth II in August.

But there was an even grimmer indication that Catholics were getting restive. Police reported more than 200 shot in the knees by guerrilla punishment squads for defying the IRA.

Catholic informants said many of their people were sickened by increased brutality shown by the guerrillas in the ghettoes and the IRA's growing involvement in racketeering in the name of patriotism.

Politically and economically the picture was as gloomy as ever.

Neither side made any moves toward power-sharing, the lynchpin of Britain's political efforts in Northern Ireland. That meant London continued to rule the province. It had done so since it suspended the Protestant-dominated provincial parliament and government in March 1972.

Proud parents, Britain's Princess Anne and Mark Phillips with their infant son, Master Peter Mark Andrew after he had been christened at Buckingham Palace

Also in December . . .

EXECUTIONS TOUCHED OFF RIOTS IN BERMUDA

The customary calm on the idyllic island of Bermuda was shattered in 1973 by a series of murders, including that of the British governor, Richard Staples, and his aide. Four years later, two blacks were hanged for the slayings and violence erupted again as hundreds of angry blacks surged through the streets of Hamilton.

The condemned men, members of a defunct terrorist group known as the Black Cadre, were Erskine Burrows, 33, and Larry Tacklyn, 25. They were put to death at dawn Dec. 2 in the fortress-like Casemates Prison at the western end of the island. They were the first executions to take place in the British colony since 1946 and they caused an uproar among the island's black colony where many regarded the act as a vendetta because whites felt threatened.

Aroused youths ran amok in the black neighborhoods of Hamilton, setting fire to stores, a school, government offices, a liquor warehouse and other buildings.

Dozens of rioters were arrested as officials estimated the damage at $2 million. The violence actually began while the court was still deliberating an appeal against the death sentences handed down two years earlier.

The case went to the Court of Appeals after Queen Eliza-

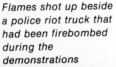

Flames shot up beside a police riot truck that had been firebombed during the demonstrations

beth II accepted a recommendation of British Foreign Secretary David Owen that she deny clemency. Later, Owen sent a letter asking Bermuda to call off the executions, but his request was turned down.

While the Appeals Court was pondering the case, police beat back about 50 persons who stormed the courthouse. There were also orderly protests. About 1,200 people attended a peaceful rally of the opposition Progressive Labor party against the death penalty and religious leaders on the island organized all-night vigils in a number of churches. Tension quickly mounted as the court refused to stay the executions.

Britain dispatched the Royal Regiment of Fusiliers from its home base outside London and a British infantry company was sent in from Belize, formerly British Honduras.

Underlying the trouble, observers said, was a feeling of political and economic dissatisfaction. Young blacks saw the British troops as an extension of United Kingdom rule and felt that Bermuda's parliament was not truly representative because of gerrymandering by the conservative multi-racial United Bermuda party. The minority Progressive Labor Party, which was predominantly black, commanded 45 percent of the popular vote, but held only 15 of the 40 seats in parliament.

Two days after the troops arrived, Britain began pulling them out as calm reappeared.

EARTHQUAKE STRUCK IRAN'S COAL BASIN KILLING MORE THAN 500 PERSONS

An earthquake struck south-central Iran in freezing pre-dawn weather on Dec. 20. Before the shocks had subsided, they had swept 16 villages in the country's coal basin killing more than 500 persons and injuring an estimated 670.

Before daybreak soldiers and civilian workers had begun digging through piles of rubble by the light of kerosene lanterns looking for bodies and trapped victims. Many of the victims were said to be children trapped by collapsing mudbrick walls. The disaster halted mining operations in the basin.

The quake left thousands of miners and their families homeless in freezing temperatures. Hundreds of helicopters were dispatched from their base in the central Iranian city of Isfahan. Led by two C-130 transport planes, the armada of choppers flew in tents, food, water, blankets, medicine and doctors. Small encampments were set up outside the stricken villages for the homeless.

Survivors sobbed and beat themselves in anguish in tents set up by the Red Lion and Sun, the Iranian equivalent of the Red Cross. In many cases, food prepared for the survivors lay untouched outside their tents until it was devoured by stray dogs.

Many of the injured were transported by train and helicopter to the towns of Zarand and Kerman. After the hospitals in that area filled up, local residents opened their homes for the victims. The stricken area lay between the agricultural town of Zarand and Kerman, a onetime Moslem fortress city.

The Red Lion and Sun reported that the quake registered 6.2 on the Richter scale, but the United States Geological Survey calculated it at 5.5. The Richter scale is a measure of energy released by an earthquake and is based on ground motion as recorded by seismographs.

It was the most devastating quake to hit Iran since 1968 when one rocked the northeastern part of the country and killed 12,000 persons. In 1962, about 10,000 persons were killed in a quake that hit the Ghazvin region, 100 miles west of Tehran.

257

TREATY ALLOWED MEXICO AND UNITED STATES TO EXCHANGE PRISONERS

The men waiting at the Mexico City airport for the plane that would take them to the United States wore short-sleeved jump suits. The women wore white-trimmed red jackets and blue pants. They laughed, shouted and waved.

It was not, however, the usual airport departure. Watching the 61 American men and women were more than 500 policemen. There also were sharpshooters stationed atop nearby buildings. Hovering overhead were two police helicopters.

Emphasizing the contrast were the words of Juan Alberto Antolin, a Mexico City prison director: "This is not a fiesta. These are prisoners—drug smugglers and poisoners of the public who are going to another prison."

The Americans all had been imprisoned in Mexico. They were being flown to San Diego, Calif., to complete the first leg of an historic international prisoner exchange. The exchange was the result of a transfer treaty that was signed in 1976 and ratified by the U.S. Senate in October of 1977 which allowed eligible Americans in Mexican jails and Mexicans in American jails to serve the rest of their sentences in their homelands.

As the American prisoners waited, a plane carrying 36 Mexican prisoners taken from U.S. jails landed. After the Mexicans debarked Dec. 9, the Americans—most of them convicted on drug charges—boarded and flew to San Diego where large crowds awaited them. The returned prisoners were not, however, allowed to speak with loved ones but were taken to a correction facility for processing. With the prisoners was an 18-month-old girl. She had been born in jail to her American mother. The child's mother had served four years and three months of a seven-year sentence for smuggling cocaine.

On Dec. 10, another 66 Americans were returned to the United States. Although the mood as the prisoners arrived was almost festive, one San Diego law official said, "They are not returning heroes, they are not returning POWs, they are criminals." A bus returned another 11 men and four women Dec. 12, and an official said as many as 44 of the 138 Americans returned thus far could be freed quickly as a result of parole hearings.

More prisoners were returned in following days and by the time the last group of Americans came back Dec. 17 the number of returnees stood at 233. James Meko, a Bureau of Prisons official, said at least 100 more Americans were expected to be returned early in 1978.

Fellow students and friends of the ill-fated University of Evansville basketball team consoled each other as they left a memorial service held in Evansville. Twenty-nine persons, including the team, were killed when their chartered DC-3 crashed on takeoff from Evansville Dec. 13

A line of tractors formed up in Washington Dec. 10 to participate in a protest. The demonstration was staged to dramatize farmers' demands for government help to get higher prices for their goods

FOR THE RECORD

KILLED. Seven women students at Providence (R.I.) College, when fire surged through the fourth floor of a women's dormitory Dec. 13. Two of the coeds jumped to their deaths seconds before firemen could have rescued them with ladders. At least 15 other students were injured. Many of the victims had stayed up late to decorate their rooms, windows and hallways for Christmas, and fire officials said the blaze could have been caused by faulty Christmas lights or by a hair dryer left on in a closet to dry clothing.

WON. The Australian national elections, by Prime Minister Malcolm Fraser and his conservative Liberal-National Country Party coalition. With 75 percent of the 8.5 million votes counted the day after the Dec. 10 election, computer predictions gave the coalition a majority of at least 42 seats in the 124-member House of Representatives. Computer analysis of the vote for the Senate, where 34 of the 64 seats were up for election, indicated the government would maintain a clear majority. Final results of the Senate election would not be known until January of 1978 because of the complex proportional representation system of voting.

EXPLOSIONS. At grain elevators near New Orleans and Galveston, Tex. The Louisiana blast occurred Dec. 22 at a Continental Grain Co. elevator while a ship was being loaded. Volatile grain dust was ignited and blew the tops off 43 giant silos in the 73-silo, 6-million bushel elevator. Thirty-five persons were killed and 11 were hospitalized. In the Texas waterfront grain elevator explosion Dec. 27, 15 persons were known dead and 23 others were injured. The blast, which was heard up to 70 miles away, twisted steel and left huge chunks of concrete strewn about the area. Nearby railroad cars were damaged by the blast.

259

Also in December . . .

Year-End Headliners

As the year 1977 came to an end, these stories were still developing

Singer Anita Bryant who led the campaign against the Gays in Florida's Dade County

ANITA VS GAYS —

Anita Bryant almost became Miss America some years ago, then went on to make a name as a popular singer. Finally, as "the voice that refreshes," the symbol of Florida orange juice, she came into full bloom, projecting an image of health and the wholesome life.

Early in 1977, Miss Bryant appeared in quite a different role as leader of a fight against gay rights in Miami that quickly had national repercussions. The 37-year-old wife and mother of four pressed a campaign to repeal an ordinance passed by the Metropolitan Dade County Commission that banned discrimination in housing, jobs or public accommodations based on "affectional or sexual preferences." As head of a church-supported group, she charged that the law was an attempt to "legitimize homosexuals and their recruitment of our children."

Miss Bryant asserted that she was not against homosexuals themselves but only the act of homosexuality. Within three months her group had produced 64,000 signatures to force the commission either to repeal the ordinance or call a special election on the issue. An election was scheduled.

Both sides in Florida rallied support from around the country. Miss Bryant said her group was receiving a thousand letters a day. On the other side, homosexuals in Boston, Chicago, Los Angeles and other cities began passing hats in gay bars and planning fund-raising dances. They also tried to mobilize political support.

A group called the Dade County Coalition for the Humanistic Rights of Gays invited local political candidates to a meeting at the YMCA to discuss discrimination against homosexuals.

"This is not just a gay issue," declared coalition leader Bob Basker. "It will have the same effect for us that it had for blacks."

Meanwhile, the Bryant forces kept on the move. Stumping in conservative, middle-class neighborhoods, they pressed their fight. Full page newspaper ads bought by the group suggested that an epidemic of child pornography might result if voters approved the ordinance.

The Bryant crusade prevailed. Gay rights leaders failed to convince Floridians that defense of the ordinance was a human rights issue that needed legal protection. In June, the voters of Dade County came out 2 to 1 for repeal of the ordinance.

"Tonight," Anita Bryant told cheering supporters in Miami Beach, "the laws of God and the cultural values of man have been vindicated."

Gay leaders were defiant in defeat. Across the country gay communities responded to the Miami vote with marches. In San Francisco, 5,000 activists staged an impromptu three-hour parade. In Chicago, 175 men and women held a candlelight vigil at midnight. In New York, hundreds of homosexuals marched through Greenwich Village for two straight nights shouting "Gay rights now!"

When Anita Bryant appeared on a TV show in New York, about 100 hostile demonstrators turned out.

"Suddenly we became a subject of national debate," said Ronald Gold, a staff member of the National Gay Task Force in New York City. "The Dade election was a setback but we're delighted with the resulting publicity."

The repeal campaign in Dade County had centered on employment discrimination, with Miss Bryant's group charging that the ordinance would allow homosexuals to teach impressionable school children.

"The Bryant bunch kept telling gays that it wasn't after their jobs, as long as they didn't advertise their homosexuality," said Gold. "But what those people were really saying was 'You pretend that you don't exist so we can go on telling our children that no responsible person is gay.'"

It appeared that, instead of driving homosexuals back into the closet, the Bryant campaign had pushed them into the open.

Also in December . . .

HUNT FOR STRANGLER—

When Yolanda Washington was found nude and strangled on Oct. 18 in the northeast section of Los Angeles, it didn't even rate a one-paragraph mention in the local papers. It was just one homicide in the city's total of 500. Besides, Yolanda Washington was a prostitute and getting killed was considered one of the risks of that trade.

Two months later, the body of Kimberly Martin, another prostitute, was found nude and strangled on a hillside a few miles from where Miss Washington's body was found. This killing was front page news across the country.

A lot had happened since the killing of Miss Washington. Beginning about the first of November, a nude and strangled body turned up every few days for about four weeks. Miss Martin was victim No. 11. Most of the victims were teen-agers, though one was only 12 and the oldest was 28. Most had been sexually molested. All but one of the bodies were found on hillsides in the northern section of the city. Police theorized the killings were related and dubbed the killer "The Hillside Strangler."

By early December, women in the city were scared. Many refused to go anywhere by themselves. Quite a few enrolled in self-defense courses. One 18-year-old girl who lived in the area said she had quit her job in a jewelry store because she was afraid to go home at night. "I don't open my windows anymore. I lock all my doors." A 19-year-old sales clerk said, "I run to my car after work."

People all over town were talking about the strangler; at cocktail parties, lunch counters, beauty shops. Everybody had a theory. There was big money for anyone whose tip led to the capture of the strangler. The county offered a $100,000 reward. The city offered $25,000. Newspapers, television stations and concerned citizens chipped in another $15,000.

Was there a common thread linking the victims? At least six of them were either Hollywood prostitutes or part of the Hollywood street scene. But the 12-year-old and 14-year-old victims were neighborhood pals last seen on a shopping trip together. Their families didn't even allow them to date. Two other victims were students with no known Hollywood connections. Perhaps they weren't all strangled by the same killer or killers. Police linked the crimes together because of what one officer termed "a number of similarities." But police said they were not certain all 11 killings were related.

Only in the case of Miss Martin was there any indication how the strangler picked up his victim. A man called an outcall prostitution service Dec. 13 and asked that a girl be sent to room 114 at a Hollywood apartment. Miss Martin was sent, and her body was found the next morning. Police later learned the phone call had been placed from the Hollywood Library and that apartment 114 had been vacant for several months.

In late November the Los Angeles Police Department set up a special 29-man task force to work on the case. That force soon grew to 42, then 50, then 55, then 65. In late December, the lieutenant in charge was replaced by a captain.

The Martin case seemed to provide some good clues. Within hours after Miss Martin's body was found, Assistant Police Chief Daryl Gates said, "We have more to go on in this case than in any of the others." The case was still unsolved a week later, and Gates told reporters, "I'm embarrassed every time I look at myself in the mirror." A week later, Gates was all set to release a composite drawing of two suspects when it was discovered the drawing depicted two police officers. They weren't the killers, and the composite was hastily canned. A week later, the scheduled news conference was canceled because there was "nothing significant to report," Gates said.

After the furious pace through November, the killer dropped out of sight for two weeks before the strangling of Miss Martin. The strangler didn't strike again before the end of the year. His total of 11 victims placed him two behind the number killed by the famous Boston Strangler, who terrorized that city in the early 1960s.

KOREA —

More than 12 months of probing into alleged Korean influence-buying had produced reams of information as the year came to a close, but the Justice Department still had not nailed down hard evidence as to which congressmen, if any, had committed illegal or unethical acts.

One significant step was taken when Washington and Seoul agreed to have Korean businessman Tongsun Park testify about any influence-buying that might have taken place in Washington. The accord reportedly called for Park to be questioned in Seoul by American and South Korean officials and then to testify in a U.S. court in return for an offer of immunity.

Free-spending bachelor Park had been accused of trying to boost support for South Korea in the U.S. capital with cash, gifts and other favors while an agent for the Seoul government.

A former director of the Korean Central Intelligence Agency says an influence-buying scheme in Congress was hatched in his KCIA headquarters office in Seoul in August 1968.

The former KCIA director, Kim Hyung Wook, testified under oath that Park and former Rep. Richard T. Hanna, D-Calif., visited him then and made a deal: if he would help make Park South Korea's exclusive U.S. rice dealer, they would use the commission money to buy influence in Congress.

"He (Hanna) said once that is done, he together with Mr. Tongsun Park would distribute that money among U.S. congressmen and have them help Korea's cause," Kim told the House ethics committee.

Kim testified he did help make Park Korea's rice dealer. Other witnesses told the ethics committee Park got $9 million in commissions out of the deal, including $1.6 million that he converted to cash.

More than 20 congressmen acknowledged Park did distribute money to them in the form of campaign contributions and other money. But they said they did nothing wrong.

They said the contributions were legal and they had no reason to suspect he was a foreign agent trying to buy their votes. They said they knew Park only as an ambitious young businessman who threw lavish parties at his fashionable Georgetown Club.

But that is not what Park was reporting back to the KCIA, according to the ethics committee. It said he boasted to the KCIA in a 1972 report that he had bought influence with 41 congressmen.

A federal grand jury indicted Park and Hanna on criminal charges of bribery and conspiring with KCIA officials to try to buy influence in Congress for the South Korean government.

The grand jury indicted another Washington-area businessman, Hancho C. Kim, on charges of conducting a second influence operation, "Operation White Snow" with $600,000 delivered by the KCIA.

Other witnesses told the ethics committee that in addition to the two businessmen's operations, Korean officials including former Ambassador Kim Dong Jo conducted their own efforts to buy influence. They said the ambassador tried in 1972 and 1973 to buy off congressmen with envelopes stuffed with $100 bills.

The witnesses said the alleged South Korean operations started to fall apart in the spring of 1976 when newspapers began exposing Tongsun Park's activities.

A recent KCIA station chief in New York City disclosed that by 1976 Seoul headquarters had cleared a grandiose plan to buy and plant a network of U.S. collaborators in Congress, the White House and top U.S. agencies.

Korean businessman Tongsun Park arrived at the Seoul prosecutor's office accompanied by his lawyer, William Hundley

Also in December . . .

A U.S. Air Force Pilot climbed aboard an F-16 fighter plane as they were silhouetted against a setting sun and orange skies

Credits

Editorial Director: Dan Perkes

Editor: Tom Hoge
Staff Writer: Phil Thomas
Copy Editor: Helen Gavzer
Black & White Photos: David Fox
Color Photos: Muche Desloovere, Jack Cerino
Photo Production: Stanley Kohler
Promotion and Distribution: Jack Elcik
Book & Cover Designs: Soho Studio

Photographs

The illustrations in this volume were selected for the most part from the news photo reports of The Associated Press and, except where specifically credited, were taken by staff photographers of The AP and its member newspapers

Feature Narratives

Hal Bock, New York
    Super Bowl
    World Series

Richard Blystone, London
    Queen Elizabeth Jubilee

Lee Byrd, Washington
    Hanafi Moslem Siege

Paul Chutkow, New Delhi
    Indira Gandhi Ouster

Frank Crepeau, Tel Aviv
    Middle East

John Gale, Amsterdam
    Moluccan Terrorists

Mary Ganz, San Francisco
    Western Drought

Larry Heinzerling, Johannesburg
    South Africa-Rhodesia

Terry Hunt, Washington
    Panama Canal

Brian Jeffries, Nairobi
    Idi Amin

Larry Kurtz, Salt Lake City
    Gilmore Execution

Dudley Lehew, New York
    Cold Wave

Andrew Lippman, Cincinnati
    Kentucky Nightclub Fire

Jules Loh, New York
    Nixon TV Interviews
    Son Of Sam
    Presidential Year

Louis Nevin, London
    British Economy

Eric Newhouse, Chattanooga
    Jailhouse Fires

James Peipert, London
    Carter Summit Debut

John Roderick, Tokyo
    China

Mike Shanahan, Washington
    Carter Inaugural

Larry Thorson, Tel Aviv
    Israeli Political

John F. Wheeler, Madrid
    Worst Plane Crash

Jane See White, New York
    New York Blackout
    Heat Wave

Contributing Reporters

Ed Blanche, London
Richard Carelli, Washington
Carol Deegan, New York
Lee Linder, Philadelphia
R. Gregory Nokes, Washington
William N. Oatis, New York
Marian Price, Washington
Andrew Rosenthal, New York

THE World IN 1977 NEWS ALMANAC

CHRONOLOGY—1977

JANUARY

1 President-elect Carter had little enthusiasm for President Ford's proposal that Puerto Rico be given statehood through processes originating in Washington.

2 Israel's minister of housing, Abraham Ofer, whose name had been mentioned in a financial scandal, killed himself.

4 Sen. Robert C. Byrd of West Virginia was chosen majority leader by his fellow Democrats without opposition as Sen. Hubert H. Humphrey of Minnesota withdrew his candidacy.

5 President-elect Carter informed President Valery Giscard d'Estaing of France that he agreed in principle with the latter's proposal for a summit meeting among Western economic powers.

6 Two Syrians and a Palestinian were hanged a few hours after Syria announced that the three had been convicted in a series of bomb attacks allegedly carried out with the complicity of Iraq. The Palestinian was executed in the main square of Damascus. The two other men were hanged in the city of Aleppo.

7 President-elect Carter and Democratic congressional leaders said they had reached general agreement on an economic stimulation package.

7 Officals said President Ford had ruled out blanket amnesty for Vietnam war deserters and draft evaders.

9 Oakland beat Minnesota 32-14 at the Super Bowl.

10 Secretary of State Henry Kissinger said no American president would ever let the Soviet Union gain strategic superiority.

11 French authorities, after a swift judicial hearing, freed a prominent Palestinian militant who had been arrested by French intelligence agents on suspicion of having been responsible for killing members of the Israeli team at the 1972 Olympics in Munich. Enraged Israeli authorities who had sought to extradite the Palestinian known as Abu Daoud, recalled their ambassador from Paris.

11 Cyrus R. Vance, who was No. 2 official in the U.S. Defense Department when American involvement expanded in Vietnam, told the Senate Foreign Relations Committee that in hindsight "it was a mistake to intervene in Vietnam."

11 Henry Ford 2nd resigned as a trustee of the Ford Foundation, complaining that the philanthropic agency his family founded was spreading itself too thin and had a staff that often failed to appreciate the capitalist system that provided the money the foundation gave away.

12 An international uproar over France's release of Abu Daoud, a suspected Palestinian terrorist leader, left the nation's leaders apparently in a state of silent shock.

12 The Department of Labor said unemployment in December 1976 declined to 7.9 percent from 8.1 percent in November.

13 French Prime Minister Raymond Barre rejected all criticism of the official decision that freed suspected Palestinian terrorist leader Abu Daoud.

14 Sir Anthony Eden, former British prime minister, died at the age of 79.

16 The State of Utah made final preparations to execute Gary Mark Gilmore at sunrise Jan. 17 and end a 10-year moratorium on the death penalty in the United States.

17 At least 48 American servicemen were killed in a collision between a Navy launch and a freighter in the Spanish harbor of Barcelona.

17 Gary Mark Gilmore, a convicted murderer, was executed by a firing squad at Utah State Prison.

17 Frigid weather put a heavy drain on natural gas and electricity supplies and forced many factories and offices across the eastern half of the nation to close.

17 More than a dozen persons were killed when a commuter train derailed and struck a bridge near Sydney, Australia.

18 Prime Minister Indira Gandhi said India would elect a new parliament in March.

18 Egyptians rioted in Cairo and other cities to protest price increases ordered by the government.

19 Egyptian consumer price increases were canceled by President Anwar Sadat after a second day of rioting in which 21 persons were reported killed.

20 Jimmy Carter was sworn in as the 39th President of the United States and said in his Inaugural Address: "I have no new dream to set forth today, but, rather, urge a fresh faith in the old dream."

20 Walter F. Mondale took the oath of office as Vice President of the United States.

20 India removed censorship of its newspapers and instructed state authorities to "expedite" the release of political prisoners.

21 President Carter granted a pardon to almost all Vietnam War draft evaders, but the status of the men who deserted during the war was unsettled.

21 President Carter asked all Americans to keep home thermostats at 65 degrees during the day and lower at night to save fuel.

22 President Carter's economic advisers worked on an economic stimulation program that called for $10 billion to $11 billion in rebates on 1976 income taxes.

23 Vice President Mondale arrived in Brussels on the first stop of a tour of Europe and Japan.

24 President Carter urged an instant and complete halt to all testing of nuclear weapons as a step toward curbing their spread.

24 President Carter rescinded former President Ford's order to end gasoline price controls.

25 Spanish workers struck to protest a wave of violence that had taken seven lives in Madrid in 48 hours.

26 The U.S. State Department accused Czechoslovakia of having violated the provisions of the 1975 Helsinki agreement by a series of arrests and harassment of human rights activists.

26 Confronting a menacing wave of political violence, the Spanish government announced that it was banning public demonstrations, expelling foreigners with "extremist" sympathies and restricting the use of private arms while at the same time continuing plans to hold general elections.

27 The two-week-old natural gas crisis bit deeper for millions of Americans as the effects of the bitter cold forced shutdowns of stores and factories in Pennsylvania and caused school closings there and in Ohio. There were new layoffs for thousands of people in a dozen states and warnings of possible further hardships. New York and New Jersey declared states of emergency.

27 The Carter Administration presented to Congress its $31.1 billion package of economic stimulants, including a $50 tax rebate aimed at 96 percent of the population as the centerpiece of plans to spur growth through greater consumption.

29 A blizzard swept across the already frozen Central states and into the East where it nearly paralyzed large areas with winds up to 60 miles an hour.

29 Soviet dissident Andrei D. Sakharov appealed in a letter to President Carter to "raise your voice" on behalf of persecuted activists in the Soviet Union and eastern Europe.

29 Three Spanish policemen were killed and three others wounded in a new outbreak of violence in Madrid.

29 At least six motorists were found dead in stranded cars around Buffalo, N.Y., which was struck by a blizzard that made the paralyzed city one of the places in the country hardest hit by the cold.

29 The snowbound Midwest states and much of the Northeast were in the grip of near-zero and sub-zero weather, bringing ordinary activities in many places to a standstill.

30 President Carter said the nation appeared faced with a "permanent, very serious energy shortage."

31 President Carter said in an economic message to Congress that his Administration would seek curbs on prices and wages.

31 Heavy snow struck northern New York State again, dropping 18 inches in the Watertown area in 24 hours and isolating and paralyzing the city of Buffalo.

FEBRUARY

1 President Carter told the Soviet envoy that the United States would not back down in its commitment for strengthened human rights in the Soviet Union and elsewhere.

2 President Carter asked Americans to unite in a spirit of cooperation and mutual effort to help him develop "predictable, long-range programs we are sure we can afford and we know will work."

2 An emergency natural gas bill, passed by Congress and signed by President Carter, allowed him to shift natural gas from surplus areas to shortage areas to keep essential services operating.

3 The Ethiopian chief of state was killed in a gun battle in Addis Ababa and seven members of the governing council reportedly were executed.

4 Eleven persons were killed and more than 150 injured in the crash of two elevated trains over one of the busiest intersections of Chicago's loop.

4 The Labor Department said unemployment declined to 7.3 percent of the work force in January, half of a percentage point below the December rate.

6 Prime Minister Indira Gandhi's principal political opponents in the March 16 parliamentary elections held a rally in New Delhi a day after Mrs. Gandhi spoke there.

7 Black nationalist guerrillas in Rhodesia raided a Catholic mission station and killed two priests, a lay brother and four nuns, all of them white.

10 President Carter offered to seek a quick agreement with the Soviet Union on a ceiling for strategic arms by postponing consideration of whether a Soviet bomber and the American cruise missile should be included.

10 Spain and the Soviet Union announced a resumption of diplomatic relations, 38 years after they were broken off at the end of the Spanish Civil War.

10 President Carter said he would move to substitute tax credits for the current personal exemptions for taxpayers and their dependents as part of his tax reform program to be unveiled later in 1977.

10 The Carter Administration launched an all-out drive for repeal of a law that had hampered U.S. relations with black African countries by allowing chrome to be imported from Rhodesia in defiance of United Nations sanctions.

11 President Carter said he planned to send an American delegation to Vietnam to discuss missing American military personnel and other issues.

12 Negotiations on the future of the divided island of Cyprus were scheduled to resume in March.

12 President Carter said he would cut the level of defense spending recommended by former President Ford, but that the revised budget still would contain a "substantial increase" over the previous fiscal year.

14 A suspended worker killed five persons and wounded five others in a shooting spree at his employer's moving company in New Rochelle, N.Y. Then, after a long siege with police, he shot and killed himself.

16 President Carter said he had indirect word the Cuba intended to remove its troops from Angola.

17 The official accounts of the death of the Anglican Archbishop of Uganda and two ministers of the Uganda government were regarded with skepticism. The three were officially reported to have been killed in an auto accident Feb. 16 shortly after they were arrested on charges of plotting to overthrow President Idi Amin.

18 The Labor Department said consumer prices rose 0.8 percent in January, for a 9.6 percent annual rate of increase.

19 King Hussein of Jordan told Secretary of State Cyrus Vance he was reluctant to foster relations with the Palestine Liberation Organization.

19 The Soviet government, in an editorial in Pravda, accused Egyptian President Anwar Sadat of spreading "lies, slander and falsification" about the Soviet role in Egypt and the Middle East.

21 Secretary of State Cyrus Vance, ending a Mideast mission, said Arabs and Israelis remained "deeply divided" on how to resolve key issues that have blocked a peace settlement.

21 The Tanzanian government's newspaper, the Daily News, said Uganda's Anglican Archbishop Janani Luwum was shot and killed Feb. 16 by President Idi Amin.

22 President Carter's budget proposal for fiscal 1978 projected a $57.7 billion deficit to make room for his economic stimulus package.

23 President Carter said he wanted to make American concern for human rights felt around the world and never intended to single out the Soviet Union as the only major transgressor.

23 Yitzhak Rabin won renomination as Israel's prime minister by only 41 votes out of nearly 3,000 cast by delegates of the governing Labor Party.

23 President Carter told newsmen he found nothing illegal or improper when he analyzed recent "controversial revelations" referring to secret funds to friendly foreign leaders.

24 The United States, according to Secretary of State Cyrus Vance, will reduce aid to Argentina, Uruguay and Ethiopia because of human rights violations in those countries.

25 All United States citizens in Uganda—estimated at 200—were told to meet with President Idi Amin in Kampala on Feb. 28. The Americans were told they would not be able to leave the country before then.

26 Uganda's President Idi Amin said it had never been his intention "to make any Americans hostages" when he ordered that no U.S. citizens leave the country until he met with them.

26 Soviet authorities refused to release figures on the number of killed and injured in the Rossiya Hotel fire Feb. 25, but unofficial sources said there were more than 20 dead.

27 The United States was invited to send a diplomatic delegation to the meeting—reset for March 2—that President Amin of Uganda has called with Americans working in that country.

28 A Uganda radio broadcast quoted President Idi Amin as saying Americans in the African nation were free to go anywhere, inside or outside of the country.

MARCH

1 President Idi Amin of Uganda dropped a demand that all Americans in the country remain there and indefinitely postponed the meeting.

1 President Carter met with Soviet dissident Vladimir K. Bukovsky, and the president said his administration's commitment to human rights was permanent.

1 President Carter said he would favor extending a federal loan program for New York City for "five of six years" after its June 30, 1978, expiration date.

1 A Soviet medical source said at least 45 persons died in a fire at the Rossiya Hotel in Moscow on Feb. 25.

2 A stringent code of ethics, including a limitation on outside earned income, was adopted by the House of Representatives in an effort to restore public confidence in Congress.

4 Hundreds of people in Bucharest, Romania, were reported killed by a strong earthquake that rocked Southern and Eastern Europe.

4 The Labor Department said unemployment rose two-tenths of a percentage point to 7.5 percent in February.

5 Romanian authorities said there were 298 known dead in Bucharest and 72 dead elsewhere, following a quake which struck March 4.

5 President Carter spent two hours answering telephoned inquiries on a nation-wide broadcast, and 42 persons calling from 26 states managed to reach and speak with the president.

6 Romanian authorities said 746 bodies had been found in Bucharest and more than 80 in other parts of the country, following a March 4 earthquake.

6 Miner Ronald Adley, 37, was rescued from a flooded coal mine in Tower City, Pa., after being trapped for nearly five days. Four other miners were reported dead and five others were listed as missing.

7 President Carter met with Israel's Prime Minister Yitzhak Rabin in Washington for talks on the Middle East.

7 Saudi Arabia said it would give $1 billion in aid to black Africa at the opening in Cairo of a conference of African and Arab leaders from 59 countries.

7 The death toll in Romania's earthquake was placed at more than 1,000 and was expected to go higher.

8 Spokesmen said President Carter would go to London in May for an economic conference with the leaders of six other industrialized countries.

9 President Carter outlined a new approach for peace in the Middle East which would urge Arabs and Israelis to agree on sovereign recognized borders.

9 Small bands of gunmen invaded three buildings in downtown Washington, killing at least one person, wounding at least 13 and taking dozens hostage.

9 President Carter asked Congress for a jobs program that would cost $1.8 billion.

9 The Food and Drug Administration announced a ban on saccharin in foods and beverages.

10 The Labor Department said wholesale prices increased 0.9 percent in February, the biggest increase in 16 months.

11 More than 100 held for nearly two days in Washington by a handful of armed Hanafi Moslem gunmen were released after three Islamic ambassadors joined in negotiations to gain their freedom.

11 Twelve Hanafi Moslem gunmen were tentatively charged with armed kidnapping after their negotiated surrender brought an end to their siege at three sites in downtown Washington.

11 Brazil canceled its 25-year-old military assistance treaty with the United States over a State Department report that criticized its alleged violations of human rights.

11 Treasury Secretary W. M. Blumenthal approved New York City's request for a $255 million federal loan to help stave off bankruptcy.

12 President Anwar Sadat told a meeting of the Palestine National Congress in Cairo that Egypt would not allow a single inch of Arab territory to remain under Israeli occupation.

13 Pravda warned that President Carter's outspokenness on human rights could damage the atmosphere in which a strategic arms agreement must be negotiated.

13 Prime Minister Yitzhak Rabin of Israel rejected President Carter's view that Israel should give up virtually all territory captured from the Arabs in the 1967 war.

13 A late winter blizzard that swept across the Middle West left at least 15 persons dead and hundreds more snowbound.

14 Riots by students in several Italian cities shook the governing Christian Democrats and the Communists and left politicians worried about the stability of Italy.

15 The confirmed death toll of an earthquake in Romania was set at 1,541, with 11,275 injured.

15 The United States said it had approved a request by Zaire for spare parts and other military equipment to help repel invading forces from Angola.

15 The value of Howard Hughes' estate was listed at about $168 million in papers filed by its administrators.

16 Secretary of State Cyrus R. Vance said forces invading Zaire from Angola had "engaged in conflict" along routes to the copper mines which were vital to the nation's economy.

16 Kamal Jumblat, the Druse chieftain who led an alliance of leftists and Moslems in the Lebanese civil war, was assassinated near Beirut.

16 President Carter told a Clinton, Mass., town meeting—his first "meet the people" tour since his inauguration—that he sought an administration responsive to the ordinary moods of ordinary citizens.

17 President Carter told the U.N. General Assembly the United Nations had allowed "its human rights machinery to be ignored and sometimes politicized."

17 Sources reported Zaire's major copper mining center of Kolwezi had been captured by rebel forces from Angola.

18 The Zaire government flew troop reinforcements to Shaba Province in an attempt to halt the advance of invading forces from neighboring Angola.

18 Hanoi handed over 12 caskets containing the remains of American pilots killed in the Vietnam War to President Carter's special commission.

18 The Labor Department said consumer prices recorded their biggest rise in nearly 2½ years in February by increasing one percent.

19 President Marien Ngouabi of the Congo was assassinated by a "suicide commando" who escaped.

20 France's opposition left made considerable gains in nationwide municipal voting, but it was defeated in Paris as former Prime Minister Jacques Chirac won the mayoral election.

21 Prime Minister Indira Gandhi was defeated for her parliamentary seat in India's sixth national election.

21 The United States was accused by Soviet Communist Party chief Leonid I. Brezhnev of using the human rights issue to interfere in the Soviet Union's internal affairs.

22 Prime Minister Indira Gandhi resigned after her Congress Party was swept from power for the first time in India's 30 years of independence.

22 President Carter told Congress he would stand firm on his concern for human rights in the Soviet Union.

22 President Carter urged Congress to propose a Constitutional amendment that would abolish the indirect Electoral College system of choosing presidents and substitute election by a simple majority.

22 An earthquake struck southern Iran and killed at least 60 persons.

23 President Carter said he would accept an invitation from Vietnam to begin a new round of diplomatic discussions in Paris.

23 The Congo's military government said the Roman Catholic Archbishop of Brazzaville, Emile Cardinal Biayenda, was kidnapped and murdered.

24 Eighty-one-year-old Morarji R. Desai was chosen to be India's fourth prime minister.

24 Direct negotiations between the United States and Cuba were begun on an agreement to regulate fishing in the waters between the two countries.

24 Morarji R. Desai was sworn in as India's prime minister.

25 President Carter's stand on human rights was endorsed by 58 senators.

25 The Carter administration lifted a ban on the spending of dollars by American visitors to Cuba.

26 Secretary of State Cyrus R. Vance arrived in Moscow for talks with Leonid I. Brezhnev and other Soviet leaders.

27 More than 550 of the 643 persons aboard two 747 jumbo jets were believed to have been killed when the planes collided and burst into flames on a foggy airport runway in the Canary Islands.

28 The collision of two 747 jumbo jets in Santa Cruz de Tenerife March 27 killed 577 persons. There were 60 survivors, 11 of them in serious condition.

28 The Defense Department said President Carter had authorized a review and possible upgrading of the other-than-honorable discharges of about 432,000 Vietnam War servicemen.

29 A Dutch official conceded that a KLM Royal Dutch Airlines jetliner had not been cleared for takeoff when it crashed into a Pan American World Airways jet on Santa Cruz De Tenerife, Canary Islands Sunday.

29 High officials in the Carter administration privately expressed fear that the $50 tax rebate proposal was in jeopardy in the Senate because of both ideological differences and political resentments.

30 Talks between Secretary of State Cyrus R. Vance and Leonid I. Brezhnev in Moscow on a treaty to limit offensive missiles and bombers carrying nuclear warheads broke down.

30 The House of Representatives voted to allow the Select Committee on Assassinations to continue through the end of 1978.

31 Soviet Foreign Minister Andrei A. Gromyko attacked the Carter administration for what he said were unrealistic proposals on arms control.

31 The loss of an important town in Zaire to invading Katangan exiles was conceded by the government.

APRIL

1 Defense Secretary Harold Brown said it was doubtful the United States and the Soviet Union could reach agreement on a reduction of their strategic weapons arsenal before the freeze on those weapons expired in October.

3 President Anwar Sadat of Egypt arrived in Washington for talks with President Carter.

4 President Anwar Sadat of Egypt told President Carter the Palestinian question was the "core and crux" of the Arab-Israeli dispute.

4 A disabled Southern Airways DC-9 crashed while attempting an emergency landing at New Hope, Ga., and 68 persons were killed.

5 Soviet Leader Leonid I. Brezhnev said "a reasonable accomodation is possible" with the United States on nuclear arms control if Washington "seeks mutually acceptable solutions not in words but by deeds."

5 Former Secretary of State Henry Kissinger urged the Carter administration to speak out forcefully about the invasion of Zaire.

5 President Anwar Sadat asked the United States to supply Egypt with many arms, including F-5E fighter planes.

6 Egyptian President Anwar Sadat said after two days of talks with President Carter that "everything will be normalized" between Israel and the Arab states once a final settlement was signed ending the state of war in the Middle East.

7 Prime Minister Yitzhak Rabin of Israel withdrew as the Labor Party's candidate for the prime ministership in the May 17 elections.

7 Britain's delegate at the United Nations received an apology from Andrew Young, the United States representative, who had said Britain was "a little chicken" on racial questions.

8 President Sadat of Egypt told the Carter administration he expected normalization of relations with Israel in about five years after a general settlement of the Israeli-Arab dispute had been achieved.

8 President Carter said the Soviet's Leonid Brehnev had assured him he was serious about an eventual agreement on the limitation of strategic arms.

9 Spain's Communist Party was legalized after a 38-year ban.

10 France lent a fleet of military transport planes to Morocco to carry troops to Zaire to support the government which was threatened by an invasion of hostile forces.

11 Israel's Finance Ministry fined Prime Minister Yitzhak Rabin the equivalent of $1,500 for having an illegal overseas bank account that led to his withdrawal as the labor Party's candidate for the prime ministership.

11 After a Soviet fishing vessel and the cargo aboard another Soviet ship were seized by the Coast Guard, the United States warned the Soviet Union that further violations of its new fishing regulations could lead to "a worsening of bilateral relations."

12 The United States decided to send $13 million worth of "non-lethal" military equipment to help Zaire resist an invasion by Katangan exiles from Angola, the State Department said.

12 President Carter commuted the 20-year prison term of G. Gordon Liddy to eight years, thus making the last of the original Watergate-burglary defendants still in jail eligible for parole in July.

13 Secretary of Defense Harold Brown said the United States was willing to revamp its strategic arms proposals but would block any Moscow attempt at bullying to win assent to a nuclear weapons control accord.

14 Moscow ordered the captains of the Soviet fishing fleet to strictly observe the new United States fishing regulations.

14 President Carter announced withdrawal of his proposed $50 tax rebate for most Americans.

15 Protest marches in Pakistan became violent and at least eight persons were reported killed.

17 The wife of Israel Prime Minister Yitzhak Rabin was fined about $27,000 for her role in maintaining bank accounts in Washington that violated Israel's currency regulations.

18 Leonid I. Brezhnev, the Soviet leader, warned that other nations seeking to "meddle" in the fighting in Zaire would bear full responsibility for the consequences.

18 President Carter said a "national catastrophe" threatened Americans if they did not respond with the "moral equivalent of war" to dwindling energy supplies.

19 President Carter decided that income tax rebates would be the best way to return to the public billions of dollars of new energy taxes he planned to propose to Congress as part of a comprehensive national energy plan.

19 The Supreme Court ruled 5-4 that spanking of schoolchildren, no matter how severe, by teachers of other school officials did not violate the Constitution's Eighth Amendment against cruel and unusual punishment.

20 President Carter proposed a national energy policy designed to raise the cost of fuels, penalize waste and bring major changes in some of the ways Americans live and work.

20 Pakistani opposition groups held strikes and protest marches in several cities in an effort to force the resignation of Prime Minister Zulfikar Ali Bhutto.

20 The Commerce Department said the nation's economic growth rose at an annual rate of 5.2 percent in the first quarter for the best gain in a year.

21 Prime Minister Zulfikar Ali Bhutto of Pakistan assumed emergency powers and imposed martial law on three major cities in a crackdown on the opposition alliance trying to force him to resign.

22 President Carter said he could not guarantee that all money collected by the federal government through taxes proposed by his energy plan would be returned to the American people through rebates and refunds.

22 New York Gov. Hugh Carey told a news conference in Dublin that members of the

Irish Republican Army were "killers" and "Marxists". He declared that they should not receive "a nickel" from Irish-Americans.

23 A pipe on an oil well in the North Sea blew out, sending a 180-foot-high fountain of oil cascading into the water and creating a 20-square-mile slick drifting toward the southern coast of Norway and Denmark's Jutland Coast.

23 The government of Ethiopia closed down a U.S. military mission and three other American offices, ordering their personnel to leave the country within four days.

24 Cuban officials in five days of frank talks with Minnesota businessmen, made it clear that their Communist-ruled nation is in serious economic trouble. "We have deficiencies," said President Fidel Castro, "lots of deficiencies."

25 President Carter sent Congress a tough hospital cost-control proposal which would force stringent financial curbs on the nation's 6,000 general care hospitals.

26 House and Senate conferees broke a deadlock and accepted President Carter's $4 billion public works jobs program by agreeing to detach controversial water pollution provisions from the legislation.

26 A change in the delicate balance of the body's sex hormones was cited as the major factor that made men susceptible to heart attacks, according to a major new theory developed by Dr. Gerald B. Phillips of Columbia University.

27 President Carter submitted legislation to Congress that would empower him to impose drastic penalties on countries found to be violating agreements designed to prevent the spread of nuclear weapons.

27 The West German government approved a four-year $2.7 billion program of energy research, focusing on nuclear power and plutonium-based reactors which were opposed by President Carter.

28 The United States and Cuba announced agreement on fishing rights in their overlapping fishing zones as a result of their first formal direct negotiations in 16 years.

28 The Federal Energy Administration charged 20 major multinational oil companies with overcharging the public by $336 million which the companies were expected to return to consumers.

29 Another futile attempt was made to repair the blowout in the oil well in the North Sea off Norway.

29 The Commerce Department said the March index of leading economic indicators was 129.7, up 1.4 percent from the revised February index and the biggest increase in 20 months.

30 The blowout on an oil well in the North Sea was successfully capped after four previous attempts had failed.

MAY

1 President Anwar Sadat said he would send Egyptian pilots to Zaire to help crush the Katangan invasion.

1 At least 39 persons were killed and some 200 injured when a May Day rally in Istanbul turned into a gunbattle.

2 A general strike in Northern Ireland was called by militant Protestants and began with the fire-bombing of several Belfast stores.

2 President Carter said the nation's welfare system "should be scrapped and a totally new system implemented."

3 The United States and Vietnam opened formal negotiations in Paris "looking toward normalizing relations," according to an American spokesman.

4 Former President Nixon said he "let the American people down" while in the White House by lying, disregarding his constitutional oath, and abetting the Watergate cover-up. But in a television interview he insisted his offenses were not criminal or impeachable because they came from political and humanitarian motives.

4 The United States and Vietnam agreed the United States would not veto Vietnam's admission to the United Nations and would lift a trade embargo after diplomatic relations were established.

5 President Carter flew to London to take part in a seven-nation economic conference.

5 Four Croatian nationalists were found guilty in the hijacking of a Trans World Airlines jet in September of 1976.

6 The national unemployment rate fell in April from 7.3 percent to 7 percent, its lowest in 29 months, and the number of people with jobs scored a strong gain of more than 500,000 for the second straight month, the Labor Department reported.

7 Leaders of the seven major industrialized democracies reached broad general agreement on a strategy for combating unemployment as they wound up the opening day of their economic summit meeting in London.

8 The leaders of the United States and six other industrial nations wound up their economic summit meeting in London with a pledge to cooperate on a series of measures to combat unemployment and the economic crisis caused by their collective trade deficit to the major oil-producing nations.

9 President Carter proposed to Congress that it eliminate the growing deficits in the Social Security System by enacting a big payroll tax increase for employers, a small rise for workers and an experimental diversion of general tax revenues to the Social Security System.

9 President Carter met in Geneva with President Hafez Assad of Syria to discuss the Middle East conflict and said at a meeting with reporters "there must be a resolution of the Palestine problem and a homeland for the Palestinians."

9 The leaders of the United States, France, Britain and West Germany warned the Soviet Union in firm language not to endanger the status quo of Berlin.

10 President Carter urged America's allies in the North Atlantic Treaty Organization to respond forcefully to a 12-year Soviet build-up in Europe that had created forces he described as "much stronger than needed for any defense purpose."

11 A federal judge, citing the primacy of federal rules, held that the ban on Concorde flights to Kennedy International Airport in New York was illegal. The ban had been imposed in 1976 pending a study of the effect of the supersonic airliner's operations on other cities.

12 Richard M. Nixon said in a television interview with David Frost that Henry A. Kissinger was an intellectual giant. But he described the former secretary of state as moody, secretive, capable of outrageous private remarks and intensely protective of official prerogatives.

13 President Carter signed two bills that were expected to create more than a million jobs.

13 The 11 members of the Organization of Petroleum Exporting Countries reportedly agreed to cancel a 5 percent oil price hike that was to have become effective in July.

14 Moscow said China was preparing for war against the West as well as the Soviet Union and warned that any aid given to China would eventually be used to start a new world war.

16 An international energy study concluded a world oil shortage by the 1980s was inevitable and carried an inherent risk of war.

16 Five persons were killed when a New York Airways helicopter idling on top of a Manhattan building keeled over on a broken landing gear.

17 To head off a sharp increase in American tariffs, Japan has agreed to limitations of its color television shipments in the United States over the next three years, American and Japanese sources reported.

18 Israel's governing Labor Party was defeated in national elections bringing to an end the party's 29-year domination of the nation's political life.

18 Douglas A. Fraser was elected president of the United Automobile Workers, succeeding Leonard Woodcock.

19 President Carter announced broad measures restricting future sales of American weapons abroad.

20 Secretary of State Cyrus R. Vance and Andrei A. Gromyko of the Soviet Union reached agreement on a formula for ending the impasse in the strategic arms limitation talks.

21 Major differences were reported holding up the conclusion of new Soviet-American strategic arms accords despite agreement on a new formula to break the deadlock in negotiations.

21 Maj. Gen. John K. Singlaub, Army chief of staff in South Korea, was ordered reassigned by President Carter after disagreeing with the President's plan to withdraw American troops from South Korea.

22 President Carter said the time was right for a settlement in the Middle East.

22 Secretary of Defense Harold Brown said South Korea's security would not be endangered by the withdrawal of American ground troops.

23 South Moluccan exiles living in Holland were holding 161 hostages in a school and a hijacked train, apparently in a new effort to force the Dutch government to help them in their fight for independence from Indonesia.

23 Menahem Begin, scheduled to be Israel's next prime minister, was hospitalized suffering from chest pains.

23 The Supreme Court refused to hear the appeals of John N. Mitchell, H. R. Haldeman, and John D. Ehrlichman from their convictions in the Watergate cover-up case.

24 Soviet President Nikolai V. Podgorny was dropped from the Communist Party's ruling Politburo in a Kremlin move seen as spelling the end of his political career.

25 Saudi Arabian Crown Prince Fahd assured President Carter there would be no oil embargo against the United States to press for concessions from Israel.

25 South Moluccans holding hostages in the Netherlands backed off from a threat to start killing them as government officials refused to honor a deadline the armed band had set.

26 The South Moluccan extremists in the Netherlands released the children they had been holding hostage but still held five teachers plus 50 to 60 other people.

26 President Carter defended a proposal to withdraw American ground troops from South Korea.

27 The House Defense Appropriations Subcommittee recommended cuts of $2.7 billion in President Carter's proposed defense budget. The amount represented a long series of small reductions.

27 Mayor Abraham Beame accepted $1.10 to settle New York City's $250,000 suit against George H. Willig, 27-year-old mountain climber who scaled the 1,350-foot South Tower of the World Trade Center.

28 Israel expressed concern to the United States that the tenor of President Carter's recent statement on the Middle East went beyond what any Israeli government could accept as the basis for negotiating an overall Middle East settlement.

28 A fast-spreading fire, pouring heavy, blinding smoke throughout one of the largest nightclubs in the Middle West killed at least 160 persons in Southgate, Ky. and injured 130.

29 Soviet Communist Party chief Leonid I. Brezhnev said "no serious forward movement" had been achieved at Geneva in negotiating a new treaty to limit strategic nuclear arms.

30 President Carter suggested that there might be stronger ties between the United States and Cuba, but he cited that nation's presence in Africa and its political prisoners as continuing impediments.

31 The U.S. Supreme Court ruled 7 to 2 that seniority systems that perpetuate the effects of past racial discrimination, placing blacks at a disadvantage to whites in the competition for better jobs and other benefits, were not necessarily illegal.

JUNE

1 After months of secrecy, Chinese authorities have described the 1976 Tangshan earthquake as the most deadly in China in more than four centuries.

2 The 27-nation north-south talks ended in Paris with major oil-producing nations and other developing countries refusing to agree to demands of the United States and the rest of the industrial world for continuing consultations on energy questions.

2 Pope Paul VI elevated his principal aide, Archbishop Giovanni Benelli, known as the second most powerful official in the Vatican, to Cardinal.

3 Cuba said it would free 10 of its 30 U.S. prisoners immediately and review the cases of the rest.

3 Vietnam delivered new information about 20 Americans who were killed in the war in Southeast Asia as the second round of talks on establishing normal United States-Vietnamese relations concluded in Paris.

4 A former director of the Korean Central Intelligence Agency, Kim Hyung Wook, broke a long silence to identify Park Tong Sun as a K.C.I.A. agent who spent millions of dollars on an allegedly illegal scheme to influence American policy on Korea.

4 Uganda's Minister of Health, Henry Kyemba, defected and gave an account in The Sunday Times of London of killings in Uganda under President Idi Amin.

5 The United States informed South Korea and Japan that it intended to pull about 6,000 American ground troops from South Korea by the end of 1978.

5 The pro-Western Seychelles government of President James R. M. Mancham was overthrown by rebels led by leftist Prime Minister F. Albert Rene.

5 Sporadic looting and vandalism continued in the Humbolt section of Chicago which was rocked by rioting that left two men dead.

6 The U.S. Supreme Court ruled 5-4 that states may not make the death penalty mandatory for anyone convicted of murdering a police officer.

6 Andrew Young, chief U.S. delegate to the United Nations, said that in describing Gerald R. Ford and Richard M. Nixon as racists "I certainly didn't mean anything degoratory about the personal lives of either."

7 In a decision expected to have national impact, residents of the Miami area voted more than 2-1 to repeal a law protecting homosexuals from discrimination in employment, housing and public accommodation.

7 Air traffic controllers and policemen in capital cities across Europe watched for an unidentified plane reported by Uganda radio to be carrying President Idi Amin to Britain for a Commonwealth conference despite warnings that he would not be welcome.

8 The House ethics committee voted to require every member of the House to disclose details of his association with South Korea in an effort to ascertain the scope of the allegedly illegal Korean attempt to influence Congress.

10 James Earl Ray, serving 99 years for the assassination of the Rev. Martin Luther King climbed over a wall of Tennessee's Brushy Mountain State Prison with five other inmates and escaped, the authorities said.

11 Dutch armed forces using fighter planes, flares and machine guns, stormed a hijacked train with 51 hostages aboard, rescuing 49 from South Moluccan extremists. Another assault group freed four teachers in a village school at Bovensmilde. The attacks took the lives of two train passengers and six of the kidnappers.

11 A force of 150 prison guards, state and local police and FBI agents used helicopters and bloodhounds to search rugged mountains of Tennessee for James Earl Ray and 10 other inmates. A sixth escapee gave up to authorities.

11 Seattle Slew won the 109th running of the Belmont Stakes and became the first undefeated horse to win racing's Triple Crown.

12 The United States suggested to the Soviet Union that each side's offensive strategic force be cut by about 10 percent below the level agreed upon at Valdivostock three years earlier.

13 Tennessee Gov. Ray Blanton called on the federal government to take over custody of James Earl Ray, recaptured after 54 hours of freedom.

13 Three black men, armed with submachine guns and grenades burst into a garage near police headquarters in Johannesburg, South Africa, and opened fire killing two white men and injuring a third.

14 Three Croatian nationalists, armed with handguns, invaded the Yugoslav Mission to the United Nations, wounded the mission chauffeur, barricaded themselves in the mission for two hours and dropped leaflets from a window before surrendering to authorities.

15 The people of Spain chose a new Parliament in the first free elections in 41 years.

16 Prime Minister Adolfo Suarez's coalition swept to victory in Spain's first free election in 41 years.

16 Leonid I. Brezhnev, head of the Soviet Communist Party, was named chief of state, becoming the first person in his country to hold both posts at once.

17 Vice President Walter Mondale said the United States believed Israel should not be asked to withdraw from occupied Arab territories unless it could obtain "real peace" from the Arab states.

19 Pope Paul VI declared Bishop John Nepomucene Neumann of Philadelphia a saint.

20 Menahem Begin became Israel's prime minister after getting a parliamentary vote of confidence for his coalition government.

20 Soviet leader Leonid I. Brezhnev arrived in Paris for three days of talks with French President Valery Giscard d'Estaing.

20 The U.S. Supreme Court ruled that neither the Constitution nor federal law required states to spend Medicaid funds for elective abortions.

20 Oil from Alaska's North Slope began to move southward to ice-free harbors through the $7.7 billion trans-Alaska pipeline which had just been completed.

21 Britain and the United States agreed on an aviation pact to replace one in effect since 1946.

22 John N. Mitchell became the first former U.S. attorney general to go to jail when he entered a prison camp near Montgomery, Ala. He had been sentenced for crimes in the Watergate cover-up.

23 The House passed a $6.7 billion foreign aid appropriations bill that put Cuba, Angola and Mozambique on a list of excluded nations that might not get aid directly or indirectly.

24 The United States and other major industrial nations of the Organization for Economic Cooperation and Development ended a meeting in Paris with a commitment for a higher average rate of economic growth in 1978.

24 A black prelate from Tanzania, Bishop Josiah M. Kibira, was elected head of the 58-million member Lutheran World Federation.

26 Forty-two persons, most of them prisoners, died in a fire that poured choking smoke through the Maury County Jail at Columbia, Tenn.

27 The Carter administration said that in return for an Arab agreement for a true peace Israel should agree to a withdrawal from some occupied lands on all fronts and to the formation of a Palestinian homeland.

27 The United States trade deficit in May was the smallest of the year, with imports exceeding exports by only $1.2 billion.

28 The U.S. Supreme Court upheld by a vote of 7-to-2 government control over Richard M. Nixon's presidential papers and tape recordings.

29 The U.S. Supreme Court held that the death penalty may not be used as punishment for rape—at least when the rape victim is an adult.

29 The Organization of Petroleum Exporting Countries said nine of its members would cancel a scheduled five percent oil price increase in an effort to achieve internal unity.

30 President Carter said he was opposed to production of the B-1 strategic bomber and said the United States would depend on existing weapons systems for its nuclear deterrent.

JULY

2 About 30 persons were hurt when a white man drove a car into a cluster of some 250 persons at a Ku Klux Klan rally in Plains, Ga.

3 Turkish Prime Minister Bulent Ecevit resigned when his center-left government was defeated in its first parliamentary vote of confidence.

4 A 26-year-old Navy enlisted man hijacked an interstate bus at gunpoint and killed two passengers before he surrendered after a nine-hour siege at New York's John F. Kennedy Airport.

4 Ku Klux Klansmen fought off demonstrators at Columbus, Ohio, when a Klan rally turned into a brawl and police were called in to end the clash.

5 Pakistan's army seized power in a bloodless coup, imposed martial law and promised new elections in October.

6 President Carter resassured leaders of American Jewish organizations that the Arab states should establish full diplomatic relations with Israel as part of an over-all Middle East settlement.

7 Five prisoners were killed and 71 others hurt when a fire swept a cell block at the federal prison in Danbury, Conn.

8 The trans-Alaska oil pipeline was shut down following an explosion and fire at a pump station about midway down the pipeline's 800-mile route.

11 Japan's Liberal-Democratic Party lost its majority in the upper house of Parliament. according to final results tallied from the election July 10.

11 Spain devalued the peseta and proposed a series of tax reforms designed to stimulate the economy.

12 President Carter, preparing for talks with Israeli Prime Minister Menahem Begin disclosed that Egypt's President Anwar Sadat had made conciliatory gestures. Officials in Washington said Carter had privately sought these gestures to improve the climate for Middle East negotiations.

13 A power failure plunged New York City and Westchester County into darkness, disrupting the lives of nearly nine million people. The power failed at 9:34 p.m., apparently when lightning struck a Consolidated Edison electrical transmission line.

14 A power blackout virtually paralyzed New York City and there was widespread looting. By 10 p.m., a bit more than 24 hours after the failure, service had been restored to all but 200,000 electric customers.

14 President Carter said a U.S. Army helicopter that was shot down, apparently by North Koreans, had strayed into North Korean airspace by mistake. Three crewmen were killed and a fourth was captured.

15 North Korea said it was willing to return to American authorities a soldier who was wounded and three others who were killed when their helicopter was shot down July 14 over North Korea.

15 The Small Business Administration designated New York City and Westchester County as disaster areas as investigations, damage assessments and cleanup operations followed a 25-hour power blackout.

16 North Korea gave the United States the bodies of three crewmen shot down in an Army helicopter over its territory and returned a fourth crewman who had been captured.

17 Israel took anti-inflation steps which were expected to increase prices of most basic commodities by 25 percent.

18 Prime Minister Ian D. Smith announced Rhodesia's Parliament would be dissolved immediately and that a general election would be held Aug. 31.

19 President Carter and Israeli Prime Minister Menahem Begin opened their two-day White House meeting with agreement to give priority to the convening of a new Geneva conference in 1977 and attainment of a "just and durable peace in the Middle East."

19 President Carter agreed to seek an increase in federal gasoline taxes of up to 5 cents to finance transportation or other government programs, according to administration officials.

20 President Carter said he felt the view of Prime Minister Menahem Begin of Israel would produce a Middle East peace conference as early as October.

20 Vietnam won Security Council approval for admission to the United Nations.

20 Leon Jaworski agreed to serve as special counsel to the House Ethics Committee to take charge of its investigation of Korean influence-buying.

20 A seven-inch rainfall caused severe flooding and at least 10 deaths in Johnstown, Pa., and surrounding areas.

21 President Carter said the United States was prepared to limit its strategic weapons programs if the Soviet Union would agree to controls on its heavy intercontinental missiles.

21 Egypt reported a major border clash with Libya. It said the Libyans were beaten back.

21 The Bureau of Labor Statistics said consumer prices rose six-tenths of one percent in June.

21 The Commerce Department said the economy grew at an annual rate of 6.4 percent in the second quarter.

22 Denying the Carter administration the power it sought to set natural gas prices, a Senate-House conference committee agreed on details of legislation to create a new 20,000-employee Department of Energy.

23 The Carter administration announced on $11.3 million program of grants and loans to help New York City recover from the looting and vandalism during the July 13-14 blackout.

23 A 27-year-old former convict, Lorne J. Acquin, was charged with the murders of his foster brother's wife, seven children and a niece. Their bodies, some of them bound, were found in a blazing house in Prospect, Conn.

24 The death toll in the Johnstown, Pa. flood rose to 51 persons, with 120 missing.

24 Egyptian President Anwar Sadat ordered Egyptian forces fighting against Libya to observe an immediate cease-fire.

25 A Senate committee accepted Budget Director Lance's contention that there was "nothing improper" in his personal or business finances and decided not to investigate them further.

26 Responding to a plea by South Korea, the United States announced that the bulk of the U.S. combat force station in Korea would remain there until the final year of the planned troops withdrawal, set for about 1982.

26 Three controversial Israeli settlements on occupied lands of the West Bank of the Jordan River were given official approval by Israeli Prime Minister Menahem Begin. The move touched off a swift negative reaction from the Carter administration.

27 A record $2.82 billion deficit in American trade in June was reported by the U.S. Commerce Department, foreshadowing further weakness of the dollar and adding to gloom on Wall Street.

27 More than 185 homes, most of them worth upward of $100,000 were destroyed by an explosive brush fire that devastated large parts of Santa Barbara, one of the nation's most scenic residential communities.

28 President Carter said Israeli Prime Minister Menahem Begin's decision to legalize three existing Jewish settlements on the Israeli-occupied West Bank of the Jordan River was an obstacle but not an insurmountable barrier to a Middle East peace.

29 Despite accidents, explosion, fire and sabotage, oil from Alaska, flowing through an 800-mile pipeline, finally began pouring into terminal storage tanks in Valdez.

30 President Carter said in an interview with a group of editors and radio and TV news directors that the American public "is not paying attention" to energy problems and has not heeded his calls for voluntary conservation.

31 With massive police patrols focused elsewhere in New York City, the killer who called himself "Son of Sam" struck for the first time in Brooklyn. He shot and critically wounded a young couple parked on the Brooklyn water front a mile south of the glit-

tering lights of the Verrazano-Narrows Bridge.

AUGUST

1 President Carter warned the Panamanian Chief of Government, Brig. Gen. Omar Torrijos Herrera, to expect no further major concessions from the United States in negotiations for a new Panama Canal treaty.

1 Stacy Moskowitz died 38 hours after she and a male companion were shot by the so-called .44-caliber revolver killer who called himself "Son of Sam."

2 The U.S. Senate killed a proposal for public financing of Senate election campaigns, handing President Carter another major setback of his package of election-law changes.

2 President Carter asked Congress to abolish all federal criminal penalties for possession of small amounts of marijuana.

3 Terrorist bombs exploded in two New York City office buildings, killing one man and injuring seven other persons. The same day, dozens of bomb threats forced more than 100,000 people to vacate their offices in the city.

4 The House of Representatives resoundingly defeated two proposals to increase the federal gasoline tax.

4 The national unemployment rate dipped in July, returning to the May level, but employment did not increase for the first time in nine months.

6 South African Prime Minister John Vorster accused the Carter administration of promoting "chaos and anarchy" in southern Africa.

6 A bomb exploded in a store in Salisbury, Rhodesia, killing 11 persons and injuring 76 others.

7 A nationwide strike by Canadian air traffic controllers began and paralyzed regular airline service throughout the nation.

8 About 150 inmates seized 14 hostages and a wing of the Eastern Correctional Facility at Napanoch, N.Y., but released the hostages and gave up after a 12-hour seige

9 Israeli leaders told Secretary of State Cyrus R. Vance they strongly opposed yielding any territory on Jordan's West Bank and in the Gaza Strip.

9 A boy and a British soldier were killed in Belfast on the eve of the first visit of Queen Elizabeth II to Northern Ireland in more than a decade.

9 Striking Dayton, Ohio, firemen watched from their picket lines as three major fires spread out of control and destroyed the homes of 13 families.

10 Negotiators announced agreement in principle on "the basic elements" of a new treaty between the United States and Panama which called for transfer of the Panama Canal and the Canal Zone to Panamanian control by the year 2000.

10 Secretary of State Cyrus R. Vance said wide gaps had to be bridged before a Geneva conference could be convened on the Middle East.

10 Queen Elizabeth II saw the first day of her visit to Northern Ireland pass without incident in her presence.

10 A man said by the police to be the .44-caliber killer who took the lives of six persons and wounded seven over a year in New York City, was taken into custody.

10 Dayton, Ohio, firemen reached an agreement with city officials on a new contract and ended a two-day strike.

11 Cuba said it would allow 84 Americans and their families to leave the country.

11 Israeli Foreign Minister Moshe Dayan said Israel's prospects for negotiating peace treaties at least with Egypt, Jordan and Lebanon were good.

11 A 24-year-old postal worker alleged to be the "Son of Sam" was arraigned on murder and other charges as police wound down a year-long investigation of a shooting spree in which six persons were murdered.

12 The first flight test of the space shuttle Enterprise was a success. The shuttle, after being released from its carrier, made a short flight and then landed in the Mojave Desert in California.

13 Secretary of State Cyrus R. Vance said final details of a plan had been agreed on by Britain and the United States for the transfer in 1978 of government in Rhodesia from white to black control.

15 The Indian government arrested four men who had been high in former Prime Minister Indira Gandhi's government on charges of corruption.

16 Soviet leader Leonid I. Brezhnev indicated at a dinner for Yugoslav President Tito that he welcomed President Carter's latest efforts to mend Soviet-American relations. He pledged that the Soviet Union would respond to any practical measures to resolve differences.

16 Former President Gerald Ford threw his support behind the Panama Canal agreement announced by the Carter administration. Ford labeled the pact "an important step forward" and called for prompt Senate approval.

17 Israel approved construction of three new Israeli settlements in territory captured from Jordan in the 1967 war.

18 The Carter administration denounced as "illegal" an Israeli decision to establish three new Jewish settlements on the West Bank.

18 Comptroller of the Currency John Heimann said criminal prosecution of Budget Director Bert Lance was not warranted, but he criticized Lance's practices while an executive of a Georgia bank.

19 An earthquake struck the eastern Indian Ocean between Australia and Indonesia, shaking buildings in Perth, Australia, 1,000 miles to the south.

20 China's Communist Party elected a new central committee at the first congress since the death of Mao Tse-tung in 1976.

20 Voyager 2 began to show signs of malfunctioning soon after taking off from Cape Canaveral on an interplanetary mission.

21 Voyager 2 flew steadily towards Jupiter on its interplanetary journey after making a fitful start.

22 Secretary of State Cyrus R. Vance began four days of talks with Chinese leaders with an appeal for mutual efforts to find ways to normalize relations between China and the United States.

23 Maryland Gov. Marvin Mandel and five wealthy business friends were convicted of some 18 counts each of mail fraud and racketeering after what experts said was one of the longest federal jury deliberations in history.

23 President Carter told a news conference that South Africa had informed the United States it had no nuclear weapons and did not intend to conduct any nuclear tests "now or in the future." A report that South Africa was about to test a nuclear weapon had been circulated originally by the Soviet new agency Tass.

25 Secretary of State Cyrus R. Vance said his four days of talks in Peking on normalizing Chinese-American relations were "candid and serious and enhanced our mutual understanding."

25 Ronald Reagan declared his opposition to a Carter administration plan to turn over control of the Panama Canal to Panama eventually.

25 Britain's air traffic control assistants went on strike over a wage issue, causing flight cancellations and delays.

26 The Securities and Exchange Commission accused Mayor Abraham Beame and Comptroller Harrison Goldin of "deceptive practices masking the city's true and disastrous financial condition," following an investigation of New York City's financial crisis.

26 A sniper who killed six persons in Hackettstown, N.J., shot and killed himself as he was about to be captured.

28 Officials said relations between Moscow and the Carter administration were less strained because of cooperation between the Soviet Union and the United States in dissuading South Africa from proceeding with a nuclear bomb test.

28 Syrian President Hafez Assad said he was ready to sign a peace agreement ending a state of war with Israel.

30 David R. Berkowitz, the man accused of being New York City's .44-caliber killer, was reported by two court-appointed psychiatrist to be mentally unfit to stand trial.

31 White Rhodesians gave Ian D. Smith an overwhelming mandate for the prime minister to negotiate a constitutional settlement outside the framework sought by the United States and Britain.

SEPTEMBER

1 Rhodesia was presented with a plan—worked out by the United States and Britain—for overcoming a constitutional impasse over transferring the government to the black majority.

2 Prime Minister Ian D. Smith said the latest British-American proposals for a Rhodesian settlement were "mad," "crazy" and "insane."

2 The Labor Department reported a rise in the unemployment rate in August of two-tenths of a percentage point to 7.1 percent of the total labor force.

3 Pakistan's former Prime Minister Zulfikar Ali Bhutto was arrested on a charge of conspiring in the attempted murder of a political opponent in 1974.

3 Former President Nixon said in a television interview he thought he had directed H. R. Haldeman to "destroy" all but the most historic of the White House tape recordings in April 1973, three months before Watergate investigators learned of their existence.

4 Three men sprayed a restaurant in San Francisco's Chinatown with rifle and shotgun fire, killing five persons and wounding 10 others.

5 Gunmen in West Germany kidnapped a prominent industrialist, Dr. Hanns-Martin Schleyer, and killed four of his bodyguards in a machine gun attack on his automobile in Cologne.

5 Sens. Abraham A. Ribicoff and Charles H. Percy urged Bert Lance's resignation as budget director on President Carter.

6 Teng Hsiao-ping, China's deputy minister, said efforts to establish normal diplomatic relations between Washington and Peking were set back during the August visit of Secretary of State Cyrus Vance.

6 President Carter welcomed Panama's chief of government, Brig. Gen. Omar Torrijos Herrera, to the White House in the start of diplomatic activity intended to build support for the Panama Canal treaties.

7 The Panama Canal treaties were signed by President Carter and Brig. Gen. Omar Torrijos Herrera, Panama's chief of government, before representatives of 26 other Western Hemisphere nations.

8 The Comptroller of the Currency accused Bert Lance and his family of abusing their positions in a Georgia bank by over-drawing their accounts for "personal gain."

8 A South Korean spokesman said his country would not accede to an American demand for an early return of Tongsun Park to the United States where he has been indicted on charges of attempting to bribe members of Congress.

9 Breaking a long-standing policy, the Carter administration approved a U.S. visit by four Soviet trade union representatives despite opposition from the A.F.L.-C.I.O.

10 The Senate Democratic leader, Robert C. Byrd of West Virginia, said the resignation of Bert Lance, director of the office of Management and Budget, was "inevitable" and suggested that Lance should quit after his appearance before the Senate Governmental Affairs Committee, Sept. 15.

11 The International Monetary Fund declared that the state of the world economy was "unsatisfactory" because of rising unemployment and "subnormal growth." It said widespread inflation had imposed both monetary and fiscal restraints that left "little room for maneuver" to improve the situation.

12 Robert Bloom, former Acting Comptroller of the Currency, admitted he misled the Senate Governmental Affairs Committee in a letter he wrote that group commending Bert Lance before he had been confirmed as budget director.

13 Joseph A. Califano Jr., Secretary of Health, Education and Welfare, announced that Medicare patients would be required to pay a greater share of their hospital bills in 1978 because of rising costs.

14 In a major blow to President Carter's energy program, the Senate Energy Committee, tentatively agreed to put aside a key section of the legislation dealing with utility rate overhaul.

15 Appearing before the Senate Governmental Affairs Committee, Budget Director Bert Lance undertook an aggressive defense of his integrity, his career as a Georgia banker and his competence to manage the national budget.

15 The House of Representatives approved an increase in the minimum wage in each of the ensuing three years and defeated by one vote a proposed subminimum wage for youths.

16 Bert Lance was confronted with evidence that, contrary to his previous assertions, a federal bank examiner said as early as 1971 that his personal checking account overdrafts violated banking laws limiting loans to bank officers.

17 Republican members of the Senate committee investigating the financial affairs of Bert Lance threw the budget director more on the defensive by emphasizing ethical questions rather than possible illegal activity.

18 Israeli Foreign Minister Moshe Dayan arrived in the United States to open a new round of Middle East diplomacy that U.S. officials said should determine whether there would be a Geneva peace conference in 1977.

19 The Carter administration strongly endorsed the argument that disadvantaged members of minority groups should constitutionally be given special consideration in university admissions. But it avoided the question of whether specific racial quotas should be used to that end.

20 President Carter's energy programs was

dealt another setback when the Senate Financing Committee killed his proposal to tax automobiles that used gas inefficiently.

21 Budget Director Bert Lance resigned from office after weeks of controversy about his past business and banking practices. President Carter said he accepted his friend's decision with "regret and sorrow." Carter told a news conference he believed Lance had "exonerated himself completely" of charges against him.

21 Foreign Minister Moshe Dayan of Israel told members of Congress his government would be prepared to allow the United States to set up a naval base at Haifa for use by the 6th Fleet.

22 The Senate handed President Carter another sharp defeat on energy by voting to keep alive a proposal to end price controls on new natural gas.

23 The House of Representatives voted 359 to 4 to increase from 65 to 70 the age at which employers might require their workers to retire

24 The United States and the Soviet Union, asserting that two days of high-level talks had narrowed their differences, said they were determined to achieve "within the near future" a new agreement limiting each side's strategic bomber and missile forces.

25 Los Angeles was selected over New York City when both the American cities bid for the 1984 Summer Olympics.

25 The Israeli cabinet approved a U.S. proposal calling for a single unified Arab delegation, including Palestinians, at the opening session of a Geneva peace conference

26 President Carter, moving to salvage his beleaguered energy program, called on the Senate to "act responsibly" and "reject narrow, special interest attacks on all segments of the national energy plan."

27 The outline of a compromise that would break a three-month deadlock between House and Senate on abortions funded by Medicaid, emerged after the House voted 252-164 to affirm support of a ban on such abortions except when the mother's life was endangered.

28 The Japanese government agreed to meet the demands of Japanese guerrillas holding 156 hostages aboard a hijacked Japan Air Lines plane in Dacca, Bangladesh. The guerrillas who seized the airliner over India and diverted it to Bangladesh, demanded that Tokyo free nine imprisoned "comrades" and pay $6 million in ransom.

29 The House of Representatives approved funds for the so-called neutron bomb, supporting President Carter's efforts to develop the controversial weapon.

30. The head of the Episcopal Church in the United States, Presiding Bishop John M. Allin, offered to resign if his fellow bishops were unwilling to accept his opposition to ordaining women as priests.

OCTOBER

2 Gunfire erupted in Dacca and rebels briefly seized the national radio and declared an "armed revolution." Later, radio officials returned to the air and said the Bangladesh army had quelled the uprising.

2 Israeli government and political leaders sharply criticized the United States for its role in issuing a joint declaration with the Soviet Union on the principles and objectives of a new Middle East peace in Geneva. One official said the Israeli government rejected the declaration "with both hands." But Palestinians and Arabs at large welcomed the Soviet-American statement as a positive step.

3 Indira Gandhi was arrested in New Delhi on two charges of official corruption. Four of her former cabinet ministers and several other associates were arrested on related charges.

3 The hijackers of a Japanese airliner surrendered in Algeria, where the plane landed after a six-day trip. The five gunmen freed the remaining 19 of their original 151 hostages.

4 The Senate approved a controversial proposal that would free newly discovered natural gas from price controls. The 50-46 vote was a setback for President Carter.

4 President Carter, calling on all governments to share in curbing the arms race, told the U.N. General Assembly the United States was "willing now" to cut its own arsenal of nuclear weapons by as much as 50 percent, if the Soviet Union would do the same.

7 A State Department official said the United States, the Soviet Union, Israel and the Arab nations had agreed informally to aim for a December start in Middle East peace talks.

7 Maryland Gov. Marvin Mandel and three business friends were sentenced to four years in prison.

7 The prime loan rate was raised by most commercial banks from 7¼ percent to 7½ percent.

8 Assassins in Spain murdered August Uncena Barraneche, president of the provincial council of the Basque province of Vizcaya, and two police bodyguards.

9 Sharbel Makhlouf, a Lebanese monk who died in 1898, was proclaimed a saint by Pope Paul VI.

11 Israel's cabinet approved a "working paper" agreement on procedures for a new Middle East peace conference.

12 The Bakke case was argued before the U.S. Supreme Court with lawyers arguing for and against special programs to favor blacks in admission to professional schools that may deny entrance to some qualified whites.

13 President Carter accused the oil industry of seeking to carry out "the biggest rip-off in history" and of not being interested in solving the nation's energy problems.

14 In an effort to facilitate approval of the Panama Canal treaty, President Carter and Brig. Gen. Omar Torrijos Herrera said the United States had the right "to act against any aggression or threat directed against the Canal."

16 Four hijackers, whose demands were rejected by West Germany, forced the pilot of an airliner carrying 86 hostages to fly to Aden despite refusal by the Southern Yemen government to give it permission to land.

17 West German commandos freed 86 hostages after storming a hijacked airliner at an airport in Mogadishu, Somalia, and killing three of four terrorists who had commandeered the plane.

17 The U.S. Supreme Court cleared the way for immediate trial flights of the supersonic Concorde airliner to New York's Kennedy International Airport.

18 Three West German terrorist leaders committed suicide in a Stuttgart prison hours after German commandos stormed a hijacked plane in Somalia and blocked an attempt to free them, officials said.

18 The New York Yankees captured the World Series baseball championship, defeating the Los Angeles Dodgers 8-4 in the sixth game.

19 A South African crackdown banned black protest groups, closed the leading black newspaper, and arrested its editor.

19 The body of Hanns-Martin Schleyer, a West German industrial leader who was kidnapped Sept. 5, was found in the trunk of an abandoned car in the French city of Mulhouse.

19 After a 19-month battle, the supersonic Concorde airliner made its maiden flight into New York.

19 The Commerce Department reported a marked slowing of the nation's economy for the third quarter of 1977.

20 Thailand's government was deposed in a bloodless coup by a military junta that installed the civilian regime a year earlier.

20 Officials said the supersonic Concorde airliner met the noise limit by a wide margin on its first takeoff from Kennedy International Airport.

21 Secretary of State Cyrus R. Vance recalled William G. Bowdler, U.S. ambassador to South Africa, for consultation on what steps the United States should take in reaction to the crackdown on blacks and their supporters.

21 A justice of the State Supreme Court in Brooklyn ruled that David R. Berkowitz was fit to stand trial for murder.

22 Senate majority leader Robert C. Byrd predicted that South Korea's refusal to cooperate fully with the American investigation into reported Korean influence buying in Washington would cause a reaction in Congress that could affect its votes on future U.S. aid to that country.

23 Panamanians voted in a national plebiscite on the new Panama Canal treaties with the United States and early returns showed votes running strongly in favor of ratification.

24 Andrew Young, U.S. chief delegate to the United Nations, said he personally favored "some form of sanctions" against South Africa which cracked down on blacks and their sympathizers the previous week. But Young added that it was his role to lay out possible alternatives and their likely consequences for decision by President Carter and Secretary of State Cyrus R. Vance.

25 In a surprising victory for the oil industry, the House Rules Committee shelved a bill designed to provide more orderly development of offshore oil and natural gas reserves. The committee voted to delay until 1978 consideration of the measure which was passed overwhelmingly in the Senate earlier in 1977.

26 The House of Representatives killed a provision in the pending Social Security financing bill that would have made Social Security coverage in 1982 for all federal employees and for those state and local government employees who do not participate voluntarily.

26 The Bethlehem Steel Corp., the nation's second largest steel producer, reported a net loss of $477 million in the third quarter, the largest ever for a quarter for a U.S. company.

27 The House of Representatives approved a bill that would require large increases in Social Security taxes in the next few years for persons earning more than $20,000 a year.

30 Andrew Young, the U.S. representative at the United Nations, ruled out an American ban on the shipment of nuclear fuels to South Africa.

30 The Israeli government's move toward a free market economy set off strikes and buying sprees.

31 The United States, Britain and France used their vetoes in the Security Council to block three African-sponsored resolutions that would have imposed stringent economic penalties on South Africa.

31 Richard Helms, the former director of Central Intelligence, pleaded no contest to a criminal charge of two misdemeanor counts of failing to testify "fully, completely and accurately" before a Senate committee.

NOVEMBER

1 President Carter withdrew membership of the United States in the International Labor Organization, a part of the United Nations.

1 Amsterdam police reported the release of Dutch millionaire Maurits Caransa—who was kidnapped Oct. 28—in exchange for about $4 million in ransom.

2 The Soviet Union moved closer to accepting a suspension of all nuclear explosions by dropping its insistence that any halt exclude blasts for peaceful purposes.

2 The conviction of Patricia Hearst for robbing a bank with a terrorist group that had kidnapped her was upheld by a federal appeals court in San Francisco.

4 The U.N. Security Council ordered a worldwide arms embargo against South Africa and also forbade its member nations to help South Africa develop nuclear weapons.

4 President Carter postponed a scheduled nine-nation tour because he wanted to be in Washington while Congress completed work on his energy program.

4 Richard Helms was fined $2,000 and given a suspended two-year sentence for having failed to testify fully and accurately to a Senate committee in 1973 when he was director of Central Intelligence about CIA operations in Chile.

5 President Carter accused South Korea of impeding justice in the United States by not persuading Tongsun Park to testify in an investigation of alleged Korean attempts to influence members of Congress improperly.

6 Israel commuted the 12-year prison sentence of Archbishop Hilarion Capucci, who had been convicted of smuggling arms into the Israeli-occupied West Bank for Palestinian guerrillas.

6 At least 38 persons were killed when an earthen dam on the outskirts of Toccoa, Ga., collapsed during heavy rains.

8 President Carter said he would sign energy legislation only if it met the basic criteria for equity and effectiveness on which he based his initial energy proposals to Congress last April.

9 Israeli planes attacked targets in and around Tyre in Southern Lebanon, and Lebanese officials said at least 60 persons were killed.

10 President Carter urged the Arab countries to follow Egypt's example and agree to an immediate convening of a Geneva peace conference with Israel.

11 Prime Minister Menahem Begin of Israel asked the citizens of Egypt to join Israelis in a silent oath of "no more wars, no more bloodshed, and no more threats."

11 Israeli planes bombed southern Lebanon for the second time in three days and Israeli artillery exchanged fire with Palestinian guns.

13 A security guard who fell asleep and left candles burning inside a freight car loaded with dynamite was blamed for an explosion that killed at least 56 persons and injured more than 1,300.

13 Somalia ordered all Soviet advisers to leave the country within seven days, ended Soviet use of naval facilities on the Indian Ocean, and broke diplomatic relations with Cuba.

13 President Anwar Sadat's offer to appear before the Israeli Parliament to aid the Middle East peace effort was described by Israeli leaders as a "positive development."

13 Longshoremen reached agreement on a new contract that was expected to end a strike that had tied up container shipping on the Atlantic and Gulf coasts for 44 days.

14 President Anwar Sadat of Egypt said he would address the Israel Parliament on Middle East peace if he received an invitation from Prime Minister Menaham Begin.

14 A hotel fire in Manila killed at least 44 persons.

14 Britain's 32,000 firemen struck for higher wages, leaving 9,000 soldiers to fight blazes across the country.

15 Israeli Prime Minister Menahem Begin transmitted a formal invitation to President Anwar Sadat of Egypt to visit Jerusalem and speak to the Israeli Parliament.

15 President Carter welcomed the Shah of Iran to the White House in ceremonies disturbed by drifts of tear gas as supporters and opponents of the Iranian ruler clashed outside the White House.

16 The Shah of Iran said before leaving Washington that as a result of his talks with President Carter his country would work against an increase in oil prices in 1978.

16 President Anwar Sadat of Egypt went to Syria for private talks with President Hafez Assad as part of Cairo's efforts to rally the Arab countries for a new Middle East peace conference.

17 President Anwar Sadat of Egypt formally accepted Prime Minister Menaham Begin's invitation and planned to visit Israel Nov. 19 for 36 hours.

18 For the first time in Israel's 29-year history, an Arab airliner touched down at an Israeli airport. Israelis applauded as 60 Egyptian officials and technicians emerged to join in feverish preparations for the historic visit of Egyptian President Anwar Sadat.

19 President Anwar Sadat made Middle East history as he arrived at Ben-Gurion International Airport, becoming the first Arab leader to visit Israel since its founding in 1948.

20 President Anwar Sadat of Egypt fulfilled his promise to go to the Israeli parliament where he delivered an eloquent plea for peace combined with a blunt reminder of deep differences still separating the two nations after 29 years of hostility.

21 President Anwar Sadat of Egypt and Israeli Prime Minister joined in pledging "no more war" as Sadat wound up his visit to Jerusalem.

22 The Indian government began a major relief effort as the official estimate of deaths from the cyclone that struck the state of Andhra Pradesh grew to 10,000.

23 Secretary of State Cyrus Vance said he had been unable to persuade Venezuelan President Carlos Andres Perez that an oil price freeze should be imposed in 1978.

24 A tomb uncovered near Salonika in October was "without reservation" that of King Philip II of Macedon, father of Alexander the Great, said Prof. Manolis Andronikos, the archeologist who discovered it.

25 The United Nations General Assembly voted 102-4 with 29 abstentions to condemn Israel's continued occupation of Arab lands, ignoring an Israeli plea that nothing be done to interfere with the "new spirit of peace" in the wake of Egyptian President Anwar Sadat's visit to Jerusalem. The United States cast one of the negative votes.

26 Egyptian president Anwar Sadat extended an invitation to all parties involved in the Middle East conflict to send representatives to Cairo for talks aimed at removing obstacles to a Middle East peace conference at Geneva. Sadat's invitation, made during a major speech to the Egyptian parliament, included Israel, the United States and the Soviet Union.

27 U.S. officials in Washington said they were perplexed over how to react to the call by Egyptian President Anwar Sadat for a preliminary Middle East conference in Cairo.

28 Israel said it would send two officials to Cairo to take part in informal talks to prepare for a Geneva peace conference.

28 Rhodesia announced raids made a week earlier against black nationalist guerrillas inside Mozambique. It said the raids killed at least 1,200 persons.

29 The Soviet Union said it would not take part in the informal Cairo talks, but the United States said it would attend the talks in preparation for calling a conference on Middle East peace.

29 Dock workers voted to accept a new contract and end a strike that had halted container shipping at ports from Maine to Texas for 60 days.

DECEMBER

1 White South African voters gave Prime Minister John Vorster's National Party the biggest majority of any government the country has had since its founding in 1910.

1 Arab leaders opposed to Egyptian-Israeli peace overtures met in Tripoli for a "summit of resistance."

2 South African security police were absolved of any responsibility in the death of Stephen Biko, a black leader, who died while in detention.

2 Blacks in Bermuda rioted in protest against the British colony's first executions in 30 years.

3 British troops were requested by Bermuda after a curfew failed to stop rioting and arson by blacks protesting the execution of two black convicted murderers.

4 A summit meeting of Arab countries at Tripoli, Libya, failed to form a united front against the peace initiative taken by President Anwar Sadat of Egypt when Iraq walked out.

4 A hijacked Malaysian airliner crashed in southern Malaysia and apparently all 100 persons aboard were killed.

4 British soldiers landed in Bermuda to help provide support for local police who had clashed with rioters since two black men were hanged for murder Dec. 2.

5 Egypt broke diplomatic relations with five Arab nations—Syria, Iraq, Libya, Algeria and Southern Yemen—that had been hostile to President Sadat's peace overtures to Israel.

5 The United Mine Workers union went on strike as it ordered out 130,000 miners covered by an expired agreement with the Bituminous Coal Operators Association.

6 President Anwar Sadat of Egypt said that if other Arab countries refused to take part in later stages envisaged for a conference in Geneva he would carry peace negotiations "through to the end" with Israel alone.

6 Eighty of the 260 British soliders sent to Bermuda to help restore order after rioting left following a second night of calm.

8 President Anwar Sadat of Egypt called his Arab critics "dwarfs" in a speech in which he urged Egypt to pursue its new course "with our heads held high."

9 An exchange of prisoners under a treaty between Mexico and the United States was made as an airliner picked up 36 Mexican nationals and took them to Mexico while Mexico released 61 Americans.

10 A decisive victory was won by Prime Minister Malcolm Fraser's Liberal Party in Australia's national election.

10 Farmers seeking higher farm prices drove tractors and trucks into Washington to protest national farm policy.

11 Secretary of State Cyrus R. Vance said the United States would do all it could to mend the rift among the Arab nations over Egypt's peace overtures to Israel.

12 Foreign Minister Moshe Dayan said Israel might accept partition of the lands of the West Bank of the Jordan River if that was what the Arabs wanted.

12 George Meany, 83, was re-elected to the presidency of the AFL-CIO.

13 Prime Minister Menahem Begin of Israel said that when the Cairo negotiations opened Egypt and Israel each would present drafts of a proposed peace treaty.

13 A flash fire in a dormitory at Rhode Island's Providence College killed seven students and injured 16 others.

13 A chartered DC-3 plane crashed in Indiana, killing 29 persons, including the entire University of Evansville basketball team.

14 Egyptian and Israeli negotiators met in Cairo to work on a framework for a Middle East peace settlement.

14 President Carter said the right to speak for Palestinian Arabs at any Middle East peace conference had been forfeited by the Palestine Liberation Organization.

16 Prime Minister Menahem Begin told President Carter that Israel was ready to restore complete sovereignty over Sinai to Egypt and to give local Palestinians control over internal affairs on the West Bank and in the Gaza Strip.

17 Thousands of Egyptians cheered as the Israeli peace delegation entered Cairo's synagogue to attend sabbeth services.

18 Prime Minister Menahem Begin said President Carter regarded Israel's latest proposal for movement toward a Middle East peace settlement as "a fair basis for negotiation."

19 Prime Minister Menahem Begin of Israel said he would meet with Egyptian President Anwar Sadat on Christmas Day in Egypt where he would brief Sadat on talks he had had with President Carter.

20 Former budget director Bert Lance agreed to sell 60 per cent of his stock in the National Bank of Georgia to an internationally known Saudi Arabian businessman for $20 a share, about $3 more than he paid for it, his lawyer announced.

21 The death toll in an earthquake which struck Iran Dec. 20 was put at at least 519.

21 Egypt's President Anwar Sadat told newsmen he would not accept an Israeli military presence on the West Bank of the Jordan as part of a Middle East settlement.

21 The Organization of Petroleum Exporting Countries said crude oil prices would not rise for the time being, after a meeting in Venezuela.

22 At least 34 persons were killed when an explosion tore through a grain elevator near New Orleans.

22 Hostages who had been held captive by a gunman for 2½ days beat him over the head and shot him to death at a bank at the American naval base at Subic Bay, the Philippines.

23 A procession of tractors was driven into Plains, Ga., by farmers protesting what they believed to be insufficient government price supports.

24 President Carter was scheduled to meet with King Hussein of Jordan in Tehran Dec. 31 in an effort to persuade the ruler to join the Israeli-Egyptian peace negotiations.

25 Prime Minister Menahem Begin of Israel met for peace talks with President Anwar Sadat of Egypt in Ismailia, Egypt.

26 Israel and Egypt said they were not able to reach agreement on the issue of a Palestinian state and Israeli withdrawal from Sinai, the West Bank of the Jordan and the Gaza Strip, but pledged to continue their peace efforts.

27 Egyptian President Anwar Sadat said that while Israel had offered to return the entire Sinai he would not back down from other demands.

28 Israeli Prime Minister Menahem Begin defended his peace plan and insisted Israeli forces must remain in the West Bank and the Gaza Strip.

28 President Carter announced the replacement of Arthur F. Burns as chairman of the Federal Reserve Board by G. William Miller.

29 President Anwar Sadat of Egypt said he was "disappointed" by President Carter's stand against a Palestinian state.

29 President Carter arrived in Warsaw, starting a seven-nation tour.

30 President Carter said in Warsaw that Americans and Poles have the same hopes for human rights.

30 Cambodia broke diplomatic relations with Vietnam, citing "ferocious and barbarous aggression."

30 South Korea agreed to let Tongsun Park return to the United States and testify at bribery and conspiracy trials.

31 Foreign Minister Mohammed Ibrahim Kamel said Egypt insisted on Israel's full withdrawal from the West Bank and the Gaza Strip and on recognition of the Palestinians' "inalienable rights" to self-determination.

31 In Tehran, President Carter and the Shah of Iran said they took "constructive steps" toward a Middle East settlement.

THE TOP 10 STORIES OF 1977

(Selected by the news editors of Associated Press member newspapers, radio and television stations)

1. Severe Winter Weather
2. International Terrorism
3. Panama Canal Treaty
4. Bert Lance Resigns
5. Elvis Presley Dies
6. Gary Gilmore Executed
7. Collision of Two 747 Jetliners
8. Energy
9. Son of Sam
10. Korean Influence-Buying

(This list was compiled before Egyptian President Anwar Sadat made his historic trip to Jerusalem.)

DEATHS—1977

JANUARY

Dzemal Bijedic, 60, had been premier of Yugoslavia since 1971. Born at Mostar in Bosnia-Hercegovina, he joined the Communist Party in 1939 and was arrested several times for his Communist activities in royal Yugoslavia. He joined Tito's partisans in 1941 and served in several important political and military posts during World War II. After the war, Bijedic became deputy minister of interior in the Bosnia-Hercegovina state government. He held other important posts in both state and federal governments finally rising to the post of federal premier in July 1971. He began a second term in May 1974. On Jan. 18, in a plane crash in central Yugoslavia.

Freddie Prinze, 22, was a beguiling young comedian and the star of the television series *Chico And The Man*. Prinze, who shot himself in a fit of despair, saw his popularity skyrocket when he took the role as a Mexican-American mechanic in the TV series. A New York native of Puerto Rican and Hungarian heritage, Prinze had acted since the age of four when he did imitations of the late Ed Sullivan. He studied drama and launched into comedy, working in New York coffee houses and night clubs. His break into television came when a talent scout caught his act at a New York club and got him onto a late night television show when Prinze was 19. In Los Angeles, Jan. 29.

Bernard "Toots" Shor, 73, was a New York saloonkeeper who served strong drinks and good stories to celebrities. Shor always said he ran his bars for his pals and didn't care that people he didn't like—he called them "crumb bums"—found him somewhat abrupt. Despite his disregard for most accepted rules of good customer relations, Shor attracted a wide and loyal following, including such notables as writer Ernest Hemingway, baseball great Joe DiMaggio, boxing champion Jack Dempsey, and the late actor Paul Douglas. Shor worked as a host at various bars and nightspots through the 1930s, before opening his own place in 1940. In New York, Jan. 23.

FEBRUARY

Roy Abernethy, 70, was an auto dealer and salesman before joining American Motors Corp. in 1954. He served as vice president for automotive sales in the years when the auto firm climbed out of the red on the strength of the compact Rambler. He became executive vice president in 1960 and then president and chief executive officer in 1962. Abernethy continued to support the Rambler but under him the company also began to produce larger cars with more powerful engines. He headed AMC for five years. In Tequestra, Fla., Feb. 28.

Queen Alia, 29, was the young, third wife of King Hussein of Jordan. She died when the helicopter in which she was riding crashed in southern Jordan during a heavy rainstorm, killing the queen and three others. The queen was tall, blonde and American-educated. She married King Hussein in 1972 after his divorce from his second wife. In 1974, they had a daughter, Haya. Noted for her informality, the queen liked to wear blue jeans and to go water skiing with her husband. She had studied in Rome and held a bachelor's degree in political science from Hunter College in New York City. Her father, Baha-Eddin Toukan, was in the Jordanian foreign service and served as ambassador to Egypt and the United States. In Jordan, Feb. 9.

Eddie Anderson, 71, was a gravel-voiced comedian who played Jack Benny's valet "Rochester" for more than 30 years. He made his first radio appearance in 1937 and appeared steadily until 1964 when Benny's television series formally ended. He used his unique voice as an instrument with which to turn the tables on his employer, played by Benny, often by just using the line, "What's that, boss?" Anderson began his show business career at the age of 14 when he appeared in an all-black revue. Then, with his older brother, Cornelius, he formed a vaudeville team and toured as a song-and-dance man. He appeared in several movies. Anderson, who in 1962 was listed as one of the 100 wealthiest blacks in the United States, went into semiretirement after the Benny show closed. In Los Angeles, Feb. 28.

John Dickson Carr, 70 was the author of 120 mystery novels and hundreds of short stories. Carr was so prolific that he wrote under two names, his own and Carter Dickson. At one time he used a third name—Carr Dickson. He once said that, "I insisted on loafing 18 hours a day at the typewriter, ever since I was old enough to know one letter from another." He created two famous detectives—Dr. Gideon Fell, an eccentric Oxford don, and Sir Henry Merrivale, of whom he said, "There's a lot of Winston Churchill in him and even a little of me." His career as a mystery writer began when his first novel, *It Walks By Night,* appeared in 1930. In Greenville, S.C., Feb. 27.

Anthony Crosland, 58, served as British Foreign Secretary for almost a year before suffering a stroke. After military service and graduation from college, he was elected at the age of 32 in 1950 to Parliament from South Gloucestershire. He was defeated five years later but returned to Parliament in 1959 and held that seat until his death. Among the posts he held were Minister of State for Economic Affairs, Secretary of State for Education, President of the Board of Trade, and Secretary of State for Local Government and Regional Planning. When the Labor Party returned to power in 1974, Crosland was named Minister of Environment and in 1975 moved to the Foreign Office. In Oxford, Feb. 19.

Andy Devine, 71, was an actor noted for his unique, squeaky voice that was the result of a childhood mishap—he fell while he had a stick in his mouth and the roof of his mouth and his vocal cords were injured. He began acting as an extra in the days of the silent movies and moved on to the talkies in the late 1920s. He usually was cast in the same secondary role—the bulky, bumbling sidekick of flashy cowboys or as a slow-witted man who, with his squeaky giggle, provided comic relief. He appeared in many films, saying in 1950 that he had made about 300 movies in 25 years. He also was active in television, appearing as a deputy in the *Wild Bill Hickok* series. In Orange, Calif., Feb. 18.

Daniel P. O'Connell, 91, was the patriarch of Democratic politics in Albany, N.Y., having dominated them in the New York State capital city since 1922. Although he was never a commanding figure in national Democratic circles, O'Connell did carve out an enclave of Democratic strength in the heart of traditionally Republican upstate New York. O'Connell's organization came to power in the early 1920s, and stood fast against several investigations, including one by Gov. Thomas E. Dewey for alleged corruption. In Albany, Feb. 28.

APRIL

Philip K. Wrigley, 82, was chairman of William Wrigley Jr. Co., the world's largest chewing gum firm, and owner of the Chicago Cubs baseball club. Wrigley, whose wealth was estimated at more than $100 million, inherited both the gum firm and the team from his father. For years, Wrigley held the price of his chewing gum to a nickel for a five-stick pack—the same price it was when his father founded the company in 1893. Only in 1971 did the price rise. Wrigley refused to put lights in Chicago's Wrigley Field for night games in deference to residents whose homes ringed the ball park. One of his proudest achievements was coming up with a chewing gum in 1975 that did not stick to dentures. Wrigley had been searching for such a gum since the 1950s. In Elkhorn, Wis., April 12.

MAY

Gen. Lewis Blaine Hershey, 83, supervised the draft of 14.5 million Americans in three wars before retiring as the oldest military man on active duty. Hershey helped set up the Selective Service System before World War II, became its director of mobilization and remained in charge of the system until 1970, having directed the draft during World War II, the Korean War, and the Vietnam War. The draftee selection system was replaced with a draft lottery in 1969, and the following year President Richard Nixon relieved Gen. Hershey of the directorship he had held since 1941 under six presidents. However, Hershey then was promoted to four-star rank and named adviser to the president on manpower mobilization. He retired from the Army three years later at age 79. At Angela, Ind., May 20.

Robert Maynard Hutchins, 78, became president of the University of Chicago at age 30 and went on to become one of the leading educators of the 20th century. Hutchins was regarded as a boy wonder when he was named dean of the Yale Law School at 28, two years after graduating magna cum laude from the school. At 30, he went to the University of Chicago and became the youngest person ever to head a major college. His controversial reforms at Chicago drew widespread attention and left their mark on colleges across the nation. He emphasized the value of general education over specialization and allowed students to enter the university after two years of high school. He also ended compulsory class attendance and granted degrees after two years to students who could pass a comprehensive test. At Santa Barbara, Calif., April 14.

James Jones, 55, was a writer whose first novel *From Here To Eternity* made him world famous and earned him the National Book Award for fiction, a feat he never again matched. The tough-faced American author, who fought as a welterweight in the Army and in Golden Gloves tournaments, enlisted in the Army in 1939 and came to know the service at a time when it attracted the jobless, misfits and adventurers. He remained in the Army until 1944 becoming a sergeant and receiving a Purple Heart. Jones once said "I write about war, because it's the only metier I've ever had." His secod novel, *Some Came Running* came out in 1958 and received mixed reviews ranging from scathing criticism to high praise. Thereafter, the hardworking, hard-living author continued to write novels with both war backgrounds and contemporary themes. The former appeared to his reading public to be realistic and authentic. The latter, according to the critics, appeared to have been written by another person. In his last book *WWII* published in 1975, Jones returned to the war he knew. It was an illustrated history for which he supplied a long text, blending his own experiences with a broad view of World War II. He once more seemed to be on familiar ground. On May 9, in Southhampton, L. I. Hospital.

JUNE

Tom C. Clark, 77, sat for 18 years on the U.S. Supreme Court and also served as attorney general in the administration of Harry S. Truman. Through much of his life he was supported by strong political friendships with Sen. Tom Connally and Rep. Sam Rayburn of Texas and Truman. Alternating between private law practice and government service he worked during World War II with the Senate War Investigating Committee headed by Truman, then senator from Missouri. At one point he was assigned to prosecute two German spies who had been landed off the coast of Maine by U-boat. Their eight-day military trial behind closed doors resulted in a death sentence for both men, later commuted to life imprisonment by President Truman. As attorney general, Clark was probably best remembered for his investigation and prosecution of Communists and other alleged subversives. Under his leadership, the United States brought the historic case against American leaders of the Communist Party for conspiring to overthrow the government. In 1949 he was made a justice of the Supreme Court. In 1957, he dissented when the high court overturned the convictions of the 14 American Communists whose prosecution he had initiated. Clark retired from the Supreme Court at the age of 67 to clear the way for his son, Ramsey, to become attorney general under Lyndon Johnson. Since then he had remained active accepting assignments to sit on the various circuits of the U.S. Court of Appeals. On June 13, in New York.

Magda Lupescu, 81, married ex-King Carol of Romania in 1947 after 22 years as his mistress. The wife of a Romanian army officer, Mme. Lupescu captivated Crown Prince Carol from their first meeting and in 1925 he abandoned his wife and his rights to the throne and took his mistress to the French Riviera, where they became one of the most publicized couples in the world. Carol became king in 1929 and for the next 11 years Mme. Lupescu was known as the power behind the throne. Carol abdicated the throne in 1940 and he and Mme. Lupescu were married in 1947. Carol died in 1953. At Estoril, Portugal, June 29.

Roberto Rosselini, 71, was a pioneering giant among Italy's postwar filmmakers. But he was perhaps best known for his much-publicized romance and marriage to film star Ingrid Bergman. The veteran director's off-camera love affairs often overshadowed his much-honored moviemaking. He was regarded as a founder of the neo-realism film movement that used documented living conditions as a setting for fiction and set a popular trend following World War II. He called the technique "the artistic form of truth." Rossellini's *Rome, Open City,* part of which was shot clandestinely in the summer in war-torn Italy in 1944 with the late Anna Magnani, was considered the first of the neo-realistic films. His later pictures included *Paisan* and *General Della Rovere* which won the 1959 Venice Film Festival Award. His first marriage, to Marcella de Marchis, mother of his son Renzo, was annulled in 1949, clearing the way for his 1950 marriage to Ingrid Bergman, after the birth of their son Robertino. The Bergman romance began during the filming of the movie *Stromboli* in which Miss Bergman starred and touched off a bitter struggle for divorce from her first husband, Dr. Peter Lindstrom. She overcame Lindstrom's opposition with a Mexican divorce and proxy marriage arrangement. Following the birth of twin daughters, Isabella and Isotta, Ingrid, Rosellini and Miss Bergman were separated in 1957 and their marriage was annulled in 1958. After another highly publicized romance, Rossellini married Sonali das Gupta, an Indian woman whom he met while filming in Bombay. They were divorced soon afterward. On June 3, in Rome.

JULY

Vladimir Nabokov, 78, Russian-American author of *Lolita,* was regarded as one of the finest prose stylists in modern literature. Nabokov spent more than half a century writing novels in both Russian and English, but it was the worldwide success of *Lolita* which appeared in 1955 that enabled him to devote the final years of his life to writing and translating his earlier Russian works into English Born to a wealthy, aristocratic family on an estate 50 miles from St. Petersburg, capital of Czarist Russia, Nabokov was bilingual in Russian and English from early childhood. Driven from Russia by the Bolshevik Revolution, Nabokov studied at Cambridge University in England, lived in Berlin between the world wars and at the onset of world War II fled with his Jewish wife to the United States where he became a citizen in 1945. His first English novels were regarded as below his best in Russian, but *Lolita, Pale Fire* and his last major novel *Ada* were hailed as the most original English prose style since James Joyce. Nabokov's wife, to whom all of his novels were dedicated, rescued the *Lolita* manuscript from a backyard incinerator at Cornell University where he taught Russian literature until 1959. The book was at first shunned by shocked American publishers and eventually was published by Paris' Olympia Press, an early promoter of what was then considered pornography. One of the most sensuous stories ever told, the book did not have a single four-letter word. The success of the novel enabled Nabokov to settle down with his wife in Montreux Switzerland. At the Palace Hotel in Montreux on July 2.

AUGUST

Alfred Lunt, 84, and his wife, Lynn Fontanne, reigned for 34 years as the leading couple of the American stage. From *The Guardsman,* their first hit together in 1924, to *The Visit,* their final triumph in 1958, they dominated this country's theater. The couple's skills filled theaters not only in New York but in London as well and jammed auditoriums in lesser towns. Perhaps their biggest hit was Terence Rattigan's *O Mistress Mine* which opened in New York in 1946 and ran for 451 performances. These were followed by three years on the road in the course of which the couple played in some 400 cities and towns from coast to coast. They found the road enriching emotionally. Said Miss Fontanne "Every night was like opening night." The pair excelled in urbane comedy, like the plays of Noel Coward who performed with them in his *Design for Living* in 1933. They played together in only two dramas which might be said to have a serious point —Robert E. Sherwood's *There Shall Be No Night* and Friederich Durrenmatt's *The Visit.* The Lunts scored their first big box office success in *The Guardsman* under the auspices of the Theater Guild. The play which had a Broadway run of 40 weeks was the Guild's first solid commercial triumph. Lunt and his wife were tireless in pursuit of perfection. Movie star Gregory Peck who served an apprenticeship in one of their plays, liked to cite practice as the secret of their seemingly effortless stage perfection. The Lunts would have little to do with the movies. Their only joint films were *The Guardsman* and *Stage Door Canteen.* On Aug. 3 in Chicago.

Francis Gary Powers, 47, burst into the news on May 1, 1960 when his U2 spy plane was downed over the Soviet city of Sverdlosk. The incident occurred at a time when the first signs of thaw were being noted in what was then called the Cold War. President Dwight D. Eisenhower and Soviet Premier Nikita Khrushchev were preparing for a major summit conference when the Soviet Union suddenly announced that an American plane had been shot down deep inside its boundaries. The incident led to cancellation of the planned summit. The National Aeronautics and Space Administration stated that the U2 was one of its planes that had strayed into Soviet air space by accident during a weather reconnaissance flight. However, Soviet officials put on display the remains of the aircraft, extensive photographic and electronic surveillance equipment and Powers himself. Powers had been one of a group of pilots working for the CIA from a base in Adana, Turkey. His crash in the Soviet Union revealed for the first time the existence of the sophisticated U2 spy plane. Powers was tried publicly in Moscow and sentenced to 10 years in a Soviet jail. However, he was released by the Russians in 1962 in exchange for Russian spy Rudolph Abel. When Powers returned home, he was not considered a hero. As a pilot for the CIA, he had reportedly been instructed to destroy his plane if capture appeared imminent. He said later that he had tried, but the destruct mechanism did not work. He said that before and during his Soviet trial he gave the Russians information about the U2. He said he believed they knew most of the facts already. On Aug. 1 in the crash of a helicopter he piloted as a reporter for a Los Angeles television station.

SEPTEMBER

Zero Mostel, 62, was a 240-pound roly-poly mass of exuberance with bulging eyes and stringy hair who starred in stage productions of *A Funny Thing Happened On The Way To The Forum, Fiddler On The Roof, Ulysses In Nighttown,* and *Rhinoceros.* He won Tony Awards for *Rhinoceros* and *Forum,* and a New York drama critics award for *Fiddler.* Regarded by many as one of the most versatile performers in the history of the theater, Mostel made his Broadway debut in 1942 and by the early 1950s he was earning $5,000 a week as a standup comic and a successful character actor. Then the Red scare intervened and Mostel, along with other famous entertainers, was branded a left-wing sympathizer and put out of work. He re-emerged triumphant a decade later, gaining acclaim for his portrayal of Tevye in *Fiddler.* In Philadelphia, Sept. 8.

OCTOBER

James M. Cain, 85, was a leading American mystery writer. He authored more than a dozen novels, including *The Postman Always Rings Twice, Double Indemnity, Serenade,* and *Mildred Pierce.* In addition to his novels, Cain produced several plays, short stories that appeared in the American Mercury, Liberty and other well-known magazines of the 1920s and 1930s. In 1931, he became editor of the New Yorker magazine, a position he held for 10 months before going to Hollywood to work as a screenwriter. In University Park, Md., Oct. 27.

Mackinlay Kantor, 73, was a prolific writer who won the Pulitzer Prize in 1956 with his *Andersonville,* a novel about a Confederate prisoner-of-war camp during the Civil War. In addition to novels, he wrote short stories, verse and reportage and produced 43 books. After writing detective stories for pulp magazines, Kantor published his first novel, *Diversey,* in 1928. His first successful novel, *Long Remember,* a story about the Civil War, was published in 1934. In Sarasota, Fla., Oct. 11.

Lester Markel, 83, was Sunday editor of the New York Times for more than 40 years and an associate editor of the paper until his retirement four years after that. By the time he stepped down, he had become a legend in his profession, the epitome of the exacting, imaginative and occasionally irascible editor whose constant flow of ideas and demands for improvement simultaneously inspired and terrified those who worked for him. He was rarely satisfied with what he saw and could turn the full measure of his sarcasm on his chosen profession. He called journalism the "froth estate" for its tendency to offer entertainment and showmanship in place of less glamorous straight news reporting and analysis. Markel kept in close touch with incumbent presidents and regularly traveled abroad and wrote magazine articles based on his discussions with world leaders. He recruited people in high places to write articles for The Times, something he clearly viewed as both a privilege for the writers and a benefit to the newspaper. In his later years, Markel became deeply involved in public television. For seven years he was editor and moderator of *News in Perspective,* a nationally broadcast public television program. On Oct. 23, at his home in New York City.

NOVEMBER

Sen. John L. McClellan, 81, of Arkansas was chiarman of the powerful Senate Appropriations Committee and the chief sponsor of much major anti-crime legislation. McClellan, who had announced he would not run in 1978 for a seventh six-year term, was a conservative pillar of the Senate establishment and was renowned for his investigations of corruption in and out of government. McClellan, who first was elected to the Senate in 1942 after two terms in the House, probably was best known as chairman of the Senate Permanent Investigations Subcommittee. He directed headline-making probes of labor racketeering, organized crime, illicit operations in overseas military clubs, and in many other areas. In Little Rock, Ark., Nov. 28.

DECEMBER

David K. E. Bruce, 79, was regarded as one of America's most gifted and seasoned diplomats. A man of great charm and sympathy, he was highly regarded in Britain, France and West Germany, where he had served as ambassador. For many years, Bruce served sporadically in the Foreign Service, breaking off during World War II to command the Office of Strategic Services in the European Theater. The agency was later to become the CIA. In 1949, President Truman made Bruce ambassador to France, and in 1957 President Eisenhower named him envoy to West Germany. President Kennedy sent him to London in 1961, an ambassadorial seat he occupied for eight years, the longest anyone ever held that post. Bruce also served in less glamorous and more vexing jobs. In 1970, President Nixon named him head of the U.S. delegation to the stalemated Paris peace talks aimed at ending the war in Vietnam. In 1973, Bruce became the first head of the U.S. liaison mission set up in Peking. On Dec. 5, in Washington, D.C.

Howard Hawks, 81, for more than four decades was one of America's most versatile film directors with such diverse movies as *Sgt. York, To Have and Have Not* and *Red River.* His long career began in 1924 when he wrote the script for *Tiger Love.* In 1926, he directed his first film, The *Road To Glory* with George O'Brien. His first major success came in 1932 with *The Crowd Roars,* a toughly realistic action film about racing-car drivers which he both wrote and directed. It starred James Cagney. This was followed the same year by *Scarface,* which starred Paul Muni and was outstanding in a wave of gangster films. Hawks directed a number of aviation films, the best of which included *The Dawn Patrol, Ceiling Zero, Only Angels Have Wings* and *Air Force.* He established a number of acting careers, including George Raft, Carole Lombard and Rita Hayworth. Hawks' last film was *Rio Lobo* in 1970, a Western starring John Wayne, one of the director's favorite actors. At the time of his death, Hawks had been making plans to return to movie making with a Western. On Dec. 26, in Palm Springs, Calif.

S. L. A. Marshall, 77, a retired brigadier general, was a noted military historian who wrote a number of books, including *Pork Chop Hill,* an account of the Korean War. Marshall enlisted in the army in 1917 and was commissioned from the ranks. He established the Army News Service and was one of three founders of the Army's historical division. He was credited with the definitive analysis of Gen. Jimmy Doolittle's historic bombing raid on Tokyo during World War II. Marshall served mostly in the European Theater in World War II and was historian for the armies of occupation. He was promoted to brigadier general in 1951 and served in Korea. Among his books were *Army on Wheels, Blitzkrieg, Men Against Fire* and *Swift Sword.* Perhaps his best known book was *Pork Chop Hill* which was made into a movie starring Gregory Peck. On Dec. 17, in El Paso, Texas.

Cyril Ritchard, 79, was an Australian-born actor whose versatile career spanned six decades and included productions at the Metropolitan Opera. He made his stage debut in 1917 as a chorus boy. Ritchard went on to win a Tony Award in 1954 for his portrayal of Captain Hook opposite Mary Martin in *Peter Pan* on Broadway. The television adaptation of that musical brought Ritchard his widest exposure to the public, but he said the lack of a live audience in TV was "the most difficult thing in the medium." In Chicago, Dec. 18.

Lady Clementine Spencer-Churchill, 92, was the wife and "darling Clemmie" of Sir Winston Churchill, Britain's World War II prime minister who died in 1965. She was known as a beauty in 1908 when she captured the eye of Churchill at a dinner party. The future prime minister, then a cabinet member, proposed soon afterward in the gardens of Blenheim Palace, his family's 16th-century estate. Lady Spencer-Churchill first went to 10 Downing Street, the home of Britain's prime ministers, when her husband took the helm of government in the dark spring of 1940. She brought a wit and courage that enabled her to remark to a friend when bombs were falling: "I have made up my mind to ignore this completely." In London, Dec. 12.

Louis Untermeyer, 92, wrote thousands of poems and produced some 90 books, most of them anthologies. Among his most popular anthologies were *Modern American Poetry* and *Modern British Poetry,* both used as textbooks. Untermeyer, who was credited with bringing poetry to more people than any other American of his generation, once said poetry was "an effort to express the inexpressible in terms of the unforgettable." In Newton, Conn., Dec. 18.

PRIZES—AWARDS

PRIZES—AWARDS
PULITZER PRIZES

Public Service—The Lufkin (Texas) News.

General Local Reporting—Margo Huston, the Milwaukee Journal.

Special Local Reporting—Acel Moore and Wendell Rawls Jr., the Philadelphia Inquirer.

National Reporting—Walter Mears, The Associated Press.

International Reporting—no award.

Editorial Writing—Warren Lerude, Foster Church and Norman F. Cardoza, the Reno (Nevada) State Journal.

Editorial Cartooning—Paul Szep, the Boston Globe.

Spot News Photography—Neal Ulevich, The Associated Press and Stanley Forman, Boston Herald-American.

Feature Photography—Robin Hood, the Chattanooga News-Free Press.

Commentary—George F. Will, Washington Post Writers Group.

Criticism—William McPherson, the Washington Post.

Fiction—no award.

General Non-fiction—William W. Warner for "Beautiful Swimmers: Watermen, Crabs and Chesapeake Bay."

Drama—Michael Cristofer for "The Shadow Box."

History—David Morris Potter for "The Impending Crisis."

Biography—John E. Mack for "A Prince of Our Disorder: The Life of T. E. Lawrence."

Poetry—James Merrill for "Divine Comedies."

Music—Richard Wernick for "Visions of Terror and Wonder."

Special Book Award—Alex Haley for "Roots."

NOBEL PRIZES

Peace—Betty Williams and Mairead Corrigan, antiwar activists in Northern Ireland for organizing a 14-month-old "Peace People's" movement to end Protestant-Catholic fighting in their homeland, and Amnesty International for its 16 years of worldwide efforts to win freedom for "prisoners of conscience" and abolish torture and the death penalty.

Literature—Vincente Aleixandre, Spain, for a half-century of "creative poetic writing which, with roots in the tradition of Spanish lyric verse and in modern currents, illuminates man's condition in the cosmos and in present-day society."

Medicine—Dr. Rosalyn Yalow, USA, for research in endocrinology, and for development of radioimmunassays of peptide hormones, and Dr. Roger Guillemin and Dr. Andrew Schally, USA, for independent competitive studies of peptide hormone production of the brain that "laid the foundations to modern hypothalamic research."

Physics—John H. Van Vleck and Philip W. Anderson, USA, and Sir Nevill E. Mott, Britain, for research on the electronic structure of magnetic and "disordered" systems.

Chemistry—Ilys Pregogine, Belgium, for expanding thermodynamic theory to explain how order can exist within seemingly disordered environmental systems.

Economics—James Meade, Britain, and Peertil Ohlin, Sweden, for their "pathbreaking contributions to the theory of international trade and international capital."

OSCARS

Picture—"Rocky."

Actor—Peter Finch in "Network."

Actress—Faye Dunaway in "Network."

Supporting Actor—Jason Robards in "All The President's Men."

Supporting Actress—Beatrice Straight in "Network."

Director—John G. Avildsen for "Rocky."

Foreign Language Film—"Black And White In Color," Ivory Coast.

Live Action Short—"In The Region Of Ice."

Animated Short—"Leisure."

Sound Achievement—"All The President's Men."

Feature Documentary—"Harlan County, U.S.A."

Short Subject Documentary—"Number Our Days."

Art Direction—"All The President's Men."

Costume Design—"Fellini's Casanova."

Original Score—"The Omen."

Song Score and Adaptation—"Bound For Glory."

Cinematography—"Bound For Glory."

Film Editing—"Rocky."

Original Song—"Evergreen" from "A Star Is Born."

Original Screenplay—Paddy Chayefsky "Network."

Special Visual Achievement—"King Kong" and "Logan's Run."

NATIONAL BOOK AWARDS

Contemporary Thought—Bruno Bettelheim for "The Uses of Enchantment: The Meaning and Importance of Fairy Tales."

Biography—W. A. Swanberg for "Norman Thomas: The Last Idealist."

Children's Book—Katherine Paterson for "The Master Puppeteer."

Fiction—Wallace Stegner for "The Spectator Bird."

History—Irving Howe for "World of Our Fathers."

Poetry—Richard Eberhart for "Collected Poems 1930–1976."

Translation—Li-Li Ch'en for "Master

Tung's Western Chamber Romance: A Chinese Chantefable."

Special Citation—Alex Haley for "Roots."

TONY AWARDS

(American Theater Wing)

Best Play, Author—"The Shadow Box," Michael Cristofer.

Best Play, Producer—"The Shadow Box," Allan Francis, Ken Marsolais, Lester Osterman, Leonard Soloway.

Best Musical, Producer—"Annie," Lewis Allen, Stephen R. Friedman, Irwin Meyer, Mike Nichols.

Best Book of a Musical—"Annie," Thomas Meehan.

Best Score—"Annie," Martin Charnin.

Best Actor, Play—"The Basic Training of Pavlo Hummel," Al Pacino.

Best Actress, Play—"The Belle of Amherst," Julie Harris.

Best Actor, Musical—"The Robber Bridegroom," Barry Bostwick.

Best Actress, Musical—"Annie," Dorothy Loudon.

Best Featured Actor, Play—"Comedians," Jonathan Pryce.

Best Featured Actress, Play—"For Colored Girls Who Have Considered Suicide When the Rainbow Is Enuf," Trazana Beverley.

Best Featured Actor, Musical—"I Love My Wife," Lenny Baker.

Best Featured Actress, Musical—"Your Arms Too Short to Box With God," Delores Hall.

Best Director, Play—"The Shadow Box," Gordon Davidson.

Best Director, Musical—"I Love My Wife," Gene Saks.

Best Scenic Designer—"Annie," David Mitchell.

Best Costume Designer—"Annie," Theoni V. Aldredge and "The Cherry Orchard," Santo Loquasto.

Best Lighting Designer—"The Cherry Orchard," Jennifer Tipton.

Best Choreographer—"Annie" Peter Gennaro.

Most Innovative Revival—"Porgy and Bess."

Special Tony Awards—Diana Ross, Barry Manilow, Lily Tomlin, Equity Library Theatre, The National Theatre of the Deaf, Center Theatre Group/Mark Taper Forum.

Lawrence Langner Award—Cheryl Crawford.

GRAMMY AWARDS

(National Academy of Recording Arts and Sciences)

Record of the Year—"This Masquerade," Artist: George Benson; Producer: Tommy Lipuma (Warner Bros.)

Album of the Year—"Songs in the Key of Life," Artist and Producer: Stevie Wonder (Tamla).

Song of the Year—"I Write the Songs," Songwriter: Bruce Johnston.

Best New Artist of the Year—Starland Vocal Band (Windsong/RCA).

Best Instrumental Arrangement—"Leprechaun's Dream," Chick Corea; Arranger: Chick Corea (Polycor).

Best Arrangement for Voices—"Afternoon Delight," Starland Vocal Band; Arrangers: Starland Vocal Band (Windsong/RCA).

Best Engineered Recording (Non-Classical)—"Breezin'," George Benson; Engineer: Al Schmitt (Warner Bros.)

Best Album Package—"Chicago X," Chicago; Art Director: John Berg (Columbia).

Best Album Notes—"The Changing Face of Harlem," The Savoy Sessions; Annotator: Dan Morgenstern (Savoy).

Best Producer of the Year—Stevie Wonder, "Songs in the Key of Life," (Tamla).

Best Jazz Vocal Performance—Ella Fitzgerald, "Fitzgerald & Pass . . . Again." (Pablo).

Best Jazz Performance by a Soloist—Count Basie, "Basie & Zoot," (Pablo).

Best Jazz Performance by a Group—"The Leprechaun," Chick Corea (Polydor).

Best Jazz Performance by a Big Band —"The Ellington Suites," Duke Ellington (Pablo).

Best Vocal Performance, Female—"Hasten Down the Wind," Linda Ronstadt (Asylum).

Best Vocal Performance, Male—"Songs in the Key of Life," Stevie Wonder (Tamla).

Best Pop Vocal Performance by a Duo, Group or Chorus—"If You Leave Me Now," Chicago (Columbia).

Best Pop Instrumental Performance—"Breezin'," George Benson (Warner Bros.)

Best Rhythm and Blues Vocal Performance, Female—"Sophisticated Lady (She's A Different Lady)," Natalie Cole (Capitol).

Best Rhythm and Blues Vocal Performance, Male—"I Wish," Stevie Wonder (Tamla).

Best Rhythm and Blues Vocal Performance by a Duo, Group or Chorus,—"You Don't Have to Be a Star (To Be In My Show)," Marilyn McCoo, Billy Davis Jr. (ABC).

Best Rhythm and Blues Instrumental Performance—"Theme from Good King Bad," George Benson (CTI).

Best Rhythm and Blues Song—"Lowdown," Boz Scaggs; Songwriters: Boz Scaggs, David Paich.

Best Soul Gospel Performance—"How I Got Over," Mahalia Jackson (Columbia).

Best Country Vocal Performance, Female—"Elite Hotel," Emmylou Harris (Reprise).

Best Country Vocal Performance, Male—"(I'm A) Stand By My Woman Man," Bonnie Milsap, (RCA).

Best Country Vocal Performance by a Duo or Group—"The End is Not in Sight (The Cowboy Tune)," Amazing Rhythm Aces (ABC).

Best Country Instrumental Performance—"Chester and Lester," Chet Atkins, Les Paul (RCA).

Best Country Song—"Broken Lady," Songwriter: Larry Gatlin.

Best Inspirational Performance—"The Astonishing, Outrageous, Amazing, Incredible, Unbelievable, Different World of Gary S. Paxton," Gary S. Paxton (Newpax).

Best Gospel Performance (Other Than Soul Gospel)—"Where the Soul Never Dies," Oak Ridge Boys (Columbia).

Best Ethnic or Traditional Recording—"Mark Twang," John Hartford (Flying Fish).

Best Latin Recording—"Unfinished Masterpiece," Eddie Palmieri (Coco).

Best Recording for Children—Prokofiev: "Peter and the Wolf"/Saint Saens: "Carnival of the Animals," Hermoine Gingold, Karl Bohm (DG).

Best Comedy Recording—"Bicentennial Nigger," Richard Pryor (Warner Bros.)

Best Spoken Word Recording—"Great American Documents," Orson Welles, Henry Fonda, Helen Hayes, James Earl Jones (CBS).

Best Instrumental Composition—"Bellavia," Chuck Mangione; Composer: Chuck Mangione.

Album of Best Original Score Written for a Motion Picture or a Television Special—"Car Wash," Composer: Norman Whitfield (MCA).

Best Cast Show Album—"Bubbling Brown Sugar," Producers: Hugo & Luigi (H & I).

Album of the Year, Classical—Beethoven: "The Five Piano Concertos," Artists: Artur Rubinstein and Daniel Barenboim conducting the London Philharmonic; Producer: Max Wilcox (RCA).

Best Classical Orchestral Performance —Straus: "Also Sprach Zarathustra," Conductor: Sir Georg Solti conducting the Chicago Symphony; Producer: Ray Minshull (London).

Best Opera Recording—Gershwin: "Porgy and Bess," Conductor: Lorin Maazel conducting the Cleveland Orchestra and Chorus; Producer: Michael Woolcock (London).

Best Choral Performance, Classical (Other Than Opera)—Rachmaninoff: "The Bells," Conductor: Andre Previn conducting the London Symphony Orchestra; Choral Director: Arthur Oldham (Angel).

Best Chamber Music Performance—"The Art of Courtly Love," David Munrow conducting Early Music Consort of London (Seraphim).

Best Classical Performance Instrumental Soloist or Soloists (With Orchestra) —Beethoven: "The Five Piano Concertos," Artur Rubinstein, piano (Daniel Barenboim Conducting London Philharmonic (RCA).

Best Classical Performance Instrumental Soloist or Soloists (Without Orchestra)—"Horowitz Concerts 1975/76," Vladimir Horowitz, Piano (RCA).

Best classical Vocal Soloist Performance—Herbert: "Music of Victor Herbert," Beverly Sills (Angel).

Best Engineered Recording, Classical —Gershwin: "Rhapsody in Blue," George Gershwin (1925 Piano Roll) and Michael Tilson Thomas conducting the Columbia Jazz Band; Engineers: Edward Graham, Ray Moore, Milton Cherin (Columbia).

EMMY AWARDS

Best Supporting Actor, Comedy Series—Gary Burghoff, "M-A-S-H."

Best Supporting Actress in a Comedy Series—Mary Kay Place, "Mary Hartman, Mary Hartman."

Best Supporting Actor in a Drama Series—Gary Frank, "Family."

Best Supporting Actress in a Drama Series—Kristy McNichol, "Family."

Lead Actor in a Single Performance in a Series—Louis Gossett Jr., "Roots."

Lead Actress in a Single Performance in a Series—Beaulah Bondi, "The Waltons."

Best Supporting Actor in a Variety Series—Tom Conway, "Carol Burnett Show."

Best Actress in a Single Performance in a Variety Show—Rita Moreno, "The Muppet Show."

Best Supporting Actor in a Comedy or Drama Special—Burgess Meredith, "Tail Gunner Joe."

Best Supporting Actress in a Comedy or Drama Special—Diana Hyland, "The Boy in the Plastic Bubble."

Best Actor in a Drama or Comedy Special—Ed Flanders, "Harry S. Truman: Plain Speaking."

Best Actress in a Drama or Comedy Special—Sally Field, "Sybil."

Best Actor in a Single Performance in a Series—Edward Asner, "Roots."

Best Actress in a Single Performance in a Series—Olivia Cole, "Roots."

Individual Award—"Tonight Show."

Best Lead Actor in a Comedy Series—Carroll O'Connor, "All In The Family."

Best Lead Actress in a Comedy Series—Beatrice Arthur, "Maude."

Best Comedy Series—"Mary Tyler Moore Show."

Best Variety Special—"The Barry Manilow Special."

Best Director of a Variety Series—Dave Powers, "Carol Burnett Show."

Best Variety Series—"Van Dyke and Co."

Best Lead Actor in a Limited Series—Christopher Plummer, "The Money Changers."

Best Lead Actress in a Limited Series—Patty Duke Astin, "Captains and the Kings."

Best Limited Series—"Roots."

Best Lead Actor in a Drama Series—James Garner, "The Rockford Files."

Best Lead Actress in a Drama Series—Lindsay Wagner, "The Bionic Woman."

Best Drama Series—"Upstairs, Downstairs."

Best Drama or Comedy Special—"Eleanor and Franklin, The White House Years" and "Sybil" (tie).

UNITED STATES GOVERNMENT

EXECUTIVE DEPARTMENT

President   Jimmy Carter
Vice President   Walter F. Mondale

CABINET

Secretary of State	Cyrus R. Vance	*Secretary of Labor*	Ray Marshall
Secretary of the Treasury	W. Michael Blumenthal	*Secretary of Health,*	
Secretary of Defense	Harold Brown	*Education & Welfare*	Joseph A. Califano, Jr.
Attorney General	Griffin B. Bell	*Secretary of Housing*	
Secretary of the Interior	Cecil D. Andrus	*& Urban Development*	Patricia B. Harris
Secretary of Agriculture	Bob Bergland	*Secretary of Transportation*	Brock Adams
Secretary of Commerce	Juanita M. Kreps	*Secretary of Energy*	James R. Schlesinger

JOINT CHIEFS OF STAFF

Gen. George S. Brown, USAF, Chairman
Gen. Bernard W. Rogers, USA
Adm. James L. Holloway, III, USN
Gen. David C. Jones, USAF
Gen. Louis H. Wilson, USMC

LEGISLATIVE

**95th Congress
Second Session**

SENATE

President of the Senate	Walter F. Mondale
President Pro Tempore	James O. Eastland (D.Miss.)
Deputy President Pro Tempore	Hubert H. Humphrey (D.Minn.)
Majority Leader	Robert C. Byrd (D.W. Va.)
Majority Whip	Alan Cranston (D.Calif.)
Minority Leader	Howard H. Baker, Jr. (R.Tenn.)
Minority Whip	Ted Stevens (R.Alaska)
Chaplain	Rev. Edward L. R. Elson

HOUSE OF REPRESENTATIVES

Speaker	Thomas P. O'Neill, Jr. (D.Mass.)
Majority Leader	James C. Wright, Jr. (D.Texas)
Majority Whip	John Brademas (D.Ind.)
Minority Leader	John J. Rhodes (R.Ariz.)
Minority Whip	Robert H. Michel (R.Ill.)
Chaplain	Rev. Edward Gardiner Latch

State Delegations

Number which precedes name of Representative
designates congressional district.

ALABAMA

SENATORS
John J. Sparkman D   James B. Allen D

REPRESENTATIVES
1. Jack Edwards R
2. William L. Dickinson R
3. Bill Nichols D
4. Tom Bevill D
5. Ronnie G. Flippo D
6. John Buchanan R
7. Walter Flowers D

ALASKA

SENATORS
Ted Stevens R   Mike Gravel D

REPRESENTATIVE
At large—Donald E. Young R

ARIZONA

SENATORS
Barry Goldwater   R   Dennis DeConcini   D
REPRESENTATIVES
1. John J. Rhodes   R
2. Morris K. Udall   D
3. Bob Stump   D
4. Eldon D. Rudd   R

ARKANSAS

SENATORS
John L. McClellan[1]   D   Dale Bumpers   D
REPRESENTATIVES
1. Bill Alexander   D
2. James G. Tucker, Jr.   D
3. John P. Hammerschmidt   R
4. Ray Thornton   D

CALIFORNIA

SENATORS
Alan Cranston   D   S. I. Hayakawa   R
REPRESENTATIVES
1. Harold T. Johnson   D
2. Don H. Clausen   R
3. John E. Moss   D
4. Robert L. Leggett   D
5. John Burton   D
6. Phillip Burton   D
7. George Miller   D
8. Ronald V. Dellums   D
9. Fortney H. (Pete) Stark   D
10. Don Edwards   D
11. Leo J. Ryan   D
12. Paul N. (Pete) McCloskey, Jr.   R
13. Norman Y. Mineta   D
14. John J. McFall   D
15. B. F. Sisk   D
16. Leon E. Panetta   D
17. John Krebs   D
18. William M. Ketchum   R
19. Robert J. Lagomarsino   R
20. Barry Goldwater, Jr.   R
21. James C. Corman   D
22. Carlos J. Moorhead   R
23. Anthony C. Beilenson   D
24. Henry A. Waxman   D
25. Edward R. Roybal   D
26. John Rousselot   R
27. Robert K. Dornan   R
28. Yvonne Brathwaite Burke   D
29. Augustus F. (Gus) Hawkins   D
30. George E. Danielson   D
31. Charles H. Wilson   D
32. Glenn M. Anderson   D
33. Del Clawson   R
34. Mark W. Hannaford   D
35. Jim Lloyd   D
36. George E. Brown, Jr.   D
37. Shirley N. Pettis   R
38. Jerry M. Patterson   D
39. Charles E. Wiggins   R
40. Robert E. Badham   R
41. Bob Wilson   R
42. Lionel Van Deerlin   D
43. Clair W. Burgener   R

COLORADO

SENATORS
Floyd K. Haskell   D   Gary Hart   D
REPRESENTATIVES
1. Patricia Schroeder   D
2. Timothy E. Wirth   D
3. Frank E. Evans   D
4. James P. (Jim) Johnson   R
5. William L. Armstrong   R

CONNECTICUT

SENATORS
Abraham A. Ribicoff   D   Lowell P. Weicker, Jr.   R
REPRESENTATIVES
1. William R. Cotter   D
2. Christopher J. Dodd   D
3. Robert N. Giaimo   D
4. Stewart B. McKinney   R
5. Ronald A. Sarasin   R
6. Toby Moffett   D

DELAWARE

SENATORS
William V. Roth, Jr.   R   Joseph R. Biden, Jr.   D
REPRESENTATIVE
At large—Thomas B. Evans, Jr.   R

FLORIDA

SENATORS
Lawton Chiles   D   Richard (Dick) Stone   D
REPRESENTATIVES
1. Robert L. F. Sikes   D
2. Don Fuqua   D
3. Charles E. Bennett   D
4. Bill Chappell, Jr.   D
5. Richard Kelly   R
6. C. W. Bill Young   R
7. Sam M. Gibbons   D
8. Andrew P. Ireland   D
9. Louis Frey, Jr.   R
10. L. A. (Skip) Bafalis   R
11. Paul G. Rogers   D
12. J. Herbert Burke   R
13. William Lehman   D
14. Claude D. Pepper   D
15. Dante B. Fascell   D

GEORGIA

SENATORS
Herman E. Talmadge   D   Sam Nunn   D
REPRESENTATIVES
1. Bo Ginn   D
2. Dawson Mathis   D
3. Jack Brinkley   D
4. Elliott H. Levitas   D
5. [Vacant][2]
6. John J. Flynt, Jr.   D
7. Larry McDonald   D
8. Billy Lee Evans   D
9. Edgar L. Jenkins   D
10. D. Douglas Barnard, Jr.   D

HAWAII

SENATORS
Daniel K. Inouye   D   Spark M. Matsunaga   D
REPRESENTATIVES
1. Cecil Heftel   D   2. Daniel K. Akaka   D

IDAHO

SENATORS
Frank Church   D   James A. McClure   R
REPRESENTATIVES
1. Steven D. Symms   R   2. George Hansen   R

ILLINOIS

SENATORS
Charles H. Percy   R   Adlai E. Stevenson   D
REPRESENTATIVES
1. Ralph H. Metcalfe   D
2. Morgan F. Murphy   D
3. Martin A. Russo   D
4. Edward J. Derwinski   R
5. John G. Fary   D
6. Henry J. Hyde   R
7. Cardiss Collins   D
8. Dan Rostenkowski   D
9. Sidney R. Yates   D
10. Abner J. Mikva   D
11. Frank Annunzio   D
12. Philip M. Crane   R
13. Robert McClory   R
14. John N. Erlenborn   R
15. Thomas J. Corcoran   R
16. John B. Anderson   R
17. George M. O'Brien   R
18. Robert H. Michel   R
19. Thomas F. Railsback   R
20. Paul Findley   R
21. Edward R. Madigan   R
22. George E. Shipley   D
23. Melvin Price   D
24. Paul Simon   D

INDIANA

SENATORS
Birch Bayh   D   Richard G. Lugar   R
REPRESENTATIVES
1. Adam Benjamin, Jr.   D
2. Floyd J. Fithian   D
3. John Brademas   D
4. J. Danforth Quayle   R
5. Elwood Hillis   R
6. David W. Evans   D
7. John T. Myers   R
8. David L. Cornwell   D
9. Lee H. Hamilton   D
10. Philip R. Sharp   D
11. Andrew Jacobs, Jr.   D

IOWA

SENATORS
Dick Clark D   John C. Culver D
REPRESENTATIVES
1. James A. S. Leach R
2. Michael T. Blouin D
3. Charles E. Grassley R
4. Neal Smith D
5. Tom Harkin D
6. Berkley Bedell D

KANSAS

SENATORS
James B. Pearson R   Bob Dole R
REPRESENTATIVES
1. Keith G. Sebelius R
2. Martha Keys D
3. Larry Winn, Jr. R
4. Daniel R. Glickman D
5. Joe Skubitz R

KENTUCKY

SENATORS
Walter (Dee) Huddleston D   Wendell H. Ford D
REPRESENTATIVES
1. Carroll Hubbard, Jr. D
2. William H. Natcher D
3. Romano L. Mazzoli D
4. M. G. (Gene) Snyder R
5. Tim Lee Carter R
6. John Breckinridge D
7. Carl D. Perkins D

LOUISIANA

SENATORS
Russell B. Long D   J. Bennett Johnston, Jr. D
REPRESENTATIVES
1. Richard A. Tonry[3] D
2. Corinne C. (Lindy) Boggs D
3. David C. Treen R
4. Joe D. Waggonner, Jr. D
5. Thomas J. Huckaby D
6. W. Henson Moore R
7. John B. Breaux D
8. Gillis W. Long D

MAINE

SENATORS
Edmund S. Muskie D   William D. Hathaway D
REPRESENTATIVES
1. David F. Emery R   2. William S. Cohen R

MARYLAND

SENATORS
Charles McC. Mathias, Jr. R   Paul S. Sarbanes D
REPRESENTATIVES
1. Robert E. Bauman R
2. Clarence D. Long D
3. Barbara A. Mikulski D
4. Marjorie S. Holt R
5. Gladys Noon Spellman D
6. Goodloe E. Byron D
7. Parren J. Mitchell D
8. Newton I. Steers, Jr. R

MASSACHUSETTS

SENATORS
Edward M. Kennedy D   Edward W. Brooke R
REPRESENTATIVES
1. Silvio O. Conte R
2. Edward P. Boland D
3. Joseph D. Early D
4. Robert F. Drinan D
5. Paul E. Tsongas D
6. Michael J. Harrington D
7. Edward J. Markey D
8. Thomas P. O'Neill, Jr. D
9. John Joseph Moakley D
10. Margaret M. Heckler R
11. James A. Burke D
12. Gerry E. Studds D

MICHIGAN

SENATORS
Robert P. Griffin R   Donald W. Riegle, Jr. D
REPRESENTATIVES
1. John Conyers, Jr. D
2. Carl D. Pursell R
3. Garry E. Brown R
4. David A. Stockman R
5. Harold S. Sawyer R
6. Bob Carr D
7. Dale E. Kildee D
8. Bob Traxler D
9. Guy Vander Jagt R
10. Elford A. Cederberg R
11. Philip E. Ruppe R
12. David E. Bonior D
13. Charles C. Diggs, Jr. D
14. Lucien N. Nedzi D
15. William D. Ford D
16. John D. Dingell D
17. William M. Brodhead D
18. James J. Blanchard D
19. William S. Broomfield R

MINNESOTA

SENATORS
Hubert H. Humphrey D   Wendell R. Anderson D
REPRESENTATIVES
1. Albert H. Quie R
2. Tom Hagedorn R
3. Bill Frenzel R
4. Bruce F. Vento D
5. Donald M. Fraser D
6. Richard Nolan D
7. Arlan Stangeland[4] R
8. James L. Oberstar D

MISSISSIPPI

SENATORS
James O. Eastland D   John C. Stennis D
REPRESENTATIVES
1. Jamie L. Whitten D
2. David R. Bowen D
3. G. V. (Sonny) Montgomery D
4. Thad Cochran R
5. Trent Lott R

MISSOURI

SENATORS
Thomas F. Eagleton D   John C. Danforth R
REPRESENTATIVES
1. William (Bill) Clay D
2. Robert A. Young D
3. Richard A. Gephardt D
4. Ike Skelton D
5. Richard Bolling D
6. E. Thomas Coleman R
7. Gene Taylor R
8. Richard H. Ichord D
9. Harold L. Volkmer D
10. Bill D. Burlison D

MONTANA

SENATORS
Lee Metcalf D   John Melcher D
REPRESENTATIVES
1. Max Baucus D   2. Ron Marlenee R

NEBRASKA

SENATORS
Carl T. Curtis R   Edward Zorinsky D
REPRESENTATIVES
1. Charles Thone R
2. John J. Cavanaugh D
3. Virginia Smith R

NEVADA

SENATORS
Howard W. Cannon D   Paul Laxalt R
REPRESENTATIVE
At large—Jim Santini D

285

NEW HAMPSHIRE

SENATORS
Thomas J. McIntyre D   John A. Durkin D
REPRESENTATIVES
1. Norman E. D'Amours D   2. James C. Cleveland R

NEW JERSEY

SENATORS
Clifford P. Case R   Harrison A. Williams, Jr. D
REPRESENTATIVES
1. James J. Florio D
2. William J. Hughes D
3. James J. Howard D
4. Frank Thompson, Jr. D
5. Millicent Fenwick R
6. Edwin B. Forsythe R
7. Andrew Maguire D
8. Robert A. Roe D
9. Harold C. Hollenbeck R
10. Peter W. Rodino, Jr. D
11. Joseph G. Minish D
12. Matthew J. Rinaldo R
13. Helen S. Meyner D
14. Joseph A. LeFante D
15. Edward J. Patten D

NEW MEXICO

SENATORS
Pete V. Domenici R   Harrison H. Schmitt R
REPRESENTATIVES
1. Manuel Lujan, Jr. R   2. Harold Runnels D

NEW YORK

SENATORS
Jacob K. Javits R   Daniel P. Moynihan D
REPRESENTATIVES
1. Otis G. Pike D
2. Thomas J. Downey D
3. Jerome A. Ambro D
4. Norman F. Lent R
5. John W. Wydler R
6. Lester L. Wolff D
7. Joseph P. Addabbo D
8. Benjamin S. Rosenthal D
9. James J. Delaney D
10. Mario Biaggi D
11. James H. Scheuer D
12. Shirley Chisholm D
13. Stephen J. Solarz D
14. Frederick W. Richmond D
15. Leo C. Zeferetti D
16. Elizabeth Holtzman D
17. John M. Murphy D
18. Edward I. Koch D
19. Charles B. Rangel D
20. Ted Weiss D
21. Herman Badillo D
22. Jonathan B. Bingham D
23. Bruce F. Caputo R
24. Richard L. Ottinger D
25. Hamilton Fish, Jr. R
26. Benjamin A. Gilman R
27. Matthew F. McHugh D
28. Samuel S. Stratton D
29. Edward W. Pattison D
30. Robert C. McEwen R
31. Donald J. Mitchell R
32. James M. Hanley D
33. William F. Walsh R
34. Frank Horton R
35. Barber B. Conable, Jr. R
36. John J. LaFalce D
37. Henry J. Nowak D
38. Jack Kemp R
39. Stanley N. Lundine D

NORTH CAROLINA

SENATORS
Jesse A. Helms R   Robert Morgan D
REPRESENTATIVES
1. Walter B. Jones D
2. L. H. Fountain D
3. Charles O. Whitley, Sr. D
4. Ike F. Andrews D
5. Stephen L. Neal D
6. Richardson Preyer D
7. Charles Rose D
8. W. G. (Bill) Hefner D
9. James G. Martin R
10. James T. Broyhill R
11. V. Lamar Gudger D

NORTH DAKOTA

SENATORS
Milton R. Young R   Quentin N. Burdick D
REPRESENTATIVE
At large—Mark Andrews R

OHIO

SENATORS
John Glenn D   Howard M. Metzenbaum D
REPRESENTATIVES
1. Willis D. Gradison, Jr. R
2. Thomas A. Luken D
3. Charles W. Whalen, Jr. R
4. Tennyson Guyer R
5. Delbert L. Latta R
6. William H. Harsha R
7. Clarence J. Brown R
8. Thomas N. Kindness R
9. Thomas L. Ashley D
10. Clarence E. Miller R
11. J. William Stanton R
12. Samuel L. Devine R
13. Donald J. Pease D
14. John F. Seiberling D
15. Chalmers P. Wylie R
16. Ralph S. Regula R
17. John M. Ashbrook R
18. Douglas Applegate D
19. Charles J. Carney D
20. Mary Rose Oakar D
21. Louis Stokes D
22. Charies A. Vanik D
23. Ronald M. Mottl D

OKLAHOMA

SENATORS
Henry L. Bellmon R   Dewey F. Bartlett R
REPRESENTATIVES
1. James R. Jones D
2. Ted Risenhoover D
3. Wesley W. Watkins D
4. Tom Steed D
5. Mickey Edwards R
6. Glenn English D

OREGON

SENATORS
Mark O. Hatfield R   Bob Packwood R
REPRESENTATIVES
1. Les AuCoin D
2. Al Ullman D
3. Robert Duncan D
4. James Weaver D

PENNSYLVANIA

SENATORS
Richard S. Schweiker R   H. John Heinz 3d R
REPRESENTATIVES
1. Michael O. Myers D
2. Robert N. C. Nix D
3. Raymond F. Lederer D
4. Joshua Eilberg D
5. Richard T. Schulze R
6. Gus Yatron D
7. Robert W. Edgar D
8. Peter H. Kostmayer D
9. E. G. (Bud) Shuster R
10. Joseph M. McDade R
11. Daniel J. Flood D
12. John P. Murtha D
13. Lawrence Coughlin R
14. William S. Moorhead D
15. Fred B. Rooney D
16. Robert S. Walker R
17. Allen E. Ertel D
18. Doug Walgren D
19. William F. Goodling R
20. Joseph M. Gaydos D
21. John H. Dent D
22. Austin J. Murphy D
23. Joseph S. Ammerman D
24. Marc L. Marks R
25. Gary A. Myers R

RHODE ISLAND

SENATORS
Claiborne Pell D   John H. Chafee R
REPRESENTATIVES
1. Fernand J. St Germain D   2. Edward P. Beard D

SOUTH CAROLINA

SENATORS
Strom Thurmond R   Ernest F. Hollings D
REPRESENTATIVES
1. Mendel J. Davis D
2. Floyd Spence R
3. Butler Derrick D
4. James R. Mann D
5. Kenneth L. Holland D
6. John W. Jenrette, Jr. D

SOUTH DAKOTA

SENATORS
George McGovern D   James Abourezk D
REPRESENTATIVES
1. Larry Pressler R   2. James Abdnor R

TENNESSEE

SENATORS
Howard H. Baker, Jr. R   James R. Sasser D
REPRESENTATIVES
1. James H. Quillen R
2. John J. Duncan R
3. Marilyn Lloyd D
4. Albert A. Gore, Jr. D
5. Clifford R. Allen D
6. Robin L. Beard R
7. Ed Jones D
8. Harold E. Ford D

TEXAS

SENATORS
John G. Tower R   Lloyd M. Bentsen D
REPRESENTATIVES
1. Sam B. Hall, Jr. D
2. Charles Wilson D
3. James M. Collins R
4. Ray Roberts D
5. James A. Mattox D
6. Olin E. Teague D
7. Bill Archer R
8. Bob Eckhardt D
9. Jack Brooks D
10. J. J. (Jake) Pickle D
11. W. R. Poage D
12. James C. Wright, Jr. D
13. Jack Hightower D
14. John Young D
15. E (Kika) de la Garza D
16. Richard C. White D
17. Omar Burleson D
18. Barbara Jordan D
19. George H. Mahon D
20. Henry B. Gonzalez D
21. Robert (Bob) Krueger D
22. Robert A. Gammage D
23. Abraham Kazen, Jr. D
24. Dale Milford D

UTAH

SENATORS
Jake Garn R   Orrin G. Hatch R
REPRESENTATIVES
1. K. Gunn McKay D   2. David D. Marriott R

VERMONT

SENATORS
Robert T. Stafford R   Patrick J. Leahy D
REPRESENTATIVE
At large—James M. Jeffords R

VIRGINIA

SENATORS
Harry F. Byrd, Jr. I   William Lloyd Scott R
REPRESENTATIVES
1. Paul S. Trible, Jr. R
2. G. William Whitehurst R
3. David E. Satterfield 3d D
4. Robert W. Daniel, Jr. R
5. W. C. (Dan) Daniel D
6. M. Caldwell Butler R
7. J. Kenneth Robinson R
8. Herbert E. Harris 2d D
9. William C. Wampler R
10. Joseph L. Fisher D

WASHINGTON

SENATORS
Warren G. Magnuson D   Henry M. Jackson D
REPRESENTATIVES
1. Joel Pritchard R
2. Lloyd Meeds D
3. Don Bonker D
4. Mike McCormack D
5. Thomas S. Foley D
6. Norman D. Dicks D
7. [Vacant][5]

WEST VIRGINIA

SENATORS
Jennings Randolph D   Robert C. Byrd D
REPRESENTATIVES
1. Robert H. Mollohan D
2. Harley O. Staggers D
3. John Slack D
4. Nick J. Rahall 2d D

WISCONSIN

SENATORS
William Proxmire D   Gaylord Nelson D
REPRESENTATIVES
1. Les Aspin D
2. Robert W. Kastenmeier D
3. Alvin Baldus D
4. Clement J. Zablocki D
5. Henry S. Reuss D
6. William A. Steiger R
7. David R. Obey D
8. Robert J. Cornell D
9. Robert W. Kasten, Jr. R

WYOMING

SENATORS
Clifford P. Hansen R   Malcolm Wallop R
REPRESENTATIVE
At large—Teno Roncalio D

DISTRICT OF COLUMBIA

DELEGATE
Walter E. Fauntroy D

GUAM

DELEGATE
Antonio Borja Won Pat D

PUERTO RICO

RESIDENT COMMISSIONER
Baltasar Corrada D

VIRGIN ISLANDS

DELEGATE
Ron de Lugo D

CLASSIFICATION

SENATE

Democrats 61
Republicans 38
Independent 1
    Total 100

HOUSE

Democrats 289
Republicans 144
Vacant 2
    Total 435

CHANGES IN CONGRESS

[1] *Arkansas, Senate*
   John L. McClellan died Nov. 28, 1977 (Democrat)

[2] *Georgia, 5th District, House*
   Andrew Young resigned Jan. 29, 1977, to become United States
   ambassador to the United Nations (Democrat)
   Wyche Fowler, Jr., sworn in April 6, 1977 (Democrat)

[3] *Louisiana, 1st District, House*
   Richard A. Tonry resigned May 4, 1977 (Democrat)
   Bob Livingston sworn in Sept. 7, 1977 (Republican)

[4] *Minnesota, 7th District, House*
   Bob Bergland resigned Jan. 22, 1977, to become secretary of
   agriculture (Democrat)
   Arlan Stangeland sworn in March 1, 1977 (Republican)

[5] *Washington, 7th District, House*
   Brock Adams resigned Jan. 22, 1977, to become secretary of
   transportation (Democrat)
   John E. Cunningham sworn in May 23, 1977 (Republican)

JUDICIARY
Supreme Court of the United States

CHIEF JUSTICE

	HOME STATE	DATE OF BIRTH	DATE TOOK COURT SEAT	APPOINTED BY
Warren E. Burger	Minn.	Sept. 17, 1907	Oct. 6, 1969	Nixon

Associate Justices

	HOME STATE	DATE OF BIRTH	DATE TOOK COURT SEAT	APPOINTED BY
William J. Brennan	N.J.	April 25, 1906	Oct. 16, 1956	Eisenhower
Potter Stewart	Ohio	Jan. 23, 1915	Oct. 14, 1958	Eisenhower
Byron R. White	Colo.	June 8, 1917	April 16, 1962	Kennedy
Thurgood Marshall	Md.	July 2, 1908	Oct. 2, 1967	Johnson
Harry A. Blackmun	Ill.	Nov. 12, 1908	June 9, 1970	Nixon
Lewis F. Powell, Jr.	Va.	Sept. 19, 1907	Jan. 7, 1972	Nixon
William H. Rehnquist	Ariz.	Oct. 1, 1924	Jan. 7, 1972	Nixon
John Paul Stevens	Ill.	April 20, 1920	Jan. 12, 1976	Ford

ECONOMICS

EMPLOYMENT

Year	Civilian Labor Force	Un-employed	Percent-age Unem-ployed
1929	49,180,000	1,550,000	3.2
1933	51,590,000	12,830,000	24.9
1940	55,640,000	8,120,000	14.6
1944	54,630,000	670,000	1.2
1960	70,612,000	3,931,000	5.6
1961	71,603,000	4,806,000	6.7
1962	71,854,000	4,007,000	5.6
1963	72,975,000	4,166,000	5.7
1964	74,233,000	3,876,000	5.2
1965	75,635,000	3,456,000	4.6
1966	75,770,000	2,875,000	3.8
1967	77,348,000	2,975,000	3.8
1968	78,737,000	2,816,000	3.6
1969	80,733,000	2,831,000	3.5
1970	82,715,000	4,088,000	4.9
1971	84,113,000	4,994,000	5.9
1972	83,542,000	4,840,000	5.6
1973	88,716,000	4,306,000	4.9
1974	91,011,000	5,076,000	5.6
1975	92,618,000	7,830,000	8.5
1976	94,773,000	7,288,000	7.7

1977 Employment — Seasonally Adjusted

Month	Civilian Labor Force (000)	Un-employed (000)	Percent-age of Unem-ployed
Jan.	95,516	6,958	7.3
Feb.	96,145	7,183	7.5
Mar.	96,539	7,064	7.3
Apr.	96,760	6,737	7.0
May	97,158	6,750	6.9
June	97,641	6,962	7.1
July	97,305	6,744	6.9
Aug.	97,697	6,926	7.1
Sept.	97,868	6,773	6.9
Oct.	98,102	6,872	7.0
Nov.	98,998	6,818	6.9
Totals from 1976 Annual Average	94,773	7,288	7.7

Source: Bureau of Labor Statistics
Department of Labor

CONSUMER PRICE INDEX - 1977

Year	All Items	Food	Apparel	Housing	Rent	Medical Care	Transportation
1913	34.5	33.6	33.8	—	55.7	—	—
1920	69.8	70.8	98.0	—	72.9	—	—
1929	59.7	55.6	56.2	—	85.4	—	—
1933	45.1	35.3	42.8	—	60.8	—	—
1940	48.8	40.5	49.6	—	63.2	—	—
1945	62.7	58.4	71.2	—	66.1	—	—
1950	83.8	85.8	91.5	83.2	79.1	73.4	79.0
1960	103.1	101.4	102.1	103.1	103.1	108.1	103.8
1961	104.2	102.6	102.8	103.9	104.4	111.3	105.0
1962	105.4	103.6	103.2	104.8	105.7	114.2	107.2
1963	106.7	105.1	104.2	106.0	106.8	117.0	107.8
1964	108.1	106.4	105.7	107.2	107.8	119.4	109.3
1965	109.9	108.8	106.8	108.5	109.8	122.3	111.6
1966	113.1	114.2	109.6	111.1	110.4	127.7	112.7
1967	116.3	115.2	114.0	114.3	112.4	136.7	115.9
1968	121.2	119.3	120.1	119.1	115.1	145.0	119.6
1969	127.7	125.5	127.1	126.7	118.8	155.0	124.2
1970	135.3	132.4	132.2	135.9	123.7	164.9	130.6
1971	121.3	118.4	119.8	124.3	115.2	128.4	118.6
1972	122.9	123.5	122.3	129.2	119.2	132.5	119.9
1973	133.1	141.4	126.8	135.0	124.3	137.7	123.8
1974	147.7	161.7	136.2	150.6	130.6	150.5	137.7
1975	161.2	175.4	142.3	166.8	137.3	168.6	150.6

1977 by Month	All Items	Food	Apparel Upkeep	Housing	Rent	Medical Care	Transportation
Jan.	175.3	183.4	150.0	183.1	149.5	194.1	172.2
Feb.	177.1	187.7	150.8	184.3	150.2	195.8	173.2
Mar.	178.2	188.6	151.7	185.5	150.8	197.6	174.7
Apr.	179.6	190.9	152.3	186.7	151.6	199.1	176.7
May	180.6	191.7	153.4	187.6	152.2	200.5	178.1
June	181.8	193.6	153.9	189.0	152.9	201.8	179.1
July	182.6	194.6	153.4	190.5	153.6	203.5	179.2
Aug.	183.3	195.2	154.8	191.4	154.4	204.9	178.8
Sept.	184.0	194.5	156.2	192.7	155.3	206.3	178.4
Oct.	184.5	194.4	157.2	193.6	156.1	207.2	178.6
Nov.	185.4	195.6	158.5	194.6	157.0	208.1	178.7
Totals from 1976	170.5	180.8	147.6	177.2	144.7	184.7	165.5

1947/49 = 100% was the base from Jan. 1953 to Dec. 1961
1957/59 = 100% was the base from Jan. 1962 to Dec. 1970
1967 = 100% was the base from Jan. 1971 to the Present.

Source: Bureau of Labor Statistics
Department of Labor

GROSS NATIONAL PRODUCT

(The total output of goods and services in the United States measured in terms of expenditures by which they were acquired.)

Year		Year	
1960	$ 503,700,000,000	1969	931,400,000,000
1961	520,100,000,000	1970	974,100,000,000
1962	560,300,000,000	1971	1,050,400,000,000
1963	590,500,000,000	1972	1,155,200,000,000
1964	632,400,000,000	1973	1,294,900,000,000
1965	683,900,000,000	1974	1,397,400,000,000
1966	743,300,000,000	1975	1,516,000,000,000
1967	789,663,000,000	1976	1,706,500,000,000
1968	865,700,000,000	1977	*1.889.900,000,000

Source: Department of Commerce

* Unofficial Associated
Press estimate based
on Commerce Dept. figures

U.S. TOTAL GROSS PUBLIC DEBT

	Total	Per Capita
1960	$ 286,331,000,000	$ 1,585
1961	288,971,000,000	1,573
1962	298,201,000,000	1,598
1963	305,860,000,000	1,615
1964	311,713,000,000	1,622
1965	317,274,000,000	1,631
1966	319,907,000,000	1,625
1967	326,221,000,000	1,638
1968	347,578,000,000	1,727
1969	353,720,000,000	1,741
1970	370,919,000,000	1,811
1971	398,129,000,000	1,922
1972	427,260,000,000	2,045
1973	458,142,000,000	2,177
1974	475,059,815,732	2,241
1975	533,189,000,000	2,496
1976 (June 30)	620,433,000,000	2,877
* 1977 (Sept. 30)	698,840,000,000	3,216

Source: Department of the Treasury

*In 1977 the fiscal year changed to a Oct. 1/Sept. 30 basis.

PER CAPITA PERSONAL INCOME

1960	$ 2,215
1961	2,264
1962	2,368
1963	2,455
1964	2,586
1965	2,765
1966	2,978
1967	3,159
1968	3,421
1969	3,687
1970	3,921
1971	4,156
1972	4,492
1973	5,023
1974	5,448
1975	5,868
1976	6,425
1977	* 7,079

Source: Commerce Department

*Unofficial Associated Press estimate based on Commerce Dept. figures

STATES OF THE UNION

State	Rank in Population*	Population*	Capital	Population of Capital*	Largest City	Population of Largest City*
Alabama	21	3,539,000	Montgomery	133,386	Birmingham	300,910
Alaska	50	330,000	Juneau	6,050	Anchorage	48,029
Arizona	33	2,058,000	Phoenix	581,562	Phoenix	581,562
Arkansas	32	2,037,000	Little Rock	132,483	Little Rock	132,483
California	1	20,601,000	Sacramento	257,105	Los Angeles	2,816,061
Colorado	30	2,437,000	Denver	511,900	Denver	511,900
Connecticut	24	3,076,000	Hartford	158,017	Hartford	158,017
Delaware	46	576,000	Dover	17,488	Wilmington	80,386
Florida	9	7,678,000	Tallahassee	72,624	Jacksonville	535,300
Georgia	15	4,786,000	Atlanta	495,039	Atlanta	495,039
Hawaii	40	832,000	Honolulu	324,871	Honolulu	324,871
Idaho	42	770,000	Boise	74,990	Boise	74,990
Illinois	5	11,236,000	Springfield	91,753	Chicago	3,369,357
Indiana	11	5,316,000	Indianapolis	746,428	Indianapolis	746,428
Iowa	25	2,904,000	Des Moines	201,404	Des Moines	201,404
Kansas	28	2,279,000	Topeka	125,011	Wichita	276,554
Kentucky	23	3,342,000	Frankfort	21,902	Louisville	361,706
Louisiana	20	3,764,000	Baton Rouge	165,963	New Orleans	589,000
Maine	38	1,028,000	Augusta	21,945	Portland	65,116
Maryland	18	4,070,000	Annapolis	30,095	Baltimore	896,900
Massachusetts	10	5,818,000	Boston	641,071	Boston	641,071
Michigan	7	9,044,000	Lansing	131,546	Detroit	1,511,482
Minnesota	19	3,897,000	St. Paul	309,980	Minneapolis	434,400
Mississippi	29	2,281,000	Jackson	153,968	Jackson	153,968
Missouri	13	4,757,000	Jefferson City	32,407	St. Louis	586,400
Montana	43	721,000	Helena	22,730	Billings	61,581
Nebraska	35	1,542,000	Lincoln	149,418	Omaha	347,328
Nevada	47	548,000	Carson City	15,264	Las Vegas	125,787
New Hampshire	41	791,000	Concord	30,022	Manchester	87,754
New Jersey	8	7,361,000	Trenton	104,638	Newark	381,930
New Mexico	37	1,106,000	Santa Fe	41,167	Albuquerque	243,751
New York	2	18,265,000	Albany	115,781	New York	7,847,100
North Carolina	12	5,273,000	Raleigh	123,793	Charlotte	241,178
North Dakota	45	640,000	Bismark	34,703	Fargo	53,365
Ohio	6	10,731,000	Columbus	539,677	Cleveland	750,903
Oklahoma	27	2,663,000	Oklahoma City	368,164	Oklahoma City	368,164
Oregon	31	2,225,000	Salem	68,296	Portland	379,967
Pennsylvania	3	11,902,000	Harrisburg	68,061	Philadelphia	1,916,000
Rhode Island	39	973,000	Providence	179,213	Providence	179,213
South Carolina	26	2,726,000	Columbia	113,542	Columbia	113,542
South Dakota	40	685,000	Pierre	9,732	Sioux Falls	72,488
Tennessee	17	4,126,000	Nashville	447,877	Memphis	623,530
Texas	4	11,704,000	Austin	251,808	Houston	1,232,802
Utah	36	1,157,000	Salt Lake City	175,885	Salt Lake City	175,885
Vermont	48	464,000	Montpelier	8,609	Burlington	38,633
Virginia	14	4,811,000	Richmond	236,500	Norfolk	283,000
Washington	22	3,429,000	Olympia	23,296	Seattle	530,831
West Virginia	30	1,794,000	Charleston	71,505	Huntington	74,315
Wisconsin	16	4,569,000	Madison	171,769	Milwaukee	717,099
Wyoming	49	353,000	Cheyenne	40,914	Cheyenne	40,914
District Of Columbia		746,000				
Commonwealth Of Puerto Rico		2,712,033	San Juan	452,749	San Juan	452,749

*Source of population totals: Estimate Bureau of the Census

UNITED NATIONS

The Secretariat

SECRETARY-GENERAL

Kurt Waldheim	Austria	

UNDER-SECRETARIES-GENERAL

Roberto E. Guyer	Argentina	Under-Secretary-General for Special Political Affairs
Brian E. Urquhart	United Kingdom	Under-Secretary-General for Special Political Affairs
William B. Buffum	United States	Under-Secretary-General for Political and General Assembly Affairs
C. V. Narasimhan	India	Under-Secretary-General for Inter-Agency Affairs and Co-ordination
Erik Suy	Belgium	Under-Secretary-General, The Legal Counsel
Arkady N. Shevchenko	U.S.S.R.	Under-Secretary-General for Political and Security Council Affairs
Tang Ming-chao	China	Under-Secretary-General for Political Affairs, Trusteeship and Decolonization
Gabriel van Laethem	France	Under-Secretary-General for Economic and Social Affairs
Issoufou Saidou Djermakoye	Niger	Under-Secretary-General, Commissioner for Technical Co-operation
George F. Davidson	Canada	Under-Secretary-General for Administration and Management
Bohdan Lewandowski	Poland	Under-Secretary-General for Conference Services and Special Assignments
Luigi Cottafavi	Italy	Under-Secretary-General, Director-General of the United Nations Office at Geneva
Faruk N. Berkel	Turkey	United Nations Disaster Relief Co-ordinator (Geneva)

Rafael Salas	Philippines	Executive Director of the United Nations Fund for Population Activities (UNFPA)
Bradford Morse	United States	Administrator of the United Nations Development Program (UNDP)
Indraprasad G. Patel	India	Deputy Administrator of the United Nations Development Program
Davidson Nicol	Sierra Leone	Executive Director of the United Nations Institute for Training and Research
Henry R. Labouisse	United States	Executive Director, United Nations Children's Fund (UNICEF)
Sir Robert Jackson	Australia	Under-Secretary-General, Co-ordinator of United Nations Assistance to Cape Verde, Indo-China and Zambia
Gamani Corea	Sri Lanka	Secretary-General of the United Nations Conference on Trade and Development (UNCTAD, Geneva)
Abd-El Rahman Khane	Algeria	Executive Director, United Nations Industrial Development Organization (UNIDO, Vienna)
Mostafa Kamal Tolba	Egypt	Executive Director, United Nations Environment Program (UNEP, Nairobi)
Lt. Gen. Ensio Siilasvuo	Finland	Chief Co-Ordinator, United Nations Peace-Keeping Missions in the Middle East
Poul Hartling	Denmark	United Nations High Commissioner for Refugees (Geneva)
Raul A. Quijane	Argentina	Chairman, International Civil Service Commission
James M. Hester	United States	Under-Secretary-General, Special Representative of the Secretary-General to the Third United Nations Conference on the Law of the Sea

GENERAL ASSEMBLY

	Year of Admission	Permanent Representative
Afghanistan	1946	Vacant
Albania	1955	Abdi Baleta
Algeria	1962	Vacant
Angola	1976	Elisio de Figueiredo
Argentina	1945	Enrique Jorge Ros
Australia	1945	Ralph L. Harry
Austria	1955	Peter Jankowitsch
Bahamas	1973	Livingston Basil Johnson
Bahrain	1971	Dr. Salman Mohamed Al Saffar
Bangladesh	1974	Khwaja Mohammed Kaiser
Barbados	1966	Dr. Donald George Blackman
Belgium	1945	Andre Ernemann
Benin	1960	Thomas S. Boya
Bhutan	1971	Dago Tshering
Bolivia	1945	Vacant
Botswana	1966	Dr. Thomas Tlou
Brazil	1945	Sergio Correa da Costa
Bulgaria	1955	Alexander Yankov
Burma	1948	U Maung Maung Gee
Burundi	1962	Artemon Simbananiye
Byelorussian Soviet Socialist Republic	1945	Leonid Aleksandrovich Delguchits
Canada	1945	William Hickson Barton
Cape Verde	1975	Dr. Amaro Alexandre de Luz
Central African Empire	1960	Jean-Arthur Bandio

Country	Year of Admission	Permanent Representative	Country	Year of Admission	Permanent Representative
Chad	1960	Beadengar Dessande	Mauritius	1968	Radha Krishna Ramphul
Chile	1945	Sergio Diez Urzua	Mexico	1945	Roberto de Rosenzweig-Diaz
China	1971	Chen Chu	Mongolia	1961	Tsevegzhavyn Puntsagnorov
Colombia	1945	Jose Fernando Botero	Morocco	1955	Vacant
Comoros	1975	None	Mozambique	1975	Jose Carlos Lobo
Congo	1960	Nicolas Mondjo	Nepal	1955	Shailendra Kumar Upadhyay
Costa Rica	1945	Fernando Salazar	Netherlands	1945	Dr. Johan Kaufmann
Cuba	1945	Dr. Ricardo Alarcon de Quesada	New Zealand	1945	Malcolm J. C. Templeton
Cyprus	1960	Zenon Rossides	Nicaragua	1945	Dr. Guillermo Sevilla-Sacasa
Czechoslovakia	1945	Dr. Ilja Hulinsky	Niger	1960	Jean Poisson
Democratic Kampuchea	1955	None	Nigeria	1960	Leslie O. Harriman
Democratic Yemen	1967	Abdalla Saleh Ashtal	Norway	1945	Ole Algard
Denmark	1945	Wilhelm Ulrichsen	Oman	1971	Mahoud Aboul-Nasr
Djibouti	1977	None	Pakistan	1947	Iqbal A. Akhund
Dominican Republic	1945	Dr. Alfonso Moreno-Martinez	Panama	1945	Dr. Jorge Enrique Illueca
Ecuador	1945	Dr. Miguel A. Albornoz	Papua New Guinea	1975	Paulias Nguna Matane
Egypt	1945	Dr. Ahmed Esmat Abdel Meguid	Paraguay	1945	Dr. Francisco Barreiro
El Salvador	1945	Miguel Rafael Urquia	Peru	1945	Dr. Carlos Alzamora
Equatorial Guinea	1968	Evuna Owono Asangono	Philippines	1945	Vacant
Ethiopia	1945	Mohamed Hamid Ibrahim	Poland	1945	Henryk Jaroszek
Fiji	1970	Berenado Vunibobo	Portugal	1955	Vasco Futscher Pereira
Finland	1955	Ilkka Olavi Pastinen	Qatar	1971	Jasim Yousif Jamal
France	1945	Jacques Leprette	Romania	1955	Ion Datcu
Gabon	1960	Leon N'Dong	Rwanda	1962	Ignace Karuhije
Gambia	1965	None	Samoa	1976	Maiava Iulai Toma
German Democratic Republic	1973	Peter Florin	Sao Tome and Principe	1975	None
Germany, Federal Republic of	1973	Baron Fuediger von Wechmar	Saudi Arabia	1945	Vacant
			Senegal	1960	Medoune Fall
Ghana	1957	Frank Edmund Boaten	Seychelles	1976	None
Greece	1945	George Popoulias	Sierra Leone	1961	Mrs. Shirley Yema Gbujama
Grenada	1974	Franklin O'Brien Dolland	Singapore	1965	Tommy Thong Bee Koh
Guatemala	1945	Julio Asensio-Wunderlich	Somalia	1960	Abdirizak Haji Hussein
Guinea	1968	Sekou Mouke Yansane	South Africa	1945	Vacant
Guinea-Bissau	1974	Gil Fernandes	Spain	1955	Jaime de Pinies
Haiti	1945	Serge E. Charles	Sri Lanka	1955	Hamilton Shirley Amerasinghe
Honduras	1945	Mario Carias	Sudan	1955	Mustafa Medani
Hungary	1955	Imre Hollai	Surinam	1975	Henricus A. F. Heidweiller
Iceland	1946	Tomas A. Tomasson	Swaziland	1968	N. M. Malinga
India	1945	Rikhi Jaipal	Sweden	1945	Anders I. Thunborg
Indonesia	1950	Chaidir Anwar Sani	Syrian Arab Republic	1945	Mowaffak Allaf
Iran	1945	Fereydoun Noveyda	Thailand	1946	Dr. Pracha Guna-Kasem
Iraq	1945	Mohammed Said K. Al-Sahhaf	Togo	1960	Akanyi-Awunyo Kodjovi
Ireland	1945	Dr. Eamonn Kennedy	Trinidad and Tobago	1962	Frank Owen Abdulah
Israel	1949	Chaim Herzog	Tunisia	1956	Mahmoud Mestiri
Italy	1955	Piero Vinci	Turkey	1945	Ilter Turkmen
Ivory Coast	1960	Amoakon E. Thiemele	Uganda	1962	Khalid Younis Kinene
Jamaica	1962	Donald O. Mills	Ukrainian Soviet Socialist Republic	1945	Vladimir Nikiphorovich Martynenko
Japan	1956	Isac Abe			
Jordan	1955	Dr. Hazem Nuseibeh	Union of Soviet Socialist Republics	1945	Oleg Aleksandrovich Troyanovsky
Kenya	1963	Charles Gatere Maina			
Kuwait	1963	Abdalla Yaccoub Bishara	United Arab Emirates	1971	Dr. Ali Humaidan
Lao People's Democratic Republic	1955	Vacant	United Kingdom of Great Britain and Northern Ireland	1945	Ivor Richard
Lebanon	1945	Ghassan Tueni			
Lesotho	1966	Mookvi V. Molapo	United Republic of Cameroon	1960	Ferdinand Leopold Oyono
Liberia	1945	David M. Thomas			
Libyan Arab People's Jamahariya	1955	Mansur Rashid Kikhia	United Republic of Tanzania	1961	Salim Ahmed Salim
Luxembourg	1945	Paul Peters	United States of America	1945	Andrew Young
Madagascar	1960	Blaise Rabetafika	Upper Volta	1960	Aisse Mensah
Malawi	1964	T. J. X. Muwamba	Uruguay	1945	Dr. Carlos Giambruno
Malaysia	1957	Tan Sri Zaiton Ibrahim	Venezuela	1945	Vacant
Maldives	1965	Fathulla Jameel	Viet Nam	1977	Dinh Ba Thi
Mali	1960	Mamadou Boubacar Kante	Yugoslavia	1945	Jaksa Petric
Malta	1964	Vacant	Zaire	1960	Kabeya wa Mukeba
Mauritania	1961	Moulaye El Hassen	Zambia	1964	Miss Gwendoline C. Konie

SPORTS

BASEBALL

FINAL MAJOR LEAGUE STANDINGS

National League
Eastern Division

	W	L	Pct.	G.B.
Philadelphia	100	61	.623	—
Pittsburgh	96	66	.593	5
St. Louis	83	79	.512	18
Chicago	81	81	.500	20
Montreal	75	87	.463	26
New York	64	98	.395	37

Western Division

	W	L	Pct.	G.B.
Los Angeles	98	64	.605	—
Cincinnati	88	74	.543	10
Houston	81	81	.500	17
San Francisco	75	87	.463	23
San Diego	69	93	.426	29
Atlanta	61	101	.377	37

American League
Eastern Division

	W	L	Pct.	G.B.
New York	100	62	.617	—
Baltimore	97	64	.602	2½
Boston	97	64	.602	2½
Detroit	74	88	.457	26
Cleveland	71	90	.441	28½
Milwaukee	67	95	.414	33
Toronto	54	107	.335	45½

Western Division

	W	L	Pct.	G.B.
Kansas City	102	60	.630	—
Texas	94	68	.580	8
Chicago	90	72	.556	12
Minnesota	84	77	.522	17½
California	74	88	.457	28
Seattle	64	98	.395	38
Oakland	63	98	.391	38½

Los Angeles defeated Philadelphia 3 games to 1 to win the National League Championship

New York defeated Kansas City 3 games to 2 to win the American League Championship

New York defeated Los Angeles 4 games to 2 in the World Series.

PRO FOOTBALL

NATIONAL FOOTBALL LEAGUE
FINAL STANDINGS

American Conference
Eastern Division

	W	L	T	Pct.	PF	PA
Baltimore	10	4	0	.714	295	221
Miami	10	4	0	.714	313	197
New England	9	5	0	.643	278	217
N.Y. Jets	3	11	0	.214	191	300
Buffalo	3	11	0	.214	160	313

Central Division

	W	L	T	Pct.	PF	PA
Pittsburgh	9	5	0	.643	283	243
Houston	8	6	0	.571	299	230
Cincinnati	8	6	0	.571	238	235
Cleveland	6	8	0	.429	269	267

Western Division

	W	L	T	Pct.	PF	PA
Denver	12	2	0	.857	274	150
Oakland	11	3	0	.786	351	230
San Diego	7	7	0	.500	222	205
Seattle	5	9	0	.357	282	373
Kansas City	2	12	0	.143	225	349

National Conference
Eastern Division

	W	L	T	Pct.	PF	PA
Dallas	12	2	0	.857	345	212
Washington	9	5	0	.643	196	189
St. Louis	7	7	0	.500	272	287
Philadelphia	5	9	0	.357	220	207
N.Y. Giants	5	9	0	.357	181	265

Central Division

	W	L	T	Pct.	PF	PA
Minnesota	9	5	0	.643	231	227
Chicago	9	5	0	.643	255	253
Detroit	6	8	0	.429	183	243
Green Bay	4	10	0	.286	134	219
Tampa Bay	2	12	0	.143	103	223

Western Division

	W	L	T	Pct.	PF	PA
Los Angeles	10	4	0	.714	302	146
Atlanta	7	7	0	.500	179	129
San Francisco	5	9	0	.357	220	262
New Orleans	3	11	0	.214	232	336

NFL PLAYOFFS

Semifinal Round

NFC—
Dallas 37, Chicago 7
Minnesota 14, Los Angeles 7

AFC—
Oakland 37, Baltimore 31
Denver 34, Pittsburgh 21

COLLEGE FOOTBALL

ALL-AMERICANS

Offense
TE—Ken MacAfee, Notre Dame
E—John Jefferson, Arizona State
E—Ozzie Newsome, Alabama
T—Dennis Baker, Wyoming
T—Chris Ward, Ohio State
G—Mark Donahue, Michigan
G—Leotis Harris, Arkansas
C—Tom Brzoza, Pittsburgh
QB—Doug Williams, Grambling
RB—Earl Campbell, Texas
RB—Terry Miller, Oklahoma State

Defense
E—Ross Browner, Notre Dame
E—Art Still, Kentucky
T—Dee Hardison, North Carolina
T—Brad Shearer, Texas
G—Randy Sidler, Penn State
LB—George Cumby, Oklahoma
LB—Jerry Robinson, UCLA
LB—Mike Woods, Cincinnati
DB—Zac Henderson, Oklahoma
DB—Bob Jury, Pittsburgh
DB—Dennis Thurman, Southern California

COLLEGE FOOTBALL CONFERENCE STANDINGS

IVY LEAGUE—Yale
SOUTHEASTERN—Alabama
ATLANTIC COAST—North Carolina
SOUTHERN—VMI, Tenn.-Chattanooga
BIG TEN—Michigan, Ohio State
PACIFIC 8—Washington
SOUTHWEST—Texas
THE VALLEY—West Texas State
BIG EIGHT—Oklahoma
BIG SKY—Boise State
MID-AMERICAN—Miami, Ohio
WESTERN ATHLETIC—Arizona State, Brigham Young
PACIFIC COAST ATHLETIC—Fresno State
OHIO VALLEY—Austin Peay
YANKEE—Massachusetts

BOWL GAMES

Rose Bowl—Southern Cal 14, Michigan 6
Orange Bowl—Ohio State 27, Colorado 10
Cotton Bowl—Houston 30, Maryland 21
Sugar Bowl—Pittsburgh 27, Georgia 3

COLLEGE BASKETBALL

MAJOR CONFERENCE CHAMPIONS

IVY LEAGUE—Princeton
EASTERN COLLEGIATE (EAST)—Rutgers
EASTERN COLLEGIATE (WEST)—West Virginia
EAST COAST (EAST)—Hofstra
EAST COAST (WEST)—Lafayette
ATLANTIC COAST—North Carolina
SOUTHEASTERN—Kentucky, Tennessee (tie)
SOUTHERN—VMI, Furman (tie)
OHIO VALLEY—Austin Peay
BIG TEN—Michigan
MID-AMERICAN—Miami, Ohio, Central Michigan (tie)
OHIO—Muskingum
INDIANA COLLEGIATE—Evansville
BIG EIGHT—Kansas State
MISSOURI VALLEY—Southern Illinois, New Mexico State (tie)
SOUTHWEST—Arkansas
SOUTHWESTERN—Texas Southern
SOUTHLAND—Southwestern Louisiana
METRO 7—Louisville
WESTERN ATHLETIC—Utah
BIG SKY—Idaho State
PACIFIC-8—UCLA
WEST COAST ATHLETIC—San Francisco
PACIFIC COAST ATHLETIC—Long Beach State, San Diego State (tie)
FAR WESTERN—Hayward State, California-Davis (tie)
NCAA CHAMPION—Marquette
NIT CHAMPION—St. Bonaventure

ALL-AMERICANS

Phil Ford, junior, North Carolina
Rickey Green, senior, Michigan
Kent Benson, senior, Indiana
Marques Johnson, senior, UCLA
Bernard King, junior, Tennessee

LEADING SCORERS

PLAYER, COLLEGE	G	FG	FT	Pts.	Avg.
Williams, Portland State	26	417	176	1010	38.8
Roberts, Oral Roberts	28	402	147	951	34.0
Bird, Indiana State	28	375	168	918	32.8
Birdsong, Houston	36	452	186	1090	30.3
Laurel, Hofstra	30	355	198	908	30.3
Natt, NE Louisiana	27	307	168	782	29.0
McConathy, Louisiana Tech	26	258	200	716	27.5
Phegley, Bradley	27	272	195	739	27.4
Reynolds, NW Louisiana	26	270	146	686	26.4
Hanson, Connecticut	27	253	196	702	26.0

RATINGS

1—Michigan
2—UCLA
3—Kentucky
4—Nevada-Las Vegas
5—North Carolina
6—Syracuse
7—Marquette
8—San Francisco
9—Wake Forest
10—Notre Dame

PRO BASKETBALL

NATIONAL BASKETBALL ASSOCIATION

Final Standings

EASTERN CONFERENCE
Atlantic Division

	W	L	Pct.	G.B.
Philadelphia	50	32	.610	—
Boston	44	38	.537	6
N.Y. Knicks	40	42	.488	10
Buffalo	30	52	.366	20
N.Y. Nets	22	60	.268	28

Central Division

	W	L	Pct.	G.B.
Houston	49	33	.598	—
Washington	48	34	.585	1
San Antonio	44	38	.537	5
Cleveland	43	39	.524	6
New Orleans	35	47	.427	14
Atlanta	31	51	.378	18

WESTERN CONFERENCE
Midwest Division

	W	L	Pct.	G.B.
Denver	50	32	.610	—
Detroit	44	38	.537	6
Chicago	44	38	.537	6
Kansas City	40	42	.488	10
Indiana	36	46	.439	14
Milwaukee	30	52	.366	20

Pacific Division

	W	L	Pct.	G.B.
Los Angeles	53	29	.646	—
Portland	49	33	.598	4
Golden State	46	36	.561	7
Seattle	40	42	.488	13
Phoenix	34	48	.415	19

PLAYOFFS

Eastern Division—
Boston defeated San Antonio 2 games to 0.
Washington defeated Cleveland 2 games to 1.
Philadelphia defeated Boston 4 games to 3.
Houston defeated Washington 4 games to 2.
Philadelphia defeated Houston 4 games to 2.

Western Division—
Golden State defeated Detroit 2 games to 1.
Portland defeated Chicago 2 games to 1.
Los Angeles defeated Golden State 4 games to 3.
Portland defeated Denver 4 games to 2.
Portland defeated Los Angeles 4 games to 0.

Championship—
Portland defeated Philadelphia 4 games to 2.

MOST VALUABLE PLAYER

Kareem Abdul-Jabbar, Los Angeles

ROOKIE OF THE YEAR

Adrian Dantley, Buffalo

FINAL SCORING LEADERS

	G.	F.	Pts.	Avg.
Maravich, New Orleans	886	501	2273	31.1
Knight, Indiana	831	413	2075	26.6
Abdul-Jabbar, L.A.	888	376	2152	26.2
Thompson, Denver	824	477	2125	25.9
McAdoo, Buff.-Knicks	740	381	1861	25.8
Lanier, Detroit	678	260	1616	25.3
Drew, Atlanta	689	412	1790	24.2
Hayes, Wash.	760	422	1942	23.7
Gervin, S.A.	726	443	1896	23.1
Issel, Denver	660	445	1765	22.3

TENNIS

WIMBLEDON CHAMPIONS

Singles, Men—Bjorn Borg
Singles, Women—Virginia Wade
Men's Doubles—Ross Case & Geoff Masters
Women's Doubles—Helen Cawley & JoAnn Russell

U.S. OPEN CHAMPIONS

Singles, Men—Guillermo Vilas
Singles, Women—Chris Evert
Men's Doubles—Frew McMillian & Bob Hewitt
Women's Doubles—Martina Navratilova & Betty Stove

U.S. CLAY COURT CHAMPIONS

Singles, Men—Manuel Orantes
Singles, Women—Laura Dupont
Men's Doubles—Jaime Fillol & Patrice Cornejo
Women's Doubles—Linky Boshoff & Ilana Klaus

U.S. NATIONAL INDOOR CHAMPIONS

Singles, Men—Bjorn Borg
Men's Doubles—Fred McNair & Sherwood Stewart

INTERNATIONAL TEAM CHAMPIONS

Davis Cup—Australia
Wightman Cup (Women)—US
Federation Cup (Women)—US

GOLF

US Open—Hubert Green
PGA—Lanny Wadkins
Masters—Tom Watson
US Amateur—John Fought
British Open—Tom Watson
NCAA Team—Houston
NCAA Individual—Scott Simpson
Women's Open—Hollis Stacey
Women's PGA—Chako Higuchi
Women's Amateur—Beth Daniel
Walker Cup-US

HOCKEY

NATIONAL HOCKEY LEAGUE

Final Standings

PRINCE OF WALES CONFERENCE
James Norris Division

	W	L	T	Pts.	GF	GA
Montreal	60	8	12	132	387	171
Los Angeles	34	31	15	83	271	241
Pittsburgh	34	33	13	81	240	252
Washington	24	42	14	62	221	307
Detroit	16	55	9	41	183	309

Charles F. Adams Division

Boston	49	23	8	106	312	240
Buffalo	48	24	8	104	301	220
Toronto	33	32	15	81	301	285
Cleveland	25	42	13	63	240	292

CLARENCE CAMPBELL CONFERENCE
Lester Patrick Division

Philadelphia	48	16	16	112	323	213
Islanders	47	21	12	106	288	193
Atlanta	34	34	12	80	264	265
Rangers	29	37	14	72	272	310

Conn Smythe Division

St. Louis	32	39	9	73	239	276
Minnesota	23	39	18	64	240	310
Chicago	26	43	11	63	240	298
Vancouver	25	42	13	63	235	294
Colorado	20	46	14	54	226	307

STANLEY CUP PLAYOFFS

Preliminary Rounds (Best-of-Three)—
Islanders defeated Chicago 2 games to 0
Buffalo defeated Minnesota 2 games to 0
Los Angeles defeated Atlanta 2 games to 1
Toronto defeated Pittsburgh 2 games to 1

Quarter-finals—
Montreal defeated St. Louis 4 games to 0
Philadelphia defeated Toronto 4 games to 2
Boston defeated Los Angeles 4 games to 2
Islanders defeated Buffalo 4 games to 0

Semi-finals—
Montreal defeated Islanders 4 games to 2
Boston defeated Philadelphia 4 games to 0

Championship Final—
Montreal defeated Boston 4 games to 0.

SCORING

	G	A	Pts.
Guy Lafleur, Mon.	56	80	136
Marcel Dionne, L.A.	53	69	122
Steve Shutt, Mon.	60	45	105
Rick MacLeish, Phil.	49	48	97
Gilbert Perreault, Buf.	39	56	95
Tim Young, Min.	29	66	95
Jean Ratelle, Bos.	33	61	94
Lanny McDonald, Tor.	46	44	90
Darryl Sittler, Tor.	38	52	90
Bobby Clarke, Phil.	27	63	90

ALL STAR GAME

Prince of Wales defeated Clarence Campbell, 4–3.

TROPHY WINNERS

Ross Trophy (Leading Scorer) Guy Lafleur—Montreal
Norris Trophy (Best Defenseman) Larry Robinson—Montreal
Calder Trophy (Best Rookie) Willi Plett—Atlanta
Hart Trophy (M.V.P.) Guy Lafleur—Montreal
Vezina Trophy (Leading Goalie) Ken Dryden, Michel Larocque—Montreal
Lady Byng Trophy (Sportsmanship) Marcel Dionne—Los Angeles

WORLD HOCKEY ASSOCIATION

Final Standings
EASTERN DIVISION

	W	L	T	Pts.	GF	GA
Quebec	47	31	3	97	353	295
Cincinnati	39	37	5	83	354	303
Indianapolis	36	37	8	80	276	305
New England	35	40	6	76	275	290
Birmingham	31	46	4	66	289	309
x-Minnesota	19	18	5	43	136	129

WESTERN DIVISION

Houston	50	24	6	106	320	241
Winnipeg	46	32	2	94	366	291
San Diego	40	37	4	84	284	283
Edmonton	34	43	4	72	243	304
Calgary	31	43	7	69	252	296
Phoenix	28	48	4	60	281	383

x-Disbanded January 20, 1977

AVCO WORLD TROPHY PLAYOFFS

Quarter-finals—
Quebec defeated New England 4 games to 1
Indianapolis defeated Cincinnati 4 games to 0
Houston defeated Edmonton 4 games to 1
Winnipeg defeated San Diego 4 games to 3

Semi-finals—
Quebec defeated Indianapolis 4 games to 1
Winnipeg defeated Houston 4 games to 2

Championship final—
Quebec defeated Winnipeg 4 games to 3

SCORING

	G	A	Pts.
Cloutier, Quebec	66	75	141
Hedberg, Winnipeg	70	61	131
Nilsson, Winnipeg	39	85	124
Ftorek, Phoenix	46	71	117
Lacroix, San Diego	32	82	114
Tardif, Quebec	49	60	109
Leduc, Cincinnati	52	55	107
Bordeleau, Quebec	32	75	107
Stoughton, Cincinnati	52	52	104
Napier, Birmingham	60	36	96

TROPHY WINNERS

M.V.P.—Robbie Ftorek, Phoenix
Best Defenseman—Ron Plumb, Cincinnati
Best Rookie—George Lyle, New England
Sportsmanship—Dave Keon, New England
Best Coach—Bill Dineen, Houston

HORSE RACING

KENTUCKY DERBY

CHURCHILL DOWNS, KY.

$267,200

Horse	Jockey
1. Seattle Slew	Jean Cruget
2. Run Dusty Run	Darrel McHargue
3. Sanhedrin	Jorge Velasquez

Margin
1 3-4 lengths

PREAKNESS

PIMLICO, M.D.

$191,000

Horse	Jockey
1. Seattle Slew	Jean Cruget
2. Iron Constitution	Jorge Velasquez
3. Run Dusty Run	Darrel McHargue

Margin
1½ lengths

BELMONT

BELMONT PARK, N.Y.

$181,800

Horse	Jockey
1. Seattle Slew	Jean Cruget
2. Run Dusty Run	Darrel McHargue
3. Sanhedrin	Jorge Velasquez

Margin
4 lengths

AWARDS

Horse of the Year—Seattle Slew
Grass Horse—Johnny D.
Two-Year-Colt—Affirmed
Two-Year-Old Filly—Lakeville Miss
Three-Year-Old Colt—Seattle Slew
Three-Year-Old Filly—Our Mims
Older Fillies—Cascapedia
Sprinter—What A Summer
Steeplechase Horse—Cafe Prince

BOXING

WORLD PROFESSIONAL CHAMPIONS

Heavyweight—Muhammad Ali.
Light Heavyweight—Victor Galindez
(WBA). Miguel Cuello (WBC).
Middleweight—Rodrigo Valdez.
Junior Middleweight—Eddie Gazo (WBA).
Rocky Mattioli (WBC)
Welterweight—Jose Cuevas (WBA).
Carlos Palomino (WBC).
Junior Welterweight—Antonio Cervantes
(WBA). Sheng Shak Muang Surin
(WBC).
Lightweight—Roberto Duran (WBA).
Esteban de Jesus (WBC).
Junior Lightweight—Samuel Serrano
(WBA). Alfredo Escalera (WBC).
Featherweight—Rafael Ortega (WBA).
Danny Lopez (WBC).
Bantamweight—Jorge Lujan (WBA).
Carlos Zarate (WBC).
Flyweight—Gutty Espadas (WBA).
Miguel Canto (WBC).
Junior Flyweight—Yoko Gushiken.

TRACK AND FIELD

NCAA CHAMPIONS

100 Meter Dash—Harvey Glance, Auburn
200 Meter Dash—William Snoddy, Oklahoma
400 Meter Dash—Herman Frazier, Arizona State
800 Meter Run—Mark Enyeart, Utah State
1,500 Meter Run—Wilson Waigwa, Texas-El Paso
5,000 Meter Run—Joshua Kimeto, Washington State
10,000 Meter Run—Samson Kimombwa, Washington State
3,000 Meter Steeplechase—James Munyala, Texas-El Paso
110 Meter High Hurdles—James Owens, UCLA
400 Meter Intermediate Hurdles—Thomas Andrews, Southern California
1,600 Meter Relay—Southern California
High Jump—Kyle Arney, Arizona State
Pole Vault—Earl Bell, Arkansas State
Long Jump—Larry Doubley, Southern California
Triple Jump—Ron Livers, San Jose State
Discus Throw—Svein Walvik, Texas-El Paso
Hammer Throw—Scott Neilson, Washington
Javelin Throw—Scott Dykehouse, Florida
Shot Put—Terry Albritton, Stanford
Decathlon—Tito Steiner, Brigham Young
Team Champion—Arizona State

AAU CHAMPIONS

100 Meter Dash—Don Quarrie, Tobias Striders
200 Meter Dash—Derald Harris, Los Medanos College
400 Meter Dash—Robert Taylor, Philadelphia Pioneers
800 Meter Dash—Mark Belger, Philadelphia Pioneers
1500 Meter Run—Steve Scott, University of California-Irvine
5000 Meter Run—Marty Liquori, Florida AA
10,000 Meter Run—Frank Shorter, Colorado Track Club
110 Meter High Hurdles—(tie) James Owens, UCLA
Charles Foster, Philadelphia Pioneers
400 Meter Intermediate Hurdles—Edwin Moses, Atlanta Pioneers
3000 Meter Steeplechase—James Munyala, Philadelphia Pioneers
5000 Meter Walk—Todd Scully, Shore Athletic Club
High Jump—Dwight Stones, Desert Oasis Track Club
Pole Vault—Mike Tully, Pacific Coast Club
Triple Jump—Milan Tiff, Tobias Striders
Long Jump—Arnie Robinson, Maccabi Union Track Club
Shot Put—Terry Albritton, Pacific Coast Club
Discus Throw—Mac Wilkins, Pacific Coast Club
Hammer Throw—Emmitt Berry, Maccabi Union Track Club
Javelin Throw—Bruce Kennedy, San Jose Stars

INDEX

299